WEB ADVERTISING
AND MARKETING

MORE COMPUTER BOOKS FROM PRIMA PUBLISHING

Build a Web Site: The Programmer's Guide to Creating, Building,
   and Maintaining a Web Presence

The CD-ROM Revolution

CompuServe Information Manager for Windows: The Complete Membership Kit
   & Handbook (with two 3½" disks)

Create Wealth with Quicken, Third Edition

Cruising America Online 2.5: The Visual Learning Guide

Cruising The Microsoft Network

Data Security

Free Electronic Networks

Interactive Internet: The Insider's Guide to MUDs, MOOs, and IRC

The Internet After Hours, Second Edition

Internet for Windows—America Online Edition: The Visual Learning Guide

Internet for Windows: America Online 2.5 Edition

Internet for Windows: The Microsoft Network Edition

The Internet Warp Book: Your Complete Guide to Getting Online with OS/2 Warp

Introduction to Internet Security

Researching on the Internet: The Complete Guide to Finding, Evaluating,
   and Organizing Information Effectively

The Software Developer's Complete Legal Companion (with 3½" disk)

Thom Duncan's Guide to NetWare Shareware (with 3½" disk)

The Web After Hours

Web Browsing with America Online

Web Browsing with Netscape Navigator

Web Browsing with NETCOM NetCruiser

Web Browsing with Prodigy

Web Browsing with The Microsoft Network

HOW TO ORDER:

For information on quantity discounts contact the publisher: Prima Publishing, P.O. Box 1260BK, Rocklin, CA 95677-1260; (916) 632-4400. On your letterhead include information concerning the intended use of the books and the number of books you wish to purchase. For individual orders, turn to the back of this book for more information.

WEB ADVERTISING AND MARKETING

JOSHUA O. TESTERMAN

THOMAS J. KUEGLER, JR.

PAUL J. DOWLING, JR.

PRIMA PUBLISHING

Dedication:

TO GOD AND THE ENTIRE CREW AT SKYLINE TECHNOLOGIES

P™ is a trademark of Prima Publishing, a division of Prima Communications, Inc.
Prima Publishing™ is a trademark of Prima Communications, Inc.

Prima Online™ is a trademark of Prima Publishing.
Prima Computer Books is an imprint of Prima Publishing, Rocklin, California 95677.

Project Editor: Jeff Ennis

Prima Publishing and the author(s) have attempted throughout this book to distinguish proprietary trademarks from descriptive terms by following the capitalization style used by the proprietor of the products discussed in this book.

Information contained in this book has been obtained by Prima Publishing from sources believed to be reliable. However, because of the possibility of human or mechanical error by our sources, Prima Publishing, or others, the Publisher does not guarantee the accuracy, adequacy, or completeness of any information and is not responsible for any errors or omissions or the results obtained from use of such information.

Screen shots of specific Web pages are provided for review, commentary, or informational purposes only. No endorsement of any company or product is either stated or implied. Further, this book is not affiliated with or sponsored by any company or product other than Prima Publishing, the authors, and their company, Skyline Network Technologies, Inc.

ISBN: 0-76150-383-8
Library of Congress Catalog Card Number: 95-72682
Printed in the United States of America
96 97 98 99 BB 10 9 8 7 6 5 4 3 2 1

CONTENTS

ACKNOWLEDGMENTS

First and foremost, all of us would like thank our acquisitions editor, Megg Bonar, for discovering us, asking us to write this book, and believing in us. Thanks to Jeff Ennis, our project editor for this book, and Dan Foster, senior project editor, at Prima Publishing. We spent numerous hours on the phone with them both, and they were truly excellent to work with while writing this book—we almost consider them a part of our family. To everyone at Prima, a big thanks—especially: John Waters, developmental editor; Sam Mills, copy editor; Danielle Foster, interior design and production; Victor Kongkadee and Michael Tanamachi, cover design and illustration; Leisa Backer-Bentley, cover layout; Katherine Stimson, index. All have done an awesome job helping us put the book together and helping us turn out the best book possible.

*   *   *

There have been many people throughout the years without whose support I would not be where I am now (you know who you are). Thank you all! Thanks to Gary S. Tosadori, Shannon H. McCall, and Marian A. Dowling, for your love and support through this entire project and for endless hours of proofreading and corrections. Thanks to all of my co-workers—your help, support, and understanding during this entire experience was greatly needed and appreciated. My family deserves thanks as well; they have always been supportive of my life and projects.

Paul

*   *   *

I want to thank my wife Elaine and my family: mom, dad, Denise, and Grant for their love and encouragement always. The teachers, educators, and coaches who have allowed me to grow into the person I am. Thank you to my co-workers and friends who have put up with me while I was working on this project. Lastly, I would like to thank all the people who ever doubted me—it was in spite of you that I was able to accomplish this task.

Tom

* * *

Thanks to mom and dad for the solid foundation and unfaltering support. To MaryAnn, Kimberly, Mandi, Melanie, and Bill for all of their love and support. To MaryAnn, again, for her contributions and advice. To my co-workers for their patience and understanding. To all of my family and friends, whose continued understanding, love, and support have always made such a difference.

Joshua

INTRODUCTION

As a business tool, the Internet—and more specifically, the World Wide Web—is fast becoming as prevalent as the office FAX machine. And like the FAX machine, the Net is drastically changing the way people do business. Companies of all sizes have embraced the Internet and found new methods of peer-to-peer, business-to-business, and business-to-consumer communications. They have discovered innovative ways to improve customer support, gather market research, and conduct new forms of advertising and sales.

The simple truth is that very few technological advances have had more impact on the business world than the Internet. And on the Net, it is the World Wide Web that rules as the advertising and marketing voice of most businesses.

WHY THE WEB?

The Web has become the mogul of the Net for several reasons. For starters, no other Internet resource offers as much creativity and versatility. The Web allows the fusion of text-based documents with graphic images, sound, and animation. It allows for complex interactions between the consumer and the advertising medium, as well as between groups of consumers.

The Web is often considered the most user-friendly Internet "application." Perhaps that is why the invention of the Web has prompted millions of consumers to go online. With estimates exceeding 17 million Web users in the United States and Canada alone, there is no question of its potential as a marketing tool. Odds are, by the time this book hits the shelves, thousands of additional consumers will be using the Web. By the time you finish reading this book, you can add even more.

To the consumer, the Web provides a rich source of entertainment, communications, research, shopping opportunities, and information (news, weather, sports, etc.). Because the Web offers so much, its usefulness has gradually moved from the business to the home, and from the spare-room to the living room. In many ways, the Web is changing home life much like it changed the business world.

Some experts claim that the World Wide Web is the fastest growing media ever developed—that the Web is growing more rapidly than television, radio, or print ever did. This rapid growth should be proof enough that most companies need to consider the Web as powerful marketing media.

WHY THIS BOOK?

There are dozens of books available that cover the World Wide Web (yet another indicator of the Web's popularity). Most of the books are intended for Web consumers—the people who browse the Web. These books help Web users find useful and interesting (and often not-so-interesting) sites.

Fewer books are available to educate and assist Web providers—those people and businesses that build Web sites. These books are an excellent tool for learning the various technical aspects of Web design.

Still fewer books are available that discuss the usefulness of the World Wide Web as a business tool. These are the books that interest business men and women the most. Such books are designed to show companies how they can make and save money on the Web (or on the Net in general).

What prompted us to write *Web Advertising and Marketing* was the need for a book that adequately discusses the vast marketing and advertising opportunities on the Web, as well as the artistic, technological, and marketing techniques required to successfully tap in to those opportunities. No other book provides the same, ideal combination of technical know-how and marketing strategy.

Web Advertising and Marketing takes you beyond finding useful information on the Web, beyond the technical details of Web documents, and beyond the general usefulness of the Web as a business tool. This book provides the experience and insight necessary to launch a successful Web marketing campaign.

WHY YOU?

This book is intended for business owners (large or small), information executives, and marketing executives. This book is even well suited for professional Web designers and consultants who want to further their knowledge. Whether or not you are already an Internet user, whether you know anything about sales and marketing strategies, this book provides virtually every piece of the knowledge you need to make educated and successful Web marketing decisions.

Even if you already have a Web marketing plan, even if you have already established a successful Web site, this book is chock-full of interesting and valuable bits of information that will make any marketing plan more profitable.

BOOK CONVENTIONS

Throughout this book, we feature several useful elements such as tips, cautions, notes, and technical notes. As a general rule, it is not necessary that you fully understand the issues covered in the technical notes—they are included primarily to allow ambitious readers the opportunity to learn some of the more technical details of the Web. We have also included several sidebars, many of which are examples from the experiences of Skyline Network Technologies, or other real-world organizations. We hope you find these sidebars relevant and insightful.

FOR MORE INFORMATION

If this book prompts you to seek more information on a particular topic, there are several places to turn:

- The front of this book contains a list of Web-related books from Prima Publishing that provide additional information.

- At the end of this book is an appendix that lists several places to look for marketing-related information directly on the Internet.

Skyline Network Technologies, Inc., has established a site that promotes and supports this book. If you have access to the Web, the *Web Advertising and Marketing* (WAM) Web site is located at:

```
http://www.skyline.net/WAM/
```

For more personalized assistance, Skyline's consultants, and many other Web professionals, are available to handle any Web-related problems you may have.

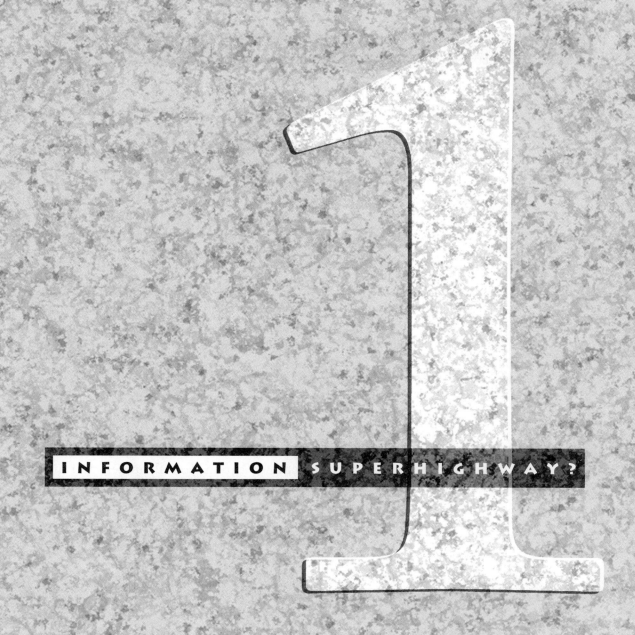

INFORMATION SUPERHIGHWAY?

It's early Monday morning and your clock radio wakes you with a story about gamblers using the "Information Superhighway" to place bets. You rub sleep from your eyes and wander out to your front step, where your morning paper greets you with the headline, "Parks and Recreation Department now on the Internet." Later, at work, the office is buzzing with the news that your biggest competitor is now on the "Web." At home that evening, the lead story on the 6 o'clock news is about shopping malls and mail-order catalogs going the way of the dinosaur: More and more consumers conduct retail business on the "electronic superhighway."

That night, sleep is slow to come. Your head is just too full of questions. "Information Superhighway"? The "Internet"? The "Web"? What does it all mean? Where did it all come from? And how will it affect the way I conduct my life and my business?

IN THE BEGINNING: A BRIEF HISTORY OF THE INTERNET

The Information Superhighway. The Internet. The Web. These familiar catchwords have become part of the public lexicon. Unfortunately, the mainstream media uses them interchangeably, with little regard for the fact that each represents a distinct concept or a particular facet of a world-changing medium of communication. To fully understand this new medium and how it will affect you and the way you'll do business in the future, you must first learn a little about its origins.

THE COLD WAR CREATES A NEED

Today's "Internet" was born during the era of the Cold War. In 1962, the Cuban Missile Crisis struck fear in the hearts of Americans. Hysteria over potential nuclear annihilation was rampant. In schools all across the country, children learned to "duck and cover" in case of nuclear attack. Average citizens spent small fortunes building and stocking personal bomb shelters. The nation's nuclear anxiety reached all the way to the Pentagon, where the Department of Defense was trying to establish a means for essential research labs and military bases to maintain lines of communication even in the face of an all-out attack.

A unit within the Department of Defense called the Advanced Research Projects Agency (ARPA) hired a research firm to create this virtually indestructible communications system. By 1972, Bolt, Bernak, and Newman had developed a network of connections between about

40 research and military establishments. They called this network ARPAnet.

ARPAnet allowed users to transfer short text messages they termed "electronic mail" from one computer location to another along the network. It also used a system called "file transfer protocol" (FTP) to transfer large files filled with text and data.

ARPAnet was the Internet in embryo.

BRING IN THE INTELLECTUALS

By the end of the 1970s, many American research facilities were creating their own small communications networks. These mini-networks typically connected three or four research centers, allowing them to share information more efficiently. Eventually, these research organizations joined with others to form increasingly larger networks. This network of networks eventually evolved into a wide-reaching scientific communications net known as the Computer Science Research Network (CSnet).

In the early 1980s, CSnet and ARPAnet existed as two distinct networks of independent mini-networks. By 1982, these two large networks had joined to facilitate the free exchange of scientific information among their many users. This union produced what we know today as the Internet.

Throughout the remainder of the '80s, the original CSnet and ARPAnet networks were modified, transfigured, and eventually supplanted by the National Science Foundation Network (NSFnet). NSFnet created a better way to connect the independent networks. Using a series of high-speed connections scattered around the country (the "backbone"), NSFnet facilitated extremely rapid data transfer from one connection point to the next. The network's original military applications gradually disappeared, and the rapid, free exchange of information among researchers in all fields became its sole purpose.

BUSINESS FINDS THE INTERNET

In 1990, an event occurred that would forever alter the direction, scope, and purpose of the fledgling communications network. The Federal Networking Council, a sort of non-binding regulatory body that governs the Internet, decided to allow Internet access to anyone who applied for it. Prior to that decision, access was possible only with a federal agency sponsorship, and applicants were required to demonstrate a specific research purpose requiring the access. This policy change opened the floodgates and allowed the first of many non-scientific entities to enter what would quickly become a freewheeling world of information exchange. Table 1-1 shows the explosion in Internet use.

Since the Federal Networking Council's decision, the Internet has expanded to every corner of the earth. Internet connections exist in more than 200 countries on every continent of the globe—even the South Pole. The subsequent commercialization of the Internet has produced unbridled growth and a level of connectivity beyond anything anyone could have predicted.

NUTS AND BOLTS OF THE INTERNET

The Internet isn't what you'd call tangible. It isn't even really a place. You'll find no official headquarters building, no single bank of computers at its heart. Just as CSnet and ARPAnet combined their mini-networks to form a larger group of interconnected researchers, today's Internet connects thousands of computer networks around the globe. Science fiction writer William Gibson called it "cyberspace." We might describe it more accurately as a global association for the exchange of

Skyline Hits the Globe

When Skyline.Net first established a Web site, our first registered users were from other countries. We had hits from Australia, Korea, Singapore, France, and New Zealand. It seemed strange that our first interested viewers would be people we had never met, and probably never would meet. What struck us in those first weeks was the enormous potential of this new communications medium for opening new and widely dispersed markets.

TABLE 1-1   PEOPLE WITH INTERNET ACCESS AT VARIOUS TIMES

Year	Number of People
1970	400
1980	3000
1990	100,000
1993	3,000,000
1995	24,000,000
2000	100,000,000

information in similar and recognizable formats. However, it may be easier to think of it as a place to go when you're on the telephone.

Internet users gain access to and utilize the Internet in a number of ways, using both established methods of data transfer, such as FTP, and evolving cyber-realms, such as the World Wide Web.

TELNET

Imagine you're sitting at home and have a sudden craving for pizza from the joint around the corner. Instead of calling and placing an order with the pizza maker, you dial the cash register directly, ordering a large pizza with extra pepperoni and indicating where you want it delivered. This, in a nutshell, is how you accomplish the procedure called "Telnet."

Telnet allows you to dial into a remote computer and gain access to that computer's programs and data. For example, if you live in Chicago but your company is headquartered in Baltimore, you could, with local Internet access, tap into all your company's activities and perform your work from the Windy City.

E-MAIL

Remember the old TV westerns, with the stagecoach racing across the prairie, delivering the mail? Nothing could keep that stagecoach from getting those letters from one end of our country to the other. The Internet can do the same thing, but without the dust and sweaty horses.

The most fundamental and widely used of all Internet features is e-mail. Using e-mail, one individual can send a message directly to another individual on the network. This message can be a simple note, a sales report, or a lengthy term paper attached to a letter. Any amount of data may be sent across the Internet, and e-mail virtually circles the globe. You can send e-mail to your brother in Buffalo, New York, and your sister studying water buffalo in Southeast Asia. And you can do it almost instantaneously. (Messages to destinations outside the United States sometimes take a day or two.)

To grasp the scope of the Internet, and specifically the use of e-mail, consider the results of a study conducted by the Electronic Messaging Association. In the study, researchers calculated that 776 billion e-mail messages were sent over the Internet in 1994. The same group estimates more than a trillion messages will have traveled from one end of the planet to the other by the end of the following year.

FTP

When you visit the public library, you're free to browse the shelves, pulling down any book you want to read. With the librarian's help, you can find books covering an incredibly wide range of topics. If you have a library card, you can even take a few home with you. The Internet's data retrieval procedures are similar to this familiar method.

The oldest and most commonly used method of retrieving data from the Internet is known as file transfer protocol (FTP). FTP allows you to grab files from another site on the Internet and transfer them to your site or computer. These files may be anything, from computer programs to journal articles, from personal essays to graphics files.

Two specific methods of FTP allow you to traffic these files across the Internet. The first allows you to transfer a file from one site to any other site. To accomplish this transfer, you must have access to both sites, and that usually means having a password to log on at both locations. The other method, called "anonymous FTP," is used at sites allowing the free and authorized transfer of files. Some sites are set up to be anonymous and some are not.

NEWS

During the 1930s, streetcorner paperboys were a common sight in every city in America. You could find them on almost any corner, a bundle of black-and-white newsprint under one arm, a soft cap pulled down over their heads, shouting out the day's headlines.

The Internet delivers the news in a similar manner (though without the caps). There are literally thousands—well over 15,000 in fact—"newsgroups" on the Net, every one devoted to a different subject. They all work in about the same way. A newsgroup is a kind of continuous listing of articles, one after another, on a particular topic. You can read any article you want, respond to it, or continue to the next article in line. You can also trace threads through these articles, so you can see how each one is connected with the newsgroup, and how each leads to the next related article.

GOPHER

If you've seen the movie *Caddyshack*, the word "gopher" probably conjures an image of the cute, cunning little animal that outwits Bill Murray and rules the golf course. The Internet has its own gophers, but they're not fuzzy, and they rarely dig holes in the ground.

Gopher is a menu-driven document delivery system that organizes and helps Internet users find information. We can also use it to measure the evolution of the Net. All the aforementioned tools will provide you with information, but they're not very helpful when you don't know where to locate that information. For example, it's difficult to FTP a file on good clam chowder recipes if you don't already know the Internet address of the cook who has them.

A gopher provides a structured search for specific types of information. It can help you search through all the information and activities at a particular college campus, or it can help you narrow your search about a very broad subject. Figure 1-1 shows a sample gopher screen.

Gophers preceded the World Wide Web, and influenced its development. The way a gopher structures information—allowing you to chose a menu item and then taking you to a specific file—is similar to the way the Web operates. The primary shortcoming of gopher is that it doesn't allow the use of graphical images or sounds. Menu choices must always connect to a very limited choice of file types, predominately text.

BIRTH OF THE WEB

As the numbers of Internet connections mushroomed in the early 1990s, users complained that it was increasingly difficult to find information. It was also difficult, if not downright impossible, to jump between related files. And there was a growing need to augment shared information with images, graphics, and sounds.

From this frustration a new Internet feature was born. What was conceived as a tiny network of scientific researchers suddenly became a

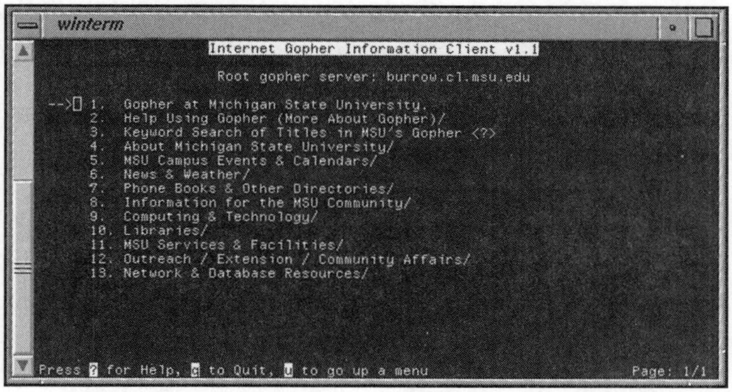

FIGURE 1-1

The initial page of the gopher at gopher.msu.edu

communications medium that would capture the world's imagination. With the birth of the World Wide Web, the Internet took its first steps into adulthood.

These useful definitions will enable you to better understand and follow along as we take you through the process of making your company a force on the Web.

Browser   *Software that allows a user to navigate the Web and retrieve documents.*

Client   *A computer or machine connected to the Web and used to display information located on a remote computer, but which does not host a site or distribute files to other computers.*

Homepage   *The initial screen for a Web site.*

Hypertext Transfer Protocol (HTTP)   *The most commonly used method for transferring Web data.*

Links   *Connections from one information file or site to another.*

Log In   *Using the Telnet function to connect to a remotely located computer.*

Provider/Web Presence Provider   *A person or company that establishes Web sites for other individuals, companies, or other entities.*

Server/Web Server   *A computer or system that hosts a Web site.*

Uniform Resource Locator (URL)   *An address used to specify the exact location of a machine, file, or piece of data on the Internet.*

Site/Web Site   *A grouping of Web pages linked so that you may easily follow from one Web page to the next. Also used to describe the information that one individual, company, or entity puts on the Web.*

INFORMATION RETRIEVAL BECOMES EASIER

The Internet is a lot like a party: If you get there early, it's easy to mingle, meet people, and learn interesting bits of information. But as more guests arrive, it becomes so crowded it's difficult to walk around, let alone meet anyone.

By the mid-1990s, the Internet was one crowded party. To alleviate the mass confusion, two physicists at the Conseil Europeen pour la Recherche Nucleaie (CERN), Tim Berners-Lee and Robert Cailliau, developed hypertext transfer protocol (HTTP). Instead of using a menu-driven system or some sort of outline, HTTP allowed users to jump from one information file directly to the next . These jumps became known as links, and with this concept, the World Wide Web was born.

GRAPHICS FIND THE INTERNET

But the Web concept wasn't enough in itself to stabilize the Internet. Without a pilot to steer users through the complexities of information search and retrieval, it was still not very useful to the public.

Then in 1993 the National Center for Supercomputing Applications (NCSA) developed a graphical Web "browser." Mosaic, as it was called, was remarkably user-friendly. It allowed Internet users to find information with a click of the mouse. Figure 1-2 shows a Web site being browsed using Mosaic.

The development of Mosaic and other graphical browsers created an explosion in Web use. The migration to the Web from other Internet uses accelerated as more and more companies and individuals recognized the ease of information transfer on the Web. It became a wonder of activity in an amazingly short period of time. Table 1-2 illustrates the increase in numbers of Web sites.

The Web continues to expand at an exponential rate. Some observers

TABLE 1-2   SITES CONNECTED TO THE WEB

Date	Number of Sites
June 1993	135
September 1993	597
October 1993	630
March 1994	1,800
June 1994	4,000
November 1994	12,000
March 1995	24,000

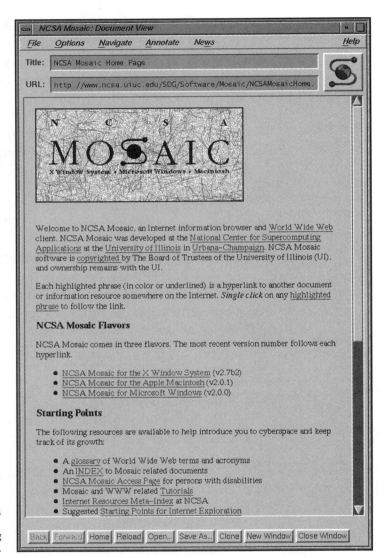

FIGURE 1-2

NCSA Mosaic home page shown using
the MOSAIC browser.

estimate that 120 to 150 new sites are added to the Web every day. It's expanding so rapidly, in fact, that no one can accurately track its growth. Adding to the Web expansion, commercial services are providing simple, easy-to-install software packages giving anyone with a computer and a modem quick and easy Web access. Services such as America Online, CompuServe, and Prodigy have contributed greatly to the skyrocketing growth of the Web. The ongoing price war fought by these large commercial providers reflects the Web's growing commercial importance.

Web growth has brought this aspect of the Information Superhighway to prime-time news. By the end of 1993, *Time, Newsweek,* the *Wall Street Journal,* and *The New York Times* had covered the growth of the Web, and the commercial world was beginning to recognize the Web as the next major marketing venue.

The Internet had become an important vehicle for getting marketing messages to a large, global audience, quickly. In April 1994, the first major commercial project, CommerceNet, was dedicated to the Web. CommerceNet was an association of large corporations working together to study the feasibility of conducting transactions and other marketplace exchanges on the Web. CommerceNet continues to develop strategies for making the Web a global marketing medium.

By the end of 1994, almost 30 percent of all Web sites were commercial in nature. To understand how the world of commerce views the Web's economic potential, look no further than Wall Street. When Netscape, the producer of the world's most popular Web browser, went public and began trading on the NASDAQ Stock Market, its shares almost instantly jumped to five times its initial offering price. UUnet Technologies and Netcom On-Line Communications Services, Inc., sell Internet and Web services and have similar stories.

The importance of the Internet in general, and the Web in particular, is not lost on software developers. Before the release of Microsoft's Windows 95, company president and founder Bill Gates, in an internal memo to some of his highest ranking employees, declared that Microsoft's presence on the Internet should be the company's number one priority.

Large corporations everywhere recognize the important marketing opportunities the Web presents. Many include Web site addresses in their print and broadcast advertising. (Check out the bottom of the screen during TV commercials. You'll be surprised how often you'll find a Web site address.)

Remember...

- The Internet emerged from concern about nuclear war during the 1960s. It expanded first into colleges and institutions, then into private enterprise, and eventually found its way to the mass market.

- The Internet's creators designed it as a way for people to communicate quickly and cheaply. It's still used that way, including Telnet, e-mail, FTP, newsgroups, and the gopher among its primary communications features.

- The World Wide Web evolved from the need for easier access to information on the Internet. It allows the quick link from one piece of information to the next. It also permits the addition of graphics and sound to text files. This addition made it a popular product for the mainstream public, and this in turn made it an effective arena for marketing and advertising.

THE FIVE WS OF WEB MARKETING

2

Before most of us commit to a major venture, we try to learn as much as possible about the project. When you planned your last vacation, for example, you probably considered a host of details and made most of your decisions before you ever stepped out the door. You chose a date, a destination, and a means of transportation. You laid out your itinerary, you packed your bags with care, and you probably took along a map or two.

Before you and your company hit the road for the World Wide Web, you'll want more than a map and the right suitcase. The following chapter provides an overview of the world of Web marketing. You'll find answers to many of your questions—everything you need for a safe and profitable trip to the Internet.

WHAT IS WEB MARKETING?

To understand Web marketing you must first understand the Web. Generally speaking, the Web is a fast-paced Net environment where citizens called Web surfers (or "netizens") make ultra-fast choices to acquire the information they want. These Web surfers tend to have short attention spans and even shorter thresholds of patience. But on a deeper level, the Web is, for all intents and purposes, a society unto itself, with its own culture, its own people, and even its own language.

One of the most important attributes of Web society is its multinational character. As we explained in Chapter 1, the Web has evolved into a culturally diverse venue, where at any given moment you'll find surfers from virtually every part of the globe. Though an American flavor dominates, every country on earth seasons this cultural stew. This confluence of cultures makes for marketing opportunities you won't find anywhere else.

Web user diversity has special implications for anyone who wants to market their products or services online using the Net. If you gear 100 percent of your advertising strictly to American audiences, you'll miss 20 percent of your potential Internet customers. It's like doing business in a street market where every fifth customer's first language is foreign.

International Conversation at Skyline.Net

Recently, a few of us at Skyline were in the MUD—a location on our site where surfers can view pictures, write notes to each other, and get responses from other surfers instantly. We conversed online with an airline manager in Luxembourg, a college student in New Zealand, and a biologist from San Jose. It wasn't until we had spoken to these people for about 15 minutes that we realized we were spanning three continents and five time zones. The genuinely international flavor of the Web, and its potential for worldwide exposure, continue to astonish even us.

Chapter 3 covers the psychological implications of such a diverse society in detail. For now, let's examine some strategies for getting your online message across. First, we'll look at two Web surfer characteristics, and how to make the most of them using Web technology.

As we've explained, you'll find people in the Web from all over the world. Most are impatient and data-hungry. One reason the Web is so popular with these Internet users is that so many Web sites feature pictures and sound. Stunning visuals and compelling music and sound effects transcend language barriers and capture the attention of fickle surfers. To be noticed on the Web, incorporate eye-catching visuals and memorable audio in all your messages.

Remember: The average surfer sees a new page of information every 15 seconds. That means he or she will view a page for only 15 seconds. Unless that page is *very* interesting, your message will be lost and forgotten before it's even noticed.

HOW DOES THIS DIFFER FROM OTHER VENUES?

Imagine running full-color ads in a publication that gives your company worldwide exposure, instantly. That's exactly what the Web can do for you. And it's just the tip of the iceberg.

In this section, we explore differences between the Web and traditional advertising media. Let's begin with print advertising.

Newspapers are among the world's most widely used advertising media. Ads range in size from a full page to an eighth or sixteenth of a page. In the last decade, many daily publications have added color to their pages, but most newsprint ads are still black-and-white.

In most papers, ad prices increasewith ad size, but circulation can determine pricing, as well. The larger the paper's circulation, the higher the ad cost. Few newspapers can claim a truly international circulation.

The disadvantages of newspaper advertising are many. Circulation largely determines ad exposure; in other words, only the people who take the trouble to buy a copy of the paper that day will have an opportunity to see your ad. We say "opportunity" because the newspaper offers more to look at than your ad. Articles, photos, features, and other ads all compete for readers' attention. Because the average reader spends about 13 minutes going through a daily newspaper—that's 13 minutes to read the headlines, check out the sports scores, do the crossword puzzle, visit Snoopy, and scan the stock exchange listings—there's not much time to spend with your ad.

Another disadvantage of newspaper advertising is that it doesn't allow you to truly target your market. Although you can (and should) learn all you can about a publication's demographics, you take a shotgun approach when you advertise in a newspaper. Your ad goes out to the general readership; you can only hope your spread was wide enough to hit a few potential customers.

Magazines offer some distinct advantages over newspapers when it comes to targeting your market. A number of niche publications have emerged in the last 10 years or so. Specialty periodicals covering everything from sailing to knitting, guitar playing to Net-surfing, have appeared on the racks. Magazine ads typically are full-color and eye-catching. Many magazines have large national—even inter-national—readerships. Because they publish weekly or monthly, magazines tend to lie around longer, making it more likely that someone will see your ad.

The great disadvantage of magazine advertising is cost. Advertising in widely circulated publications, such as *Time* or *Sports Illustrated*, is expensive. You can spend well into five figures on a single ad. Most large periodicals put out regional versions offering less expensive ad space, but saving ad costs this way reduces the scope of your marketing strategy, reducing its effectiveness in turn.

Broadcast advertising differs from print in a number of ways. A radio ad can be anything from an elaborately produced pre-recorded spot to an on-air plug read by a DJ or talk-show host. These spots are always intermingled with the programming, and the entire listening audience hears them. Buying air time on a single radio station is simple and inexpensive. The cost of each spot is determined by the station and the time slot or show that airs it, but compared to other forms of advertising, it's rather inexpensive.

A primary disadvantage of radio advertising is that it's highly local. Each station reaches only the listeners within its broadcast range. No matter how powerful the station's signal, there's always a limit. You can compensate for this limitation somewhat by running ads on several stations (you can even run ads on stations across the country), but this significantly increases your costs, eliminating one of the features that makes radio so appealing in the first place. And even then, you won't reach an *international* audience.

Another disadvantage is that radio doesn't allow you to target a very specific audience. Although radio stations and advertising firms that buy radio spots for clients can tell you which time slots and what shows appeal to which audiences, radio simply can't target your message to a narrow group. You waste 60 to 70 percent of your radio advertising dollars on listeners you don't want to reach.

One of the most widely recognizable advertising media is television. Delivering color, movement, sound, and music, a TV ad can be as expensive to produce as a short movie, or as simple as a stand-up in a used-car lot. Advances in computer video production technology allow you to deliver virtually any image you can conceive. With the advent of cable and satellite technology, television audiences continue to expand. Millions of people around the world can view a single program almost simultaneously. The American public utilizes television widely as a communication medium. Studies suggest the average American spends up to three hours a day in front of a TV set, which means they're seeing approximately 30 commercials every day.

Unfortunately, television advertising is expensive. An effective television marketing campaign can cost millions of dollars. A single 30-second spot for a large-audience event, such as a Super Bowl, can cost $500,000. Television provides instant exposure, but it also can destroy all but the most expansive marketing budgets.

Finally, there's direct mail. Direct mail has been around for decades, but recently it's reached a kind of apex. Households and workplaces across America receive thousands of pounds of so-called "junk mail" every business day. Most direct-mail pieces take the form of some kind of brochure, usually accompanied by a letter.

Direct mail is a very effective way to get your company's message to a specific type of customer. When you send a direct-mail piece, you know exactly who you're spending your marketing dollars on. With direct mail, market size is virtually limitless. You can mail your advertising to anyone with an address. You can even reach an international audience, though it's more difficult.

But direct mail isn't cheap. It must be designed, written, printed, and mailed. The postage alone can run from 30 cents to a few dollars per article.

Direct mail's other great drawback of direct mail is its limited effectiveness. An average piece of direct mail generates responses from only about 3 percent of recipients—a rather low response rate for such an expensive marketing tool.

As an advertising medium, the Web stands head and shoulders above traditional print, broadcast, and direct-mail avenues. It's relatively inexpensive, sometimes downright *cheap*, delivering your message—with color, sound, and motion—in a split second, anywhere in the world, at a fraction of the cost of most other media.

And we can't overstate the potential *reach* of online advertising. While the Web touches an astoundingly large domestic and international market, it also allows you to narrow-focus your message in those markets. In later chapters, we'll show you how you can use the Internet to target very specific markets all over the world.

But the Web also gives you something other media can't deliver in any form—*interactivity*. Imagine running a television or radio commercial, and permitting the viewers to respond—by touching the screen or the radio dial—and let you know what they thought about it. And what if your audience could also order your product or service from your commercial instantly, without even having to pick up the phone to call those operators who are always standing by? Most marketing professionals would call that a miracle. We call it the Web.

No other information delivery system gives you virtually instant interaction with your potential customers. The Web enables you to get

TABLE 2-1 HOW THE WEB STACKS UP AGAINST
OTHER ADVERTISING AVENUES

Marketing Quality	World Wide Web	Radio	Newspaper	Periodicals	Television	Direct Mail
Large National Audience	Yes	Maybe	Maybe	Maybe	Maybe	Yes
International Exposure	Yes	No	No	Maybe	Maybe	No
Can Be Targeted to a Specific Audience	Yes	No	No	Maybe	No	Yes
Audience Has Option to View Ads at Their Convenience	Yes	No	Yes	Yes	No	Yes
Relative Expense	Low	Medium	Medium	High	High	High
Instant Customer Interaction	Yes	No	No	No	No	No

unprecedented feedback on the effectiveness of your advertising. It allows you to learn immediately what your audience thinks about your product and your message. And it even makes it possible to take product orders directly from your Web page.

Although the Web has distinct advantages over all other forms of marketing media, we don't expect it to replace print, broadcasting, or direct mail anytime in the near future. There are markets the Web can't reach, but as it expands, the World Wide Web will touch an increasing number of potential customers. That's why we believe the Web should have a place in every company's marketing scheme.

And General Motors agrees with us. GM recently announced it has signed a $20 million contract with a large ad agency to conduct Web marketing in 1996. This project will augment activities on GM's in-house Web site (Figure 2-1) and current advertising on other sites around the Web. The contract represents the largest advertising investment ever made in an online marketing plan, yet it constitutes only a portion of the company's annual billion-dollar-plus advertising budget.

 You'll find many Web sites representing large corporations. What follows is a partial list of recognizable URLs.

```
http://www.xerox.com

http://www.chryslercars.com

http://www.wal-mart.com

http://www.citicorp.com

http://www.motorola.com

http://www.boeing.com

http://www.cocacola.com

http://www.americanexpress.com
```

WHO CAN BENEFIT FROM WEB MARKETING?

How do you know whether online marketing is right for you and your company? After all, you're not General Motors. Your company is far more local or regional, and your advertising budget wouldn't pay for a month's worth of paper clips at some corporations.

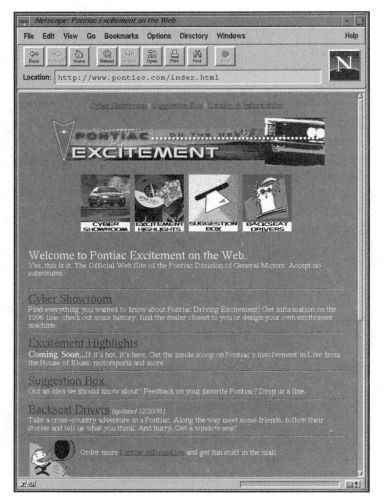

FIGURE 2-1

The Pontiac homepage is part
of General Motors' online
marketing scheme.

Perhaps yours is a service business. What can the Web do for you?
Maybe you think your product isn't technical enough, or it's something
that won't appeal to the age group you perceive to be surfing the Net.

Whether your customer base is international or local, whether your
company offers products or services, whether your advertising budget
would pay off the national debt or barely cover the lunch check at
McDonald's, the Web has something to offer you.

PRODUCT, PRODUCT...WHO'S GOT A PRODUCT?

Companies with product offerings typically fall into one of three categories—manufacturer, wholesaler, or retailer. Each can find marketing success on the Web.

Economically speaking, a manufacturer is any person or company that makes a product offered for sale. This definition includes everyone from GM to the local custom leather shop. Some manufacturers involve themselves in every sales level, from marketing to direct sales. Others do virtually no marketing and have little direct involvement with the final sale. No matter how a manufacturer handles its marketing, the Web can add support and increase product visibility.

If you're involved in the direct sale of products to another manufacturer or the general public, the Web's advantages are obvious: It increases your exposure to potential clients by providing ready access to information about your current products, as well as products in development. It can allow customers to place orders directly from your Web page. It even makes it possible to collect survey information so you can learn what kinds of products your customers want.

Manufacturers who depend on vendors for most of their product marketing may find the advantages of using the Web to be less obvious. One Web area these manufacturers can use to great advantage is in receiving bids from suppliers. Your suppliers can access your Web page and examine the your requested specifications, the proposal due date, and even view project diagrams. Instead of dozens of salespeople taking up your day with annoying phone calls, you can simply refer them to your Web site.

You can also set up your Web site to accommodate online orders from vendors. Instead of establishing an 800 number—which costs your company money with every call—vendors can place shipment requests online at no extra expense to you. You can even provide a form for their sales projections.

Novell Corp., a software company, has utilized the Web in some of these ways. Novell's Web site, (http://www.novell.com) provides its customers with useful information about its current products, breaking news about new products, and discussions of future offerings. The site includes information about where to buy Novell products. Although

Novell doesn't necessarily sell its products directly to the consumer, the company does use its site as a marketing device (see Figure 2-2).

Wholesalers are the middlemen of the commercial world. They buy products in large quantities from many manufacturers, mark up the prices, and then resell them to retail establishments, or to consumers through special wholesale outlets. They exist because it's sometimes easier and more profitable for the manufacturer to sell a large quantity at a slightly reduced price to one customer than it is to sell fewer products to many clients at a higher price.

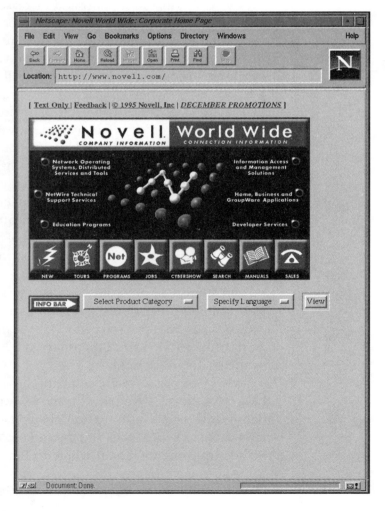

FIGURE 2-2

The Novell Corporation homepage

Vertical Market Examination: Auto Parts Manufacturers

Market Overview:

An industry where companies manufacture parts for automobiles, usually selling them to wholesale establishments, retail stores, or automobile manufacturers.

Web Marketing Strategies:

- Arrange bids and proposals from suppliers of raw materials

- Allow customers to place orders to replenish their inventories using an online order form

- Allow the general public to receive information on utilizing parts in their automobiles

- Provide a list of retail stores offering the company's parts

- Establish an online public survey to learn how the company's parts stack up against its competitors'

- Use the Web to debut parts now in development

The Web offers a number of advantages to wholesalers. They can set up Web-based catalogues for retailers, with direct, online ordering, significantly reducing their sales forces. By targeting online "mailings" to potential customers' sites, they can solicit new business. They can even surf other Web sites to scout out new products to carry in inventory.

Potomac Distribution (http://www.cais.com/potomac//home.html), a wholesale distributor of sports cards and related memorabilia, uses the Web to facilitate ordering and to bring in new customers, with great results. The company's customers can conduct online transactions using credit cards, checks, or COD. Figure 2-3 shows Potomac's homepage. Notice how the company groups its products in general categories to make it easy for its customers to find what they want.

Retailers are the last link in the product food chain, and are the companies that most often deal directly with the consumer. Retailers operate in several ways. Some operate retail outlets with on-premises inventories. Others utilize catalogues. Still others rely on advertisements and customer phone inquiries. Some combine these strategies (JCPenney, for example, operates department stores along with its catalogue business.) Web marketing can benefit all three retail modes.

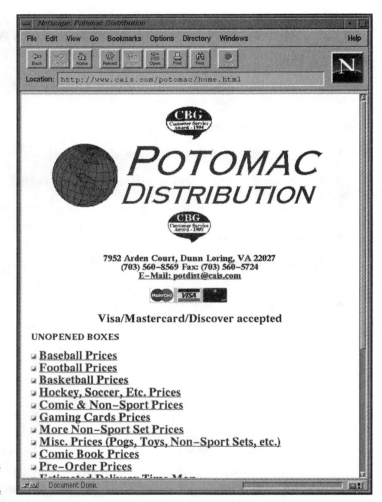

FIGURE 2-3

The Potomac Distribution homepage

In many ways, the Web is already another place for consumers to shop. It's a kind of storefront, catalogue, and mail-order form all rolled up into one. A consumer can view the merchandise, compare colors, sizes, and prices, and place his or her order without leaving the Web.

Most retailers won't have to change their marketing approach much when they venture onto the Web. The technology may be different, but the nuts and bolts of marketing retail products on the Web is not unlike marketing in other media. A good example of this is 1-800-FLOWERS (http://www.800flowers.com). Here's a company that, after years of selling flowers using an 800 number, decided to establish a

Vertical Market Examination: Candy and Sundry Wholesalers

Market Overview:
Deals in the procurement and delivery of candy, cigarettes, tobacco products, and other small retail items. The company's customers are usually retail stores or vending companies.

Web Marketing Strategies:

- Establish an online catalogue with online ordering capabilities, including delivery time and proper billing arrangements.

- Put accounts receivable on the site so that current customers can access their billing information and realize the state of their account.

- Advertise Easter candy specials without having to print up and distribute a flyer.

- Work with established customers to put out a directory of product outlets.

Vertical Market Examination: Grocery Stores/Supermarkets

Market Overview:
Usually a storefront where the consumer arrives to purchase vegetables, fruit, canned goods, meats, dairy products, and other household items.

Web Marketing Strategies:

- The outlet can develop an ordering service on the Web where customers can order groceries for either delivery or pick-up. The store can charge a fee to cover the cost of ordering groceries in this manner.

- Instead of mailing weekly circulars or posting sales specials in a newspaper, a Web site could host the store's weekly specials.

- The site could offer a section of consumer information, recipes, and nutritional data to promote store products.

presence online and sell its products there. Today, the company processes around $20 million worth of orders a year from its Web site.

No matter what segment of the product market your company falls into, you can improve your business with these simple online marketing strategies. No product is too regional or specialized to be effectively advertised online. As a rule, we say anything you can sell through conventional venues can find a niche on the Web.

CAN THE WEB SERVE SERVICE INDUSTRIES?

When the concept of advertising on the Web began to gain acceptance, many believed only companies with products to sell would benefit from Web marketing. No one saw a place for service industries on the Web. Many service companies did, however—lucky for them. In this section, we discuss how service industries everywhere have used the Web successfully, and what they did to make their online strategies work. We also examine some specific vertical markets, and offer advice for those business areas.

You run across plenty of service companies in your daily life. Auto repair garages, travel agencies, barber shops, dry cleaners—all are service industries. These companies generally don't provide their customers with tangible products, but they do have something to sell. The question is, how can they sell it on the Web? Let's look at a few examples of service industries with successful Web-marketing strategies.

The airlines have embraced the Web with open arms and used it in a big way. United Airlines (http://www.ual.com), for example, has a site on the Web where you can locate flight information. You can access frequent flyer information, look up destinations, airplane seating arrangements, and even examine airport maps. You can also ask the company questions directly from its Web site. United releases information about new products and programs on its Web site, as well.

The one thing United Airlines doesn't offer on its site is online ticket ordering. This site, and most of the other airline sites we know about, exist as part of the companies' overall marketing schemes. Even though they don't sell tickets directly through their sites, they believe their Web presence enhances their public image. We believe that eventually all airlines will sell tickets and other services online.

NOTE *To receive an interesting overview of airlines on the Web and to get an index to airline sites, check out a site put together by a graduate student from the University of California at Berkeley (http://haas.berkeley.edu/~seidel/airline.html). This site provides several examples of service companies— airlines particularly—that are utilizing the Web.*

Another type of service company taking the Web by storm is financial services. Everything from banking to investment research, accounting to legal advice, has found its way to the Web. Online banking seems to be getting the most press lately. Though very few U.S.

Vertical Market Examination: Travel Agencies

Market Overview:
A business that organizes travel arrangements for customers. It also purchases tickets and makes reservations for all stops along the itinerary.

Web Marketing Strategies:

- Establish a search mechanism so customers can choose their own itinerary and travel arrangements.

- Post online "brochures" of popular destinations to entice customers to take certain trips.

- Allow customers to fantasize about trips that they would like to take, including menu items and recreation they will enjoy.

- Design online tours, complete with pricing and availability. The tour can show what they'll eat, where they'll sleep, and where they'll spend their spare time. This can be a virtual tour complete with video and sound.

banks current offer online services, hundreds of banks have Web sites. One of the more interesting and well-developed of these is the site set up by NationsBank (http://www.nationsbank.com). This site lists services, branch locations, the latest press releases, and other company news, such as NationsBank's sponsorship of the 1996 U.S. Olympic Team. The NationsBank site also includes an interesting feature for a bank, an online catalogue where visitors can browse for products with the bank's name on them (see Figure 2-4). The site doesn't provide for online ordering.

NationsBank does not currently offer online banking, but the company has announced that it's developing software that will soon enable its customers to conduct many banking transactions online.

As the banking industry continues to consolidate, expect to see more online banking services becoming available. The growing numbers of newly merged banks will want to serve larger and more geographically diverse areas—what Web marketing is all about.

Financial services from accounting firms to stock brokerage houses are also establishing themselves on the Web. Most use their Web sites to relay financial advice or news. Some charge fees for this information; often it's a flat fee for access to certain portions of the site. This is very similar to publishing a subscription newsletter or financial magazine. Only the most successful and well-known of these financial institutions can get away with charging information fees on the Web, but some of them have succeeded.

One well-set-up site that doesn't charge membership fees is CNN-Financial Network (http://www.cnnfn.com). This site was set up by

FIGURE 2-4

A glimpse at the products that are being sold by NationsBank

the Cable News Network and is packed with financial news and information. The site allows visitors to search news articles for financial information, and receive market quotes on any publicly traded stock or mutual fund. (Figure 2-5 shows the initial search page for this feature.) Another excellent feature is its "Topic of the Day," which allows users to express opinions on topics and questions is raised by CNN-Financial Network's creators.

CNN utilizes this site much like it does its cable channel. It's really an extension of CNN's present operations, and sells advertising space to companies looking for Web exposure.

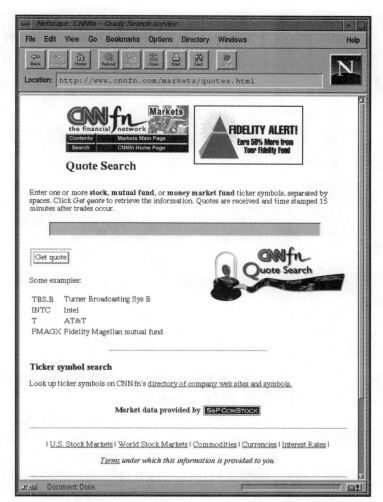

FIGURE 2-5

A view of the search page for CNN-Financial Network's feature for stock and mutual fund quotes

United Airlines, NationsBank, and CNN-Financial Network are just a few of the thousands of service companies with sites on the Web. Some are well-developed and some are, let's say, less developed. But a common thread runs through all these sites: Each is designed to expand the company's area of influence and reach new customers beyond those it reached with traditional forms of advertising. If your company is a service-based business, you too can introduce yourself to new markets with a Web site.

Vertical Market Examination: Securities Firm

Market Overview:

Works in the trading of stocks, commodities, and bonds for individuals, companies, or organizations.

Web Marketing Strategy:

- Allow individuals to track their portfolios online.

- Offer advice and tips on the stocks the firm recommends to buy and sell.

- Include articles on different financial matters (401K plans, when to buy high-risk stocks, or how to build a retirement nest egg).

- Include financial-planning programs showing how much users would have now if they had invested in the firm's recommended stocks on a certain day in history.

- Offer a program demonstrating the differences between dollar-cost averaging and lump-sum investing.

WHO *SHOULDN'T* BRING THEIR MARKETING TO THE WEB?

Up to now, we've characterized the World Wide Web as a kind of marketing Superman, faster than a speeding competitor, more powerful than traditional advertising, able to leap tall customers in a single bound. But you're probably wondering if there isn't a little kryptonite somewhere on the Internet.

The Web does have its shortcomings, though fewer than you might think. Some businesses may not do so well on the Web. If yours is a highly local concern—say a small, local liquor store—there may be no reason for you to take your business to the Web. It probably won't generate much business locally, and you can't realistically expect to increase your sales to a national level. Why would anyone order a six-pack of beer from you from across the country when they can buy it much more easily and less expensively from their local store?

Companies targeting older clients are also unlikely to gain much from Web marketing. Currently, most Web surfers are under 40. This may not always be the case, but if your clientele is older, don't expect immediate sales results from marketing on the Web. (Chapter 3 goes into more detail about Web demographics.)

WHY SHOULD I INVEST IN WEB MARKETING?

When television first came on the scene in the 1950s, many people called it a fad. Americas wouldn't be excited for long about sitting in front of a little screen and watching little fuzzy pictures, they said. At the time, radio was king of home entertainment, and many people believed it would never be replaced. Today, as we all know, television is entrenched in American culture. Much more than a form of entertainment, it's become an integral part of our lives. It influences how we think, eat, spend our money, even dream. Imagine yourself as a 1950s business owner. Would you be one of those who doubted the future of television, or would you have jumped at this marketing juggernaut?

Many things said of TV in its early stages are now said of the Web. In this section, we put forth some of the reasons we believe the Web is the next television.

MAKING YOUR MARK IN THE NEXT CENTURY

The 1990s mark the end of a century of change. At the beginning of this century, America's primary mode of transportation was the horse and buggy; at the close, nearly every adult American owns a car, and most have never even been on a horse. By the same token, just a few generations ago, everyone received their information from local newspapers, and they were the only places to advertise your wares; as the century draws to a close, we find ourselves in a veritable information storm where marketing vehicles are many and varied.

The 21st century promises to be another period of great change. The companies that will fare best in the coming years are those riding the cutting edge of technology. The Web, though still in its infancy, promises to be a driving force in the world of communication for many years to come. To make the most of this opportunity, you must jump into this medium now, so your firm is seen as one of the companies that helped the Web to grow, and not a parasite cashing in at the end.

GETTING IN ON THE GROUND FLOOR

The World Wide Web hasn't even begun to reach its full potential. Pioneering companies that go online *now* are in a position to grow with the Web, and expand and enhance their sites as the technology matures. It's like being one of the forward-thinking marketers who first advertised on television. They were in on the ground floor of what would become one of the most powerful and effective advertising medium the world has ever seen. By having your strategy in place on the Web early in its development, you, too, will have a leg up on the competition.

IS THIS COST-EFFECTIVE RIGHT NOW?

Another reason to get involved with Web marketing now is cost. Many Web consultants and Web presence providers are trying to lure companies onto the Web with extremely low introductory prices. As the business community comes to recognize the Web as a viable advertising medium, prices are sure to escalate. In its early stages of development, television advertising was relatively inexpensive. A spot on one of the early Super Bowls, for example, cost only a few thousand dollars. Today, that same spot could easily cost $500,000 or more. Advertising costs on the Web undoubtedly will escalate the same way, but on the Web, you can often lock in some of your costs if you start now. We'll continue this discussion of Web business costs in later chapters.

Direct comparisons between advertising rates on the Web and traditional media can be difficult to make. But Table 2-2 will give you some idea of how they stack up.

Ad rates may vary slightly from region to region, but in terms of cost effectiveness, the Web comes out head and shoulders above every other marketing vehicle. Dollar for dollar, the Web can put your message in front of more people for less money than any other medium.

As we have shown in this section, there's little reason not to include the Web as part of your total marketing strategy. Companies that establish a presence on the Web are viewed as cutting-edge trendsetters; companies that establish that presence early enjoy all the advantages of charter membership. We also showed you that the Web may be the most cost-efficient information delivery system ever devised.

WHEN'S THE BEST TIME TO GO ONLINE?

In comedy, love, and business, timing is everything. That's true of Web marketing, too. Once you've made the decision to take your company online, you still must determine the best time to make your move. The following section asks questions you should answer before venturing

TABLE 2-2 WHAT DOES $350 BUY YOU THESE DAYS?

Radio	Newspaper	Periodicals	Television	Direct Mail	The Web
Two 30-second spots on a morning show of a major metropolitan station	One week of 3-by-5-inch ads in the classified section of a largely circulated newspaper	A small classified ad in a trade or hobby-related magazine	Two 30-second spots during the morning news show of television station metropolitan or 10 non-prime-time spots on a cable station	About 700 mailers sent to clients throughout the United States	Development and one-month publication of a three page Web site

into cyberspace. What's the best time to go online? After you've answered the following:

HAVE YOU DONE YOUR HOMEWORK?

When we were in grade school, our teachers wouldn't let us go to recess if our homework wasn't finished. Not doing your homework before going online will cost you more than a session on the monkey bars.

We believe that, to prosper on the Web, you must be fully prepared to be there. The first step in that preparation is reading our book. OK, so we're a little biased. But whether you chose our book or another one, you need to find a reliable Web guide to take you through all the steps necessary to establish a credible Web site.

You must also accumulate some serious surf time on the Web. You can't possibly create an effective Web-marketing strategy without it. Pages of a book, no matter how expertly written (excuse us once again for being biased), can't come alive in the way the Web itself can. We suggest you get an account with a provider that will allow you to spend time on the Web. Check out the sites we discuss in the book, and look for related sites. To really understand the Web, there's just no substitute for direct experience.

The Internet has its own unique language, with which all true Net surfers are intimately familiar. What follows are some of the most commonly used terms and their definitions.

Flamers   *People who send negative or derogatory e-mail or news postings.*

Netizen   *A person who utilizes the Web or the Internet in general.*

Surfing   *Traveling from site to site on the Web or, generally speaking, spending time on the Web.*

Finally, prepare to stay on the Web for the long haul. As we say on numerous occasions in this book, the Web is an animal that is constantly evolving. Your advertising and marketing strategy must evolve with it. Some things will work, and some won't. The key is to keep changing and upgrading what you offer. The Web is the medium of the future; it's in your best interest to stick around, do your homework, and mark its progress.

DOES YOUR PRODUCT OR SERVICE FIT THE WEB'S CURRENT DEMOGRAPHICS?

Earlier in this chapter we discussed who may not be good candidates for Web marketing. Part of that discussion centered on the Web's current demographic makeup. At this time, the Web doesn't offer much to companies with products or services geared to older clientele, but the Web's audience is expanding. As users age, and as the Web becomes even more mainstream, some products that weren't right for the Web may find an online niche.

Before you go to the trouble and expense of setting up a Web site, make sure your product or service will appeal to a significant number of Netizens. Some products and services simply don't match the Web's current demography. On the other hand, if you're going online to enhance and reshape your overall marketing strategy, there's really no wrong time to take your company onto the Web. In the long run, the Web will prove to be the world's greatest marketing venue.

WHERE DO I GO TO MAKE ALL THIS HAPPEN?

Imagine you're in a strange town, using a map to try and find your way around. Your map shows your destination clear as day, but when you try to get there, you find a set of railroad tracks blocking your way. The tracks are uncrossable *and* they weren't on the map. Now you have a terrible dilemma. You know where you want to go, you can see it on the map, but you have no idea how to get there.

When you decide to put your company on the Web you have a similar predicament. You're convinced that this is all perfect for you and your company, but you're unsure how to make it happen. The following section will help you get the ball rolling, both technically and with your marketing plan.

CAN I DO IT ALONE?

Tales of the American West are rife with images of lawmen standing alone against the lawlessness of the frontier. The Web may not be the Wild West, but it's definitely frontier territory, another way of saying that attempting to establish a Web page on your own can leave you pushing up daisies.

But Web marketing can be a solo enterprise. Round up your research, prepare a marketing strategy, and, with a little technical know-how, you can even set up your own site. Even if you don't have all the technical knowledge you need to establish your presence on the Web, you can gain a lot of technical expertise just surfing the Web.

Depending on your company's size, you may want to assign one of your employees the task of becoming a Web master. You may even want to hire a new staff member who already has the training and knowledge you need.

If you do decide to set up a Web site yourself, remember to allow plenty of time to acquire some new skills and enough room to make a few mistakes. Nobody becomes a Web master overnight. The effort you put into such a project will yield great rewards, but it will be frustrating at times, and it can be expensive. If you don't think you have the patience, the resources, or the time to give to the project, you're better off hiring a Web consultant.

Skyline.Net is Soup-to-Nuts

Recently the managers of a large periodical approached Skyline.Net about setting up a Web page. They were looking for advertising development, marketing strategies, technical expertise, and overall Web-presence development. This periodical wanted an outside consulting firm to handle all their software and hardware purchasing and configuration. They also were interested in a long-term training program so their employees could become Web-capable. They even requested that we advise them on the hiring of extra full-time staff for the technical aspects of their project.

At press time, negotiations with this company are still underway.

Skyline Network Technologies, Inc., is an all-inclusive consulting firm. We have created single homepages for customers who already had their marketing plans in place, developed Web ads from client suggestions, and customized software to fit specialized Web applications.

In addition to simple Web-presence development, we also have taken companies from no Web presence to a complete, technically viable Web setup, including training current staff and advice on the hiring of new personnel. Our motto is: "If you can dream it on the Web, we can make it reality."

IS THERE HELP OUT THERE?

To continue our Western metaphor…When settlers circled their wagons against Indian attacks, the cavalry always seemed to come to the rescue. Many parts of the business world have begun to rely on a new form of cavalry. They're called outside consultants, and they represent one of the biggest business trends of the '90s.

Setting up a Web site on your own may be possible, but it isn't always the best use of your resources. The project could cost you more time and money than you have to spare. Depending on your circumstances and in-house expertise, you might want to hire consultants to develop at least part of your Web site and your Web marketing plan.

You could also approach the project with a hands-off attitude and hire consultants to do it all. The right Web consultant has the expertise to handle everything from the technical aspects of site construction to the development of online advertising. A good consultant should provide all the software and hardware you need, as well as in-house training. Some consultants will even help you set up an in-house Web department for your ongoing online marketing effort. Others will advise you on hiring new technical personnel.

Remember...

- Web marketing is an avenue for communicating your company's message in a dynamic, visual way. It offers the unique ability to communicate your message quickly and clearly to a worldwide audience. It offers a feature found nowhere else in the marketing world—the potential for instant customer response.

- No matter what your business is or what you sell, service or product, you'll find a niche on the Web. Creating a Web presence is a bad move for very few companies.

- The Web promises to be the marketing venue of the next century. Taking steps to get on the Web now ensures your company of being viewed as a trendsetter in this new medium—not to mention that it's usually cheaper to get in on the ground floor.

- It's important to prepare your company to take the Web plunge. You should be well-versed in what it's going to take to devise an expert Web marketing plan. Luckily, you have a road map for this new land of advertising—this book.

- It's possible to handle all the technical and marketing work on your own, but a consultant's expertise can bring your Web marketing strategy to life.

3

STRAIGHT TALK ABOUT WEB MARKETING: MYTHS AND FACTS

Today, what business person hasn't heard of the Internet and the World Wide Web? Even if they've never actually used or witnessed the Net, a growing number of business owners, CEOs, and vice presidents have used phrases like "surf the Net," and "Information Superhighway" at an important business meeting or luncheon. Newspapers, magazines, television programs, books, and even movies have painted both realistic and exaggerated pictures of the Internet. Unfortunately, all this media attention and street talk has led to a lot of confusion. It can be difficult to separate the real Net from the rumors and empty claims.

Adding to the confusion is a veritable blitzkrieg of conflicting reports on Net proprieties and legalities. Just a few months ago, we were told that using the Internet for business purposes was worse than clubbing baby seals on Christmas Eve. Before that, we were told it would violate federal laws to use this government-funded network for such personal or corporate gain. Despite all the misinformation, and obfuscation, it's become standard corporate practice to tap the profit potential of cyberspace. Did the rules change, or just their interpretation? Are the changes expanding business opportunities on the Net, or reducing them? What is the future—both short- and long-term—of business on the Net? In this chapter, we answer these and other questions often asked by business professionals considering "going online."

YES, YOU CAN! (MAKE MONEY, THAT IS)

First, let's debunk a popular myth: Companies are *not* striking virtual gold all over the World Wide Web. Despite what you may have heard, the Web will not solve all your marketing problems. However, many Web projects have, in fact, been extremely profitable for many companies. The Web has given large and small enterprises alike unprecedented access to lucrative worldwide markets.

THE INTERNET GOLD RUSH

Whether or not *thar's gold 'n them thar hills* (virtual or otherwise), it's clear that American business has joined the rush to the Web, eager to take advantage of this vast expanse of marketing opportunities. In many cases, that eagerness has been highly rewarded. Several companies have literally found overnight success, using the Web as their major (and sometimes only) marketing medium. Others have turned fledgling home businesses into flourishing enterprises. Figure 3-1 shows the Web site for Hot Hot Hot, a specialty shop dealing in exotic hot sauces. The tiny company sold more that $60,000 worth of sauce through the Web in 1994, nearly a quarter of its total business. And that doesn't include the off-line business the Web site helped generate. The final sales figures for 1995 are expected to be significantly higher. On a larger scale, Ceram, Inc., a Colorado Springs electronics firm, invested $100,000 in its Web site and was rewarded with nearly $4 million in sales in one year. Through further use of the Web, the company expects to increase its annual sales to $10 million.

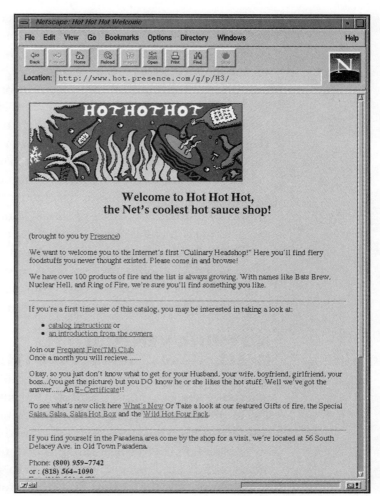

FIGURE 3-1

Hot Hot Hot has sold more than $60,000 worth of sauce through this Web site. URL=http://www.hot.presence.com/g/p/H3/

THE DEATH OF THE SALESMAN

As a marketing tool, the Web continues to grow at a phenomenal rate, attracting a staggering list of business enterprises. In the face of this growth, many business owners and managers ask themselves, "Will the Web cause the everyday, coat-and-tie salespeople and downtown dealers to become obsolete?" The answer is a decisive "*No.*" Most companies that have made the move to Web marketing will attest to its value, but few give the Web much credit for final sales. At least for now, salespeople have no reason to fear displacement.

What effect will Web growth actually have on the traditional sales force? Although the typical salesperson will not be replaced by the Web anytime soon, the Web is fast becoming a useful mechanism for generating traditional sales. You might say it's become a tool of the trade. When your company spends its dollars putting valuable product information and online brochures on the corporate Web site, your entire sales force must learn to use that resource in their customer interactions. They must also familiarize themselves with your competitors' Web sites. Why? Because a growing number of your customers are finding your competition's Web sites are just a click away from your own. And on the Web, sellers can change prices almost instantly, as often as they want.

Jem Computers, for example, is a liquidator of surplus computer equipment. They incorporate "interactive pricing" in their Web site. Simply put, interactive pricing allows Jem to adjust their prices from moment to moment as demand and inventory status change. As goods remain in the stockroom, prices drop; as demand increases, prices stabilize and rise. Companies competing with Jem Computers must prepare their sales force to handle consumer reaction to this remarkably flexible form of pricing.

NOTHING VENTURED (WELL...PRACTICALLY NOTHING)

It seems every company tells a different tale about their level of Web marketing success, yet two aspects continue to drive businesses onto the Information Superhighway—price and coverage. The plain and simple truth is, a business can publish product information and online order forms on the Web for millions of consumers to see, at a fraction of the cost of a full-page advertisement in a popular magazine. Obviously, the potential for reward clearly outweighs the risks.

MARKETING—IT'S NOT JUST FOR SELLING ANYMORE

On average, businesses spend three to 12 months just deciding whether to enter the online marketplace. But while Company A weighs the sales potential of the Web, Company B (and probably Companies C, D, and E) is launching its Web site. While Company A estimates the sales potential of going online at formal board meetings and in casual discussions around the coffee machine, Company B accumulates instant market research, sales leads, and an enhanced corporate image. The Web is used to achieve a broad range of objectives:

- market research
- generating sales leads
- pre-sale support
- post-sale support
- inventory verification
- image-building
- press releases
- catalogs
- parts lists
- online discussions
- demonstration tools
- personnel recruitment
- support for traveling personnel
- parts lists
- personnel directories
- company policies
- memoranda

Most of these objectives apply to marketing; all can make or save a lot of money. Though most corporate Web sites typically don't produce direct online sales, successful sites draw visitors who take away product or service information and buy later, through a sales representative or from a local merchant. In fact, most of the larger corporate Web sites don't provide for direct, online ordering, though they could.

The important thing to remember is, just because you didn't made the sale online, that doesn't mean your Web site failed to generate the interest, name recognition, and product confidence necessary to make that sale. And don't forget, many companies are saving a lot of money by going online. Computer industry giant Sun Microsystems, for example, provides product information and customer support services through its popular Web site (Figure 3-2). While Sun doesn't conduct online sales, the firm boasts substantial cost savings through the online distribution of product literature, software updates, and other vital information. In a single month, Sun's Web site saved the company nearly $950,000—money it otherwise would have spent on more than 7,500 software modules and 5,000 literature packages.

IT'S A BIG WORLD—OR *IS* IT?

Another common misconception about the World Wide Web concerns its size and the efficacy with which it delivers information. We often hear that the Web has an audience of over 30 million in countries around the world. (They don't call it *worldwide* for nothing.) Some people believe the Web makes it easy to reach all those people, and in a way, it does. Information posted on the World Wide Web instantly becomes available to practically every Web user in the world. It's hard to believe any single medium can draw such an audience, but it's absolutely true. And that audience continues to grow.

But just because your information is out there, that doesn't mean everyone, or *anyone*, will see it. Look at it this way: If you drop your business card on the sidewalk in downtown New York, the information on that card is instantly available to the hundreds of thousands of people who will walk by it on any given day. But chances are, you're not going to get a lot of calls from them.

So take the available-audience claims of an overenthusiastic (or dishonest) Web marketing consultant with a grain of salt. Ask yourself (or the consultant), "How much of that audience can I actually capture?"

FIGURE 3-2

Sun's Web site is an excellent marketing tool, yet offers no opportunity for online sales.

THE NEEDLE IN A HAY MOUNTAIN

With 24,000 sites currently available, and hundreds more appearing daily, the Web is the world's most diverse source of information. This is one of the reasons it attracts thousands of new users from around the world every day. However, the odds of the user you want to reach stumbling on your little site can be overwhelmingly unfavorable. A Web site rarely generates its own audience. Fortunately, many ways exist to funnel Web users to your site; unfortunately, they all take time and money. Internet newsgroups, mailing lists, and search sites are just a few techniques to increase your audience. (See Chapter 9, "Attracting Customers," for an in-depth discussion of these and other techniques.)

JUST HOW POPULAR IS WEB MARKETING?

Pick up a magazine and look at the advertisements. Depending on the publication, you'll find from 5 to 80 percent of those ads refer readers to a corporate Web site. Now, pick up today's newspaper and do the same thing. Now turn on your TV. Notice how many car manufacturers and motion picture companies have put up Web sites and announce them in their conventional ads.

Many experts claim the World Wide Web is the fastest growing communications medium ever developed. That is, the Web is growing more rapidly than television, radio, or print ever did. And the numbers seem to support this claim. For example, in 1993, Web traffic increased by a factor of 187. In early 1994, the number of Web servers more than tripled in a single three-month period. Today, there are more than 24,000 Web servers worldwide.

A significant portion of this growth results from the explosive increase in Web commerce. There are so many "malls" on the Web, the next time you surf the Net you'll think you're on Long Island! If you were waiting for Web commerce to become popular, you waited too long.

NOTE

Skyline's research shows that the most popular businesses on the Web are Internet-related concerns, such as access providers and other relevant services. But also at the top of the list are businesses dealing in:

- *Computer hardware*
- *Music*
- *Computer software*
- *Publishing (electronic and traditional)*
- *Financial services*
- *Books*
- *Internet-related consulting*
- *Telecommunications*

- *Travel*
- *Food*
- *Advertising*
- *Media services*
- *Non-Internet-related consulting.*

The last time we checked, it was estimated that 2,000 companies joined the Internet community each month. By the time this book goes to print, that number will be significantly higher. And these are not just Fortune 500 companies. In fact, small firms are doing more business on the Net than corporate giants.

KNOCK-KNOCK. WHO'S THERE?—DEMOGRAPHICS OF THE NET

All the talk about the growth of the World Wide Web population has prompted marketing departments and advertising agencies to seek out demographic information on Web users. Unfortunately, World Wide Web demographics are hard to come by, and the available research is inconclusive. Nobody knows with any certainty how many users, Web servers, or corporate Web sites currently exist. Several studies have been conducted, but no two studies have generated the same numbers, and it's no wonder—the Internet is a faceless society. On the Web, people can communicate, learn, and shop with almost total anonymity. The Web does not reveal race, gender, age, or income. It's a refreshing atmosphere for many, but it's a nightmare for marketing departments.

Fortunately, many Web users are willing to provide demographic information to anonymous surveys. So far, only a handful of such surveys have been conducted, and their results vary significantly. However, definite trends are emerging.

THE EARLY DAYS

The Internet was founded for government and educational use, so it's no surprise that its earliest users were teachers, students, and scientists. This segment of the population dominated the Net throughout the pre-Web years and even during the Web's early development. These users were primarily middle-class males with a college education (or seeking one) and a technical or scientific career.

Web Demographics

A recent CommerceNet/Nielsen study, released late 1995, has provided advertisers with the hard figures they need to make Web marketing decisions. The study shows that 24 million people over the age of 16 use the Internet in the United States and Canada alone. That figure translates to 11 percent of the population above the age of 16. Moreover, a residual market of 13 million people have access to the Net but don't use it regularly. The study also found that 2.5 million people (14 percent of Web users) have conducted at least one online transaction over the Web. Other findings include:

- Typical purchases tend to be under $100 or over $500, with fewer in between.

- 25 percent of all men who use the Web for business purposes have purchased products or services online.

- 62 percent of Internet users have access to the Net from their homes.

- 54 percent of Internet users have access to the Net from their place of employment.

- 30 percent of Internet users have access to the Net from school.

- Males account for 77 percent of all Internet use.

- The average Web user is well-educated and works in a professional field.

- The average Web user has an annual income above $80,000.

TODAY

With the advent of the Web, a great variety of people found they could turn to the Net for information and entertainment without having to master tedious software and complicated interfaces. Today's Web is more diverse than ever. More and more professionals, managers, and clerical workers find themselves using the Web for their occupations or while pursuing higher education. The Web attracts an increasing number of females and even school-age children. With such a large user base, you can find individuals of all combinations of race, nationality, income, gender, age, and personal interests visiting the Web.

CommerceNet gathered the demographic information in Table 3-1. Other interesting statistics gathered by others include:

> At-home users of the Net and other private online services watch
> 25 percent less television. They also read fewer newspapers and

magazines. This means conventional advertising may not reach those consumers.

Home PC users represent 40 percent of all buying power but only 15 percent of the population. But be careful with this statistic. It does not mean that households with PCs have 40 percent of all buying power. It means the regular PC users within those households have the buying power. The important thing to remember is, the vast majority of Web users also fall into the category of home PC users. And a growing number of home PC users—the ones that watch 25 percent less television—are becoming Web users.

WOMEN IN CYBERSPACE

Women are responsible for 70 percent of real-world purchases, but only a small portion of online sales transactions. This is in part because fewer women than men log on. But even the women who *are* on the Net shop less than their male counterparts. Instead, research shows that women turn to the Net for social interaction and convenience.

These findings have prompted advertisers to personalize their Web sites and incorporate a sense of community. And because women in professional fields seem to find their own way into cyberspace, many companies now target their content to homemakers (male and female).

The Web site for Homers, a division of Hearts New Media and Technology, incorporates features from *Redbook, Good Housekeeping, Popular Mechanics,* and *Country Living* in an attempt to develop a virtual gathering place for people interested in home life. To further appeal to female shoppers, clothing companies are considering technology that allows consumers to select body types and view potential purchases on models of similar build. At some sites, one shopper can ask another shopper's opinion before making a purchase. This concern with attracting female consumers has generated a demand for female Web designers. In the male-dominated field of Web design, female designers can add a refreshing woman's touch and attract more female shoppers.

Skyline recently has seen significant increases in the number of women visiting our Web site. We credit this to our exceptionally high rate of social interaction and easy Web access via private networks like Prodigy.

TABLE 3-1 BASELINE WWW USER DEMOGRAPHICS REPORTED BY COMMERCENET

Gender		Highest level of formal education completed	
Male	64.5 %	Less than High School	4 %
Female	35.5 %	High School	8 %
		Technical School	1 %
Age		Some College	24 %
16–24	22 %	Completed College	29 %
25–34	30 %	Some Post Grad	9 %
35–44	26 %	Post Grad	26 %
45–54	17 %		
55 or older	5 %	**Household income**	
		Under $10K	1 %
Occupation		$10–19.9K	4 %
Professional	37 %	$20–29.9K	7 %
Full-Time Student	16 %	$30–39.9K	10 %
Administrative/Managerial	14 %	$40–49.9K	10 %
Technical	12 %	$50–59.9K	11 %
Sales	5 %	$60–69.9K	9 %
Clerical	3 %	$70–79.9K	10 %
Service Worker	2 %	$80–89.9K	7 %
Laborer	2 %	$90–99.9K	4 %
Military	2 %	$100K or Over	14 %
Retired/Not Working	2 %	Don't Know/Refuse	14 %
Craftsperson	1 %		
Homemaker	1 %		

PROJECTIONS

As the World Wide Web and Web commerce become more popular, user numbers will continue to grow, along with their diversity. The Web is rapidly becoming a significant part of our daily lives. In some parts of the U.S., people can walk into a sidewalk cafe and surf the Net over a cup of cappucino. Elsewhere, hundreds of business owners turn to the Web instead of traditional media for up-to-date news and stock reports. The Web has become such a valuable information and business tool, it will soon be considered a business necessity, as indispensable as the telephone or copy machine. Likewise, business-to-business Web purchases will continue to increase.

Over the next few years, you can expect current user trends to continue. We'll find more women on the Web (some predict they'll outnumber the men), and a wider distribution of ages. Technical professionals will continue to shape the Web, but as the Internet enters more homes, the number of non-technical professionals, blue-collar workers, and full-time homemakers exploring the Web will grow exponentially. In addition to an obvious increase in online purchases, their presence is destined to provoke a more diversified offering of products and services, and renewed dedication to the creativity and aesthetics of traditional advertising media. Companies will be forced to offer competitive prices and advanced product features as comparison shopping moves to an entirely new level. Comparison shopping is another factor encouraging the growth of Web commerce. Consumers (especially women) will be captivated by the convenience of browsing the prices and features of competing products from the privacy of their homes.

The growth of the Web as an information and entertainment tool is sure to generate an increased reliance on the Web for marketing opportunities. More Web users means more consumers. That means big bucks for innovative companies willing to spend time and money establishing a foothold in this new domain.

Cyber-sexism

The November 6, 1995 issue of *Information Week* magazine contains an interesting complaint from a California UNIX system administrator. She'd read about the Web site for Speedware (a Canadian company selling application development tools) in a previous issue of the magazine. Believing she would find something useful on the site, she visited the home page. "[Her] interest in the company turned to shock and then to disgust" when she saw the full-size image on the Speedware home page. The image contained two businesspeople: a gentleman in "California casual attire" and a woman wearing a miniskirt and shirt that bared her midriff. She complained "I don't know of any self-respecting female technical professional who would show up at the office in that type of sexist attire. You can believe that I crossed Speedware off my list of possible purchases...It's hard to take such a company seriously."

NUMBERS CAN LIE

At Skyline, we like to caution our clients against putting too much faith in demographic Web data. Survey results vary remarkably. This is understandable considering the biases and errors that plague the survey process.

Self-selection is one of the unfortunate biases found in any voluntary survey. The very fact that a user has chosen to complete the survey injects a significant bias into the data. This is especially damaging when the user can read the survey questions before answering them. If a survey question offends or causes the respondent discomfort, he or she may discard the survey or complete it dishonestly. For example, many people won't choose the smallest household income in a list, even if it accurately reflects their actual income. Likewise, many people won't place themselves in the oldest age group.

Another self-selection issue deals with the number of Web surveys. The average user will only complete one or two surveys, even if he or she comes across many more. The bias here is that users are likely to fill out only the first couple of surveys they encounter. This skews the sampling by selecting only users who are fairly new to the Web.

The bottom line is that current demographic data provides only a rough sketch of the Web community. Nonetheless, even the most conservative interpretation of available statistics paints an encouraging picture of a Web full of educated consumers with average to above-average incomes. And recent trends indicate the Web is fast becoming a marketplace rich and diverse enough to support extensive commerce.

THE INTERNET VS. PRIVATE NETWORKS

Some of the most common misconceptions about the Internet result from its confusion with the private networks commonly known as commercial online services. While widespread Internet use is a recent phenomenon, the commercial services have been fairly popular since the 1980s. Companies like America Online, CompuServe, and Prodigy (referred to collectively as the "Big Three") provide services for which subscribers pay a monthly and/or hourly fee, to connect (using a PC and a modem) to private networks and mainframes. These services initially allowed users to locate news, weather, sports, and other information via the Internet. In recent years, online services have expanded to include entertainment and expansive shopping opportunities.

THE COMMERCIAL SERVICES

Commercial online services differ from the Internet in many ways. These services were developed strictly for commercial reasons, paving the way

The Big Three Enter the Web

The popular perception of the Internet as primarily a scientific tool has deterred many would-be Web advertisers. These advertisers want to reach *consumers*, not just researchers and students. Thanks to recent changes in private networks and online services like CompuServe and Prodigy, several million consumers now access the World Wide Web. These private networks, which have boasted a large and diverse consumer base for many years, now add Web access to their list of services.

for the development of the first forms of electronic commerce. Most information sent to a commercial online service subscriber is commercially driven, so the companies that operate these services receive much of their income by marketing products and services for their sponsors. Each of these private networks is maintained by its respective corporation, and until recently, there was no way to send or receive data (even e-mail) between the networks. The rate structure of the commercial services tends to discourage users from spending large amounts of time online. Table 3-2 contrasts typical monthly fees for commercial online service access and Internet access as a function of the amount of time spent online. In addition to the Internet access providers shown in the table, there are other national providers and a large number of small, local access providers. The local providers are acquiring a growing portion of residential Internet users by offering unlimited use of the Net for prices as low as $30.

TABLE 3-2 ESTIMATED CHARGES FOR ONLINE SERVICES

Service/Network		Monthly Online Hours			
		5	10	40	60
Private Networks	America Online	$9.95	$24.70	$113.20	$172.20
	CompuServe	9.95	24.70	63.95	102.95
	Microsoft Network	9.95	19.95	59.45	99.95
	Prodigy	9.95	24.70	59.45	118.45
National Internet Access Providers	Internet MCI	9.95	22.45	97.45	147.45
	Netcom	19.95	19.95	19.95	59.95
	Pipeline USA	5.00	12.50	19.95	19.95
	PSINet	29.00	29.00	45.50	75.50

THE INTERNET

In contrast to private, commercial services, the Internet is a public network. This means no one person or company controls it. Each segment of the Net is controlled by its owner, making it a complex network of private networks. When you connect to the Internet, your network (no matter how small) becomes the Internet. What you do with that section of the Net is entirely your concern.

Compared to the Big Three, the Internet is in its commercial infancy. Businesses, organizations, and the U.S. government are still working to develop the best ways to use the Internet as a marketing tool. For instance, the Internet community has yet to agree on a secure method of conducting credit-card transactions. On the other hand, because the World Wide Web is still developing, there are more opportunities for creative businesses to establish themselves as leaders and innovators in matters of Web marketing.

The lack of central control has helped the Web become one of today's most affordable marketing mediums. For these reasons, the Web has proven very successful for a number businesses.

The *Chicago Tribune* recently launched "Career Finder," an online version of the newspaper's "Help Wanted" section. The *Tribune* found that 60 to 70 percent of its advertisers will pay the additional dollar per line to place their ads on the Web. The newspaper expects to generate hundreds of thousands of dollars in revenues in 1995 alone. The *Chicago Tribune* has a long history with America Online, but the newspaper

TABLE 3-3 HOW THE INTERNET DIFFERS FROM PRIVATE NETWORKS

The Internet	Private Networks
Has no central authority	Controlled by a single company
Limited demographic statistics	Good demographic information
Publishing information is fairly inexpensive	Much more expensive to publish information
Providing interactive information is easy	Interactivity is limited and expensive
Most users have intermediate to advanced computer skills	Many users have only beginner computer skills
No trusted method of secure transactions	Secure transactions are commonplace
More than 24 million users in North America	CompuServe, for example, has over 2 million users
Home of the Web	No Web access until very recently

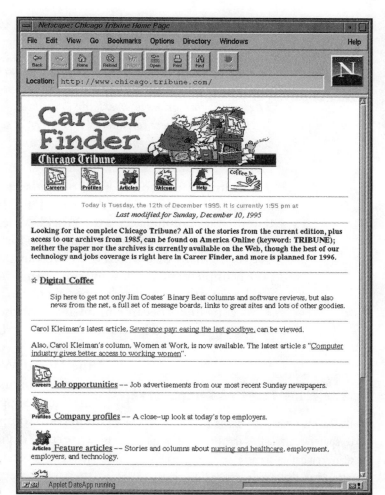

FIGURE 3-3

The *Chicago Tribune* "Career Finder"
contains job opportunities and more.
URL=http://www.chicago.tribune.com

reports that, until the new Web site, it hadn't made much money online.
The *Tribune* still maintains current news stories and archives on America
Online, but plans to move more information to the Web in 1996.

WHY IS THERE CONFUSION?

As the Internet became more popular (and especially with the birth of
the Web), commercial online services rushed to duplicate its features.
Many made exaggerated claims. Some even called themselves "the Net"
and the "Information Superhighway." Many also claimed to provide
"Internet access" when, in fact, they were merely allowing their

subscribers to exchange e-mail and news with previously unreachable Internet users.

When Big Three users were finally able to exchange news and e-mail with those on the Internet, much of the Internet community responded with scorn. These swarms of new users, or "newbies," were totally uneducated in "netiquette" and were considered intruders. It wasn't uncommon for an otherwise acceptable newsgroup posting from an America Online user to generate harsh responses from Internet regulars.

Eventually, the commercial online services gave in to the pressure and began providing what they called "full Internet access." This meant that their users could access the World Wide Web in addition to Internet news and e-mail. This was a major step forward for the users of private networks; many discovered their Web access was extremely limited and poorly implemented. Plus, swarms of Internet applications pop up every week that private network subscribers can't use.

As consumers became more aware of the limitations of commercial online services, and local Internet access providers lowered their prices, the online services raced to compete with the World Wide Web. Now the online services are rushing to come up with more interactive applications to hold subscriber interest. CompuServe even created its own Internet division providing ordinary Internet access that actually competes with its private network services.

The Many Faces of CompuServe

The largest commercial online service, CompuServe, started in the 1970s selling time-share computing services on its mainframes. later, when the market changed drastically, CompuServe began hosting interactive forums and providing access to news and business databases. These services evolved into the CompuServe we know today. CompuServe responded to market changes brought about by the Internet and the Web by purchasing Spry, the developer of *Internet in A Box*, a product that provides affordable and easy-to-use access to the Internet. CompuServe is now in position to become one of the world's largest Internet access providers.

SO, WHICH DO I CHOOSE?

Perhaps we're a little biased, but we don't see a role for commercial online services (as they are today) in the future of electronic commerce. The services offered by these private networks are limited and proprietary, and a growing portion of their users spend most of their time accessing the Web instead of the services' internal features. But for the immediate future, they still hold a considerable share of the online market, and offer secure and reliable purchases and transactions.

We can expect some drastic changes in both services and price structure from the commercial services over the next couple of years as they become more and more Web-like. Several services are likely to split into two divisions. One will offer complete Internet access, like an ordinary Internet access provider. The other will continue to offer subscriptions to their usual information services, except these services will be Web-based. This move will enhance the marketability of these information services, allowing millions of Web users to subscribe without obtaining additional software or learning a new interface. The new Internet access divisions will use pre-existing telephone services available now in many locations.

> ### Take a Lesson from America Online
>
> In 1994, America Online became America's fastest-growing commercial online service. It accumulated more than 2 million subscribers, rivaling CompuServe, the long-time giant among online services. America Online's phenomenal success is directly attributable to its colorful, easy-to-use interface, live chat rooms, abundance of available software, news and financial information, online magazines, and features catering to children and senior citizens. To capture the Internet audience, Web designers are well-advised to look closely at the success of America Online, and the many features that made it so popular.

THE ONE-WAY MIRROR

Understand that even though users of commercial online services have some access to the Internet (and usually the World Wide Web), this relationship doesn't hold in the other direction. Web users have no easy way to browse the commercial content of America Online or CompuServe. So by placing your business on the Internet side of this one-way mirror, you are available to the largest possible market.

A LITTLE CHANGE GOES A LONG WAY

Web marketing research shows that users respond best to information that constantly changes. This finding concurs with conventional marketing wisdom. Imagine your magazine advertisements saying something different each time a reader turns to them, or having the ability to change an image (maybe even animate it) right before that reader's eyes. You can accomplish this and more on the World Wide Web. In fact, static advertising—static *anything*—is obsolete on the Web, and Web publishers are expected to provide content that keeps up with such changes. After all, you wouldn't waste your money broadcasting a radio commercial over a television network. Likewise, you shouldn't waste your money marketing via limited commercial online services when the interactivity of the Web is so easily available.

OPEN 24 HOURS

The World Wide Web is a full-time marketing medium. Aside from occasional problems, a corporate Web site can be up and running long after your marketing department has gone home for the evening. A Web site doesn't take holidays, vacations, or lunch breaks, so you can be sure it's ready to greet prospective customers whenever they happen to visit. Or can you?

A current trend for small to medium companies is to hire what some call "bargain-basement Web-presence providers." These are the mom-and-pop companies that recently have become so popular. They're typically one-person operations. That person often spends most of his or her time at a day job and a few hours each evening creating Web documents, then storing them on a small Web server in the basement or a spare bedroom.

This kind of operation is not a bad choice for many businesses. These amateur Web designers often do excellent work at a fair price. But the reliability of small-time Web sites can leave a lot to be desired. Many of these sites have unreliable electrical power sources or poor Internet connections. Some have no backup server in case the primary server needs repairs or upgrades. If the operator has a day job, you can bet all upgrades will take place in the evenings, when most consumers browse the Web. A seemingly 24-hour operation can actually end up keeping bankers' hours. Every minute that a Web server is down, businesses lose valuable marketing opportunities—and that can be *very* expensive

TIP *It's always a good idea to visit the office of your perspective Web service provider before making your final decision. It's the best way to get a feel for the amount of resources available to that company. Don't shy away from a small-time operation, but prepare for a few headaches, and expect lower rates for your trouble.*

OVERPOPULATION

In conventional media, businesses want to place their advertisements in high-traffic areas. The larger audience increases the potential for sales prospects. The same holds true on the World Wide Web. But it's possible for a Web site to have so much traffic that a company's advertisements actually receive *less* exposure. Web browsers load a Web page in stages. First, they retrieve the text for the page. Then they retrieve the images that should appear with the text. At an overpopulated site, image transfer slows drastically. A user may stare at a graphic-less Web page for several minutes before an image appears. Typically, users won't wait more than a few seconds before moving on, so odds are the images that provide Web advertising's real impact will seldom be seen.

TOO MANY COOKS

Because the Internet is a unique, cooperative effort of many companies, universities, and governments, unexpected problems crop up at unexpected times. When a customer tries to connect to your corporate Web site, for example, they might have to travel through three or four—sometimes as many as twenty—different networks. If any one of those networks isn't working, your customer won't be able to connect to your site. Plus, it may appear to that customer that your Web site is not working properly.

The effect of this occasional unreliability is that you can't count on your site being available 24 hours a day. If you have salesmen who connect to your site when they visit with customers (and you should), they should prepare for possible problems. This includes bringing along a set of literature in case he or she can't access the online information.

Remember, the odds are very small that you will have a connection problem at a crucial time, but it always pays to prepare. As time goes on and the Internet becomes more reliable, the already slim chances of a serious connection problem will become even smaller. For now, place your web site on the most reliable network and server you can afford.

Be Prepared

When Skyline first started out, we often took notebook PCs to the offices of potential clients, used a modem to connect to the Internet, and showed the potential client exactly what we do online. We were wise enough to store some samples directly on the PC's hard drive so we could have something to show if we ran into problems connecting to the Net. This insurance paid off on several occasions.

THE FINAL FRONTIER (BIG FISH, LITTLE FISH?)

For the first time in history, the pen is no longer the only weapon mightier than the sword, and freedom of the press no longer requires a slew of reporters and editors. With the arrival of the Web, millions of individuals and many small businesses now have inexpensive access to mass communication and global markets throughout the world. Consequently, many call the Web the next frontier—the ultimate democracy for the free-market world. Admittedly, the World Wide Web has a long way to go before it replaces traditional publishing methods, but it's rapidly changing the way advertisers and consumers perceive the media. It's giving a voice to practically anyone with a message. And, these days, every business (large or small) has a message.

BIGGER IS BETTER

In traditional advertising, big corporations have a significant advantage over the little guys. Money has always bought the most colorful graphics, the coolest slogans, the catchiest jingles, and the best air time and placement. In many ways, bigger has always been better. The World Wide Web threatens to change all of that by allowing every corporation the same level of exposure at an affordable price. The good news for major corporations is that exposure is no longer everything. Companies with large advertising budgets and talented marketing departments will always rule the advertising world. Successful advertising still requires colorful graphics, cool slogans, and catchy jingles. And the concept of air time will probably exist even on the Web, as businesses vie for ideal advertising space on other Web sites.

The only reason large companies haven't overshadowed the little guys in the arena of Web marketing is that they've been pulling their punches. They're afraid to invest too much time and money into a medium that has yet to prove itself. A little more aggressiveness could bring many of these companies instant Internet success. The market's there for the taking. And the first business in each field to make a name for itself on the Web will reap the benefits for years to come.

DAVID VS. GOLIATH

On the other hand, small businesses have a fighting chance. The Web seems to be the land of the underdog. For now, the Web community is consistently more impressed by innovative ideas than catchy slogans.

FIGURE 3-4

Silicon Graphics' "Silicon Surf" has long been regarded as one of the largest and most advanced sites on the Web. URL=http://www.sgi.com

Realize, however, that this is changing as the average Internet user becomes less technically oriented and more interested in flashy graphics. When users don't understand the technological advances or the creative ingenuity behind a Web site, they'll rely on appearance and ease of use to maintain their interest.

It's imperative, then, that small companies carefully allocate their resources between developing new ideas and using old ideas in an appealing way. If you keep this in mind, a small budget doesn't have to be your downfall. Because all businesses on the Web have the same

Innovation Brings Mixed Results

Skyline Network Technologies has developed a Web application that turns an ordinary Web site in to a "virtual world." Using *S.N.T.MUD*, users can walk around, meet and talk to other users, and interact with objects and businesses. When Skyline began alpha testing *S.N.T.MUD* software with a Virtual Baltimore Tour, we received understandably mixed responses. Longtime Web users, who understood the technological difficulties overcome by *S.N.T.MUD*, were extremely impressed. In fact, several other Web development companies expressed interest in obtaining the software for themselves. But many users simply found the feature entertaining, and had little appreciation for the software behind it. These users were more interested in the online pictures of Baltimore Harbor. This experience taught us that we must provide both innovative ideas for Web veterans and interesting multimedia for less technically oriented users.

potential audience, it's like anybody can afford to run an advertisement during Super Bowl half-time: The successful companies will be the ones with advertisements as appealing as the game itself.

IT'S OKAY TO MARKET ON THE INTERNET

About half the people we talk to still believe the Internet is not supposed to be used for commercial purposes. That may have been true a couple of years ago, but now the Internet is open for business. The government no longer maintains the backbone of the Internet, and many early restrictions have been lifted. The question is no longer "Will the government let us market products on the Internet?" Instead it's "Will the Internet community let us market products on the Internet?"

The key to effective advertising is knowing what services are available for a particular medium, and exploring how other companies have exploited those services. On the Net, advertisers can participate in online forums, discussion groups, and chat areas to get a feel for consumers' views. Sending tons of e-mail and news messages to consumers is not the answer—unless, of course, you believe that any publicity is good publicity.

TIP

Don't have time to surf the Net looking for creative ways to tap its resources? That doesn't mean you have to jump in blindly. Hire a Web consultant to do the vital research for you.

RESPONSIBLE INTERNET MARKETING

The vast majority of Internet users are not opposed to the current commercialization of the Web. Instead, they oppose the flagrant abuses committed by advertisers on many of the other Internet applications. The only resistance to Web commercialization is based on the fear that the Web, too, will be overrun with commercial messages. This fear has created a hypersensitivity that has forced many companies to think twice about their marketing strategies.

THE SUBSIDIZED CONTENT MODEL

Most Internet users realize that the marriage of advertising and media production must occur on the Net just as it occurred in traditional media. And nearly all Web users would rather put up with advertisements than find their favorite Web sites asking for monthly access fees. So the subsidized content model, where advertisers pay the media producer (in this case the Web site owner) so the viewers don't have to, is finding a welcome home in the Internet community. In fact, because this trend is almost certain to increase Web site quality and creativity, this form of commercialism will be a welcome change to that of the private networks, where high production costs hinder advertiser creativity.

BAD NEIGHBORHOODS: SECURITY ON THE WEB

Security on the Web has been a major concern since its inception. In truth, the Web is no less secure than most other Internet applications. The difference is that no other Internet application is used so heavily for commercial purposes.

THE BIGGEST HURDLE

Ask any Web marketing specialist what the biggest hurdle he or she faces is. If the answer isn't "security," they're in the wrong business. Security will continue to be a thorn in the side of Web marketers until somebody comes up with a reliable standard for encrypting financial transactions and valuable data. Until that happens, and people begin to develop confidence in that standard, Web marketing won't develop to its full potential.

But current fears about the insecurity of Internet transactions are in many ways overblown. Most people are concerned that their credit card numbers may travel unencrypted across the Internet from their PC to the online retailer. And the potential does exist for credit card numbers posted on the Net to be intercepted by riffraff who'll use those numbers to make unauthorized purchases. But for average consumers, the risk they take sending their credit card numbers this way is negligible, especially if they're in the habit of verifying all the charges on their credit card statements (an excellent practice for all credit card customers). Most credit card number misuse can be traced to a dishonest retailer or employee who was given the number directly by the cardholder. Unencrypted Web purchases can actually be even safer than mail order. This is partly because credit card numbers from Web purchases often pass through fewer hands, providing less opportunity for theft. Nevertheless, the risk of theft is there and it must be dealt with before electronic commerce can reach its full potential.

Simply put, encryption is the process of taking valuable data and turning it into what looks like meaningless chatter. The encrypted data can be sent over the Internet or other network without the fear of somebody intercepting it. When the appropriate party receives the encrypted data, that party will use a previously agreed-upon code to unencrypt the data back to its original form.

THE TRUTH ABOUT HTML

We've talked about HTML and its importance to the development of the World Wide Web. Now, you're probably wondering exactly how much you'll need to know about this Web language to get your site up and running. But before you go out and buy one of the many books on this subject, lets look at a few HTML basics.

THE LANGUAGE OF THE WEB

HTML (HyperText Markup Language) is the language of the World Wide Web. An HTML document is the text and codes that produce a Web page. There is no mysterious witchcraft behind HTML. It even looks a lot like plain text, except that it has some formatting codes mixed in. HTML is fairly easy to learn, but it can take a lot of experience and practice to truly master it. Most of the best HTML documents are written by professional HTML authors. (If you're interested in learning the language yourself, the appendix in the back of this book lists a number of helpful resources.)

What follows is the HTML used to create the document in Figure 3-5. Notice that formatting codes, called "tags," surround certain sections of the text. A tag is the name given to any element of an HTML document used as instructions to format the document. Designers use tags to make certain text show up as bold or underlined. Tags can also create links between distinct HTML documents.

```
<head>

<title>Skyline Network Technologies, Inc.</title>

</head>

<body background=/icon/Clouds.jpeg>

<h6>

<center>

<img vspace=1 src=header.gif>

<hr width=75%>

P.O. Box 43162 <img align=absmiddle src=/icon/
redball.gif>

Baltimore, MD 21236 <img align=absmiddle src=/icon/
redball.gif>

(410)882-3781<br>

<hr width=75%>

</h6>

<b><font size="+1">Skyline Network Technologies,
Incorporated</font></b>

is a full service internet publishing and consulting
firm specializing in
```

```
<b>interactive advertising</b>.

<p>

<b>Interactive advertising</b> is an extremely
effective method of reaching

potential customers. Click <a href=foryou/>here</a>

to see if your company could benefit from
<b>interactive advertising</b>.

<p>

<img align="absmiddle" src=check2.gif>Check out our
complete list of

<a href=services.html>services</a>.

<p>

How may we help you? Fill out our <a href=foryou/
AdForm.html>inquiry form</a>.

We'd love to hear from you.<p>

<h6>

<img src=/headers/bottom.gif><br>

<A href=/top/>Top</A> |

<A href=/legal/copyright.html>Copyrights</A> |

<A href=/legal/disclaimer.html>Disclaimer</A> |

<A href=/home/>Boom Town</A> ]

<p>

&copy Skyline Network Technologies, Inc.

</h6>

</center>

</body>
```

FIGURE 3-5

Compare this page to the HTML in the Technical Note. URL=http://www.skyline.net/home/skyline/

LIMITATIONS

Just like any spoken language, HTML has many limitations. These include:

- HTML tags give only basic instructions to the Web browser. The browser is free to interpret them any way it chooses. For example, the tag used to denote bold text may be interpreted by the browser to mean underline or italics.

HTML doesn't readily allow for the absolute placement of images and text on a page. That is, it doesn't work like your word processor, where you can drag an image, chart, or table anywhere on the page. And it can be quite complicated (and sometimes impossible) to set text exactly where you want it on the page.

HTML is actually a set of standards agreed upon by the makers of Web browsers. The companies that design the browsers are free to deviate from the standards and use their own tags. When this happens, Web publishers are forced to create HTML that's compatible with all popular browsers.

TIP

The more complicated an HTML document becomes, the more difficult it is to ensure compatibility with all popular browsers and PC configurations. An experienced Web consultant can guide you to create Web pages that all will enjoy.

Every user has a unique combination of browser, PC, network connection, and software configuration, so an HTML page can appear drastically different from one user to the next. One user may only be able to display 64 colors, while another may use a laptop with a very limited screen size. Yet another may have poor eyesight and configure his browser to display text much larger than normal. The challenge is to create Web pages that will look good regardless of idiosyncrasies.

DYNAMIC ADDRESSABILITY

The two most important issues in advertising are appeal and relevance. The easiest way to ensure that your information is relevant to a particular person is to let that person select the information. That's why the Web's biggest advantage over all other media is its use of *dynamic addressability*. Dynamic addressability allows specific content to be sent to an individual based on that person's behavior. This allows a Web site to guide the consumer to the content that best addresses his or her needs. Most traditional media do not allow for the conveyance of specific advertising messages to specific individuals for specific reasons.

Only non-broadcast media, such as direct mail and selective binding (print), allow customized addressing of targeted individuals. And neither of these media allows for customized addressing in real time.

The simplest form of the Web's dynamic addressability is built directly into HTML language. By designing a web page so that it contains links to other Web pages, the advertiser creates the opportunity for dynamic addressability. A user can follow the links he or she believes are the most suitable. And by choosing the most suitable information, the user automatically targets the advertiser's message to meet his or her particular needs. Allowing the reader to choose the path shifts the interaction's balance of power. The advertiser no longer provides a single well-orchestrated message to the consumer. Instead, the consumer is free to pick and choose information at his or her discretion.

THE REMOTE CONTROL DILEMMA

To further understand this shift in the balance of power, think back to the days before remote control TV. That box in the living room held the attention of the entire family for several hours every day. And every 15 minutes, we all sat obediently and watched 3 minutes of commercials (unless we had to leave the room). But now, we often surf from channel to channel, especially during commercial breaks. If it weren't for the fact that nearly all television broadcasters insert commercials at the same intervals, we might never watch a single TV commercial.

The Web confronts us with hundreds of thousands of "channels," each with its own brief program (a single Web site). Each has its own combination of entertainment, information, and commercialization, and each constantly entices us to switch to another channel. This leads to a dilemma for the Web marketer—how to get consumers to sit obediently through the commercials when thousands of other channels call to them, channels that may have no commercial information at all.

THE COMMON GATEWAY INTERFACE

Regardless of its dynamic addressability, a Web page is a still a static document. It simply sits there and waits for the user to choose to read it. The page is displayed only when the user chooses to display it. And the page is displayed as it was written, even if it doesn't exactly suit the user's needs. But what if the advertiser wants to modify that page based on the user's previous behavior? A more advanced dynamic addressability is needed to achieve such a level of interactivity. The Common Gateway

Interface (CGI) was developed for just this purpose. The designer can use a CGI-compliant program to make highly interactive modifications to HTML or to generate completely new documents. The use of CGIs greatly enhances a site's dynamic addressability and shifts the balance of power back to the advertiser (often without the consumer's knowledge).

The use of CGI programs within a Web site is generally best left to professional programmers who understand CGI security issues.

Most people have no need to understand the details of CGI, but Web marketers should understand that the CGI standard allows real-time creation and modification of HTML documents. Instead of sending a canned reply based on a single user preference, the CGI standard can run a program that generates a highly customized response. Rather than trust the user to choose the appropriate information, programmers can write a CGI-compliant program to analyze the user's behavior or available demographics and react accordingly. For example, a hotel company may automatically display its government room rate when a user connects from a government facility. (Yes, there are ways to determine who connects from a government facility.) This adds another dimension to Web site interactivity. Because all successful advertising incorporates both appeal and relevance, this ability to dynamically address content to specific users and to guide those users to additional relevant content provides the advertiser with a great advantage.

Even a simple CGI can make users feel welcome. When users note that a site has responded to their actions, they feel appreciated. Ask an experienced Web consultant what you can do to make users feel at home.

Remember...

- You can make money on the Internet. Thousands of companies use the Web successfully to increase sales and overall productivity.

- Selling isn't the only reason to establish a Web presence. The Web can save your company thousands of dollars, for example, by providing convenient and inexpensive customer support.

- The demographics of the Web make it a rich market for nearly any type of business. As the Web population increases and diversifies, the demographics will continue to improve.

- With careful planning, and a reliable Web server, your corporate Web site can sell for you 24 hours a day, every day.

- The economics of Web marketing help level the playing field between major corporations and small businesses.

- Dynamic addressability is the key feature making the Web an excellent marketing medium. To be successful, companies must exploit this feature and provide Web sites that respond to users' desires.

4

INTERNET PSYCHOLOGY: UNDERSTANDING THE INTERNET MIND

It's been said that marketing is psychology at its finest, and few business marketing professionals would argue that point. Since it's virtually impossible to address and market products and services to an audience effectively without first understanding how that audience thinks and reacts, we devote this chapter to an exploration of the psychological and sociological makeup of the Internet community.

THE MAKINGS OF A SOCIETY

The Internet is a society, and like any society, it has its own culture. If you doubt the truth of this statement, just spend some time online. You'll find a unique community, with its own arts, sciences, customs, and standards of behavior. The Net has its social activists, its singles groups, and its own peculiar methods for handling grievances. Soon, it may even have its own money.

We define society as a group of human beings broadly distinguished from other groups by mutual interests, participation in characteristic relationships, shared institutions, and a common culture.

Culture is the totality of socially transmitted behavior patterns, arts, beliefs, institutions, and all other products of human work and thought characteristic of a community or population.

Admittedly, Internet culture comprises a heterogeneous conglomeration of real-world cultures modified to fit the limitations and advantages of the online world. But, historically, that's how cultures form—by subcultures coming together. As those subcultures interact and develop together, a new and unique culture is born. The Internet community may never become a truly homogeneous society in the traditional sense, but this electronic nexus of disparate subcultures already manifests what can truly be called an identity.

This unique culture presents many opportunities to the marketing world, but it also holds dangers for the ill-prepared. When a company sets out to establish itself in a foreign culture, it must first examine that culture and adapt both its products and its marketing strategies to the new markets. The same is true for any business entering the world of Internet commerce. Each business must find its own way to adapt to Internet culture.

Because Internet society is subject to more cross-cultural influences than any other society in history, adaptation can be a fairly simple task.

Members of the Internet community are all members of other real-world societies, so we can use traditional marketing history and a little common sense to guide our online endeavors. Since most Internet users are male, many advertisers have taken what they already know about that audience and used it to design their Web marketing strategies. College students make up a significant portion of the Web, so companies are adapting marketing techniques used on college campuses into successful World Wide Web campaigns.

Perhaps the biggest difference between the Internet community and other cultures is the lack of central authority on the Net. No governing body tells Net users what they can and cannot do online. The individual corporations and educational institutions providing Net access establish acceptable use policies for their users, but these policies hardly affect the millions of homes connecting to the Net each day. These users pay good money for Internet access and, understandably, they don't want anybody telling them what they can and cannot do.

SKELETONS IN THE CLOSET

Most Internet users respect the Net and would do nothing to diminish its usefulness as a tool for businesses and communication worldwide. But as in any society, some seek to exploit this revolutionary medium in ways that are clearly immoral and often illegal. Some recent developments in online delinquency include copyright violations, pornography, and crimes against children.

Internet copyright violations can be as innocent as scanning a comic strip out of the Sunday paper and passing it around the Net, or as heinous as making the entire set of WordPerfect installation disks available via FTP (see Technical Note). Regardless of its seriousness, copyright violations have become commonplace on the Internet, and it's often nearly impossible to catch the culprits. For example, software pirates have been known to break into the FTP sites of small corporations and post entire software packages there. Other pirates are then free to log on to the site and download the software. Many businesses are surprised to find that these kinds of activities have been taking place on their site for years. Catching the pirates can be difficult, especially because many businesses are reluctant to admit they've been violated in such a manner. (The business may be prosecuted in the culprits' absence.)

TECH NOTE

In Chapter 1, we briefly discussed File Transfer Protocol (FTP). An FTP site is a computer hosting a large number of files so that appropriate Internet users can download the files to their own computer using FTP. This is similar to the way a Web site holds a large number of Web documents so that Web users can receive and view the documents using a Web browser.

A software pirate *is an individual who engages in the illegal distribution or use of copyrighted software.*

PORNOGRAPHY

Pornography has a long-standing presence in the Internet community. It's simple to transmit obscene pictures around the world using the Net, but this practice has been limited to a few obscure areas. Today, you must look hard for online pornographic material to find it. Until recently, few people complained about this seamy side of the Internet. But the presence on the Internet of more and more households, school systems, and even churches—and their concomitant "family values"—is triggering a groundswell of concern about Net pornography. It's unfortunate that so many households and schools waited so long to join the Internet because of sensational stories about cyberporn. After weighing the risks, many finally have gone online.

In many cases, the only crime involved in sending pornographic materials around the Net is copyright violation. Most Internet pornography consists of previously published photographs that have been scanned and distributed illegally. The recent spate of complaints about online pornography stems largely from very real concerns about the newest and most serious crimes to be committed on the Net.

Making the Web a Safer Place

A new type of software can help prevent children and sensitive adults from viewing pornographic or other potentially offensive material. An entire line of products is now available to limit access to World Wide Web sites. Corporations use these products to limit Web access during work hours, and schools and parents use them to eliminate access to pornographic material. The software locates a database of sites and blocks access to those sites deemed inappropriate. Most software packages are configurable to block only specific categories or levels of offensiveness. Some can even be configured, for example, to block certain sites only during work hours. This way, employees confined to work-related sites during the day may surf the Net after-hours. Tools like this provide another reason not to include offensive material on commercial Web sites.

CRIMES AGAINST CHILDREN

Nobody likes to admit it, so let's just say it and get it over with: The Internet has been used to commit serious and vile crimes against young children. The most common crimes is probably the distribution of child pornography, but more serious offenses involve adults who befriend children online and use that friendship to commit some form of child abduction or abuse. The FBI and other law-enforcement agencies find and prosecute many of those who commit these crimes. Unfortunately, recent media attention to this subject has generated unreasonable fear that the Internet is a breeding ground for perverts.

The truth is, any society with more than 30 million members will have its share of criminals. Statistically, the Internet will always be a generally safe place for both children and adults. But just as a street-corner drugstore owner wants to keep his neighborhood free from riffraff that might scare away customers, Internet advertisers have a definite stake in making the Web a safe place to do business.

THE FIRST AMENDMENT

The Internet community has always been very protective of its right to free and unfettered speech. We've been looking at the Internet from a business and marketing perspective, but the Net is also an important vehicle for political and social discourse. The understandable value people place on this new venue for democracy has lead to an extreme sensitivity to anything that may threaten this freedom. Many have come to perceive affordable Internet access as a right.

The Internet community has interpreted the right to free speech very loosely. Somehow it's come to mean "free exchange of information." In other words, people want to pay no more to send images and data around the world than they pay to write a simple e-mail message. More importantly, people are demanding access to a limitless amount of information from the Internet without paying additional fees. Some companies have tried to refuse these demands. Most have failed.

With the advent of the Web, many individuals and companies began providing valuable information online, hoping that eventually people would be willing to pay for such information. Instead, they discovered that Internet users not only want more information than ever, they want that information better organized. Interestingly, information providers rushed to comply, even after realizing that their plans to charge fees for information probably won't succeed.

THE GIFT CULTURE

The Internet is the first-ever user-driven mass medium. Its growth and development are entirely the result of user contributions. Consequently, the Internet—and especially the World Wide Web—has evolved into a "gift culture." Thousands of individuals and companies use the Web to give things away. Advice, entertainment, software, images—it's out there and it's free to millions of Web users all over the world. Companies in every field are learning they must give something of value to Web users to be taken seriously.

Internet users historically have been unwilling to pay for online information. The most common exceptions are financial and business information. For example, a handful of electronic newsletters have surfaced dealing with Internet marketing. Originally, there was no charge to receive these newsletters via e-mail, but eventually the demand became so great that publishers could charge several hundred dollars a year for this information. Incidentally, such financial and business information is far less prone to copyright violation than other types of information. Most businesses won't pay for information just to distribute it—and risk putting it in their competitors' hands—for free.

BIRDS OF A FEATHER

In many ways, the Internet is an experiment in social interaction. Sociologists are amazed by the levels of interaction and organization in the lawless Net frontier. From the beginning Internet users organized themselves around common interests, careers, and geography. Newsgroups, mailing lists, and now special-interest Web sites have provided an outlet for people to express their feelings, experiences, and goals on a variety of topics. Consequently, many Net users have formed strong bonds with one another. These bonds don't often manifest as true friendships, but exist as a spirit of brotherhood and a desire to work together. The failure to understand this spirit has been the downfall of more than a few businesses on the Net.

Because Net users tend to stick together and share good and bad experiences, businesses must tread very lightly. You only have to anger one or two users to turn the mass-media capabilities of the Internet against you. Internet users are not afraid to tell the world about any problem they have with your company. While a single disgruntled user is unlikely to single-handedly to destroy your company's reputation, plenty of consumers will take another's complaints to heart.

Although we don't take the story seriously, we can't count the number of times we've received the famous cookie recipe complaint through our e-mail. The e-mail message was allegedly sent by a woman who was so impressed with a popular cookie company's product that she called them up and asked for the recipe. She was told she would have to pay for it, and that the charge would be "three-fifty." Thinking that meant three dollars and fifty cents, the woman agreed to pay and gave the company her credit card number. She was given the recipe, but was surprised to learn that she had been charged $350. The woman tried to convince both the cookie maker and her credit card company that the charge was unfair, but in the end, she footed the bill. She took her

Homework on the Net

The following e-mail message was posted to the Internet and has crossed our desk several times. We've been told this young girl received thousands of responses to her message. It shows just how successfully and quickly the Internet can be used to pass along a simple message. You may notice that, although the girl stated specific dates she wanted to receive her messages, she failed to include the year. This message, and several others like it, have floated around the Internet for years. Imagine how a negative message about your company can spread through the Internet. Note: We have changed the girl's name and her e-mail address avoid encouraging more responses.

Hi. My name is Mary Mailer. I am an 11-year-old sixth-grader
in DeLand, Florida. I am doing a science project that will attempt
to demonstrate the scope and reach of the Internet by gauging
how many messages I can receive in a 24-hour period.
Please send a brief message (even just one word, like "Hi")
to my dad's e-mail account: <dad@some.email.address> between
9 a.m. Wednesday, November 29 and 9 a.m., Thursday, November 30
(adjust for your time zone).
I would also very much appreciate it if you could forward THIS
message to as many people and groups as you know on-line so they
can send me messages, too!
Thank you very, very much,
Mary Mailer
<dad@some.email.address>
Southwestern Middle School
DeLand, Florida

revenge by posting her story and the valuable recipe all over the Net. We won't include the recipe (or the name of the cookie company) here. If you want it, you'll have to get an e-mail account and wait for the message to come your way.

E-mail isn't the only venue for frustrated consumers. Consider the DIVE! site (see Figure 4-1). In January 1995, Mary Feller launched a Web site she believed could save the NBC series *seaQuest* from its ratings dive. The site was designed as a public protest against what Mary considered to be "NBC's tinkering with what could have been the best sci-fi series in years." The use of this new method of protest was discussed in the February 13, 1995, issue of *Interactive Age.* The Newspaper printed a story about the Web site just three weeks after the site first appeared on the Web, but NBC executives did not head the warnings of the Web community. The Web site reports that on November 16, 1995, the cast and crew of *seaQuest* were informed that the show had been "canceled due to very low ratings." As this book went to press, the DIVE! site had changed its name to "DIVED" and continues to follow the final days of the television series.

INSTANT GRATIFICATION

The Internet is a medium of communication. And like any such medium, its strength lies in the speed with which it can pass along its information. If it were faster to send a letter through the postal service, e-mail would not have become the medium of choice for so much business-to-business communication. Likewise, if a customer could learn about your products faster at the store than he can click on them with his Web browser, you'd waste your money going online. The Web is just another manifestation of a world where everybody is rushed and everything must be done right now.

HISTORICALLY SPEAKING

The Internet first became popular because it was the fastest way to send written communication from one place to another. Soon, people realized it could transmit images and data just as quickly, and cheaply. Suddenly, the Internet was providing better speed and pricing than the postal service or even the fax machine. Without this speed the Internet would never have become so popular. The thrill of instant gratification drives the Internet to expand, and makes it a valuable marketing tool.

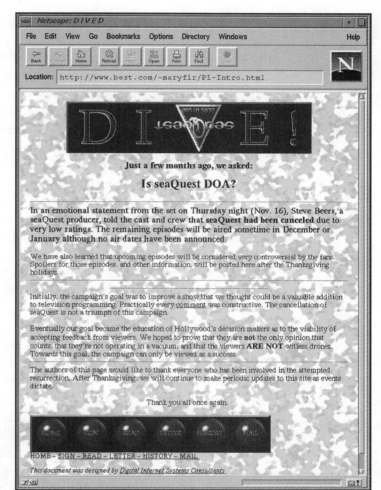

FIGURE 4-1

The DIVED site recaps the efforts of Web users to revive NBC's television show *seaQuest*.

GIVE IT TO ME NOW!

A desire for instant information is even more prevalent on the Web than elsewhere on the Internet. Internet users (like the rest of the modern world) are impatient. They know what they want and they want it now. Every time a user connects to your Web site and must wait for your server to respond or for an image to transmit, that user is inconvenienced, by your company. People don't go to the Web for inconvenience. They want convenient forms of information, entertainment, and commerce. If you plan to go online, our advice to you is, "Give them what they want, and give it to them *now*."

As an online marketer, you'll want to keep potential customers moving and interested from their first visit to your homepage right up to the final sale. Your Web site is essentially a self-guided tour of your business, so it must respond quickly to users' desires. The Web captivates its audience by providing instant feedback to users' wishes. Any salesman will confirm the importance of keeping a prospect moving toward the sale. And a corporate Web site—your virtual salesperson—must be designed to serve the same purpose. In later chapters we'll discuss ways to hold your visitors' interest in your Web site, and how to use that interest to make a sale.

There are other ways to benefit from this desire for instant gratification. The most common method is the online order form. Allowing customers to order and pay for products directly through your Web site (often from the convenience of their home PC), taps into the power of instant gratification. More importantly, you encourage convenience purchases and discourage comparison shopping.

CONVENIENCE PURCHASES

Convenience purchases are those purchases made to save a little time. For instance, a customer may know that one store offers a better price or selection, but he or she chooses to buy at another store simply because that store is closer, or because the buyer was there anyway, buying something else. In today's fast-paced society, our time is so valuable we actually spend money to save time. That's why location is the single most important factor for retail stores in the '90s.

Consider convenience stores: They exist solely because people won't take the time to travel to larger stores with better prices. Businesses have learned that if you can give people what they want, quickly and conveniently, they will reward your efforts by paying top dollar.

COMPARISON SHOPPING

As we said before, comparison shopping is so easy on the Web that businesses are forced to provide competitive pricing. Those businesses that can't (or won't) provide such pricing can always hope that offering convenient payment options and online order forms balances the scales somewhat. By offering online forms at your Web site, you tap into the customers' urge to buy.

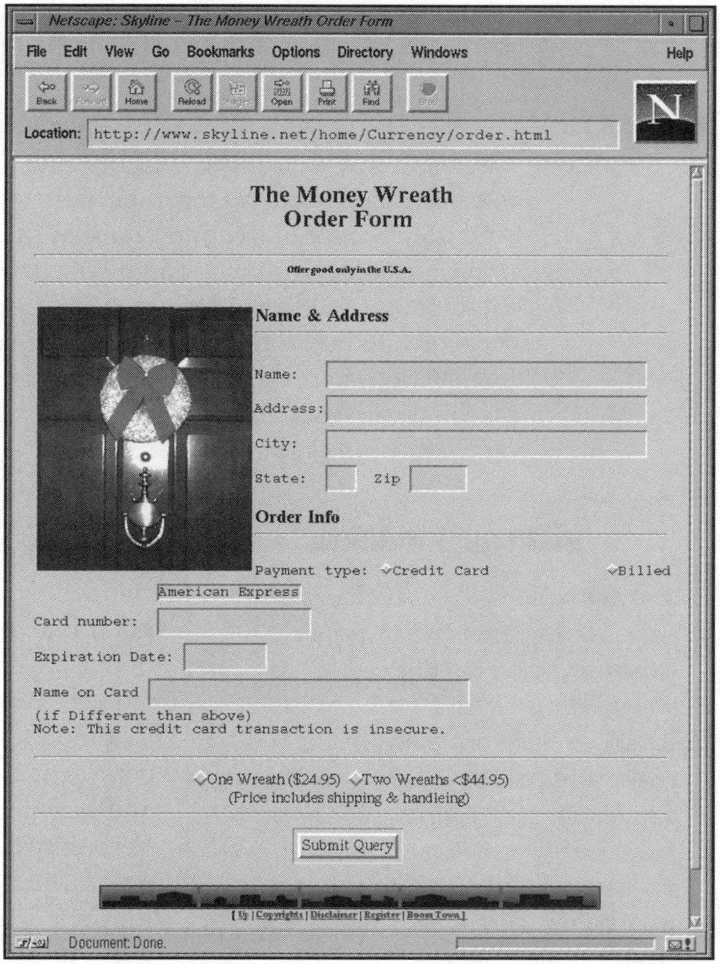

FIGURE 4-2

Online forms allow customers to spend money on a whim.

OTHER IMPLICATIONS

Merely allowing customers to make online purchases isn't enough to ensure their instant gratification. Businesses must further enhance purchase speed and convenience by expediting the shipping process. Remember, a customer can usually visit a local merchant, make a purchase, and return home with the product in hand. Online merchants probably never will compete successfully with real-world retailers in turnaround time. But Web customers still expect you to make an honest effort. And more and more businesses find that Web users will pay a little extra for services like overnight delivery.

NEWBIES

Newbies are a special breed of Internet user. They're the new kids, the inexperienced users taking their first tentative steps into cyberspace. And they behave like country mice in the big city—a strange combination of scared, confused, and amazed. Fancy graphics easily impress these people, and they love to fill out online forms (even if it means they have to buy something). They actually enjoy participating in online surveys, and they're very willing to provide feedback about your products, services, and Web site. Together these factors make newbies excellent sources for market research.

An interesting characteristic of newbies is their tendency to believe anything they read on the Web. They don't yet understand how easy and inexpensive it is to publish information there, and tend to give undue credit to Web sources. When a consumer buys a book on repairing automobiles, he or she can be reasonably confident that an expert wrote the book and provided accurate information. On the Web, however, nearly everyone is a self-proclaimed expert on something, and they're not afraid to show off their expertise—or lack of it. What newbies (and even some experienced Web travelers) fail to realize is that the person providing the information may have no more knowledge of the subject than they do. (As newbies become more "street smart," it will become necessary to provide some form of credentials when making expert claims.)

Be Kind to Newbies

At Skyline, we're visited by lots of newbies asking questions about the Web and the Internet. We do our best to be helpful and patient with these visitors, and it pays off. Through our advice and encouragement, we've developed relationships with these new Web users. Through these relationships, we've found unique learning opportunities, and several additional customers. For us, it has paid to remember that everyone we interact with is a potential customer. Refer to Chapter 5 for more information on establishing beneficial relationships with consumers.

Since the Web population is growing so rapidly, newbies will continue to be an important Internet subgroup for the next few years. Consider this group's special needs and characteristics when you devise your Internet marketing strategy. This can be as simple as offering reassuring explanations about the privacy of their transactions, or as involved as providing a question-and-answer forum for new users to seek expert advice on Internet issues.

TO CLICK OR NOT TO CLICK

We have said the Web is not a linear medium. As its name implies, the Web is a somewhat irregular lacework of interconnected sites. Users travel between sites directly and (usually) quickly along linkages spread around the Web. The most effective Web sites conform to this model. They allow users to travel swiftly to topics that interest them rather than forcing them to wade through large amounts of unwanted information. That is why the average corporate homepage contains six to nine links to other pages that take users instantly to specific Web sites.

Yet most business will probably want to funnel users to specific pages within their own Web site. They expect to be able to arrange the data on their sites like grocery and department stores arrange their merchandise—so that each item receives the proper amount of attention from the customers most likely to buy.

You can arrange a Web site so the right users find the most relevant information. The question becomes, how do you allow users the freedom to choose their destinations, while encouraging them to follow the path you desire? Web site designers accomplish this using three common techniques not much different from those used in the retail environment. Although we discuss these techniques as they apply to online catalogues, you can use them to create any style Web site.

"Online catalogue," or online product catalogue, refers to a common Web site design style. In its simplest form, it lists company products on a page. Web users can click on the name of a specific product for detailed information about that product, and perhaps the opportunity to order it. Grouping products into categories, allowing searches, and incorporating cross-references to related or accessory items enhance the online catalogue.

ARRANGE THINGS LOGICALLY

Just as a supermarket puts the ketchup next to the mustard, you should arrange a Web site so that each page flows logically to the page it links to. This structure makes for more pleasurable shopping and actually increases sales. We see companies spend thousands of dollars putting a product catalogue on the Web without bothering to organize it logically. Group related products in a way that encourages the most profit. Say Joe's Leather Goods sells three saddle styles, including the very popular and very expensive "Texas Throne." Joe should arrange his catalogue to draw users in to examine the Texas Throne. If the user is not impressed, he or she should be made instantly aware of the other two saddle styles.

Companies that don't offer an online catalogue can still profit from arranging their site in a manner that encourages browsing. Keeping common navigational buttons is one way to encourage Web users to explore. Navigational buttons are images, or text, that appear on Web pages to help users find their way around. (Figure 4-3 shows one example

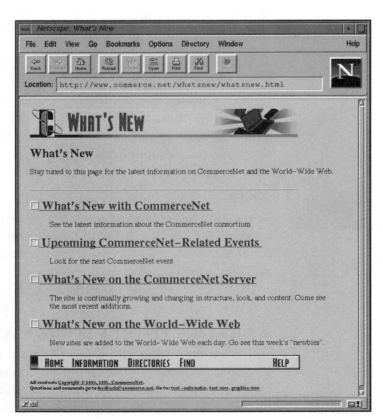

FIGURE 4-3

CommerceNet makes excellent use of navigational buttons.

of navigational buttons.) By keeping these elements consistent throughout a Web site, businesses can make Web customers feel comfortable.

COLOR AND POSITION

Color and position will always be the most important tools for directing consumer attention. In the grocery store, certain items are always placed in plain view. These are usually products that don't appear on the typical grocery list, like photographic film, snack foods, and magazines. By placing them strategically, the store attracts shopper attention to items that might otherwise have been ignored or forgotten.

Similarly, you should arrange your Web site to call attention to information that might otherwise go unnoticed or unsought. The best way to encourage users to read specific information or click on specific links is to make it stand out. Our studies show that users most often click on brightly colored, rectangular links appearing a third of the way down the *visible* Web page. As we said in Chapter 3, visible pages may differ slightly from user to user, so you should keep important information and links high enough on the page that every user will see them as soon as they arrive. Figure 4-4 shows the Allergy Relief Home Page (yes...they are serious!) which has important links that appear too far down the page.

MULTIPLE PATHS

Several years ago, retail stores almost always arranged their products so that no product ever appeared in two locations. Now you commonly find some items with shelf space in several store locations. Retailers have learned that customers sometimes need more than one chance to choose an item. Limited shelf space provides this strategy's only drawback.

On a Web site, however, "shelf space" is virtually endless. A single product needs only one entry in an online catalogue, but it can be referred to in several ways. That is, customers should be able to locate a product by following any of several paths through the Web site. For example, Joe's Leather Goods might sort its online catalogue into boots, saddles, hats, jackets, and accessories. Each category may form its own page, but each page may still contain items like leather cleaners and

FIGURE 4-4

Poor placement of links on the Allergy Relief homepage requires the typical user to scroll down to find the site's most important information.

conditioners, which also appear in the accessories category. Other Web data can be organized in the same way without a significant cost increase.

PREDICTING WHAT WILL BE POPULAR

At Skyline, we focus much of our effort on developing Web features that will entertain the Internet community and bring more visitors to our Web site. Consequently, we have spent a lot of time studying the Web's most popular sites and looking for common traits. We're sad to report that our best efforts have yielded no significant discoveries. The only themes common to successful Web sites seem to be originality and usefulness.

Take the George Goble homepage (Figure 4-5). This page shows readers how to barbecue with 60 pounds of charcoal and 10 gallons of liquid oxygen. It's been read approximately 2.6 million times, and counting. Dave Barry made it the subject of a newspaper column, and other articles have mentioned it. It is perhaps one of the most popular documents on the Web. No company sponsors the page—it's simply the product of a few creative minds at Purdue University.

At Skyline we pride ourselves on our ability to develop some of the most exciting and interactive features on the Web. One of our Web site's most popular features is also our simplest—the *Mortgage Calculator*.

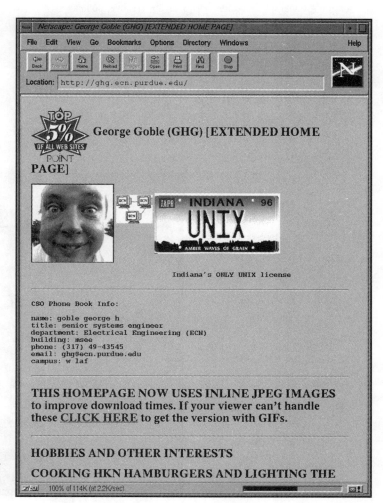

FIGURE 4-5

The George Goble homepage teaches readers to cook with 60 pounds of charcoal and 10 gallons of liquid oxygen. Don't try this at home!

This little program allows users to enter loan information to amortize it instantly (see Figure 4-6). The results display in a tabular and graphic format. One of our programmers wrote the loan calculator as his first attempt at CGI programming, but it has become an all-time favorite among our visitors.

Creating corporate home pages as popular as George Goble's is no easy feat. One reason so many corporate sites are less than mesmerizing is that many Web advertisers believe they must provide professional-looking documents that meet the same standards as conventional advertisements to represent their businesses. This version of "professionalism" severely limits the creativity of many Web site designs.

Encouraging Creativity

At Skyline, we advise our clients to encourage employees to create personal homepages, which can be designed with much less regard for professionalism. This often yields highly creative, popular documents. As long as they aren't offensive or utterly *un*professional, personal homepages can be an effective way to attract Web users to the corporate site. (The bonus is that some employees will become skilled at writing HTML.) Later in this book, we will discuss some of the steps you can take to ensure that personal homepages do not damage your company image.

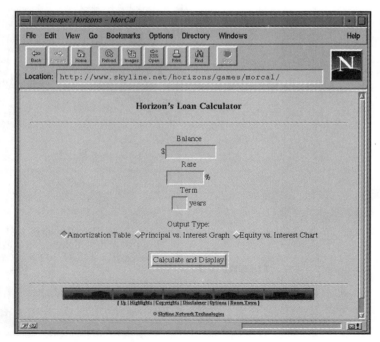

FIGURE 4-6

Skyline's Mortgage Calculator had become more popular.

THE BALANCE OF POWER

An important characteristic of Web advertising is its unique advertiser/consumer relationship. Traditional media fosters an advertiser-initiated relationship, where the advertiser carefully selects and orchestrates information and presents it to the consumer. The advertiser provides a 30-second message, for example, that the consumer can heed or ignore. The Internet shifts the balance of power in this relationship from the advertiser to the consumer. Potential customers on the Net deliberately select the content they want. This shift has prompted many advertisers to ask themselves, "Why would anyone choose to view advertising?" Truth to tell, the Internet is the world's largest collection of trivial information. Any medium that houses a continuously updated coffee pot (http://www.cl.can.ac.uk/coffee/coffee.html), a usage monitor for the toilettes of a university restroom (http://enity.vuse.vanderbilt.edu/project/), and "The Amazing Fish Cam" (http://www.mcom.com/fishcam/fishcam.html) IS the perfect place for any type of information to flourish and gain popularity.

In traditional broadcast media, time is a commodity, so much so that detailed product information can't be provided to consumers in any practical way. But on the Web, it's perfectly acceptable for an automobile manufacturer, for example, to provide detailed information about the features and design processes of its cars. In Internet marketing, the

Sex Sells...or Does It?

We've already discussed the history and availability of pornographic material on the Internet. What we didn't mention was that, while cyberporn traditionally has been confined to isolated corners of the Net, large amounts of pornographic material have recently surfaced on the World Wide Web. The popularity of this material has prompted some small companies to consider using sex to sell their products on the Web. For the most part, they are not succeeding.

On the Web, sex sells sex, and nothing more. The only companies to profit from using lewd pictures on their Web sites are enterprises in the business of selling lewdness. This may not be the trend in other media, but companies that try to use sex to sell traditional products on the Net will be very disappointed. For reasons we've already discussed, pornography and lewdness on the Web have become sensitive issues. Eventually, users may be as comfortable with sexual imagery on the Internet as they are in traditional media. Then, perhaps, sex and sexuality may find a place in Web marketing. But until that time, we advise everybody to keep their clothes on.

challenge is no longer to buy as much network time as you can afford. Instead, it's to capture as much of the Web users' time as they will allow. And you need not compress your message into a spare, uninformative slogan. On the Web, consumers expect to find lots of useful information about products and services. It's the advertisers' job to host the information and resources on their Web sites in such a way that consumers return again and again. They can do that only by stocking their Web pages with rich and compellingly presented content.

Our advice to anyone seeking the recipe for a popular Web site is, good luck! In all our surfing and searching, we've found no magic formula that guarantees a site's popularity. (And we've looked!) The best any of us can do is to strive for originality and creativity in our Web site designs.

TRENDS AND PREDICTIONS

As the price of Internet access continues to drop, the availability of good Web browsers continues to increase, and the features of those browsers continue to multiply, the cultural blend of Internet society will undergo some major changes. Most of those changes will be prompted by the diversification of an already highly diverse population spending more and more time online. Until now, most Internet users have browsed the Web alone, but we're seeing more groups and families spending time together online, instead of in front of the TV. That trend will persist as the desktop computer continues its migration from office to home, and from the home office to living rooms and rec rooms.

As the Internet culture grows and matures, netizens will form more online groups. Most users will belong to more than one group, but those will be more loosely organized. Currently, users tend to remain devoted to a single large group. As the Net diversifies, these groups will become smaller (relative to the entire Net population), lessening the opportunities for users to share their views about a particular company.

Remember...

- The Internet is a society in itself. It has its own culture, including its own arts, sciences, institutions, and criminals. Businesses must take the time needed to learn about the Net culture before they go online, or hire a consultant to handle such matters.

- The Internet began as a "Gift Culture," and the Web has encouraged the practice even more. Companies are expected to provide some value to the Web community before they will be taken seriously.

- Internet users tend to stick together by passing along both good and bad news to each other. In other words, your experiences with one customer may affect a lot of other potential customers.

- Web surfers are looking for instant gratification and convenience. To market successfully on the Web, you must provide both.

- By carefully planning your Web site, you can make the user's visit more enjoyable and direct their attention to the information you feel is most profitable. Arrange the site logically for the user, and strategically for you.

5

Up to now, we've given you what might be described as a scouting report on the World Wide Web. We've talked about the origins of the Web, its makeup, and the needs and expectations of the online community. And we've examined many of its strengths and weaknesses. Pardon the sports analogy, but now it's time to huddle up and call a few plays.

CHOOSING YOUR STRATEGY

How your company approaches Web marketing depends largely on what you want to accomplish with the project. You can spend a ton of money establishing an impressive site with lots of features, but if all you're after is a corporate presence, you'll probably be wasting your resources. Similarly, if you pinch every penny developing a site to establish an online catalogue for direct Internet sales and move your company into new markets, you'll probably be unhappy with the results.

Whatever the extent of your commitment to marketing your company online, some fundamental principles apply to every successful Web site.

HOW DO I PUT THIS ALL TOGETHER?

Setting up a Web site is a lot like baking a cake. If you want it to turn out right, you have to assemble the appropriate ingredients in the correct amounts and then combine them in the proper way. Every cake is different, as is every Web site, but all cakes have a few things in common, a basic recipe, so to speak. The basic formula for a successful Web site includes the following steps:

1. Define your commitment to the project.

2. Incorporate the right ingredients.

3. Mix the ingredients to perfection.

4. Put the icing on the cake.

DEFINE YOUR COMMITMENT TO THE PROJECT

Here you must decide whether to use a mix with easy-to-follow instructions, or to make it from scratch? In cake-making and Web-site design, each approach requires a different commitment of materials, time, and money. The resources you commit to developing your site should be proportionate with the role you expect the World Wide Web to play in your company's overall marketing plan.

INCORPORATE THE RIGHT INGREDIENTS

You must add the ingredients in this cake we're baking in the right proportions. Thoughtfully designed, dynamic graphics are this recipe's primary ingredient. They set the Web apart from the rest of the Internet. You'll also want to add a cup or so of audio, but don't overdo it. You might want to throw in a dash of video, though it's a rare and costly spice right now.

MIX THE INGREDIENTS TO PERFECTION

Just as you would sift, separate, stir, mix, fold, and blend the ingredients for your cake, you'll use a long list of techniques to combine the online marketing elements of your Web site. You'll provide samples, offer discounts, and give away free information. You'll give your site an interesting storefront to draw visitors from all over the Internet community. And you'll put it all together with an understanding of the technological variations and limitations with which Web surfers will view your site.

PUT THE ICING ON THE CAKE

A good icing can make an average cake into something special. In our Web marketing recipe, the icing is the interaction your site facilitates between you and your visitors. It is this interaction that sets your Web site apart and builds the rapport that leads to a successful marketing venture.

BUYING A STORE-MADE CAKE

We've geared our basic Web-site "recipe" for do-it-your-selfers, but it also contains important information for those planning to use consultants to develop their Web presence and online marketing strategy. If that's your plan, make sure the company or consultant you hire follows our recipe. Before you sign a contract, reread this section of the book. Make a checklist and use it to make sure all proposals you receive incorporate our recommendations.

LET YOUR IMAGES DO THE SELLING

As we explained in Chapter 1, the Internet has grown steadily since its inception, but it wasn't until the emergence of the World Wide Web that the Net manifested the explosive growth of the last few years. The Web is the multimedia arm of the Internet. As such, it has made images, sound, animation—and, increasingly, video—integral aspects of the online neighborhood. As you and your company take up residence in this neighborhood, make the most of the Web's ability to utilize a variety of media to deliver your marketing message.

In this section, we show you several sites that incorporate these Web features effectively in their online marketing efforts. We cover specific graphical features you'll want to exploit, as well as the most effective ways to use sound and the Web's developing animation capabilities.

INCORPORATING GRAPHICS INTO YOUR SITE

In the offline world, a picture is worth a thousand words; on the Web, it's worth a million. More than any other aspect of the Web, it is the ability to deliver *pictures* that sets it apart from the rest of the Internet, and arguably, it was this graphical capability that fueled its phenomenal growth.

The Web's graphical capability allows online marketers to promote their products and services with the same sophistication as offline advertisers. Slick, full-color magazine ads have nothing on well-designed Web pages. Web graphics also make it possible to present appealing, user-friendly interfaces that will make less technically adept Web surfers feel right at home.

Its Web graphics are also highly functional. Van-Mungo Graphics T-shirts (http://www.vanmungo.com) is a good example of a company that depends on graphics for the success of its Web site. The small T-shirt company specializes in wild, creative designs, utilizing illustrations on its site to display its latest creations online to curious surfers. Without these illustrations, the site would lose its power; no amount of text description could equal the impact of the colorful display of the Van-Mungo designs (see Figure 5-1).

The Harbour Galleries Web site (http://www.best.com/~webforce/R3890.html) also uses Web graphics as an integral part of its marketing plan. Harbour imports and creates fine jewelry and antique jewelry reproductions. For every product offered on the site, Harbour provides

FIGURE 5-1

A Van-Mungo T-shirt depicting a jester.

#19 Jester $12.50

a corresponding picture. The site includes text descriptions of the pieces, but without the graphics, they'd fall flat. Would you shell out $1,500 for a bracelet without seeing at least a picture of it?

Here's a sample description of a Harbour selection: "A 1935 Platinum w/calibre cut rubies and approximately .75 cts of diamonds." Compare the impact of the text (which, we admit, could be punched up a bit), with Figure 5-2, a picture of that same piece of jewelry. Which of these would most influence your decision to buy? There's really no contest.

The images on both these sites do more than merely decorate the space. They're key to their respective companies' marketing plans. Without them, they might as well take out ads in the classifieds.

Although you'll want to include eye-catching and dynamic graphics on your Web site, keep in mind some technical issues as you design these visual aspects. First, remember that Web surfers use a wide variety of browsers; your Web pages won't look the same to every visitor. Since most surfers use *Netscape Navigator*, start with visuals that look good on that browser.

Second, when you design the visual effects of your Web site, go for high contrast. Many browsers and computers don't recognize all 256 colors. If your pictures and graphics use lot of shading and subtle hue variations, the images may not be crisp for some surfers. For example, a pale blue sky with a few wispy clouds might not even register on some browsers. As you look at your design, try to imagine it rendered in black and white. If it holds up as a dynamic composition without the colors, you're pretty safe.

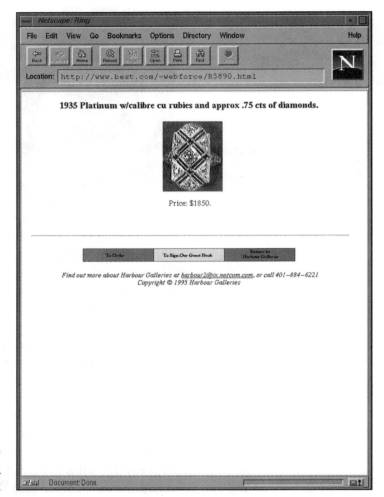

FIGURE 5-2

The Web-site illustration of a ring for sale online from Harbour Galleries.

Finally, consider download time. The graphics you so painstakingly assemble on your Web site ultimately must be downloaded by visitors. Complex images can take forever to reach the Web surfer, who, if you believe the statistics, is a very impatient information consumer. And if the surfer has a slow connection, the wait can be excruciating. It's safe to say that most visitors to your site won't wait long to see your stunning layout. Adding nonessential graphics only bottlenecks your operation.

The bottom line here is this: If your site is technically difficult to access, visitors won't hang around for long. Many of those you want to reach won't have the latest, greatest software and hardware. Some Web surfers will come to you from online services such as *America Online* or *CompuServe*, slowing the process even more. You could put together the greatest marketing plan in the world, including sharp, precise graphics, a free trial offer of your product, and a money-back guarantee, but it won't do you any good if nobody waits around to see it.

An excellent strategy for dealing with disparate Web browsers and variations in computer technology is to allow visitors to your site to choose how they want to view it. Usually, surfers click on a homepage icon or text link to view either all the site's graphics or a text-only version (see Figure 5-3). Providing a text-only version of your site seems to go against everything we've said about the advantages of the Web, but including this option makes your site available to those who might not otherwise be able to access it.

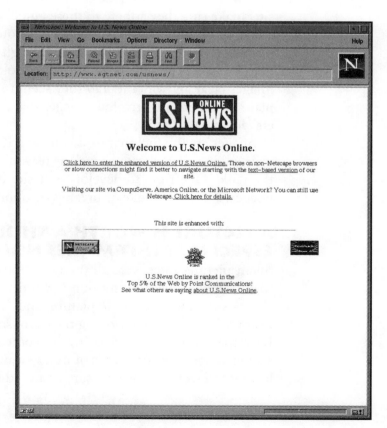

FIGURE 5-3

U.S. News & World Report offers surfers a text-only option.

When you select images for your site, remember to choose pictures and graphics that enhance your marketing plan. Every picture on your site should help you sell your product or service. Don't scatter pictures arbitrarily around your site. Tie them into your product or service. Each image should have a purpose. It should be, in a word, *relevant*.

Images should also be vivid and clear. If your images are muddy, it really doesn't matter what your plan is; Web surfers won't spend much time on your site, anyway.

The images you include on your site reflect on your company. They must be of the best quality you can manage. Your site's graphical presentation must meet or exceed expectations formed by broadcast television and Hollywood movies. Otherwise, you risk losing credibility in the Internet community. Once you lose your credibility, your site ceases to be an effective marketing tool. In other words, if your pix are cheesy, your site could actually *hurt* your company's image.

If you're utilizing outside consulting firms to create images for your site, make sure they adhere to these guidelines. Don't be lured by price alone. Creating a quality site with top-notch graphics may cost a few more dollars, but the rewards far outweigh the costs. Check out other sites prospective firms have created. Look at design details. Are the images clear and vibrant? Do they seem to enhance a clear marketing plan? Are there any frivolous images that do nothing but take up surfers' download time?

Images are the fuel that runs your site. If you put low-grade gas into your engine it won't run as well as it would with high-octane juice in the tank. Take time to develop your site design around high-quality images. They will make or break your online marketing plan.

A PICTURE IS WORTH A THOUSAND WORDS, ESPECIALLY IF IT MAKES NOISE

Silent pictures once were all the rage. Stars like Charlie Chaplin rose to great heights without speaking a word. As the technology developed sound was added to motion pictures and the silent era came to an end. Many Web sites are developing the use of sound as a marketing feature. It's rather impressive to have a voice come through your modem from a site that may be thousands of miles away. Imagine hearing a blaring locomotive as you view a picture of an old steam engine.

Several individuals and organizations have done a good job incorporating this impressive feature into their Web site marketing schemes. An excellent example is a site called "Spanish Lessons by Tyler Jones" (http://www.williamette.edu/~tjones/spanish/Spanish-main.html). As you might guess, this site is a Spanish language tutorial. It includes lessons on vocabulary, grammar, and verb tenses for which visitors can download audio recordings of correct pronunciations.

A company effectively utilizing sound with more of a marketing purpose is Virgin Records (http://www.vmg.co.uk). As you might imagine, this site promotes the company's recording artists and their CDs. On the Virgin site, visitors can preview audio demos of both new and established artists. What better industry to make the most of sound as an Internet marketing tool?

Now, before you go out and hire the Boston Philharmonic to record your company theme song, remember that online audio is still a fairly new feature, and using it has a few drawbacks. One is that many computers can't process it. The machines simply lack sound cards or speakers. You could spend a lot of time and money developing innovative music and sound effects many of your visitors won't even hear.

Online audio takes up a lot of space, as well, so audio-heavy sites can take a long time to load. Remember, many surfers aren't working with the fastest technology available, and they may have slow Internet connections. And never forget that Web surfers aren't the most patient computer users. If you jam your site with audio effects that take forever to load, many visitors will just skip to the next site. Cool sound effects won't do you any good if most people won't even hear them.

These shortcomings shouldn't stop you from utilizing audio effects altogether. Audio may very well have an important place in your scheme—as Mr. Jones and Virgin Records will attest—but in most cases you shouldn't make it the primary thrust. If you have a famous spokesperson or a highly recognizable jingle, by all means, include them in your site design, but offer it as an option. That way, those who don't want to wait for the audio file can click through to other features of your site.

Figure 5-4 is an example of a site that presents its audio feature as an option. Notice that they show the amount of memory the audio takes up. This gives the visitor an idea of how long it will take to download

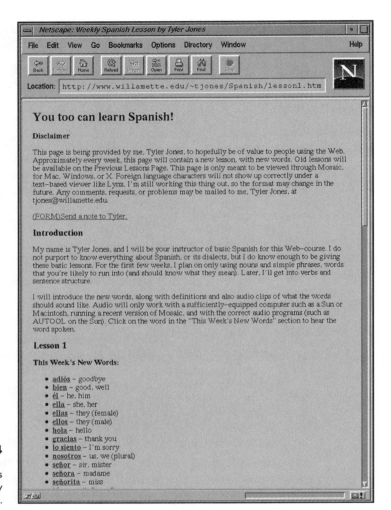

FIGURE 5-4

"Spanish Lessons by Tyler Jones" offers optional audio that surfers may download at their discretion.

the file. Many surfers find this kind of information helpful, and you should include it if you plan to utilize audio.

Trying to accommodate every visitor who comes to your site can be exhausting. But in these early stages of Web evolution, it's essential—especially if you want your marketing message to reach the greatest possible audience.

ANIMATION—BRINGING YOUR PICTURES TO LIFE

When people talk about animation on the Web, they aren't necessarily referring to Disney cartoon figures that move and speak like Aladdin or Pocahontas. Usually they mean full- or partial-motion video. Many Web sites use video effectively to market their products or services. In this section, we look at some of those sites and discuss the part animation can play in your marketing scheme.

An interesting site incorporating video effectively belongs to software designer Galt Technologies (http://www.galttech.com). Galt specializes in developing screen-savers for personal computers. The Galt site allows visitors to download sample screen-savers and watch them go in full-motion video. This is an excellent use of video on the Web because it matches the feature to the product. It would be difficult for a customer to get a true feel for the quality of Galt's products without seeing the screen-savers in action. Although these screen-saver samples are rather large and take a while to download, they're integral to the marketing scheme. This site also utilizes a marketing technique we deal with in greater detail later in this chapter—offering free samples.

ESPN provides another great example of a Web site effectively utilizing full-motion video to market its products and services. Called ESPNet (http://ESPNet.sportszone.com), this site is superbly organized and offers many technically advanced features. You'll find optional full-motion video highlights of sporting events from around the world. You can click on clips of college football in Southern California, or watch highlights from an NBA game in New York. The site benefits from a lot of offline support. Currently, the site doesn't utilize video for its advertisers, but the potential is there.

Impressive as it is, online video has a few drawbacks. Just as many surfers use browsers or computers that prevent them from processing online audio, fewer utilize browsers that enable them to correctly view video clips. All the work and money you spend to produce cool video for your site—and your prospective clients won't even process it.

And like audio files, video files take up a lot of disk space. Video files can take a long time to load, increasing the risk of losing your audience. If you build your entire site around a five-minute video spot, many surfers will simply pass you by.

Probably the greatest shortcoming of online video at this time, however, is cost. Running full- or partial-motion video on your site requires an extra investment in special hardware. You'll also need a fast connection to avoid bottlenecks; nothing says "small potatoes" to Web surfers like a slow-loading site. (There are no slow lanes on the Information Superhighway.)

Our advice when it comes to online video is the same as for online audio: Make it an optional feature. Also, if you plan to ease your company onto the Web, video is probably not something you should think about right now. On the other hand, if you're working with an unlimited budget and your company wants to go online in a big way, video can be important element.

You Can't Buy a Diamond Ring for Ten Cents, Unless You Want a Ring That Isn't Worth a Dime

Skyline was once approached by a company that wanted to go all out to establish a major Web presence. The execs and managers asked for the works. They wanted a multipage setup, with search engines, plenty of customized graphics, full-motion video capabilities, and the ability to receive fax-on-demand from remote locations. Needless to say, we were excited about the possibilities of designing a site with so many bells and whistles—that is, until the discussion turned to the company's budget. The amount of money they wanted to spend on their site wouldn't have supported a single homepage on our system. Our biggest challenge on that job was bringing the clients' expectations into line with their budget.

If and when you incorporate video into your site design, follow these guidelines: First, video should *not* be the only thing on your site. Video should be an *option*. The memory the video requires should be clearly labeled to help visitors decide whether to download the file.

Also, since video production is expensive, it should be both important and integral to your company's marketing scheme. It makes no sense to utilize video if it won't help you with your marketing plan. In other words, video for its own sake is a waste. For example, there's almost never a need to offer a full-motion video of someone speaking—a talking head. This image is simply not dynamic enough. You risk infuriating surfers who spend their valuable time downloading such a clip. And you can bet they won't stick around to view any genuinely worthwhile images you might offer them. You'll be lucky if they come back.

In the future, the Web probably will involve video in a big way, especially as high-speed Internet connections become the norm. Web browsers' ability to display video also will improve. Even if full-motion video doesn't fall into your current marketing plans, keep it in mind as the technology changes.

SOMETHING FOR NOTHING

People love to get something for nothing. On the Web, where "something for nothing" is practically a commandment, giving something away is one of the most effective draws you can give your site. In fact, it's almost mandatory for online marketing success. The something you give away can be almost anything, from a product or service sample to a discount you offer only on the Web, to free information available only at your site.

In this section, we discuss the importance of the something-for-nothing approach to online marketing, and explore how some companies use giveaways to bring traffic to their sites.

SAMPLES: JUST GIVE THEM A TASTE

Offering free product samples is a tried and true marketing technique. In grocery stores, product reps entice customers with cold cuts on toothpicks and hot microwave pizza. Direct-mail campaigns send out blizzards of trial-size product samples. On the Web this practice has a variety of highly effective applications.

The software industry has used the free-sample strategy on the Web since its inception, primarily via something called "shareware." Shareware is software surfers can downloaded from a Web site. Some shareware programs, commonly called "freeware," are offered at no cost. Other shareware programs are presented as samples of larger and more powerful programs; only a shell demonstration version is available for free on the Web. Still other shareware programs are meant to be downloaded and tried out for free, but paid for later, in kind of an Internet honor system; shareware users are expected to send the developer a check if they decide to continue using the product.

A software company that recently utilized shareware to release a new software package is Viacom New Media. The company released a demonstration version of its latest computer game, *Zoop*, onto the Net through its Web site (http://www.demon.co.uk/noonien/zoop.html). The shareware version includes only three of the game's 99 levels. Viacom New Media offers this shareware free of charge and doesn't expect people to pay for this demo version. The company released the shareware hoping surfers would try the game, like it, and buy the full-length version.

The company announced the release of this shareware in its mainstream advertising, and in standard Web advertising avenues. This gave the demo version a lot of exposure, and created an opportunity for many people to download and try this new game. This tactic seems to have been successful for Viacom New Media; *Zoop* has proved to be one of their top-selling computer games.

Perhaps the most famous freeware of all time, not to mention the most successful, is *Netscape Navigator* (http://www.netscape.com). Starting in 1994, Netscape Corp. released its Web browser online. This enabled thousands of people to try out the software package, and helped establish the program as a standard Internet tool.

Netscape eventually capitalized on the success of its freeware Web browser by charging a fee to commercial clients for its use. Individuals could still use the program for free, but companies had to pay. Netscape also went on to develop its secure server, which made it possible to conduct secure online commercial transactions. The company didn't offer this software—which only worked with *Netscape Navigator*—as a freeware. Of course, by this time *Navigator* had become the preeminent Web browser, and thousands of users were happy to pay for the new secure server.

Offering freebies is a great way to generate interest in your site. But to make the most of the marketing potential of giveaways, you should follow some simple guidelines. First, all giveaways should in some way relate to or symbolize your company. It does you no good to offer free T-shirts advertising a popular brewing company if your firm has nothing to do with beer. If you can't give away exact samples of your product or service, at least make sure the giveaway items feature your company *name* in some way—coffee mugs, T-shirts, pens, pocket knives, and a host of other "premiums" can all display your company name and logo. And you can make the giveaway contingent on the visitor filling out an online survey or trying out your product.

Second, if your company offers something for free online, it had better be something you're proud of. Remember, your purpose is to entice the surfer to come back and become a buyer. If your giveaway item is a piece of junk, most people will conclude that your product or service is, too.

DISCOUNTS: ONLINE COUPONS

Have you ever tried out a new restaurant just because you got a coupon in the mail? Ever bought a particular brand of kitchen appliance because of a rebate? In these budget-conscious times, many consumers make their purchases, large and small, based on rebates and discounts.

You can dramatically increase traffic at your Web site by offering such incentives. In fact, the concept of the Web as a commercial environment is so new to so many people, you may have to offer incentives to get them to act.

In this section, we look at some companies that use online discounts to entice surfers to become shoppers, and discuss ways you can use discounts effectively on your site.

Online discounts are fast becoming an effective means of generating Web site traffic. Digital Discounts (http://www.digidiscounts.com) has made a real impact using this strategy. This site is a cybermall (discussed in Chapter 7); that is, it's home to several companies offering products or services for sale. The stores at this site give discounts to all their online customers. Customers visiting the site receive passwords they use later when they phone the stores to place their orders. Site traffic has increased because the discounts are only available to online buyers. This process also gives the store owners a gauge of their online marketing plan's effectiveness. When they hear lots of passwords, they know it's working.

Before you use this strategy, keep in mind a couple of things about online discounts. To have the desired effect, they must be perceived as valuable. You can't offer a meaningless discount and expect anyone to care. Would you rush to a new car lot to take advantage of a $100 rebate on a $25,000 car? Probably not. It's in your best interest to assume the Web community thinks the same way.

Also, your online discounts should only be available *online*. It makes the surfers feel special because they're doing business with your company on the Web. This entices them to buy more readily through your Web site, and gives you some great feedback on your Web marketing strategy. If you don't use the Web for direct sales, you can offer a special discount to anyone who places an order with your company and mentions something they'll find only on your Web site, like Digital Discounts' password.

Finally, make sure the discount you offer is easy to figure out. As we have said many times, surfers are an impatient bunch. Offers requiring a pencil and calculator will be ignored. Make sure the online description of the discount is clear and uncomplicated. Confusion is the quickest way to lose an online sale.

FREE INFORMATION: SURFERS LOVE LEARNING SOMETHING NEW

As we have explained repeatedly throughout this book, the Web, and the Internet in general, was created for the free exchange of information. It was meant to be a bastion of the information age, sending ideas streaking around the globe in the flash of an eye. Because to this day most Web surfers primarily seek free information, that's one of the most effective "premiums" you can offer. The trick, of course, is to work your marketing materials into the data. This is a lot like putting sugar into medicine to get a child to take it. (Thank you, Mary Poppins.) In this section we explore some sites that use that "spoonful of sugar" to help their marketing medicine go down. We also provide some do's and don'ts of giving away information as a Web marketing device.

The Little Employment Group, Inc., site (http://www.netaccess. on.ca/~leg) offers interesting free information. This site is run by an employment agency that connects qualified applicants with interested employers for a fee. As an enticement, the company offers applicants free job-hunting tips and employers information generally helpful for choosing the right applicant. Although these pointers are free information, they also act as teasers for the Little Employment Group.

Another type of information offered free on the Web is financial advice. This is currently extremely popular on the Net, and many Web sites offer it. Atlantic Financial Consulting (http://www.af.com), for example, uses free financial advice very effectively as a marketing tool. The site describes the company's services, throwing in a few pieces of free financial information. The company's "Twelve Tips of Investing" is particularly popular and effective. These tips provide generally useful information while also highlighting the company's expertise and giving surfers a preview of what to expect if they hire the firm.

The cardinal rule about offering free information on the Internet is that it must be *100 percent accurate*. You don't want to develop a reputation for inaccuracy in cyberspace. If that happens, you might as well fold up your tents and go home. And don't think you can put anything over on Web surfers. They have an uncanny knack for ferreting out erroneous data. That's what many of them do for *fun*. Once they can prove your information is "bogus," they'll delight in spreading the word throughout the Internet. On the Web, your company's reputation is a valuable commodity that should be preserved at all times. If it's soiled in any way, the damage may be irreparable.

It's important the information you give away on your site is actually useful. It need not be earth-shattering news, but it must be of value to someone. It's a bonus if the information is special or unique, but usefulness is essential. For example, informing the online community that your favorite color is fuchsia probably won't draw crowds to your site. On the other hand, the *history* of fuchsia, with the origins of its name, and so on, may be considered a worthwhile piece of information. You may consider the history of a color completely trivial, but Web surfers exist who'll be drawn to this type of information.

And finally, free information on your site should be *relevant* to your marketing plan. This guideline isn't set in stone, but it makes sense to tie information to your company, product, or service. Unrelated information can be a successful draw, but tends to create extra work for your site. For example, offering the latest stock quotes on your site may be an effective draw, but it probably won't help your company much if you're a wholesale flower distributor. You'd be far better served in terms of expense and time offering information and pictures about various buds and blossoms.

EVERYBODY CAN WIN: ONLINE SWEEPSTAKES AND CONTESTS

People love contests. The proliferation of state lotteries and direct-mail sweepstakes is proof of that. This concept has gained some momentum on the Web, as well. In this section, we examine some sites effectively utilizing this technique. We also explain some good ways for you to utilize sweepstakes and pitfalls you should watch for.

Online sweepstakes aren't new. Sites have been running sweepstakes since the Web first debuted on the Net. One interesting Web site offering a sweepstakes is "The Vail Valley" (http://www.vail.net). This organization promotes businesses and other organizations located in Vail, Colorado. The Vail Valley sweepstakes draws surfers to the site, and entices them to fill out an online survey, enabling the group to collect important demographic and marketing data used for targeted mailings. Even the prize—a set of lift tickets good on the slopes of Vail—is a way to promote the subject of the site!

A site with a slightly different approach belongs to a California consumer electronics firm, Fuga Corp. (http://www.fuga.com). This company's main product is an electronic planner. To help market this product and their site in general, Fuga conducts an online sweepstakes with a $100 prize. (Cash will always motivate a surfer to fill out an entry form, but it may serve Fuga better to offer one of its products as a prize. Doing so would get people to try its merchandise.)

Fuga uses an online form as an entry blank. This form allows the company to gather great amounts of demographic information from the surfers who enter its contest. Fuga can determine the buying preferences of its surfers, as well as the types of planners they currently use. All the information Fuga gathers is vital to its uniquely effective marketing plan. By setting up a sweepstakes, the company is able to gather the data it needs without alienating the surfers who visit its site.

A sweepstakes is really just a kind of giveaway device. It's less expensive than a true giveaway because only the winners receive items. But everyone is lured into entering the contest because they *might* win something for nothing. And because you give away fewer items, you can give away cooler stuff. The more valuable sweepstakes giveaway item will reflect positively on your company.

Another advantage of online sweepstakes is their ability to cull extensive demographics information about those visiting your site. Many surfers are reluctant to offer honest information about themselves online. Many feel it's an intrusion into their privacy. But sweepstakes have a way of overcoming this resistance. Surfers, and people in general, will offer all kinds of information about themselves if they think they might win something. Information you may want to ask for includes actual (as opposed to online) name; postal address; e-mail address; phone number; place of employment; annual income; occupation; ages, hobbies, and any information pertinent to your marketing plan.

Sweepstakes offer a unique opportunity for a you to tie the Web world into the real world. Some surfers attempt to live out a separate identity on the Web. By offering a chance to win something for free, you can bridge this gap.

There is, however, one small sticking point when it comes to online sweepstakes: They must be legal where they're offered. The Internet, remember, is not bound by geographic borders, and contest laws vary widely from state to state and country to country. To ensure that your company stays within the law, have an attorney put together a disclaimer you can publish on your online sweepstakes form.

ONLINE STOREFRONTS

If you've ever shopped along downtown Chicago's Michigan Avenue, you know that window-shopping is alive and well in America. This downtown section of the street is called the "Magnificent Mile" because of its seemingly endless stretch of storefronts. Shops of every type sell everything you can imagine, but you don't have to go in to find out what each one sells. Most of the stores have large and impressive display windows.

Companies selling products and services on the Web should take a tip from the merchants on the Magnificent Mile.

WINDOW-SHOPPING ON THE WEB

"Window-shopping" is a popular Web activity. In fact, that could very well serve as one definition of "Web surfing." Links between sites make this online window-shopping possible, whisking people from site to site as if they were shoppers strolling down the sidewalk.

Your site should include plenty of links, but you also want surfers to linger awhile. (In other words, don't make the links the most prominent feature of your site.) You hold their attention, of course, by making your site as interesting as possible.

And remember that a surfer may enter your site at any page, not necessarily your homepage. Make sure that every page on your site is interesting. Unlike real-world storefronts featuring one or at most two display windows, a Web site has almost unlimited "windows" to stroll past. The key is to make as many of your site's windows as possible provocative and eye-catching. You may only hold your surfers' attention for a few seconds if your key pages don't impress them.

The good news is that you can control fairly well which pages will be key pages. You link to these specific pages by submitting the appropriate URLs to popular search mechanisms and by posting the specific page address in your other advertising. We provide details on how to do this later in the book. The thing to remember here is that you control which pages will make up your "storefront."

MAKE YOUR WINDOW DIFFERENT

We've said your site can have as many storefront pages as you like. Your next job is to figure out what to display in them. Your storefront pages should be your site's true highlights. Nothing you offer on these pages should be the least bit shabby or second-rate. If you want eye-catching graphics, this is the place to put them.

If you use product or information giveaways, or if you run a contest or sweepstakes on your site, mention it on all your storefront pages. Preferably, provide a link directly to this unique feature. For example, if you offer a sample of your widgets to anyone who fills out an online form, make sure your storefront page has a link directly to that page.

Another feature that can spruce up your storefront pages is an icon that, when clicked on, sends visitors to another page within your site. This feature encourages surfers to view everything your site has to offer. This way you can make all your site's features intricate parts of your marketing plan. You should still make your key pages your best and most unique, but don't forget that you have the ability to spread the wealth throughout your site.

Be sure and include your company's name, logo, and, if you have one, slogan on every page of your site—especially storefront pages. It's like hanging a sign out in front of your business. You want to leave an impression with surfers who visit your site, even if they only stay to see one page. Your company's name and slogan should take a secondary role on other pages, but on these linked storefront pages they should be large and prominent.

Again, those linked pages are the most important on your Web site. They're your storefront windows to the Internet, and you must use them to entice surfers to come in and spend some time. When surfers cruise by, they must want to stop and explore. Even if they only make it to your storefront pages, your prominent company name and slogan enable you at least to capitalize on some added name recognition.

LET PEOPLE KNOW WHO YOUR FRIENDS ARE

It's often said that people can tell things about you by the company you keep. If you hang out with losers and creeps, people get one impression; if you pal around with successful, ambitious people, they'll associate you with success. Of course, they also say you can't tell a book by its cover, but we're talking about marketing here, where perception *is* reality.

That's why it's so important to be selective about the sites you link to. You want a link-rich site, but you should take great care to make sure the links you provide are to high-quality sites, and that the sites linked to you are of the same quality. Surfers remember and appreciate these associations.

TARGET MARKETING

One of the great things about marketing on the Web is that you can gather so much information about your prospective clientele. This has always been possible in other marketing media, but only after some extra effort and expense. The beauty of the Web is that this quality is inherent in the medium. On the Web, it's readily apparent who looks at what sites and for what information.

In this section we discuss target marketing on the Web and how to utilize it in your design. We also point out some pitfalls of target marketing and how to avoid them. We included some proven online "press releases," and tips on how to use them to create a target market you can build on.

IF YOU KNOW YOUR TARGET MARKET, GO GET 'EM

One of the great attractions of the Web for marketers is that it's a *pull* medium. Niche magazines are pull mediums; they draw people interested in the subject covered—sailing, woodworking, stamp collecting. The ads are almost as interesting to these readers as the articles. Television and radio are *push* mediums; few viewers or listeners actually look for ads, so marketers have to "push" their ads at the audience. But on the Web, searching for stuff is what the experience is all about. Many surfers will stop and look at anything if they think it will be interesting.

Target marketing in a pull medium differs a little from target marketing in other media, because the audience actively seeks out the information provider, whether it's an impartial source or an advertiser. On the Web, the marketers usually provide the information Web surfers seek, putting them in a unique position to spread the word.

Word gets around on the Web mostly by "word of mouth" (that is, e-mail). You should compile a sort of online Rolodex of people you meet on the Web. This happens naturally as you spend time surfing and as people come to your site and spend time there. Get their e-mail addresses and any other information about them you can. This will enable you to contact them later, when you offer a new site feature, for instance, or when you develop a new product or service. This is the simplest and maybe one of the most personal ways to target your market.

If you use a consulting firm to conduct your Web marketing, you may want to confirm that they'll conduct this type of personalized advertising research for you. If they do offer this service, expect to pay extra for it. If they don't, this is something you may want to handle on your own, which will add a personal touch to the process.

WHAT YOUR TARGET LIKES TO HEAR AND HOW TO TELL THEM

In the last section, we talked about utilizing e-mail to target potential customers online. However, never forget that blatant commercialism is still frowned on, even on the Web. You must, therefore, frame your target marketing efforts as offers of new, and what you believe to be exciting, information. Take care not to sound like you're trying to sell something; you're just a helpful messenger conveying information that might be of interest. You might also want to drop a line to these surfers when you're not offering such information, as well. This may make them feel more at ease when you come bearing other material. Send a little note introducing yourself; tell them you're just someone seeking friends on the Net, and that they can return the e-mail if they like. This may mean you'll get a lot of e-mail from people that you may not know, but of course there's no better way to meet people. Later in this book, we'll walk you through some specific methods of utilizing e-mail to target surfers and provide some specific ways to accomplish this task.

SPECIALIZED PRESS RELEASES: GETTING THE MESSAGE TO YOUR AUDIENCE

The press release is a long-established and often-used marketing device, a standard lure in the PR/marketing tackle box. Press releases are used primarily to communicate new information about companies to news media in hopes they'll report the information in their publications. It's a way of generating publicity, which often amounts to free advertising. Press releases are also used on the Web, though in a specialized form.

These specialized press releases provide a unique vehicle for targeting a specific population of the Web world.

On the Internet, press releases are usually submitted to newsgroups for publication. Newsgroups are forums of a sort, where related information is exchanged on a given subject. More than 15,000 newsgroups currently are active across the Internet, covering subjects ranging from aardvarks to zoot suits and everything in between (literally). Posting to newsgroups permits you to target those most interested in the subject of your release. Later on in this book, we discuss in detail the ways you can utilize newsgroups in your marketing plan.

BUILD RAPPORT WITH YOUR SURFERS

It's the oldest adage in sales: Customers buy from salespeople they like and trust. Effective salespeople build a rapport with their customers. They try to find something they have in common and make a personal connection. They strive to make their customers feel as though they're buying from a friend. And who could turn down a friend?

The Web's greatest single sales and marketing asset is that it facilitates this kind of rapport-building. In this section, we cover this important Web marketing aspect in detail.

PROVIDE A PLACE FOR YOUR CUSTOMERS TO TALK

Web marketing differs from marketing in any other medium in that when you advertise on the Web, you join a community, a community with its own culture, language, and code of ethics. Above all, it has a sense of togetherness. People communicating on the Web can connect instantly. Many report feeling as though they'd known each other for years. Part of the reason for this "connectedness" is that Web surfers do, in fact, have a lot in common, or they wouldn't have found each other on the Internet.

The challenge for Web marketers is to support this sense of connection and allow it to flourish on your site. To accomplish this, you must provide an interactive venue, a place where surfers can "talk" to each other, and where you can "talk" with them. Let's look at three types of interactive environments you can create on your site: message boards, chat lines, and MUSEs.

MESSAGE BOARDS

Message boards are online areas where Internet users can post messages about specific topics. Others can respond to those postings with postings of their own, and in this way carry on a kind of conversation. Message boards almost always are dedicated to specific subject areas usually established by whoever runs the site. Sometimes their focus can be rather narrow. For example, a message board may be dedicated to the "Best Restaurants in Baltimore." One Web surfer may post a statement saying that The Prime Rib is Baltimore's best restaurant. Having read this message, another surfer could respond that, yes, The Prime Rib is a fine restaurant, but there's nothing like the Italian food at Chiparrelli's. Before long, a dozen other surfers post responses and responses to responses, generating this unique kind of conversation.

You can direct a message board on your site to address topics in which your company is involved. You can even create message boards dedicated to your company's specific products or services. For example, to continue our theme of restaurants, you might establish a message board dedicated to a discussion of just Italian food, or you might devote a site specifically to your restaurant.

The one caution: If you plan to keep the focus of the message boards on your site very narrow, be sure to offer quite a few different message boards. Remember, the key here is to generate interaction on your site, not just discussion about your company.

One drawback of message boards is that online "conversation" usually doesn't take place in real time. When a surfer posts a message, it may not show up immediately, because many message board systems have built-in automatic waiting periods. These delays can be anywhere from a few minutes to days or even weeks. Some message board operators intentionally add their own delays to screen out inappropriate messages.

CHAT ROOMS

Another interactive online venue you might want to feature on your Web site is the "chat room" (also referred to as "chat areas" or "chat lines"). Chat rooms are parts of a site where surfers can "meet" and exchange messages. They can converse freely in real time as if they were on the phone. Chat rooms also allow more than two people to

FIGURE 5-5

A Skyline.Net message board
dedicated to the city of Baltimore.

converse at one time. Other participants can "eavesdrop" and join in as the spirit moves them. In some chat rooms, you can do something called *whispering*, to isolate your message to only one party.

Like message boards, chat rooms are usually established to cover specific topics of discussion. You'll want to offer a variety of chat rooms on your site, including some related to your business and others of general interest.

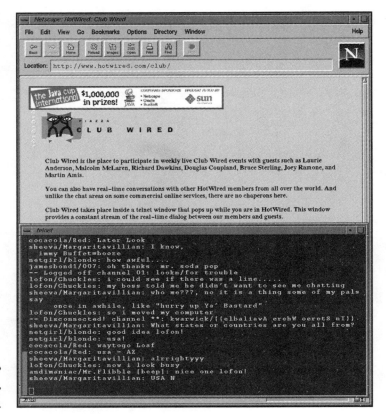

FIGURE 5-6

A popular chat room on "HotWired!,"
one of the Web's most popular sites.

MUSES

One final form of interactive Web site venue we'd like to mention is
called a MUSE (multi-user simulation environment). A MUSE
allows interaction similar to a chat room, usually in the context of a
game. Many of these games are adventure- or fantasy-related,
allowing surfers to assume imaginary roles or characters. MUSEs
are popular on the Web because they offer surfers the chance to
interact in a competitive way. Many MUSEs are text-driven, but
some do incorporate graphics and other visuals. Graphics-driven
MUSEs offer surfers the chance to see where they are and what
they're doing in an animated virtual game space.

You can incorporate MUSE technology into your Web strategy, creating an online interactive store or office. You can even incorporate
office personnel or store clerks into MUSE scenery, giving surfers real

people from your company to interact with "face-to-face" online. You can also provide visitors to your MUSE store with "free" simulated money they can spend while they "shop." This simulated shopping won't necessarily add to your real-world bottom line, but it can get potential customers in the habit of shopping on your site. If they practice simulated shopping enough, eventually they might buy something. You can use this MUSE setup to create truly dynamic interactive catalogues.

MUSEs can go almost anywhere your imagination wants to go. Give your imagination free rein and incorporate them into your marketing plan as much as possible.

GET THE WHOLE GANG INVOLVED

There are several ways to incorporate interactivity into your online marketing scheme. When we started this section, we told you that interaction was important because it allows you to build rapport with your customer. This connection between surfers and your company develops when you and your employees spend time in the interactive environments of your site. Encourage your employees to post messages on your site's message boards. This will give your company personality and demonstrates responsiveness to surfer cares and concerns.

If you set up chat rooms, you and your employees should spend time in them conversing with the surfers. You should facilitate lively interactions and even direct the conversations toward specific areas. Although you should take care not to alienate surfers with a hard sell, you can definitely give your company a face. During these chat sessions you and your employees may develop relationships with surfers that eventually can turn into sales.

The same thing can happen on your MUSEs. If you've set up a MUSE as a tour of your office or store, your employees can become a nonthreatening online sales force, guiding surfers to products or services, and pointing out the advantages of what your company has to offer. Or your staff can simply meet people and talk about the MUSE and anything else comes up in conversation. This is a surprisingly effective way to build rapport and watch sales grow.

By allowing your whole company to get involved in your site's interactive environments, you give the Internet community the opportunity to meet the people who *are* your business. They'll learn that the administration department has a sense of humor, that the guys in production are knowledgeable, and that your people in personnel care deeply about their company. This kind of interaction allows visitors to your site to get to know you and your people, develop relationships, and become customers.

Remember...

- Creating a successful marketing plan for the Web is like baking a cake from scratch; you must assemble the appropriate ingredients in the correct amounts, and then combine them in the proper way.

- Determine the scope of your online commitment *before* you start the project. This decision will greatly influence your Web-marketing strategy.

- Images and graphics are Web specialties. Make sure to intersperse them through out your site.

- Sound and video are excellent features you can use in your Web site design, but use them cautiously. As online technology improves, so will the efficacy of these features.

- Surfers, like the rest of us, love to get something for nothing. Be sure to include free product samples, discounts, and free information in your online marketing plan.

- A Web site is like a storefront window. Use it to lure customers deeper into your marketing plan. Make sure your site is eye-catching and memorable.

- Target marketing is easy on the Web. Utilize press releases and other target marketing devices to attract your Web clientele.

- Building rapport on the Web is as easy as providing a place for surfers to converse. Get out there and talk with them yourself. Use the interactivity of the Web to ensure the success of your Web strategy.

6

DO'S AND DON'TS OF WEB MARKETING

The World Wide Web provides a universe of opportunity for companies that carefully plan their marketing strategies and target their markets. But no matter how much time they spend planning specific strategies, every company should take some very important steps before going online. Likewise, there are some actions that each company should carefully avoid. We discuss some of those do's and don'ts of Web marketing in this chapter.

DO: LOOK BEFORE YOU LEAP

The most important step to take before designing a Web site (or even hiring somebody else to design one) is to browse the Web yourself. After that, browse some more. Get an Internet connection and browse on your own, or hire a consultant to show you the ropes. The following sections include tips and strategies to help you find your way around the World Wide Web.

GETTING ACQUAINTED WITH THE MEDIUM

The Web is the most sophisticated communications medium ever created, offering advantages and limitations very different from those of television, radio, and print. If you try to use this new medium for marketing without first acquainting yourself with it, you're setting yourself up for trouble. Without a thorough working knowledge of the Web, you risk being mislead or ripped off by an unscrupulous Web designer or consultant; hiring too much staff to develop and manage your Web site; offending or boring the Web community with an inappropriately designed site; poor online sales, and just generally wasting your time and money.

If you're willing to take those risks, feel free to skip this step and the next two chapters. But to make your company's initial move onto the Web a successful one, there's no substitute for comprehensive, first-hand knowledge. In this book we've tried to give you almost everything you need to understand the World Wide Web and its marketing potential. But a book can't give you the experience of browsing the Web. Going online yourself is the only way to get a real feel for the medium and your potential audience. Take some time now and do a little surfing. (It doesn't have to take more than a couple hours, although it should.) You'll save yourself a lot of time, money, and headaches later on.

IF ALL YOUR COMPETITORS JUMPED OFF A CLIFF...

Most companies go online today for one reason—their competition is going online. Odds are, if you're reading this book, you have a competitor who already has a Web site or is in the process of building one. If that's your situation, you have a terrific opportunity to conduct a little research into their marketing strategies. What better way to ensure that your Web presence keeps a step (or more) ahead of your competition than checking out their sites? If you hire a professional Web designer, be sure he checks out your competition, too.

NOTE *If your current market is limited geographically, don't forget that the Web may have allowed more businesses to compete within your market. In other words, you may have more competitors than you think.*

You can use any of the various Web search sites to locate competing businesses. Figure 6-1 shows one of the more popular search sites. *The ISP Internet Yellow Pages* contains the URLs of thousands of different businesses around the world. Its excellent interface and huge database make it easy to locate your competitors' sites.

When visiting your competitors' Web sites, make lists of the things you like and dislike about each. You'll find these lists very helpful when you, or a professional Web designer, design your company's Web site.

DO: GIVE, GIVE, GIVE

In the offline world—and especially in business—everyone knows you don't get something for nothing. On the Internet, however, that isn't the case. We've already discussed how the Internet developed as a gift culture. Most of the software used for Internet applications (like the Web) is available free in some form, and nearly all information on the Web is available at no cost.

To establish a powerful Web presence, your site will have to do more than flaunt your company's products or services. There's no reason to insist that all the information on your site relate directly to your company. It's just as important to attract people who may become customers in the near future. Companies that advertise on television don't just run their ads during programs relating directly to their products or services; they advertise on programs that have the greatest appropriate audience.

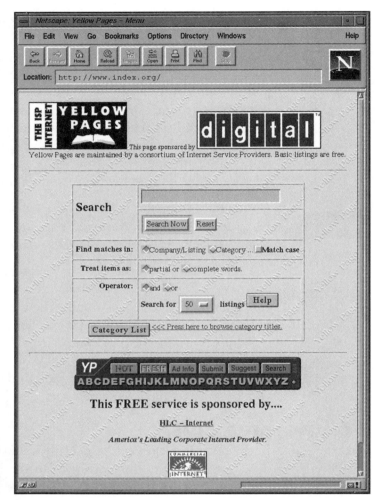

FIGURE 6-1

The Internet Yellow Pages is an excellent resource for anybody looking for businesses on the Web.

On the Web, you provide the program and the advertisements. Your "programming" should attract a diverse audience. If nothing else, it increases your name recognition. And on the Net, so much information passes from person to person, sooner or later it will bring you additional business. If Kim's Florist becomes known around the Web for its online European tour guide, that's all the better for Kim. Not only has she constructed a roadside billboard with her online florist, she's built the highway that runs past it.

Many businesses try to offer an index of interesting Web sites so that visitors will use their site as a starting point for their Web surfing. It's a good idea, but it usually doesn't work. Why would you want to spend so much time and money developing a site only to send people away once they get there? That's exactly what happens—when people see an interesting link, they follow it. They won't wait until they finish looking around your site. Of course, an index is useful in some cases. Skyline, for instance, hosts the World Wide Web Resource EXchange (REX), which features a growing list of Web sites organized by topic. This makes sense for us because serving the Web is our business.

Never forget that commercial sites are still considered intrusions by many in the Internet community. Giving something back to the community can pave the way to acceptance. If your site offers something totally unrelated to your business, nobody can call your generosity a marketing ploy.

DON'T: OFFEND THE NATIVES

When visiting a new culture, rule number one is, "Don't offend the natives." This applies both to individual travelers and to businesses expanding into new markets. It's also important for businesses to remember that rule when dealing with the Internet. As we've said before, the Net has a culture of its own, with its own beliefs, customs, trends, arts, and sciences. A successful marketer, like a successful traveler, learns to adapt to new cultures.

SPAM KILLS

The Internet is the biggest experiment in freedom of speech the world has ever seen. Within the Internet, Usenet is the most common method of mass communication. (That's two-way communication among large groups of users. The Web is generally a one-way form.) But Usenet's openness makes it vulnerable to a type of abuse that jeopardizes its very existence. That abuse often takes the form of something called "spam." Spamming is the easiest way to offend the Internet natives. It refers to the flooding of Usenet with large numbers of identical, or similar, messages.

To fully understand how spamming works, consider one of the most well-known examples. It involves two Arizona lawyers, Laurence Canter and Martha Siegel. They distributed thousands of advertisements for their immigration-law practice, Canter & Siegel, on Usenet. Below is an example of their post:

```
Green Card Lottery 1994 May Be The Last One!

THE DEADLINE HAS BEEN ANNOUNCED

The Green Card Lottery is a completely legal program
giving

away a certain annual allotment of Green Cards to
persons

born in certain countries. The lottery program was

scheduled to continue on a permanent basis. However,

recently, Senator Alan J. Simpson introduced a bill into

the U.S. Congress which could end any future lotteries.

THE 1994 LOTTERY IS SCHEDULED TO TAKE PLACE SOON, BUT IT

MAY BE THE VERY LAST ONE.

PERSONS BORN IN MOST COUNTRIES QUALIFY, MANY FOR THE
FIRST

TIME.

The only countries NOT qualifying are: Mexico; India;
P.R.

China; Taiwan, Philippines, North Korea, Canada, United

Kingdom (except Northern Ireland), Jamaica, Dominican

Republic, El Salvador, and Vietnam.

Lottery registration will take place soon. 55,000 Green

Cards will be given to those who register correctly. NO

JOB IS REQUIRED.

THERE IS A STRICT JUNE DEADLINE.

THE TIME TO START IS NOW!!
```

```
For FREE information via Email, send

request to cslaw@indirect.com

************************

Canter & Siegel, Immigration Attorneys
```

The lawyers included the firm address, phone number, fax number, and their fees for helping people enter the Green Card Lottery. While the actual lottery was free, the firm charged $95 per person or $145 per couple to help fill out the applications.

As a single message, this offer would have caused little reaction among netizens. The fact that it was basically a scam might have annoyed a few people. If the message had been cross-posted (see technical note) to several newsgroups, a few more people might have complained. But this message appeared so frequently and in so many unrelated newsgroups, even the most forgiving users grew irritated. Not surprisingly, the issue quickly became a controversy—a controversy the law firm claimed was a clash between legitimate advertisers and the anti-commercial culture of the Net.

Cross-posting is the "polite" way to send messages to several newsgroups at the same time. When a message is cross-posted, it's sent only once (saving space and money for the Usenet sites) and usually read only once by a given user. Still, it's available to a larger number and a wider variety of users because the message is seen by readers of several newsgroups. Abuse of cross-posting is a serious issue nonetheless.

Companies advertising via Usenet take advantage of a service paid for by others. Economists call such companies "free riders." Their abuse of the service significantly diminishes its value to those who pay for it. Because the foregoing message was sent 6,000 times, every major news system in the world had to download it 6,000 times. Many of these sites are university- and government-sponsored sites and may pay (in some form) for each message that comes in. That's why the Internet community responded so harshly. The Canter & Siegel spam generated hundreds of thousands of angry e-mail, postal mail, and telephone responses.

Spamming can be so damaging that the act of spamming is often called a "spam attack." It's considered an attack on the entire Usenet community. And it's bad press. Spamming is the worst form of blatant commercialism on the Internet.

Consider the volume of junk mail you receive every day through postal mail (often called "snail mail" on the Net, for obvious reasons). You don't want to open it. You don't even want to sort through the envelopes. But you have to, because somewhere among the credit card offers, sweepstakes entries, and unwanted advertising is your phone bill. People who use e-mail and Usenet news feel the same way about junk on the Internet. They use these services for fast communication among colleagues, customers, and family members. The last thing they want to do is spend time searching through their (electronic) mailboxes or newsgroups to find the useful information among scores of advertisements and offers.

Spamming can be a huge temptation when a company enters the online world. If not for the harsh consequences, it would be an excellent way to announce your new Web site. Usenet reaches millions of people every day all over the world. There is no faster way to disseminate information. Besides, the Internet is devoted to the free exchange of information and ideas—why shouldn't businesses tap into it.

The problem is that spam—while viewed by some as the simple exercise of free speech—actually inhibits the free exchange of information by destroying the usefulness of the medium. Internet users have worked hard to categorize information on the Net so it can be used effectively. If businesses violate the sanctity of these categories by broadcasting messages to thousands (or even dozens) of Usenet news groups, they litter the Information Superhighway with information pollution and make it difficult for legitimate users to find the information they need.

Spamming isn't the only way to offend the Internet community. Any unsolicited or non-contextual advertisements are sure to anger users. Within your own Web site, however, just about any form of advertising is considered solicited because the user chose to visit your site.

As long as you're careful when you advertise your site throughout the Net (see Chapter 9), and you don't violate the standards of the collective Internet culture within your site, you'll be fairly safe. But if you want to do more than just coexist with Internet natives, read on and learn about the soft sell.

STICK TO THE SOFT SELL

It's been said that a good business finds a need and fills it. And yet consumers constantly are bombarded with commercial messages that attempt to *create* a need and fill it. In a medium like the Web, where consumers choose only the content they want, nobody wants to be told what's fashionable and popular or what they need to be successful. Those kinds of traditional advertising messages just won't work in cyberspace. No self-respecting netizen would willingly choose content that tells him how dingy his whites are, or that a single pimple will turn her into a social outcast. Such messages will only alienate consumers on the Net. Always remember that practically every user to visit your site has conscientiously chosen to do so. You can assume that they are already interested in your products, services, or at least the added value of your site.

Lately, we've seen a rebirth of the soft sell even in the bastions of conventional sales. Many car dealers, for example, now encourage their salespeople to be less aggressive. The customers already know they need a car, the reasoning goes. They've even expressed a specific interest in the dealer by visiting the lot. If allowed to browse the lot at their own pace, without the usual hovering sales force, shoppers generally will explore the lot more thoroughly, and will be drawn naturally to the cars and features they find most interesting. After they've had a chance to wander around the lot undisturbed, many customers actually ask the salespeople to answer questions and help them reach a decision.

Consumers have taken to this sales approach, and that reaction has prompted other businesses to reconsider the merits of the soft sell. On the Web, it's a must.

THE VIRTUAL PEACE PIPE

The Internet community responded harshly and swiftly to the Canter & Siegel green card incident. The law firm received an incredible amount of hate mail, both electronic and postal. To make it difficult for the lawyers to identify serious inquiries, many users falsely claimed that they needed the firm's services. They also bombarded the firm's Internet access provider with hate mail, claiming it shouldn't have let the law firm get away with sending out all that spam in the first place. In fact, so much hate mail went out over the Internet it caused bandwidth problems for the provider and the law firm. The provider responded by refusing future service to Canter & Siegel, and posting a message defending its actions to the Internet community. Most Net users quickly forgave the provider.

GETTING FLAMED

The process of sending hate messages through e-mail or Usenet is called "flaming." Flames are verbal attacks in electronic form. They can be vulgar and they often generate more flames, either in support of or against the original flamer. In the green card incident, both the law firm and its provider were flamed. Flaming is common practice when businesses offend the Net community.

Anyone on the Internet—and many people who aren't on the Net—can be flamed. You don't have to spam Usenet or send unsolicited e-mail to provoke an attack. You may do nothing more than launch a new and inoffensive Web site to suddenly find yourself being flamed. You may be flamed even before you go online. Perhaps somebody out there is unhappy with one of your products. Maybe they on't like your company name. You could even become the victim of a contentious competitor willing to go to great lengths to injure your reputation.

Flaming occurs every day, and unless it ignites a chain of flames, it usually has no direct consequences. Generally, flames that don't concern free speech or blatant commercialism are quickly forgotten.

FORGIVE AND FORGET

If you find yourself or your company on the receiving end of a flame attack, the first thing you should do about it is…nothing. Remember, millions of people worldwide have access to Usenet and e-mail. If only one or two have harsh words for you, consider yourself lucky. If you respond to the flame, you'll probably only make matters worse. Your best bet is to wait it out. Most people will have forgotten about the flame by the time you respond, anyway.

If the flame against you generates a significant online response, and people *aren't* forgetting about it, you may have to defend yourself. Post a calm, rational response. Your message should explain that everything was a misunderstanding, that your company would never think of violating the sanctity of the Internet, and that you harbor no hard feelings for the rotten scoundrel who sent the original flame.

Whatever you do, don't send your response in haste. Have a public relations expert read it first, preferably one with Internet experience. A Web marketing consultant may also be able to advise you.

DO: CATER TO THE MASSES

One of the biggest sins of many of today's Web designers is their failure to understand the limitations of the computer and Internet connections of the average consumer. They sit in their offices all day with advanced graphics workstations and high-speed Internet access, and they begin to take it for granted that the rest of the world has access to the same state-of-the-art technology.

ALL BROWSERS ARE NOT CREATED EQUAL

Every Web user has a unique combination of equipment and other factors affecting his or her Web experience. These factors include:

- browser software
- computer architecture (IBM, Macintosh, SGI, etc.)
- computer processing speed
- operating system (Windows 3.1, OS/2, UNIX, etc.)
- Internet connection speed
- video capabilities
- audio capabilities
- browser configuration
- personal preference

These elements combine variously with your Web pages to produce an impression on your audience. It's important to create Web documents that make a good impression on most available configurations.

One of the most important differences between users is often ignored by Web marketers. That difference is "bandwidth"—the speed at which a computer can receive data from the Internet. Many medium to large corporations, most universities, and several government agencies enjoy a high-speed connection to the Internet. This means even highly detailed graphics and audio files can transfer very quickly. But average users connect to the Net from their homes, using a modem, and making the connection as much as 100 times slower than typical high-speed corporate networks. Because browsing the Web requires that every document a user views—every image, every sound file, and every animation—be downloaded to his or her computer, the user may spend several minutes waiting for the document to transfer. The same document may require only a couple of seconds to download with a high-speed connection. Rather than wait, average consumers may give up on the site and move on.

Another difference between users is computer power, specifically, graphical capabilities. The two most significant measures of graphical capability are resolution and color depth. "Resolution" refers to the number of addressable dots (called pixels) on the screen. For example, a PC may have a resolution of 640 by 480; that is, 640 columns and 480 rows of pixels. The monitor in a graphics workstation, on the other hand, may have a resolution of 1280 by 1024, more than four times as many pixels as the PC. An image that stretched the entire width of such a monitor would not fit on an ordinary PC screen.

"Color depth" refers to the number of colors a screen can display at one time. The average home PC can display 256 colors at a time, while many high performance PCs and graphics workstations can display millions of colors at once. Designers usually should limit the colors on a page to fewer than 256. In fact, it's often wise to keep the number as low as 64. Some older browsers and many computer configurations won't allow the full 256 colors to be displayed.

THE GREAT DIVIDE

In the early days of the Web, there was only one popular graphics-capable Web browser—NCSA's *Mosaic*. (A program called *Lynx* allowed text-only Web browsing for those without access to an graphics-capable Internet connection. Today, people rarely use *Lynx* to browse the Web.) Because practically everybody used the same browser, it was fairly easy for a Web designer to see how a Web document would look to most users. And since *Mosaic* was available for most combinations of computer architectures and operating systems, Web documents were automatically compatible with almost every system. But before long, new browsers began to appear.

Extensions to HTML

HTML provides the standard set of codes used in all Web documents. It was invented by Tim Berners-Lee while working at CERN. Mosaic is one of the original programs designed to display HTML documents. Early Mosaic users could browse any Web document written in HTML.

To further the development of the Web, a team of Web experts formed the W3 Consortium, which was given the task of expanding the HTML standard so designers could implement new features. The consortium was to approve new standards to which all browsers would conform thereafter. Once they'd agreed on the expanded standards, Web designers could begin incorporating them into their documents.

Netscape Communications Corp. (and other companies) grew tired of waiting for the consortium to approve new HTML standards, so the company developed its own "extensions" to the HTML standard. These extensions are additional codes that can be used in Web documents. A browser equipped to interpret these extensions (like the Netscape browser) can properly display documents that use the extensions. Browsers that don't recognize the new codes will ignore the extensions and display the document as it would appear without them. Sometimes, this makes the document appear drastically different from what the designer intended. Correspondingly, this divergence from the approved HTML standard has caused a few problems for Web site developers.

Luckily, Netscape was kind enough to model their extensions after the standards being considered (but not yet approved) by the W3 Consortium. This allows Web designers the freedom to use the Netscape extensions in their documents, and be reasonably certain they'll be compatible with future Web browsers.

The most noteworthy browser to emerge since *Mosaic* first appeared is *Netscape* (also called "Mozilla"), from Netscape Communications Corp. Netscape Communications was founded by some of the same talented people who developed the original *Mosaic* program.

At first, *Netscape* behaved basically the same way *Mosaic* always had. But eventually, Netscape programmers—working to improve Web marketing opportunities—added new features to their product. The browser soon began supporting HTML extensions (see the foregoing technical note). These extensions added so much flexibility to Web-page layout, that a growing number of Web designers, starved for fresh layout tools, began modifying their documents to make use of the new extensions. These extensions have allowed designers to build a more colorful, attractive Web for users of the *Netscape* browser.

Netscape's decision to support HTML extensions divided the Web community; a page that looked great using one browser might look terrible with another. Images that line up neatly within *Netscape* often appear in a muddled heap within *Mosaic*. The problem only grew worse as more Web browsers were developed and each acquired its own peculiar features. Web content providers (marketers and designers) faced

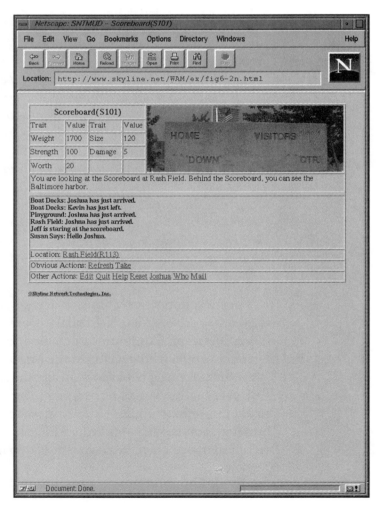

FIGURE 6-2A

S.N.T.MUD software is written for use with *Netscape* browsers.

a difficult issue. They could set up a basic site any browser could access equally, or they could create a flashy site that would look great to *Netscape* users and risk alienating non-Nescape users. (Figure 6-2A shows a Web page as it would appear using Netscape and Figure 6-2B using Mosaic.)

Imagine what would happen if television stations suddenly changed the way they broadcast their programming. Suppose each station chose a different broadcast standard, and we had to have TV sets compatible with each. Odds are, a lot of us would spend more time listening to the radio (or surfing the Net). Well, the same thing is happening on the Web. It's common to connect to a Web site and see a message like

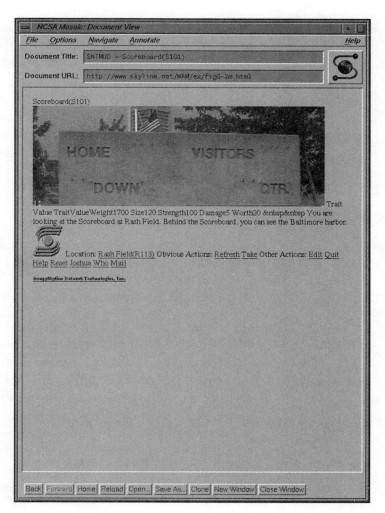

FIGURE 6-2B

S.N.T.MUD software displays its incompatibility with this version of Mosaic.

"This site is *Netscape* enhanced." Whether or not such a message is a badge of honor depends on your point of view.

Even at Skyline, we had to design our S.N.T.MUD software to use a large number of *Netscape* extensions. No other popular browser was versatile enough to handle such a complicated application. Sadly, this means that only *Netscape* users can access S.N.T.MUD. (Fortunately for us, it's the most widely used browser.) As other browsers try to catch up to *Netscape*, they generally aim to maintain *Netscape* compatibility, becoming more and more compatible with *Netscape*-enhanced sites and features like S.N.T.MUD.

Luckily, most Web users can obtain several popular browsers free of charge (at least on a trial basis), so it isn't terribly difficult to switch from one browser to another. But the unfortunate users who access the Web through a commercial online service, like Prodigy, don't have the option of choosing their browser. They can only use the browser their online service provides. We're sorry to say these services seem to be making no significant attempt to incorporate advanced Web features and extensions into their browsers.

What's In a Label?

At Skyline Network Technologies, we discourage Web marketers and designers from using labels such as, "This site enhanced for *Netscape*." Such labels tell non-Netscape users and visitors from commercial networks such as the Microsoft Network, Prodigy, and America Online, "This site isn't constructed for you."

NOTE *We don't like to spread rumors, but there's a growing belief that commercial online services purposely designed their Web browsers with limited capabilities. It's speculated that commercial services hope to keep their users in the dark about the abilities of the Web so their own services will appear more advanced in comparison.*

Whether or not this is true, we encourage all members of commercial online services to e-mail their service requesting improved Web access.

What effects have these browser variations had on Web design? Web designers must now make design decisions that weigh universal access against cutting-edge presentation. It's increasingly difficult to design a Web document incorporating the advanced layout capabilities of *Netscape*, while providing an elegant appearance on other browsers.

Some sites offer a separate link for non-*Netscape* users. Such users select a different version of the same information—a version that follows the official standard for Web layout. This policy can make users feel second-rate. A more complicated and technically sophisticated approach is to have the Web site choose the page best suited to the visitor's browser automatically (see the sidebar on page 138). This can be done without the visitor's assistance (or even knowledge), but it requires that page design and maintenance take two or more forms. This means more time and money for development.

The big plus in all this for Web designers is that online marketers have more need than ever of professionally designed Web sites. It takes a lot of experience to understand both obvious and subtle differences between browser displays. And the emerging practice of designing two or more versions of each Web page means more headaches for do-it-yourselfers and more bucks for professional designers.

YOU CAN'T PLEASE 'EM ALL

When deciding between universal access and cutting-edge presentation, consider your audience. If you are marketing to a technologically savvy crowd, you can be reasonably sure your customers have better-than-average computer systems and Internet connections. These users appreciate, even expect, impressive, graphically sophisticated sites. If you are marketing to a mass audience, limit your use of full-color images, animation, and sounds. A large portion of your market will only be frustrated by the heavy use of multimedia.

BUSINESS-TO-BUSINESS MARKETING

The CommerceNet/Nielsen demographic survey found that most Internet use occurs at the user's workplace. Presumably, a significant portion of these users browse for business-related information or products. The study also showed that more than half of Web users have used the Web to search for information on products and services they plan to purchase either on- or offline. For this reason, business-to-business marketing has influenced the Web significantly. If your target audience is other businesses, you're in for an exciting time designing your Web site. In general, business Web users have better Internet connections, faster computers, enhanced multimedia capabilities, and a generally higher screen resolution (more pixels). And if you market to high-tech businesses, your customers are even better equipped.

The greater your market's computing and communications capabilities, the freer you are to develop cutting-edge Web pages. If these are your customers, your Web site can, and should, include high-resolution, full-color graphics, interactive features, and multimedia presentations. Your customers are used to such flashy sites and expect one from any serious Web advertiser—especially one *they'll* be doing business with.

Medium-sized and large companies desiring such sites are well-advised to bring in consultants to help with the design, but may also hire Web design teams to maintain and/or improve the site. Smaller companies that can't afford to develop advanced Web strategies will have a harder time competing. They must take care with their Web advertising budgets and stress originality and creativity over technological superiority.

BUSINESS-TO-CONSUMER MARKETING

Business-to-consumer sales on the World Wide Web have just begun to take off. As more and more home users begin to connect to the Net via modem, and the commercial online services continue to expand Internet access to millions of others, business-to-consumer sales will continue to increase.

Because business users once accounted for the majority of Web users, Web designers often forget about home users. The average home Web user isn't nearly as well-equipped as the average business user. Most have slower computers; smaller, lower-resolution monitors with less color depth; slower Internet connections (usually much, *much* slower), and, often, outdated or otherwise limited Web-browser software. They can't be expected to appreciate the Web's newer or more advanced features.

A Site by Any Other Browser

Skyline, like a few other Web development firms, has refined a solution that combines cutting-edge presentation with universal access. Our solution, designed for companies with significant financial interest in the Web, includes the high-tech design of Web documents that best suit the upper 25 to 50 percent of their audience. But these sites also include a less complicated set of documents created to provide a clear presentation on all but 2 to 5 percent of the advertiser's audience. The Skyline Web server automatically chooses the most appropriate version of the documents and sends it to the user.

The drawback to this scenario is price. It's much more expensive to include two or more versions of each page. One solution is to design multiple versions of only a few key pages. The remaining pages could be designed so that one version suits virtually any user.

Interactive documents and features (like S.N.T.MUD) can be very difficult to develop this way. Because they create pages on the fly, interactive features would require considerable programming effort to provide output automatically compatible with any browser. Sometimes developers are forced to exclude some users to create a hot site that appeals to the majority.

Companies marketing to the typical consumer are under less pressure to create elaborate, leading-edge presentations. Instead, they're expected to provide clear and concise information using very little bandwidth that doesn't require a top-of-the-line PC. This doesn't mean these Web sites must be boring. They simply require less investment in multimedia and interactive applications. The sites also must be extremely easy to navigate, because visitors generally have less Web experience and are less "computer literate" than their business-user counterparts.

As home PCs become cheaper (and prices are dropping fast) and more feature-rich, home Internet users will come to expect Web sites that live up to the expanding capabilities of their machines. So designers must continue to improve sites to keep pace with the technology and consumer expectations. Don't discount these users just because they're the minority.

IT'S NOT THAT EASY

It's a mistake to assume that all business-to-business shoppers have access to state-of-the-art technology, while all business-to-consumer shoppers use inferior systems. Many major corporations still use outdated computer systems and slow Internet connections; many home PC users have top-of-the-line systems and high-speed ISDN Internet connections.

DON'T: GO ONLINE BEFORE IT'S TIME

One of the most common mistakes new Web advertisers make is launching their Web sites before they're ready. Because Web sites often change from day to day, it can be tempting to launch a half-built site and expand it while it's being used. One school of thought holds that posting a teaser message (or teaser site) touting upcoming features is a sound marketing strategy. Such a sampling, the thinking goes, entices dedicated users and casual surfers to make a mental note to return to the site when it's complete.

These half-built sites often include "under construction" messages telling visitors the feature they've chosen will be available shortly, often accompanied by an image of a yellow-and-black road construction sign (a practice that's become tediously popular).

The problem with this message is that it's usually provided *after* the user selects the feature. This frustrates users, especially those with slow

Internet connections. The last thing they want to do is wait for a document to arrive only to discover it's just another annoying road sign. Several sights on the Web offer nothing more than a homepage with six or seven links, with each link pointing to another road sign. A site like this has no business being online.

The other school argues that no site should go online until it's reasonably close to completion. Users interpret "under construction" messages as "incomplete," and will simply leave, this argument goes. Most users have neither the time nor the inclination to return at a later date, so, until your site is operational, you're just wasting users' time.

In our opinion, neither school has it right. A teaser offers the advantage of telling a user that a new feature will arrive soon, but it should encourage a return visit, without frustrating the user. Wait until your Web site is reasonably complete—offering some useful and quality information, with most available links pointing to attractive, complete pages—before going online.

It's perfectly okay to list features in the works, but follow a few simple rules: First, don't create a link to a feature if it displays only an "under construction" message. If the page offers nothing useful, let users know before they follow a link to it. At least put a miniaturize road sign (or, better, a "coming soon" notice) next to the link so the user has fair warning.

Second, let users know when the feature will be completed, and make sure you complete it by that date. Don't get yourself into trouble by underestimating the time you'll need. You don't want users coming back only to find it still under construction. They won't return.

Third, do not keep too many sections of your Web site under construction at once. Users should believe they're visiting a completed site, not just browsing your plans.

An organization that used this strategy to great effect is the National Football League. Andrew Fry, a consultant for the NFL Web site, suggested making the site publicly available with very little content for a few weeks before the complete package was ready for posting. During those weeks a message at the site relayed the number of days remaining to completion, a countdown to the site launch that heightened excitement among potential visitors.

There are a few valid reasons to announce a Web site or feature before it's complete. One of the best is to outflank imitators. Like conventional trademarking, first use of a concept in a publication can establish proprietary rights to that concept. In other words, launching a Web feature that's not yet fully functional can prevent other businesses from launching a similar feature while you complete your development.

Another reason to announce early is to solicit user feedback. If you want Web users' input about a Web feature, you can announce the basic concept and ask users to send you their ideas. This makes users feel like they have an impact on the site, and it can provide your company with some great ideas.

DO: ENCOURAGE EMPLOYEE INPUT

While a sophisticated, professionally produced site may be the goal of most businesses on the Web, it's not the only way to attract attention. Everyday people—not marketing departments—have designed and maintained many of the most popular Web sites. For this reason, some companies encourage their employees to develop personal Web pages as a way of enhancing the corporate Web site. We see this trend primarily in businesses that have their own Internet connection and operate their own Web site. Such companies often have Web-savvy employees and the resources to host a large site.

The most common method of providing access to personal Web pages is the tilde (~) method. This allows a Web user to access the personal Web pages of a corporate employee by adding `~employee_name` *to the corporate URL. For example, if Skyline had an employee named Jim, we might let him create his own Web pages. Web users could then access Jim's personal Web pages by using the URL* `http://www.skyline.net/~jim`.

The tilde method allows employees to create their own pages without giving them access to the corporate Web pages. Each employee can protect his or her page so other employees don't modify them, making it easy to hold employees accountable for content.

THE SOUL OF THE WEB

Personal pages are the soul of the Web. Internet users historically have shown less interest in using the Web for commerce than as a means for creative expression and a tool for the free exchange of ideas. In fact, today's Internet community is in many ways a rebellious group. The Internet is a lawless frontier, and users are often viewed as social mavericks. To the dismay of many of these mavericks, the commercialization of the Net has been accompanied by the threat of government intervention. Despite the gradual acceptance of commerce on the Net, people still tend to associate corporate Web sites with the inevitable taming of the Net. The Internet community fears the taming of the Net will lead to a broken spirit. Companies can help keep that spirit alive by encouraging employee participation on the Web.

Using personal Web pages is in some ways a license to thrill. A company using employee pages (even fictitious employee pages) can get away with just about anything. From subtle (and we do mean subtle) jabs at the competition, to embarrassing photos from last year's company Christmas party (tastefully done, of course), employee pages can add a personal touch to an otherwise stuffy corporate Web site. And Web users will be impressed by a company that allows employees to express themselves. Remember how sensitive the Internet community is about free expression? That sensitivity can work for you as well as against you.

CAUTIONS

Allowing your employees to represent your company to an audience as large as the Web's presents definite risks. Like it or not, every employee with access to your Web site represents your company on the Net. There's always the chance an employee will post something that will embarrass the company or offend customers and potential customers.

The posting of pornography on an employee page, for example, could have dire consequences for your company. This can happen as the result of a joke, or one or two of your mild-mannered workers might harbor a secret urge to publish dirty pictures. To avert a disastrous situation, management must prohibit such use of company facilities and prevent any association between the company and such material.

Pornography isn't the only potentially offensive material to worry about. Some employees may belong to extreme political or religious groups whose views may offend customers (and even co-workers). Or they may simply have other strong opinions—and you've just given them a place to voice those opinions. No company has the right to interfere with the speech, religion, or beliefs of its of employees, but likewise employees have no right to use the company's Web site to wreck its corporate image. You may have to prohibit employees from including political or religious views on their personal Web pages.

In addition to potentially offensive material, you should watch your employees' personal pages for comments about company products, services, prices, or policies. For instance, a misinformed engineer could post incorrect product or pricing information. If it appears the employee was representing the company when making such claims, the company can be held responsible (legally, perceptually, or both) for the claims.

A company may also be held legally responsible for any laws employees violate using company resources. They may (knowingly or otherwise) violate copyright laws, slander laws, import/export laws, or FCC regulations. In many cases, the company managing the network and the Web server can be held liable for the actions of its users and employees.

This last risk associated with employee personal pages will send chills up the spines of every manager reading these pages. That risk is…the disgruntled employee. The Web can be a very useful tool for such employees to communicate dissatisfaction over lost promotions or raises,

Taking the Blame

A couple of years ago, an America Online (AOL) user posted some very unflattering comments about another online service provider to an AOL forum. That company asked AOL to remove the comments from the forum, claiming that the comments were untrue and slanderous. AOL denied the request on the grounds that their forums allowed free discussion among AOL users. The AOL policy was basically to permit all messages not extremely offensive in nature, a common practice among online services and even Web sites.

When the company failed to get a satisfactory response from AOL, they filed suit. AOL contended they couldn't be sued because the comments were made by a third party. A preliminary hearing was held to determine whether AOL could, indeed, be sued for the comments of its members. The court ruled that AOL *could* be held responsible for such comments, allowing the suit to go forward. It would take a second trial to determine whether the comments actually were slanderous.

In the end, the company dropped all charges against AOL in exchange for a public apology. But the legal precedent set in the preliminary hearing has forced all online service providers and Web sites to take some level of responsibility for the actions of their users. This means that companies that allow their employees to maintain personal Web pages may be held responsible (at least in part) for what is published on those pages.

health benefits, and work atmosphere. It can be embarrassing enough to find an employee bad-mouthing you on the Net, but imagine if they vented their complaints via the corporate Web site.

Many corporations providing direct Internet access to their employees are so concerned about the content of personal employee pages they prohibit their workers from participating on the corporate Web site. These companies cite fear that employees will post adult-oriented or politically incorrect material as their number one reason for prohibiting such use.

What makes this fear an even greater concern is the fact that offensive material need not originate directly from employee pages. An employee's page could include a link to his or her favorite Web site (besides the corporate site, of course). If that favorite site links to five more sites, and one of those sites has offensive material, users may associate that material with your company. After all, they may have begun their Web exploration at your site, and may not realize they followed a link to another site altogether.

While we at Skyline encourage most companies to utilize personal pages, many experts will disagree. Several companies (especially very large corporations) have found that the legal risks and potential damage to public image make personal pages a virtual nightmare. Consider all of the issues we discuss in this section before making your own decision.

Despite the drawbacks, however, prohibiting employee personal pages is unwise, and often unenforceable. With products like Vermeer's *Personal Web Server* for Windows-based PCs and BIAP Systems' *MacHTTP*, virtually any employee with access to the corporate net can have a Web server up and running on their desktop computer before you can print the policy that bans them. All of your employees may not possess the tact or the experience to represent your corporation in an official capacity. Still, the fact that you hired them and that they continue to work for you betokens your faith in their ability to conduct themselves within corporate guidelines. Besides, an employee with Internet access can just as easily (if not more so) misrepresent your company using e-mail, Usenet news, or other Internet applications. If you take away all the "dangerous" tools, what will your employees have to work with?

GUIDELINES

The best way to protect yourself from the perils of personal pages, and to encourage personal pages that enhance your company's image, is to educate and supervise your employees. Follow these guidelines to ensure successful employee participation:

- Let them know what information is acceptable—by legal, Internet, and corporate standards—to include on a personal page. Take nothing for granted; most employees have no concept of the intricacies of public relations or the legalities of publishing.

- If you have employees who would use the Net to vent their disapproval or to air dirty corporate laundry, you really have bigger problems to consider. Find a constructive way to handle employee gripes, such as a complaint/suggestion box monitored by middle or upper management.

- Don't allow your employees to spend so much time creating Web pages that they neglect their company responsibilities. The communicative and creative power of the Web can be addictive. Don't allow competing departments, for example, to develop a Web-page contest.

- Make no attempt to inhibit free expression that you cannot defend clearly to your employees. Whether or not your company is new to the Net, we guarantee that your employees will quickly adopt the widespread belief that the Internet should provide and encourage the free and uninhibited exchange of information.

- On the other hand, take steps to prevent your employees' personal pages from becoming so unprofessional (in appearance or content) that they have a negative effect on the company image. Each of these precautions must be fully justified and laid out for employees from the beginning. It's much easier to prevent certain forms of expression than it is to take those forms away.

Don't forget to tie the personal pages into your corporate Web pages, where appropriate. Many companies provide a "Meet the staff" link on their homepage. Web users who click that link receive a list of employees and links to each employee's personal page. As customers get to know your employees through their personal pages, they feel more comfortable with your company and are more likely to do business with you.

Encourage your employees to tie corporate philosophies and corporate Web pages into their personal pages. A customer is much more likely to take seriously an employee's opinion than anything that comes out of the marketing department. Your employees should feel free to brag (subtly) about their own qualifications and those of the company. Employees should discuss their current projects, and link those discussions with related corporate pages.

Lead by example. Your employees will take their cues from the corporate Web pages. Their individual creativity (and the fact that they're not professional designers) will create important differences between their pages and those of the corporation, but a professionally designed corporate site will set the example.

DO: BE INNOVATIVE

Web marketing, like traditional marketing, isn't an exact science. It's difficult to predict consumer reaction to any given marketing strategy. Consequently, your Web site may not become the instant success you'd hoped. Sure, you can follow the guidelines in this book, and even seek the advice of a professional Web design firm. You can say all the right things in all the right places, have the best graphics, maybe include some animation. These factors can make for a successful Web site, but no one can guarantee that your site will in fact be a huge success. Web marketing is so new, and there is still so much to learn, you may have to rely on trial and error to learn what works.

In Web design, you'll find *imitators* and *innovators*. Imitators look around the Web for successful sites, and incorporate appealing elements from those sites into their own. The imitated sites offer at least some insurance of the copies' future popularity. The nature of the Web makes it very easy to imitate the Web documents of other businesses, so this school of thought has many adherents.

Innovators, on the other hand, focus on originality. They're not interested in doing what's been done. They ask themselves, "What can I do that no one else has tried?" These individuals and companies keep the Web fresh and interesting. Their sites often draw floods of visitors searching for something new. And just about as often, their sites fall flat. Too much originality creates unnecessary risk; an original idea hasn't proved itself. The more original ideas you bring to your site, the more risk that your efforts won't be appreciated.

Consider how conventional advertising has changed over the years. Modern television advertisements look nothing like the ads of the 1950s—and we're not just talking about color and the coming and going of bellbottoms. It's easy to watch an old TV ad and guess the era in which it was created. But these changes occurred gradually, as each ad agency took a conventional idea and improved on it.

We recommend taking basic, time-proven strategies and techniques, and using them to lay the groundwork for your Web site. Feel free to incorporate a few ideas from around the Web into your site. Then, after you've developed a working Web site, look for innovative improvements. These might include a flashy homepage design, a new idea for multimedia, or an elaborate interactive feature (see the following section, "Do: Be Dynamic"). A professional Web designer can help you discover and develop innovative ideas. But take care: Many Web design firms haven't the skills or the resources for much more than basic document design.

Experimenting on the Web offers two advantages: You can receive instant consumer feedback, and trying something new is fairly inexpensive. By setting up the basic framework of a conventional (but certainly not boring) Web site design, you ensure that your visitors won't feel lost. And you'll have a base from which to launch a few experiments.

Innovative ideas created—and will always support—the Web. Its community won't hold it against you if you try something new. And don't discourage too quickly. It may take a little while for your ideas to catch on.

DON'T: OVERDO IT

A common mistake among Web designers is focusing too much on creating graphics-rich Web sites, fancy layout techniques, sounds, and animation. The site is a marketing tool, not an experiment in Web technology. Don't use your Web site to show off features of the Web. Use it to show off your business and the features of *your Web site*. If you spend more time and money incorporating bells and whistles into your site than you spend incorporating marketing strategies, you're probably overdoing it.

Overdoing it can be expensive. A wowee-zowee site costs a lot more to build and maintain, and the emphasis on special effects could cost the site its focus for both company and user. The company may lose track of the reasons it went online in the first place, and users will be so distracted by the bells and whistles, they won't notice the marketing material. They'll have a great time browsing your site, and never learn your company's name.

To be effective, each element of your Web site should contribute to your company's overall marketing strategy. Use Web technology to highlight your services, not to overshadow them.

DO: BE DYNAMIC

dynamic   adj. [Fr. dynamique < Gk. dunamikos, powerful < dunamis, power < dunasthai, to be able.] 1. Of or relating to energy, force, or motion. 2. Marked by continuous change, activity, or progress. 3. Marked by vigor and energy.

A Web site should be dynamic, in every sense of the word. It must be vigorous and energetic and move the user in a particular direction. It must change constantly and maintain user interest. When we say a Web site is dynamic, we're usually referring to its constant state of change. A site can be dynamic in any of these ways (listed in the order of their complexity):

- hypertext documents

- regularly updated documents

- active documents
- search tools
- interactive features

HYPERTEXT DOCUMENTS

Hypertext documents provide the simplest and most obvious way to create a dynamic Web site. Any document that contains links to other documents is considered hypertext. If you've used the hypertext Help systems common on PCs and Macintoshes, you have a good idea how hypertext works. Each page contains hyperlinked words or images you can select with a mouse. When you select a hyperlinked item (called a link), a new page is retrieved. As we discussed in Chapter 3, creating hyperlinks is the simplest way to achieve dynamic addressability. In hypertext documents, users choose content that suits their specific needs.

REGULARLY UPDATED DOCUMENTS

Regularly updated documents can also give you a dynamic Web site, although they involve a little more work on the part of the Web marketer. Regularly updated documents are easy to understand: They're designed to be updated on a regular basis. They may be updated anywhere from every 10 minutes to once a month. Generally, if the updates occur more often than once a day, they're accomplished in some automated manner.

Note to Small Businesses

Many small businesses have small, inexpensive Web sites maintained by Web presence providers and changed infrequently. Small businesses often can't afford the cost of maintaining their own sites, and they usually can't pay the provider to constantly update and expand them. That doesn't mean such sites can't be effective. They're like online business cards or brochures offering consumers around the world access to ready information, 24 hours a day, about these companies.

The main difference between static sites and regularly updated sites is that static sites get fewer repeat visitors. When users returning to a site see that nothing has changed, they often decide there's no reason to come back again. Our advice to small companies is to go ahead and put up a static Web site if that's all your budget can support. But choose a provider that can make inexpensive updates on occasion. Be sure to provide information that suits your users' needs—this will attract repeat visitors.

Topics best suited for regularly updated documents include sports, news, stocks, and weather information. Several sites post links to a new "cool" Web site every day. Others offer an astute quote every morning. Readers of such information understand that the content is always changing, and therefore they regularly re-visit the site. These kinds of sites develop regular visitors. If the information is timely and useful enough, these visitors learn to depend on the site, visiting weekly, daily, even hourly. If you ever intend to charge for access to the information on your site, regularly updated documents are essential to your development.

FIGURE 6-3

Purdue University provides updated weather maps each and every hour.

Not Guilty!

The *San Jose Mercury News* (San Jose, California) does an excellent job of updating its Mercury Center Web site. When the O.J. Simpson trial concluded and the verdict was announced, Mercury Center posted a "Not Guilty" headline within 18 seconds.

Irregularly updated documents can also establish a certain level of Web dynamics. The only difference between these two types of Web documents is that one is updated at unpredictable times. When a Web page is modified just for the sake of change, or to add more information, that's an "irregular update." These updates, while important, are less likely to encourage return visitors, since they have no way of knowing when an update occurs.

Whether you do it regularly or randomly, it's important to the success of your Web site to change your Web pages frequently, even if it's just a change in the appearance. A Web site that remains static for more than a month isn't likely to inspire return visits. Users need to see something different each time they visit your site.

ACTIVE DOCUMENTS

Sometimes it's difficult to tell the difference between updated documents and "active" documents. Like updated documents, active documents change, but they also have the potential to change each time a user accesses them. In other words, every time a user retrieves an active document, the Web site executes a program that actively decides what to send the user. For instance, some popular sites sell advertising space on their pages. Rather than use an automatic regular update to change the advertisement every ten minutes, an active document can select a new advertisement each time it's retrieved.

The advantage of active documents is their ability to "choose" the ad that best suits the user. An active document may be smart enough to realize that the user just viewed a page about Ford Mustangs. It could use that information to select an advertisement for the Ford Motor Company, and send that advertisement to the user.

SEARCH TOOLS

Search tools are an easy way to add some interaction (and convenience) to your Web site. If your site contains large amounts of information (product specifications, databases, and so on), you may want to make your information searchable. While a search engine isn't exactly what most people consider interactive, it gives the user some control of the information he or she views. This significantly enhances the users' experience, saves time, and contributes to your site's dynamic addressability. Monitoring your users' searches also helps track some audience demographics.

INTERACTIVE FEATURES

The highest level of dynamic development on the World Wide Web is an interactive feature. When properly implemented, these features achieve an impressive level of user involvement by letting them *experience* the Web, not just view it. The three most common interactive features are games, chat rooms, and Web MUSHes.

GAMES

Shopping, research, and reading interesting Web pages aren't the only ways to spend time on the Web. Many people turn to the Web for more direct forms of entertainment. Online games are becoming the "in" thing on the World Wide Web. The games available now provide anything from mindless amusement to brain-teasing puzzles. The sidebar on page 154 lists some popular Web games. We show a well-written twist on the classic, "Hangman," in Figure 6-4. If you think your company could benefit from providing online entertainment, consider these examples.

To be honest, the current crop of online games hasn't even come close to harnessing the entertainment potential of the Web; most games are popular only as novelties. Few online games allow the player to interact with other Web users, either cooperatively or competitively. Games that allow direct interaction between players flourished on the Internet during the years before the Web, so expect to see an increased interest in online games in the near future. Most of these kinds of games fall into the MUSH/MUD category (discussed later in this chapter).

CHAT ROOMS

Chat rooms are quickly becoming one of the hottest trends on the Web. Interestingly, the Internet had chat rooms long before the Web came along. The most common interface to chat rooms was *Internet Relay Chat*, a program that let hundreds of users share the same text-only conversation. Chat rooms have always been popular, but their migration to the Web has brought with them an entirely new breed of

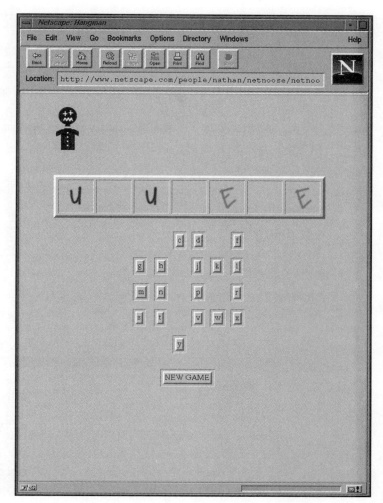

FIGURE 6-4

A programmer at Netscape
Communications has written a
refreshing version of the
classic game, "Hangman."

user. From the user's view, chat rooms provide a virtual conference call
where each person can "talk" (by typing messages) with every other
participant in the chat room. From the view of the chat room provider,
it's simply a Web page that acts as a gigantic chalkboard, on which
each participant writes messages for the world to see.

Yes, the concept sounds too simple, even dull. But, chat rooms have
evolved into an art form. They have been improved on in small but
significant ways. They can be organized by topic, limited to particular
users, and sometimes incorporate their own forms of comic relief—

Web Games

Thinking of providing online entertainment to your Web visitors? Check out these Web games for ideas.

NetNoose http://www.netscape.com/people/nathan/netnoose/index.html
This is a new twist to the old-time classic, "Hangman." An excellent example of a simple game on the Web.

Scrambler http://www.skyline.net/horizons/games/scramble
Remember the old nine-tile puzzles where one tile was missing? The tiles are all scrambled, and you slide them around to solve the puzzle. Another classic.

S.N.T.MUD http://www.skyline.net:8000
The Web's most interactive game. Players move in a virtual world centered around Maryland's Baltimore Harbor.

Tic-Tac-Toe http://www.bu.edu/Games/tictactoe
Part of the collection from Boston University. Players compete against a university computer.

Pegs http://www.bu.edu/htbin/pegs
Another game from Boston University. A game of strategy against a computer opponent.

Hunt the Wumpus http://www.bu.edu/htbin/wcl
A multi-user game from Boston University.

crazy things might happen to the participants while they're talking. Compared to e-mail, chat rooms are an excellent, speedy form of communication. They're used for collaboration among co-workers and students, and provide an excellent bridge between the deaf and the rest of the world. But mostly, they're used for fun.

Chat rooms provide real-time communication among people from all over the world. They provide more social interaction than nearly any other Internet application (the Web included). We've already talked about how Internet users, especially women, are seeking more social interaction. Chat rooms provide that interaction. They're different each time the user visits (different people, different discussions, different moods). Chat rooms have started lasting friendships and steamy romances—including a few marriages. (Remember, your results may vary....)

Companies can best benefit from chat room exposure by hosting discussion sessions and user groups in which the company fields questions related to your field. They can also present non-intrusive advertisements to chat room participants. Even though chat rooms are text-only applications, advertisers can use the graphical features of the Web to display advertisements while the users chat.

Occasionally, a company will pay a well-known musician, sports figure, or Hollywood celebrity to participate in a chat room. The company advertises the event like they would any other public appearance, and generally collects a cover charge from each participant.

MUSES, MUDS, AND MORE

MUSHes (Multi-User Shared Hallucinations) and MUDs (Multi-User Dungeons) fall into the more general category of MUSEs (Multi-User Simulation Environments). (Don't get hung up on the strange names; it's not important that you understand the subtle differences between these services. We'll refer to them all as MUSEs.)

MUSEs began as online arenas for popular role-playing games like "Dungeons & Dragons." Role-playing fanatics designed computer programs that allowed users from all over the world to connect (over the Internet) and join in on a continuous role-playing game. Though entirely text-based, these programs matured quickly and acquired enough features to make the players feel as though they were truly a part of the game's virtual world.

Before long, the mainstream crowd (those who were not interested in fantasy games) realized the value of these programs, and a new generation of MUSEs was born. These MUSEs had more realistic themes than their MUD counterparts. Such themes might include sunny beaches; a college fraternity house where users build their own rooms, furniture, and pets; or a virtual city where users build their own homes. Admittedly, all of this may sound a little weird to non-MUSErs, but their popularity among mainstream Net users is truly astounding.

Web-based versions of MUSEs have existed for only a short while. The Web provides a point-and-click interface filled with images—one that appeals to a much broader audience. With this type of interface, today's Web users can visit an online location, whether fantastic or realistic, and perform some or all of the following actions:

- walk from room to room, building to building, and street to street

- look at objects and people that are in the same location

- pick up, use, and drop objects

- purchase real or virtual products

- talk to other users in the same location (each room is also a chat room)

- send mail to other users

- fight with and steal from other users (prohibited in some MUSEs)

Both the entertainment and commercial value of MUSEs should be of interest to Web advertisers. We're not suggesting that every online business create a virtual fantasy world, but there's no question that this kind of interactivity attracts consumers. When 25 people (or 250) connect to a single Web site, adopt a new character and personality, and enter a simulated world made of connected rooms and movable props, dynamic addressability compounds in elaborate and sometimes astounding ways.

Web MUSEs are still in their infancy, but innovative applications like S.N.T.MUD are getting commercial attention that could eventually translate into development capital. In the next year or two, you'll see a growing number of MUSEs appearing on the Web. They'll be used for social experimentation (kind of like rat mazes), highly interactive games, and virtual shopping centers with real salespeople and customer communication.

Remember...

- There's no substitute for a few hours (or a few days) of browsing the Web before you make any decisions about your online future. Take the time to get acquainted with the medium and your competition.

- On the Net, it's wiser to give than to receive. Always remember the Internet is a gift culture. Don't enter the online world asking for business. Ask the Web what you can do for them.

- Usenet spam and other Net offenses will win you no friends on the Web.

- Most flames are best ignored. If you try to respond, you'll probably just fan the fire.

- Companies that learn to use the soft sell will be very successful in the new "find a need and fill it" atmosphere of the Web.

- Differences in Web browser software, computer hardware, Internet connection speed, and personal preference make it difficult to design a Web site that is innovative while catering to the majority of Web users. Design your pages to meet the tastes and capabilities of your audience.

- Personal Web pages are the soul of the Web. Establish a policy that encourages employee Web pages but prevents liability problems and damage to the company image.

- If your site isn't dynamic, you'll attract few return users. Interactive sites will soon be the norm, so start thinking about it now.

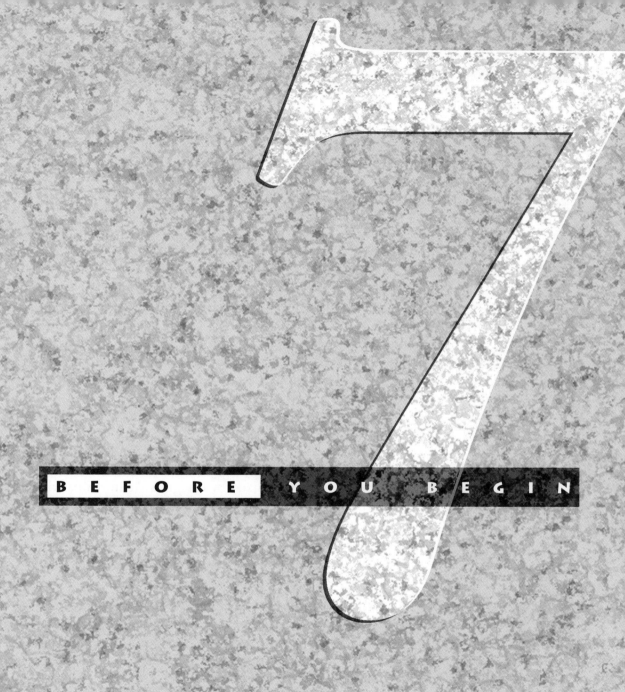

BEFORE YOU BEGIN

In the previous chapter, we listed a number of do's and don'ts every company should consider before launching a Web site. But before you take your company online, take the time to consider the look and feel you want your site to have. Learn a bit about essential Web-site design principles, and do some surfing with design and style in mind. In this chapter, we discuss Web site styles and online design principles, as well as the basic steps you'll take as you and your company go online.

CHOOSING A DESIGN STYLE

Before you launch your Web site, you'll have to make some decisions about the style of its design. You'll find many popular Web site design styles to choose from. It's also possible to combine elements from different styles to create a style unique to your site. Surfing the Web is, of course, the best way to see how other companies use the Web site designs described in this chapter. While you're there, you just might find a few styles we missed.

CYBERMALLS

A cybermall is a collection of online storefronts on a single Web site. Cybermalls usually have the look and feel (see note) of real-world shopping malls, and they're often organized by category. As in real-world malls, the stores in cybermalls generally deal in retail products rather than services. The stores are almost always small businesses, usually specialty shops offering only a handful of items. Generally, each business in a cybermall has only one or two simple Web pages, and each store looks very much like the next.

When Web designers talk about the "look and feel" of a site or Web page, they mean the ways a document may be designed to reflect a real-world location or item. The look and feel of a Web site or page relates directly to the theme of that site or page. For instance, a site with an island theme may use images and terminology that create the look and feel of a beach. A site with an outer-space theme would use dark backgrounds, pictures of planets, and appropriate terminology to create the look and feel of being in space. Essentially, "look and feel" refers to the mental images and emotional resonances a given design evokes.

The cybermall design offers three advantages—price, turnaround time, and the ability to share customers. Cybermalls are generally the least expensive Web design style. The company operating the mall will design your pages (usually one or two, and not very original) and fit them in among the other stores. The simplicity of this design allows new businesses to get online very quickly, and the other stores in the mall provide an instant pool of shoppers for newcomers.

Some cybermalls provide the stores on their sites with online purchasing services that allow customers to buy directly from the stores over the Internet (a growing trend). In other cybermalls, stores list telephone numbers for customers to call to place orders. Unfortunately,

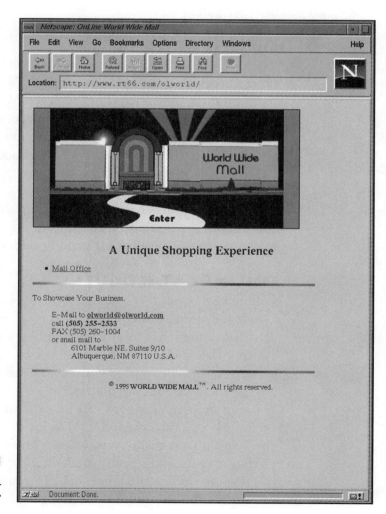

FIGURE 7-1

The World Wide Mall provides "over 100 Exciting Stores plus Classifieds."

cybermalls are often poor-quality sites. The lack of integration between stores on these sites prevents shoppers from buying products from more than one store at a time. The lack of original page design makes it difficult to stand out. Fact is, they're simply not very popular among Web surfers.

All cybermalls don't necessarily imitate the look and feel of real-world shopping malls. Many web design firms provide an online listing of some or all of their clients. Users can select a client from the list and visit the corresponding online storefront. If the storefront, in turn, provides a link back to the original list, this setup becomes a simple form of cybermall.

ONLINE BROCHURES

The online brochure is a popular Web site design style. Basically, an online brochure consists of one to five Web pages describing a company, product, or service. The "typical" Web site takes the form of an online brochure. It includes a front page, called the homepage, that usually lists general information about the company, some additional pages with specific information about products or services, and a page explaining how to contact the company for more information or to make a purchase.

Online brochures can be fairly inexpensive to design and maintain and can hold as much or as little information as you want. They may or may not provide a means for making online purchases.

ONLINE CATALOGUES

Online catalogues incorporate readily into a brochure-style Web site. Catalogues provide a complete listing of all of the products and services a company has to offer. Much like a conventional catalogue, an online catalogue is usually organized by category. Each item has its own page, or shares a page with several similar products. Prices generally are included, but not always.

Large online catalogues can be expensive to create and maintain. Including a picture of each item helps to liven up the site, but it can also liven up the price considerably. You'll probably want to include pricing information in your catalogue, but if your prices fluctuate and you need to update them periodically, you can bet your Web designer will expect you to pay for each change.

Because an online catalogue can display all of your products and services, it can be an invaluable resource for your customers, distributors, and sales force. Large online catalogues provide many opportunities for your company to display its name and logo to browsing Web surfers.

Most medium-to-large online catalogues provide some method for making online purchases. But users are still more than a little wary of this technology. If you set up an online catalogue, let customers know how to order your products or services offline, as well.

SHOPPING CARTS

You most often see virtual shopping carts in small-to-medium catalogues, where they encourage the purchase of more than one product at a time. Users browsing catalogues with virtual shopping carts are able to "load" their carts as they browse. Each time they find an item they want to buy, they simply add it to the cart. When they're finished, they pay for everything at once.

Without virtual shopping carts, visitors to your catalogue must pay for each item separately or remember items on their own and combine them manually.

To understand the technicalities involved in developing a virtual shopping cart, you must first understand that the World Wide Web is a stateless application. That is, the Web server doesn't keep track of users as they move from page to page. When a user visits a Web document, the Web browser contacts the Web server and says "Give me page xyz." The Web server then says "Okay, here it is." The server then sends the documents and "hangs up" on the browser. When the browser comes back for another document, the server doesn't remember that it just talked to that browser.

To design a virtual shopping cart, the programmer must develop a way for the server to remember the user. Otherwise the user would put a product in his or her cart and the server would simply forget it was there. The server would always think the cart was empty. To prevent this, Web programmers send a kind of "token" to the Web browser. When the browser requests a new document, it gives the token back to the server and the server uses the token to figure out which user (and which cart) is visiting.

Virtual shopping carts have the advantage of providing the customer with an easy way to purchase several products at once. They make it just as easy to purchase three products as it is to purchase one—a definite marketing advantage. Unfortunately, the carts confuse many users. The concept may even scare them away. The technicalities involved in using virtual shopping carts can also create Web design complications that ultimately make them fairly expensive.

The virtual shopping cart doesn't always have the look and feel of a real-world shopping cart. Sometimes it takes the form of a check list. As shoppers browse the online catalogue, they simply check off boxes next to the products. When they're ready to pay, the server remembers all the items they selected.

VIRTUAL VENDORS

The most complicated style of online storefront design is the virtual vendor. Like virtual shopping carts, virtual vendors remember what objects users select from the catalogue. But virtual vendors can incorporate so many additional features, they can seem more like MUSEs (see Chapter 6).

In its simplest form, a virtual vendor is a virtual shopping cart with the look and feel of a store. This sort of interface can be more fun than a simple online catalogue, allowing browsers to walk around a store, looking at products. Though the results are the same—the user has access to product details and the opportunity to collect and buy several things at a time—the entertainment value of the virtual vendor encourages continued browsing and return visits.

The most sophisticated virtual vendors are actually MUSEs, with the look and feel of retail stores. In these versions, browsers not only feel as though they're walking around the store, they might actually meet store employees or other shoppers with whom they can interact. This highly advanced mix of social interaction and online shopping is just beginning to emerge on the Web, but will quickly bring Web commerce into the mainstream, especially among female shoppers.

Virtual vendors do, however, have disadvantages. Web designers are only beginning to use this technology on the Web, so there are bound to be kinks to work out. Virtual vendors also can be expensive to build, and may become too graphically intensive for typical home users dialing in to the Internet with a modem. And unless they're carefully implemented, they can be confusing and even off-putting to users.

MAINTAINING CONSISTENCY

Your Web site must be exciting, engaging, and unique if you want it to get real attention from the Internet community and command a respectable number of return visitors. But your site also must maintain a certain level of consistency in its style and design.

When we talk about Web site consistency, we're talking about several factors, including a common look and feel, uniform navigational tools, a consistently displayed company hallmark, and consistency over time. All these factors contribute to a Web site's ability to flow together logically, or its "coherence factor."

COMMON LOOK AND FEEL

For a site to flow well from page to page, each page must have a similar look and feel. It's important to be creative and keep each page from looking just like the last one, but it's also important to let users know they're still looking at the same Web site. The Web's nature makes it easy to jump from one site to the another. You don't want users to forget where they are.

Earlier, we told you that "look and feel" refers to the sum of the mental and emotional images conveyed by the design of a Web document. But the concept also applies to the overall physical appearance of a page or site. Maintaining a common look and feel among Web pages involves keeping the mental and emotional images consistent with the theme and *keeping the general appearance, or layout, of the pages consistent throughout the site. This may also include providing the same navigational buttons on each page.*

You can create a common look and feel on your Web site by using a similar page layout on each major page, using the same background or image on each page, or keeping a consistent theme throughout. Don't, however, make the pages look *too* similar. You're after consistency, not monotony.

CONSISTENT NAVIGATIONAL TOOLS

One way to develop a consistent look and feel among Web pages is to include the same navigational buttons on each page. In Chapter 3, we discussed how navigational buttons can encourage a user to explore your site more thoroughly. Users want to feel like they're navigating the site, not like the site is navigating them. And if you've ever gotten lost on a Web site, you know how frustrating that can be. Utilizing clear and consistent navigational buttons throughout your site will make visitors feel at home.

Varying your navigational buttons significantly will cause them to lose their usefulness. Imagine trying to find your way around an unfamiliar city where the streets aren't named consistently, and the signs are all different styles and located in different places. You'd get lost in no time. How soon will you want to return to that city?

You owe it to your visitors to make their stay on your Web site as effortless as possible. That means not only providing consistent navigational buttons, but also consistent and easy-to-follow links. Link consistency is very important to the success of your Web site. All the links on your site should behave as expected. Links that look like they point to the same document should, indeed, point to that document. For example, many Web designers place a "Home" or "Back" button on each Web page. The Home button takes the user back to the site's homepage (usually the first page users connect to). A site loses link consistency when Home buttons take the user back to pages other than the homepage.

The Back button is an even more common source of link inconsistency. If there's no obvious page to go back to, the user often has no idea what effect clicking the button will have. In an online catalogue, for instance, one Back button may take the user from a product description to the overall Table of Contents. Another Back button may take the user from a product description to a list of similar products (a single category's "table of contents"). If the button itself doesn't indicate where the link will take the user, the site loses link consistency.

COMPANY HALLMARK

A compelling reason to establish a corporate Web site is to increase name recognition. Even if your site contained no product information and didn't allow any form of online purchasing, you could still use the Web to expose millions of people around the world to your company name. You simply attract an audience (covered in Chapter 9) and bombard them with the company "hallmark."

A hallmark can be your company logo, your company name, an identifying image, or a copyright notice appearing on every Web page. We

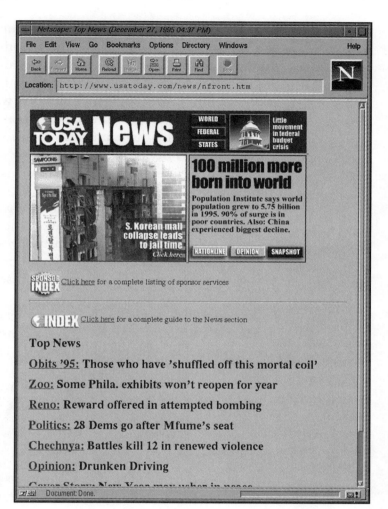

FIGURE 7-2

The *USA Today* Web site makes excellent use of consistent navigational tools at the top and bottom of each page.

call them hallmarks because they act as certificates of authenticity. Including your hallmark on every page says, "We are Acme Widgets and we are proud to bring you this Web page." Your hallmark creates an impression on the user. If a user views five Web pages, each with your hallmark, he or she receives five impressions of your company.

Placing the company hallmark on a Web site isn't much different from the practice of including the company name and logo on products. When you buy a case of Coca-Cola, you see the name and logo on every can. When you drink the soda, you're constantly reminded who the manufacturer is. Everybody around you knows you're drinking a Coca-Cola (assuming you drink from the can), and can easily go to the store and look for the same name and logo on the shelves.

Similarly, you want to remind visitors to your Web site constantly that they are on your company's site. You want them to know where to turn for more online information or to make purchases. You want anyone who walks by their terminals to see that they're on your site. If those passersby decide to check out your site, you want to make sure they see the same hallmark and know instantly they've come to the right place.

Visitors should receive impressions of your company from any page on your site. Include your hallmark somewhere on every Web page. Users should never have to ask themselves, "Whose site is this?" Try putting your hallmark in the same position on each page, say, near the navigational buttons. That way, when users look for direction, your hallmark reminds them of your company.

Enough of these hallmark impressions can make a significant difference in consumer attitude. When a consumer thinks, "I've seen that name before," it lends credibility to your company and makes it seem more enduring. For this reason, you may want to tie your online hallmark directly to your conventional logo. You might even want them to be identical. That way the two will work together to increase overall consumer recognition.

REPETITION IS KEY

Remember the rule of sevens: Consumers must receive seven impressions of a product or company to find it familiar. Arrange your site so the average visitor will read your company name or see your logo at least seven times during each visit. This isn't always easy. If your site is a one-page brochure, for example, you don't want to plaster your company name seven times across the page. Be subtle. Make sure that when the user leaves your site, he or she remembers your company name, not just the colorful graphics you featured there.

CONSISTENCY OVER TIME

In Chapter 6, we advised you to strive for a dynamic Web-site design, and we suggested that one way to inject dynamism into your site is to update it continually and expand it with new and changing features and content. In fact, we said, if you don't change your site regularly and often, you risk losing repeat visitors.

Ironically, while you're injecting all that variety into your site, you've also got to make sure that it's *consistent over time*. The idea here is to avoid changing your site so drastically that return users fail to recognize it, or get lost. You don't want what was once familiar ground to become strange and confusing.

Avoid this problem by expanding your site in such a way that the user doesn't have to learn new navigating skills each time he or she visits. If users return to your site a second or third time, it's because they found something they liked the first time.

It's also important to make sure they can find your site again if they decide they want to come back. The existence of "bookmark" features on Web browsers makes this even more important. Modern browsers can be told to remember the locations of Web documents, so users can more easily return to their favorite sites. Bookmarks make it simple for users to revisit your Web site—unless, in your efforts to remain dynamic, you move the site; in that case, a true fan might never find you again.

If you've ever been away from your hometown for a few years, and then returned to find new buildings everywhere, you'll understand the need for consistency over time on your Web site. The changes in your hometown may have been for the better, but it no longer feels like home. Now imagine instead if a few streets and buildings were moved and renamed. Even the old familiar places are now somewhere clear across town. That's how it feels to visit a favorite Web site that's been radically changed. It leaves your visitors lost and confused.

Your Web site should strive to make visitors feel at home, even though that home is growing and improving. Make your changes as gently as possible, and be sure to provide plenty of road signs (navigational tools) to help users navigate the new features.

WHAT'S NEW

One such navigational tool is the "What's New" page. A What's New page lists recent changes to your Web site, and allows users to find new features quickly without searching the entire site. Admittedly, forcing users to browse the entire site could be to the advertiser's advantage, but very few Web surfers have the time or inclination to do this. If you don't make the changes obvious, they'll assume everything is still the same.

Companies with sites that include a What's New page quickly find it to be the most popular page on the site. Users will often set their bookmarks to this page and never visit the site's front page, or homepage. Take advantage of this. Include information about a new product or service on the What's New page, even if that information has nothing to do with Web-site additions. Tell the user what's new at your company, not just on the site. If nothing's new, use the space to post some sort of reminder about an older, popular Web page, or to push a specific product.

To encourage users to visit their homepages, some companies include lists of new features there. Most homepages are designed to make the company's first and best impression, so it makes sense to make it the most popular page on the site.

CORPORATE PREPARATIONS

Adding a Web site to your current marketing plan is a simple way to increase public exposure and cut marketing expenses. By itself, a Web site can do much for just about any company, large or small. But many companies look at the Internet with a much broader vision. They see the Net as more than just a home for their newest advertising tool. They see a medium that can change the way they do business.

For these companies, it's not enough just to throw up a site. They know that establishing an address on the Web is just one step toward building the business model of the near future. They understand the benefits of training their employees in the use of the Net and the Web. They realize the importance of knowing and understanding the rules of Internet etiquette, and of training their personnel to handle complaints received from the Internet.

The following section is aimed at those companies who grasp the enormous potential of the Internet. But it includes important information for any company considering Web marketing. Sooner or later, nearly every company in the world will have to deal with these issues. In fact, many of the following topics could apply to businesses with only an e-mail account and no other Internet presence.

TRAINING

Properly trained employees are critical to the success of any business enterprise. Yet, in our business, we often see companies make huge investments in sophisticated computer equipment, and then fail to train their employees to utilize it fully. An investment they thought would yield greater productivity only breeds stagnation and frustration from employees who haven't the skills they want and need.

We see this is happening in business every day. Equipment from copy machines to desktop PCs, cutting-edge software to heavy construction machinery is wasted because employees received little or no training.

Look at the Internet as another piece of business equipment, albeit a sophisticated one. Whether a company uses the Net for Web marketing, exchanging e-mail, finding and buying equipment and supplies, or any of a host of other tasks, to get the most out of it, you must train your employees to use it properly. The time you invest in training now will pay big dividends down the road.

PREPARING FOR E-MAIL

Chances are, you've already used electronic mail to communicate with colleagues and customers, as well as family and friends. But if you're like most people, you've probably never stopped to consider the content of an e-mail message—that is, the *form* of your message. Just as style guidelines and sophisticated techniques exist to help create powerful and successful letters and memoranda written offline, certain techniques have been established to help create effective e-mail.

In the hands of someone with no training, e-mail can be a dangerous thing. Its improvisational form makes it difficult to convey a sense of professionalism; it's so easy to write and send that people often fail to take the time to think about what they're writing. And once an e-mail message is sent, there's almost no way of getting it back before it reaches its destination.

Most companies setting up shop on the Web will probably find a use for e-mail in the near future. Your Web site may even include a user feedback or order form that's e-mailed to your company. Let's examine some aspects of e-mail we've found to be important to companies using it as a business tool.

E-mail Builds a Reputation

At Skyline, we always respond quickly and thoroughly to user e-mail, even when the user only wants free advice. Often, users are so impressed they write back to express their surprise and gratitude. Apparently, consumers have become so used to being ignored by corporations they deeply appreciate an attentive response. As more companies use the fast turnaround time and the low cost of e-mail to serve their customers, the Web will change the business/consumer relationship. Web users will come to expect this new level of attention from all companies, both online and off.

SIGNATURE ETIQUETTE

A "signature" is the three to five lines of text that appear at the end of an e-mail message. Signatures usually include the name and e-mail address of the person and/or company sending the message, along with their phone number, address, Web-site location (URL), and a brief description of the company. If the e-mail is a personal message, the signature may contain the sender's favorite quote instead of a company description.

Many e-mail programs include a feature that will add a signature to every message automatically, without the sender's intervention. The signature file for our Webmaster at Skyline Network Technologies looks like this:

```
+ - - - - - - - - - - - - - - - - - - - - + - - - - - - - - - +
| Skyline Network Technologies, Incorporated | webmaster@skyline.net |
| Internet Publishing, Consulting and Marketing | http://www.skyline.net |
|      Home of HORIZONS Magazine        |    (410)882-3781    |
+ - - - - - - - - - - - - - - - - - - - - + - - - - - - - - - +
```

The "webmaster" address in the Skyline signature is the e-mail address users write to with general comments or questions. A Webmaster is the person responsible for organizing and maintaining a Web site. He is almost always responsible for answering e-mail message from users. Webmasters are becoming common among companies that maintain their own Web sites.

Notice how the signature takes up only five lines. Many people include signatures using 10 or more lines. Most Internet-savvy circles consider this quite rude. An oversized signature distracts from the actual message and wastes network bandwidth, e-mail storage space, and the recipient's time. If you have something important to say about yourself or your company, included it in the message. Attaching a large amount of unrelated company or personal information to a signature quickly turns your serious e-mail message into electronic junk mail.

The left side of the signature incorporates our corporate name, a brief description of our services, and a quick plug for one of our features, *Horizons Magazine*. We include this information to increase our name recognition and to let the recipient know that we offer services they may want.

On the right side of the signature, you'll find our e-mail address, our Web-site URL (http://www.skyline.net), and our phone number. We've given the reader three ways to contact us if he or she would like more information. For example, say we e-mail a price estimate to a potential customer. When that customer reads the estimate and decides to purchase our services (as we hope), our phone number is instantly available. No need to look it up in the phone book. If instead the customer wants to browse our Web site and see what kind of work we do, the URL is just as available.

Think of your e-mail signature as another kind of business card. It contains your vital information, and nothing more. It should be neat and concise, and encourage name recognition.

QUOTING ETIQUETTE

One of the handiest features of today's e-mail software is its ability to quote another person's e-mail message. Quoting an e-mail message isn't quite the same as quoting Shakespeare. You simply precede the lines being quoted with a "greater than" symbol (>).

Quoting can be a useful tool when responding to e-mail messages. It helps the other parties remember what they wrote to you. Because e-mail is so easy, people often send out messages with very little thought. By the time you respond, they may have forgotten they contacted you. By quoting the first few lines of their message, you ensure they understand your purpose for writing.

The following example demonstrates the successful use of quoting. The first few lines show the quote as it might be created by an e-mail program. The remaining lines contain the reply.

```
At 12:28 PM 01/14/96, you wrote:

>Mr. Jones,
```

```
>I was wondering if you could tell me more about your
line of widgets. I am

>especially interested in how your widgets differ from
those of my current

>supplier —Will's Widget Works.

>

>Thank you very much,

>Albert Smith, Smith's Widget Distributors, Inc.

Thank your for you interest in Acme Widgets. You have
contacted us at a very

exciting time. We've just released our new line of blue
widgets. These

beautiful trinkets are hand crafted and come is all
shades of blue.
```

...(the message continues)...

SIMPLE PRECAUTIONS

Anyone using e-mail for professional messages should take these simple precautions:

- Take care to word things so they can be clearly understood. Often we forget that e-mail doesn't convey our facial expressions or our tone of voice. You must convey these things with your words. Limit your use of sarcasm and humor; e-mail has a way of making such things sound rude or confusing.

- Likewise, take care not to misinterpret incoming e-mail. The sender may not have followed our advice about limiting sarcasm and humor. If a message seems rude or offensive, more often than not you've just misunderstood.

- For important messages that are not urgent, compose the message, wait an hour or two, read it again, then send it.

Catch major mistakes or easily misinterpreted phrasing *before* you send a message.

- Don't expect your e-mail to remain private. Unless you take special measures (discussed in Chapter 13), your e-mail is subject to "eavesdropping."

- If your e-mail software automatically quotes a message when you reply to it, feel free to remove unnecessary information from the quote. There's usually no need to quote an entire e-mail message. Be careful not to modify the meaning of the quote.

- If your e-mail software doesn't quote automatically, it's OK to manually quote a message in the same form. Just type the greater than sign and a small portion of the message.

- DON'T USE ALL CAPITAL LETTERS. It's the e-mail equivalent of yelling. It denotes anger. For emphasis, indicate an underline with underscore characters before and after, like _this_.

- Your signature should never be longer than your message. If you send a one- or two-line e-mail message, forgo the signature and just use your name and company name.

- Avoid ASCII art in both the message and signature. ASCII art is the use of everyday text characters to create an image. If you don't know what we're talking about, you've probably never used ASCII art. Keep it that way, at least in professional communications.

It's OK to use "smileys" occasionally in your e-mail, as long as you're writing to a seasoned Net user (not some stuffy corporate executive who's just gotten his first e-mail account), and the tone of the e-mail isn't very formal. Smileys, or "emoticons," convey facial expressions or moods. Table 7-1 shows some popular smileys. We don't recommend using other faces (there are hundreds) except among friends. Alternatively, you may prefer the more concise "mood tags." Mood tags actually use whatever word you think best conveys your intended mood.

TABLE 7-1 A FEW POPULAR SMILEYS AND THEIR EQUIVALENT MOOD TAGS.

Mood/Message	Smiley	Mood Tag
Funny, that was a joke	:) or : -)	\<grin\> or \<g\>
Happy	:) or : -)	\<smile\> or \<grin\> or \<g\>
Sad	: (or : - (	\<frown\>
Surprise	:o or :-o	\<suprise\>
Wink	;) or ; -)	\<wink\>

PREPARING FOR COMPLAINTS

When you establish a Web site, or any other Internet service, chances are you'll also establish some means for consumer response. It may be a phone number, an online form, or an e-mail address; whatever it is, you'll provide the Internet community with some way to contact your company. (There wouldn't be much point to all this if you didn't.) And you'll undoubtedly develop a plan for responding to customer contacts.

What most companies fail to do is plan for *complaints*. When you publish corporate information where 30 million people all over the world can see it, you're going to get a few complaints. That's the nature of the Net. If Mother Teresa had a Web page, she would get complaints. These complaints may be about your Web pages, product offerings, prices, the spelling of your name, or even the weather.

Generally speaking, you can handle these complaints the same way you handle traditional complaints in the offline world. Problem is, these complaints may arrive through non-traditional channels. If your Web site includes the phone number of your sales department, but not your support department, you can bet your sales department will receive calls they're not used to handling.

If your site displays no e-mail address specifically for complaints, your unfortunate Webmaster (or the Webmaster of your Web-presence provider) will receive customer e-mail of every type, from complaints to sales questions to personnel inquiries. Usually the Webmaster isn't equipped to reply to his own e-mail.

The Baltimore/Cleveland Conflict

Because Skyline Network Technologies is based in Baltimore, Maryland, and we focus a lot of our attention on the city, we were once the target of an offensive complaint during the negotiation of the deal to move the Cleveland Browns to Baltimore. In fact, the message is too offensive to include in this book. The point is, the price of exposure is *exposure*. When you open yourself up to the Net audience, you open yourself up to all kinds of people and their discontent. Prepare your employees to handle such issues calmly and professionally.

The best way to prepare your employees for complaints (and other responses) is to educate them. Let them know they shouldn't try to field questions or complaints they're not trained to handle. If you don't, the wrong people will give the wrong answers to your suddenly very dissatisfied customers. Make sure those who are responsible for responding to complaints do it in a timely manner—especially if the complaint was received via e-mail. You can soothe many an angry customer by simply responding quickly. If you maintain your own Web site, provide your Webmaster with an e-mail account. And make sure the person responsible for answering that e-mail has access to the necessary resources. It's becoming the norm in large companies for the Webmaster to work very closely with corporate executives. In fact, the Webmaster may double as an assistant to a vice-president just so they can keep each other informed on company issues and consumer responses. If you don't maintain your own Web site, make sure your Web-presence provider will pass along e-mail meant for your company.

PREPARING FOR HACKERS

Nobody likes to think about it, but the fact is, the Internet is full of hackers. And, as we explain in Chapter 13, they can do a lot of damage. Every business on the Web must prepare for hacker activity. Even the small business that hires a Web-presence provider to create and maintain a three-page online brochure needs to take steps to protect its site.

Small businesses can start by choosing a Web-presence provider with a valid security policy. The most important thing to look for in that policy is frequent backups of customers' Web sites—especially *yours*. Your provider should make copies of the important files on his Web server on a regular basis. It's the only way he can be sure that, should a hacker invade the server and delete or modify your files, he can have you up and running again quickly and easily. By the way, these backups shouldn't cost you a penny.

Larger companies that maintain their own Web sites should have a more complete security policy, especially if they have confidential information on the same network as their sites. Still, the best protection for your Web site to back up your Web files often.

FOLLOWING CONVENTIONAL MARKETING DESIGN PRINCIPLES

The songwriter and humorist Tom Lehrer once claimed, "The reason most folk songs are so awful is they were written by 'the people.'" The same is often true of Web design. Most poor Web sites are poor because they were designed by "the people," not Web-site designers.

Remember when desktop publishing tools first became available to the average home-computer user? Suddenly, anybody "publishing" a church newsletter or PTA update could become an editor, typesetter, and graphic designer overnight. Would you want any of these overnight publishers working on your annual report?

As in any form of publishing, one can't properly design a Web site with mediocre tools and minimal know-how. Any 12-year-old can design a PTA newsletter on his or her home PC, and there are probably several 12-year-olds who can create Web documents. But unless the child is a genius, neither the newsletter nor the Web document will have the look and feel of a professional publication.

Proper Web design requires the same high levels of talent, experience, and technology required by the rest of the publishing world. In many ways, Web design follows the same design principles used for decades by traditional, offline designers. In other ways, however, the process of designing a Web site is unlike anything that's gone before.

It's beyond the scope of this book to teach you how to design a Web site, but we strongly believe that anyone joining the Web community should have a least a passing understanding of Web design. Even though you'll probably hire someone to design your site (and maybe especially because you will), you should familiarize yourself with the following design considerations:

- Positive vs. negative space
- Complementing colors
- Type manipulation

- Textures
- Eye movement
- Element unity
- Aesthetics

Each of these elements must be considered in the design of a successful Web site.

POSITIVE AND NEGATIVE SPACE

Simply defined, positive space is the area on a painting, document, product package, or any visual display, that contains text, images, or some other design element. Negative space is simply the area around these elements, the region of a design perceived as "empty."

The proper balance of positive and negative space is crucial to design success, but Web designers often ignored it. Without such a balance, the eye becomes confused; there's no visual progression to follow, and the viewer loses interest.

On the Web, early design strategies focused almost exclusively on cramming as much information onto a page as possible. This approach contradicts conventional design wisdom.

COMPLEMENTING COLORS

When marketing through conventional media, designers have always focused on the careful selection of color combinations. Each color must not only "match" the others, but the colors must combine for mood or effect, as well. The right colors can make certain objects stand out, and others go nearly unnoticed. They can convey a feeling of excitement, urgency, warmth, or contentment. When the colors are chosen so they complement each other, they enhance every other design element. Conventional designers may spend hours choosing the appropriate green from a book containing thousands of shades and hues of green.

In the offline world, designers are free to choose from a nearly unlimited rainbow of very specific colors. But in Web design, color choice is a little more complicated. It's impossible to guarantee that a color you choose will be the color that appears on the user's display. In fact, the color the user sees may be very different from your intended color. If you've ever shopped for a TV set, you've probably noticed how color tones vary slightly from screen to screen. Internal differences among TV sets make it impossible for a broadcaster to display the identical color on every TV. The fact that all sets also allow you to adjust picture elements, like brightness, hue, and saturation, only makes displays more varied.

Computer monitors vary similarly. Some have more red, some are brighter, and some have a low level of contrast. There's just no way to be sure how your documents will look on every computer. You must also consider the graphics capabilities of individual netizens. A series of color gradients in a sunset may show up as a single color, or worse, as a blotchy, striped mess.

TYPE MANIPULATION

The concept of type manipulation is just beginning to take hold on the Web. Type manipulation involves using different fonts, text sizes, text colors, and text positioning to create an effect. Type always has been an important conventional design consideration, but many Web designers continue to overlooked it.

Until recent improvements in Web browsers (specifically *Netscape*), it was difficult to control text size, color, and positioning in a Web document. Online text historically has been set flush left or centered. Previously, designers could choose from only six font sizes, and couldn't even know for sure what those sizes were (see Tech Note). New browsers make text position, color, and size much more flexible.

Unfortunately, documents designed to have interesting layouts on these improved browsers will look completely different on other browsers. And there's still no way to change the basic display font. For these reasons, many designers replace normal text with images that contain text. In other words, they "take a picture" of the text set in the typeface they want to use, and then paste that picture into the Web document. That way, everyone who looks at it sees the same thing no matter what their base font.

In the original HTML standard, designers indicated text size primarily with heading tags. These tags looked something like this:

```
<H1>This is the largest text available.</H1>

<H2>This text is almost as large.</H2>

<H3>This text is not so large.</H3>
```

```
<H4>This text is medium.</H4>

<H5>This text is small.</H5>

<H6>This text is tiny.</H6>
```

The standard also provides tags for bold and italics (<B> and <I> respectively), but they're rarely used. The actual appearance of headings, bold, and italics depends on the browser and the way it's configured. Figure 7-3 shows the Web page produced by the six headers above.

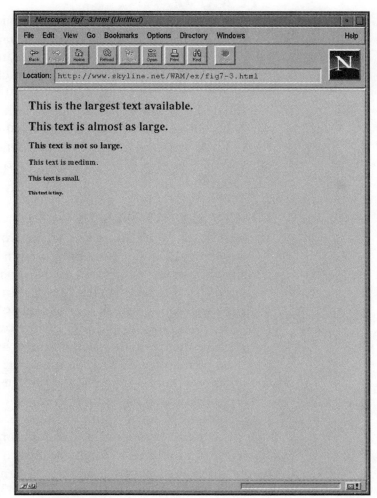

FIGURE 7-3

This example of HTML headings shows the limited capabilities of text manipulation on the Web.

TEXTURES

Along with solid colors, designers can incorporate a variety of simulated textures into their designs. Textures may be part of the background, or used in a foreground element. On the Web, textures can be difficult to use because of the limitations and inconsistencies of computer displays. The subtle variations of a marble or stone texture, for example, won't be recognizable on many displays.

Difficulties aside, Web designers should try to use (carefully chosen) textures where appropriate. These textures can significantly enhance the appearance of a Web site.

EYE MOVEMENT

Conventional offline designers pay special attention to the placement of text and images, arranging them in a way that encourages the eye to take in everything the viewer should see, in the order that best serves the design. Like the frames of a movie, each element contributes to an impression, a feeling, or an idea.

Web designers have virtually ignored the concept of eye movement, partly because of the layout limitations of early Web browsers. But as the HTML standard improves and expands—as more and more layout tools become available—there ceases to be any excuse for neglecting such an important aspect of graphic design.

UNITY OF ELEMENTS

With the birth of the Web came a rebirth of clip art. Never before have so many prepackaged images been used in corporate publications—or perhaps they've just never been used so poorly. The ease of use and low cost of Web publishing can lead designers to believe the design process itself is easier and cheaper. Consequently, they often take any image that suits their purpose and toss it onto the Web page. Too often, designers take little care to ensure that the image on the left side of the page complements the image on the right. Designers haphazardly mix stick figures with photographs, and sketches with detailed illustrations.

Designers should undertake Web-page layout with care and purpose, and an eye toward unity of design. Each element on the page should be there for a reason, and should combine seamlessly with other elements to produce the intended effect. Without unity, design elements fail to work together and the design fails to do its job.

AESTHETICS

Naturally, all Web design should be aesthetically pleasing. But take care—this aspect of Web-page design isn't simply a matter of personal taste. The "I know what I like" attitude will get you nowhere. And you can't simply ask your co-workers what they think of your Web page. It takes a lot of research and experience to learn what visual elements appeal most to which audience.

Unfortunately, an in-depth examination of online aesthetics is beyond the scope of this book. We only ask that you think hard about your audience. Find out what appeals to them, and ignore your personal taste. If your audience has any cultural, racial, or educational similarities, use them to choose designs with the most potential appeal. Concentrate on audience age, gender, interests, and marital status to develop appealing design strategies.

THE DESIGN PROCESS

Many of the less design-oriented Web designers consider the creation of Web documents to be a simple matter. These designers will never create truly effective Web pages. Proper Web design, like conventional offline design, is a complex process.

It begins with the development of an overall site concept, considering the purpose of each individual page. Then the designer carefully chooses elements that support that concept. When choosing these elements, the designer must consider each of the foregoing principles.

DO-IT-YOURSELF VS. OUTSOURCING

The single most important decision you'll make about marketing your company on the Web is how much of the work to do yourself. A wide variety of services exist to assist companies in creating and maintaining a Web site, from full-service "turnkey" contractors to Web design consultants who can help at any point along the way.

First, let's consider what's involved in building a site yourself.

DO IT YOURSELF

Are you sitting down? We're about to tell you something that may upset those of you who already have spent a large amount of money on outsourced Web development. We'll probably upset a few professional Web designers, as well. Ready? Okay, here goes:

It's easy to create a Web page.

The HTML standard was designed to be easy to learn. The developers of HTML knew that unless the average person could learn HTML quickly and effortlessly, the standard wouldn't catch on. Remember, the task force that developed the standard wasn't trying to make anybody rich. It wasn't out to develop tools only companies with large amounts of time and money to invest could use. In fact, the task force wasn't thinking about companies at all. The HTML standard was created to be used by scientists, students, and government agencies to promote the free exchange of information.

Web pages are so easy to create, many companies opt to build their own Web sites. After all, if 16-year-olds are creating their own pages on the Web, why shouldn't you? To build a basic Web site, you need only four things:

- A Web server (hardware)

- Web server software

- A high-speed, full-time Internet connection (not just a modem)

- One computer expert (preferably a UNIX systems administrator)

If your company already has an Internet connection, you may already have a machine that can be used as the server hardware. You can obtain an acceptable version of the Web server software on the Internet for free. All you really need is someone capable of setting it all up.

If your company doesn't already have a full-time, high-speed Internet connection, get one, along with the server hardware and probably a "router" (a machine that controls your Internet connection). These will cost several thousand dollars (see Chapter 12 for detailed cost estimations).

Once you have everything, you can begin building your site immediately. Most companies can rely on their marketing departments to provide the content and the information services department to set up the Web server and put the content in HTML format.

OUTSOURCING

For those businesses that don't want to devote their own resources to building their sites, hundreds of companies exist to help. These offer a wide variety of services, from simple training in HTML design to complete Web packages customized for your company. By hiring a professional Web designer, you eliminate many of the headaches associated with Web design. You may also save a lot of time and money, and end up with a more effective site.

The following sections describe the steps involved in setting up a Web site. They also describe how—and when—a consultant should be brought into the process.

DECIDING WHAT TO OUTSOURCE

As we said, you'll find a variety of services and products to help you establish a presence on the World Wide Web. To help you decide when and whether to hire one of these companies, we've divided the site-building process into eight steps.

Note to Small Businesses
The potential cost of these steps may frighten many small businesses. If you feel you can't afford such things as your own Internet connection or a high-speed workstation, consider the "no-hands" method of getting online, discussed later in this chapter.

1. Acquiring an Internet connection and domain name

2. Purchasing and installing server hardware

3. Purchasing, installing, and configuring server software

4. Developing basic Web strategy and structure

5. Designing Web pages

6. Designing interactive Web applications

7. Marketing your site

8. Monitoring, maintaining, and improving your site

1. ACQUIRING AN INTERNET CONNECTION AND DOMAIN NAME

This step puts your company online. It generally involves three more steps:

- 🌐 Purchasing Internet service from an Internet access provider (sometimes called Internet service provider, or ISP)

- 🌐 Purchasing a data circuit from a local telephone company (telco)

- 🌐 Contacting the Internic and requesting a domain name (see Tech Note)

Companies unfamiliar with the Internet often hire a consultant for this first step. An Internet consultant can help you decide what type of Internet connection is right for you, and he or she will have the necessary experience to effectively deal with the ISP, the local telephone company, and the Internic (all of which can be a headache).

Additionally, a consultant can save you a lot of money by steering you away from unnecessary services and equipment the ISP and telco often try to sell.

Consider a number of factors before choosing your Internet connection, including how much initial Web traffic you expect; how much you expect your site to grow; your budget constraints; current ISP and telco pricing schemes (they constantly change), and your geographic location.

Companies on limited budgets often elect not to acquire an Internet connection. Instead they hire a Web-presence provider to host the Web site. Web-presence providers maintain a single Internet connection, and use it to provide Web service to several companies. This lowers the cost of operating a Web site.

Companies that hire a Web-presence provider usually won't need to purchase server hardware or software (steps two and three), making for an even less expensive Web site.

TABLE 7-2 INTERNET ZONE NAMES AND WHAT THEY MEAN

Zone	Used for
com	Commercial organizations
edu	Educational institutions
gov	Government agencies
int	International organizations
mil	Military agencies
net	Networking organizations or companies
org	Clubs, consortiums, and professional societies

This step is usually no problem for companies already on the Net, or firms whose employees have some Internet expertise. If you're willing to deal with the ISP and the telco yourself, and you're confident you can communicate your needs to them and resist investing in unnecessary products and services, you can save a little money by going at it alone.

The Internic and Domain Names
The Internic is the authority that assigns domain names to companies and organizations. A "domain name" is the name used to locate your company online. It may or may not be the same as your trade name. For example, Skyline Network Technologies' domain name is "skyline.net," so our Web site URL is "http://www.skyline.net" and our e-mail address is "webmaster @skyline.net". Your domain name will be used every time a user tries to contact you.

Domain names make more sense read from right to left. The right-hand portion of the name ("net" in "skyline.net") is the "zone name." In the United States, most domain names fall into one of the three-letter zones (see Table 7-2). Most company domain names fall into the "com" zone. The next piece of the domain name ("skyline" in "skyline.net") is chosen by the company or organization.

When addressing a specific machine in a domain, add the name (or nickname) of that machine to the left of the domain name. For example, we nicknamed Skyline's Web server "www", a common practice on Web servers. That is why our URL is "http://www.skyline.net". When you type this into a Web browser, you're saying you want to use the hypertext transfer protocol (the Web protocol) to connect to the machine named "www" at the site that chose "skyline" for its name. You're also saying that the site is part of a networking organization.

2. PURCHASING AND INSTALLING SERVER HARDWARE

You can run a Web server on just about any computer. There are servers for Windows PCs and Macintoshes, as well as for high-powered workstations and mainframes. But most busy servers are run on high-powered workstations from Sun Microsystems or Silicon Graphics (SGI), or on top-of-the-line Pentium PCs. In each case, the systems usually run some version of a UNIX operating system (see following Technical Note).

What is UNIX?

AT&T developed the UNIX operating system in the early 1970s as a multi-user system that would run on various hardware platforms. Most high-performance, multi-user computer systems now use UNIX in some form. Both Sun and SGI have developed their own version of UNIX for use on their computers. PCs often use "Linux," a cost-free version of UNIX that was designed through the contributions of thousands of people throughout the Internet community.

Many large companies already own several UNIX workstations or other computers capable of supporting a Web site. These companies should make certain someone in the company can install and manage such a workstation.

Companies that don't use UNIX workstations may have no idea what type of hardware to purchase, much less how to install and manage it. Companies that do have UNIX machines may have no one on staff who knows how best to configure the system to run a busy Web site.

A Web consultant can help you choose the best hardware for your needs and budget. He or she can work alone or train your staff in the skills needed to maintain the server. Ask yourself if your staff has the experience necessary to choose, install, and manage what may become the most important computer in your organization.

3. PURCHASING, INSTALLING, AND CONFIGURING SERVER SOFTWARE

If you hired a consultant to help with the Step 2, the same consultant can probably install your server software. Server software is a program that runs continuously on your server hardware. The program waits for a user to request a Web document, then sends the document and waits for another request.

If you installed your server hardware yourself, you'll have to decide whether to hire a consultant to install the server software. To be honest, if your staff is capable of installing the hardware and setting up a UNIX-style operating system, they should be able to install the Web server software. In other words, you'll probably only hire a consultant to install your software if you hired one to install your hardware.

Regardless of who installs the server software, you may still seek the advice of a consultant when choosing which software to use. There are dozens of available software packages, and more pop up every month.

Each package has its pros and cons. A consultant can explain all the features and help you choose which package is best for you. If you're lucky, he or she may find that you don't need to purchase the software. Your company may only need one of the free Web server packages available on the Net.

4. DEVELOPING A BASIC WEB STRATEGY AND STRUCTURE

Easily the most complicated and crucial step in the process, this is where you sketch out a plan for the development of your Web site. As we've said before, your online strategy should complement your overall marketing plan.

This is also the point in the process when most companies are better off hiring a consultant. Unless members of your staff possess abundant experience using the Web and designing Web pages, you should seek the advice of a professional.

A professional Web consultant can take your ideas and mold them to fit the limitations of the World Wide Web. Without this expertise, you may find yourself planning an impossible site. You may also find yourself wasting a lot of time and money re-inventing the wheel. An experienced consultant has probably worked with clients whose goals are similar to yours, and will know how best to achieve them.

5. DESIGNING WEB PAGES

Finally, the step you've all been waiting for—designing your Web pages. This is where you get to create, and draw on the vast pools of artistic talent within your organization. You say there is no artistic talent in your organization? Well, you're not alone. We've seen plenty of Web sites that looked like the accountants designed them.

There are actually three phases to the design of a Web page:

- Artistic design
- Marketing design
- Technical design

During the artistic design phase, you decide which images to use on your Web pages, how to lay them out most effectively, and what colors to include. Marketing design incorporates traditional marketing strategies into your Web pages. During this phase, you write product descriptions and select which products to market most aggressively. During the technical design phase you write the HTML code that makes the design work online.

Often, Web advertisers contribute to the artistic and marketing design processes by providing the Web consultant with pre-existing brochures, logos, and other materials the designer can adapt to the Web in the technical design process.

While these are three distinct phases of Web design, you must consider them together. The folks in the art department, for example, must design the images to fit the needs of the marketing department, and they can't plan a page layout that's technically impossible. This is where a skilled Web consultant can be of great help. He or she can coordinate your artistic ideas with your marketing ideas and ensure they're all technically feasible.

Most Web consultants are only skilled in the technical design of Web pages. Don't expect a simple Web-presence provider to contribute to the artistic design or the marketing value of your site. For these steps, you'll need an advertising firm or a full-service Web firm, providing publishing, marketing, and consulting services.

6. DESIGNING INTERACTIVE WEB APPLICATIONS

If Web pages are the meat and potatoes of your site, interactive applications must be the gravy. Interactive Web applications add flavor and character to your site that you could never achieve with a typical static Web page. The proper design of interactive applications requires all of the skills of a seasoned Web site designer, plus the following:

- Programming skills (usually in C++ or Perl)

- A thorough understanding of the Hypertext Transfer Protocol (HTTP)

- Kknowledge of the Common Gateway Interface (CGI)

- A thorough comprehension of Web-browser variations

- An understanding of security principles, specifically UNIX, CGI, and Internet security

- Creativity and patience

Needless to say, designing an interactive application isn't a simple task. It's the part of the process that's really best left to professional programmers. If you have programmers in your company who can design Web applications, then you're fortunate; hiring a professional to design interactive Web applications can quickly become your largest Web-related expense. If you don't have your own programmers, we suggest talking to a professional Web designer about adding some level of interactivity to your site. You can add as much or as little interactivity as your budget allows.

As we said before, many Web designers are only skilled at designing simple, static Web pages. There's a big difference between designing a static Web page and planning and programming interactive applications. Before you hire a Web designer to create an interactive application, ask to see previous work. It's the only way you'll know whether he or she has the skills and experience to create the application you need.

7.   MARKETING YOUR SITE

When you build a Web site, you construct an island. Forget the "Information Superhighway" analogy. The Web isn't a stretch of road lined with sites everyone sees as they drive by. The Web is much more like a vast ocean of information—an ocean with very few navigational tools. The success of your site depends on your ability to make enough waves to attract the surfers.

In Chapter 9, we discuss in greater detail the strategies and tools you need to market your Web site effectively. The chapter covers simple and complex techniques to attract attention to your site. Anyone, even the smallest company, can apply most of these techniques. But a professional Web marketing firm can usually apply them more efficiently and effectively. These firms devote a lot of time and effort to keeping up with the various site marketing services, and can make these services work well for you.

8.   MONITORING, MAINTAINING, AND IMPROVING YOUR SITE

The final step in this process is really a continuing effort to ensure the success of your Web site. These ongoing efforts include:

   Operating the server and the Internet connection

- Counting "hits"
- Counting interested "hits"
- Counting visitors
- Registering users
- Conducting market research
- Making improvements
- Training your staff
- Restructuring your site
- Contacting your visitors
- And much more....

We discuss this list in greater detail in Chapter 11. For now, we just want to make the point that most of these tasks can be farmed out to marketing firms or advertising agencies.

LOOK MA, NO HANDS!

Of course, you can always just forget all this stuff and hire somebody to do *everything*. You can contact a Web-presence provider by telephone and be online in two days. We call this technique the "no hands" approach to Web marketing. (Well, you might need one hand to dial the phone.)

There's nothing wrong with the no-hands approach. Even Skyline offers a full line of turnkey systems. But businesses that choose this route should understand that there's very little marketing expertise involved in designing most basic turnkey sites. You can't expect someone who barely knows you to design a Web site that reflects your company's character and enhances your current marketing strategies. A very few companies do provide turnkey systems that incorporate your current marketing strategies, but these companies are exceptions. They're more expensive and require more cooperation, which makes hiring them a little less "no hands."

The vast majority of Internet-presence providers (at least 95 percent) create simple Web pages that incorporate very little marketing value. This is the most common and least expensive form of no-hands Web advertising.

For small businesses, the low cost and minimal hassles of no-hands Web sites makes them the perfect vehicles for developing an online presence. With this approach, you don't need an Internet connection, an e-mail address, a domain name (although it's optional), or any Web expertise. The Web-presence provider creates your Web pages and maintains them on its own server. The presence provider can even issue reports showing how much traffic your site receives. It's really very painless.

Companies opting for the no-hands approach should understand that not all Web-presence providers are created equal. Some won't provide quality pages. Others won't complete their work in a timely manner. Some have Web servers that are so prone to crashes and network problems that your site may be down more than it's up.

When you look for a turnkey Web-presence provider, look for more than a low price. Find a couple of companies in your price range, and choose the one that seems the most professional. Don't discount a company just because it's small and young, but make sure the company has the talent and desire to grow along with your needs. If you choose a company that provides only the services you're looking for now, they won't be of much use to you when you're ready to expand your site and include advanced features.

WebTech Goes Bankrupt

In August of 1995, WebTech, a 1-year-old, Florida-based Web-presence provider, filed for bankruptcy, stranding nearly a hundred advertisers. This company's failure has prompted concerns among Web advertisers and other Web firms.

WebTech had promoted its services throughout the Tampa–St. Petersburg area using seminars and radio advertisements. The company had provided several cost-free, no-hands Web sites to a variety of area businesses in an attempt to heighten interest and establish a client base. When the company filed for bankruptcy, it stranded both paying and non-paying customers by turning off its Web server and disconnecting the phone.

WebTech's failure and similar incidents may presage an inevitable shakeout among Web-presence providers. During 1994 and '95, at least 900 new Web design firms opened their doors. Only a small fraction of those firms have the capital to sustain the cost of providing Web services for any length of time. The rest are gambling on instant success just to meet expenses.

What does all this say to potential Web advertisers? Beware of "freebies," and watch out for the price-cutters.

WHAT'S IN A NAME

Companies that pay Web-presence providers to host their Web sites (either as a separate service or part of a no-hands package) need not maintain their own Internet connections or domain names. This can translate into significant savings for many companies. Most businesses will still benefit from establishing their own domain names, however, as the following parable illustrates:

> *The Widget Mart has just asked Skyline Network Technologies to provide a turnkey Web site. The company doesn't want to worry about maintaining the server or even having an Internet connection. Skyline agrees to host the company's site on the Skyline Web server, and establishes a directory on the server that contains The Widget Mart's Web site, (http://www.skyline.net/wmart).*
>
> *Meanwhile, Tom Jones wants to purchase some widgets, and he's heard that The Widget Mart now has a Web site. But he can't remember the URL. Tom is an experienced Web surfer, so he tries http://www.widgetmart.com and http://www.widget-mart.com, with no luck. Eventually he decides to use a Web directory service. He goes to Skyline's Resource EXchange (REX) and looks up "widget." He finds four widget stores and visits the first—not The Widget Mart—and finds exactly what he wants. In the end, he purchases his widget online from the first store without ever visiting The Widget Mart's Web site.*

If Widget Mart had acquired its own domain name, it could still let Skyline maintain its site on the Skyline server. But that server could be set up to answer to the Widget Mart domain. In that case, our parable would have gone more like this:

> *Tom Jones wants to buy some widgets, and he's heard that The Widget Mart now has a Web site. He can't remember the URL. Tom is an experienced Web user, so he tries http://www.widgetmart.com and is instantly rewarded with The Widget Mart homepage. Tom finds exactly what he's looking for at an excellent price so he makes his online purchase.*

It may cost a little bit extra (very little), but most companies find that it's worth it to have their own domain names. It makes their URLs shorter and easier to remember, and it allows them to change

Web-presence providers (or even move their Web sites to corporate headquarters) without changing URLs; the new site can be configured to answer to the original URL.

Plus, when a company obtains its own domain name, it can be sure another company won't come along and use that name. Domain names are dispensed on a first-come, first-served basis.

PROS AND CONS

We've discussed some of the reasons you might want to hire a Web consultant to complete any or all of the eight Web-site-building steps. Now let's look at the overall pros and cons of doing it yourself vs. outsourcing.

The biggest advantage of doing it yourself is the fact that you maintain total control of the site. The biggest disadvantage is also that you maintain total control of the site. Companies that develop and maintain their own Web sites can quickly (and maybe cheaply) change direction, add documents, and develop new interactive features. But they're also stuck dealing with all of the headaches of Web publishing, including maintaining (and paying for) the Internet connection; providing security; making transactions, and keeping up with the newest Web browsers and development layout tools.

Advantages to no-hands Web development include low cost, short setup time (no time spent training staff), and no additional personnel or training.

Disadvantages to no-hands development include the risk of poor quality, the lack of control, and the possibility that the site may not complement current marketing strategies. In almost every case, the best choice lies somewhere between the self-sufficient approach and the no-hands approach. Each company should start by considering the most appropriate extreme, then look through the eight steps of building a Web site and decide which steps warrant deviating from the extreme. Consider the following example:

> *The Widget Mart started by considering the no-hands extreme. The company knew it didn't want to manage the Web site, and therefore had no need for an Internet connection. This meant they had no need to purchase server hardware or software (steps two and three). But the company did want to establish a domain name. It decided to let the Web consultants handle everything, but found that they could*

save money and time on step five (designing Web pages) by provid-
ing brochures and a copy of the logo (on floppy disk).

Another company might start with the self-sufficient approach and look for steps for which their staff has neither the time nor the skill. For example:

The Fictitious Broadcasting Company (FBC) began with the self-
sufficient approach to building a Web site. FBC already had a
high-speed Internet connection and a computer that could be used
as a Web server. What the company didn't have was someone who
knew how to create Web pages or write interactive applications.
So FBC hired a consultant to teach Web-page design to four mem-
bers of its staff. They contracted the same consultant to write two
interactive games based on two of FBC's television shows.

OUR ADVICE

You'll find a wide variety of products and services to assist you in set-ting up a quality Web site. If you can afford them, use them—especially as an alternative to hiring or training personnel. But don't think that hiring a consultant frees you of all responsibility. If you want an effec-tive site, you must work closely with any consultants you hire. If your consultant doesn't encourage, or at least welcome, your participation, you've probably chosen the wrong consultant.

If you can't afford expensive Web products and services, don't worry. Create a Web site that's within your budget and hope that it pays for itself quickly. When choosing consultants on a budget, don't completely sacrifice quality and professionalism for price. And look for hidden costs—not all consultants are as inexpensive as they seem.

As we said before, 16-year-olds can create Web pages. The problem is, the pages they create look like they were created by 16-year-olds. Don't equate *creating* pages with *designing* pages. Designing requires careful planning and appropriate skills. Don't overestimate the design abilities of your employees (or some Web designers, for that matter).

Finally, remember that no job is so large or so small that you can't find a consultant to handle it. You can hire a consultant to design a single page or to fly out to your Tokyo branch and spend six months building a fantastic site. At the same time, however, not every consultant can handle every job. Don't expect the small-time Web-presence provider to supply any marketing or artistic value to your Web site. You must provide that value yourself, or find a firm that specializes in the marketing side of Web design.

Remember...

- Web advertisers can choose from several design styles. The most popular and least expensive style is the online brochure. Online catalogues, while more expensive, are becoming popular. Virtual vendors are the wave of the future.

- Build a consistent site to enhance your coherence factor. Consistency encourages the exploration of your Web site; increases name, logo, and hallmark recognition, and leads to more return visits.

- To get the most out of going online, companies should prepare for changes the Internet will bring to the way they do business. Don't rely on an untrained Webmaster or your Web-presence provider to respond to the feedback your site will generate.

- If you expect your employees to use the Net to benefit the company, you must train them to use the Net effectively.

- Conventional design principles are just as important on the Web as they are in conventional media.

- When building your site, there's no step so large or so small that you can't outsource it to a quality Web-marketing and -publishing firm.

- Not all Web consultants are created equal. If you want basic Web design, hire an ordinary Web designer. If you want marketing expertise, hire a Web-marketing firm. Few companies can provide the gamut of marketing, publishing, and consulting expertise required to build a successful site.

- The no-hands method of establishing a Web presence can be a cost-effective way for small companies to test the online waters.

- Don't look for the lowest price, unless you have to. You usually get what you pay for.

8

MIGRATING TO ELECTRONIC PUBLISHING

So you're taking the plunge and expanding your operations to include the World Wide Web. Having made it this far through the book, you should understand what makes a successful Web marketing strategy. After all, you now know how to attract surfers to your site and where to get help if you need it. What may not be clear to you, however, is how you can adapt your existing marketing plan to the Web.

The first question to ask yourself is rather straightforward: Does your current marketing plan work? That is, does it tell your customers what you want them to know about your company? Be completely honest. If you find it difficult to judge your marketing efforts objectively, solicit opinions from your friends and colleagues. Such simple research is cheap, easy, and effective. For example, if you use television or radio marketing, record your spots, give them to your friends, and have them review them at their convenience. Sending out direct mail pieces to selected friends and family can also prove revealing—especially when those who throw away their junk mail as soon as they get it fail to respond to your inquiries.

To make the most of this informal critique process, ask your participants the following:

- 🌐 *Does your marketing piece—print ad, radio spot, direct mail, etc.—deliver a clear and precise message?*

- 🌐 *Does it portray the correct image of your company?*

- 🌐 *Is it memorable?*

- 🌐 *If you could change one thing about it, what would that be?*

- 🌐 *Does it provide enough incentive to entice customers to respond?*

This review strategy may sound like a simple and even obvious one—one you have practiced many times before. If so, congratulate yourself. You would be surprised at the number of business people who don't take the time to find out if their marketing efforts actually work.

The response you receive from this "market research" will offer you valuable insights. Depending on the verdict you receive from reviewers, you may choose to refine your current marketing plan—or completely rehaul it. Either way, making the necessary changes will not only improve your conventional marketing vehicles, it will also set the stage for effective marketing on the Web.

If the response is largely favorable, fine. If not, you must address some crucial issues before you can proceed. Are you running your television or radio spots on the right channel or station and in the right time slot? Are you running your print ad in the right publications as frequently as needed? And are you sending enough direct mail pieces to the right people?

If budget constraints necessarily limit your marketing opportunities, make sure that the those you can afford are the best that you can do. For example, it's better to run fewer print ads of better quality than to run many poorly conceived and poorly designed ads. (Remember, it's important that your current marketing program is in tip-top shape before you venture into the new domain of Web marketing.)

So far we've talked only about such marketing efforts as print ads, TV and radio spots, and direct mail. Now let's examine the nuts and bolts of your marketing plan: the promotions, specials, and enticements you use to draw your customers to your business. Are you offering enough to bring in the customers you need? Promotions are the key to your whole marketing plan and as such, they require your utmost attention. To determine the effectiveness of your current promotions, survey your new customers. Find out why they initially came to your business. If specific advertised promotions drew them in, then your promotions have been effective. But if you hear a variety of responses, then your promotions probably are not working as well as they should. Try some alternatives. Remember, for promotions to work they must only provide perceived value to the customer; they don't have to cost an arm and a leg. In other words, if your customers believe they're getting a deal, then your promotion is a success. Most great promotions only have to be creative to be effective.

If you find that your potential customers are reluctant to spend their hard-earned money on your products or services, try offering samples. Samples are great enticements, because quality products and services typically sell themselves to potential customers.

Some products or services, usually large-ticket items such as cars or houses, are impossible to offer as samples. Consider offering a no-risk guarantee, allowing customers to try out your products or services for a designated short length of time. If after this time they are unsatisfied, then customers can return the products or services, no questions asked. This may sound risky to those without confidence in their businesses. But if you are confident of the quality of your products or services, then you should have little to worry about. You will satisfy the great majority of your customers—and you will lose nothing. Keep in mind that customers often experience difficulty making buying decisions, especially for large-ticket items. So give them the peace of mind they need by promising them a refund should any unforeseen circumstance arise.

REDESIGN EXISTING MARKETING STRATEGIES FOR THE WEB

To determine if your current plan will work on the Web, we offer you another little self-examination. This one consists of just two questions:

1. Can your current marketing plan accommodate instant customer interaction?

2. Does your current advertising effectively incorporate graphics and other attention-grabbing features?

The first question asks whether or not your current plan will allow you to use multimedia effectively. The word "multimedia" refers to the combining of multiple types of media to create one new media venue. The Web is a multimedia venue because it combines the action of television with the information of print media, offering the exceptional feature of instant interaction.

Does your current marketing plan enable you to incorporate this instant interaction with customers? For example, can you offer your products or services as samples that Web customers can avail themselves of instantly? Or can you use an interesting subject related to your business to establish a message board, chat room, or MUSE? Even a survey related to your company, or industry as a whole, can capitalize on this interaction process. Is there any way you can make surfers feel like they are interacting with you, your staff, and/or your company?

The best Web marketing challenges and engages surfers. This means using colorful, cutting-edge graphics, audio clips, even full-motion video. Does your marketing plan offer any of these elements already?

DINOSAURS ON THE WEB

Having reviewed your current marketing efforts in light of the Web's unique opportunities, you've come to one of two conclusions—he first, that your current plan is well suited for the Web, and only requires technical transfiguration and slight adaptation to make the jump; the alternative, that you must develop a completely new marketing plan for the Web. In either case, your first impulse may be to send your current plan back to your marketing department or outside advertising agency for revision. How sound this decision may be depends upon the capabilities of those resources.

Just because you have an in-house advertising or marketing department doesn't mean you have the in-house expertise needed to develop a working Web strategy. You could try to educate your staff: buy them this book and have them spend some time exploring the Web themselves. This way they'll better understand what strategies succeed on the Web. Another option: have the marketing department work hand-in-hand with the computer or technical department of your company. This may be of some help; still, there's no guarantee that the technical department has the expertise needed to make this transition to the Web either. The Internet is a specialized portion of the computer world; the people who run corporate computer systems are not always well-versed in the World Wide Web.

A final alternative: hiring outside consultants who will work on ad-hoc development of Web pages or help coordinate the evolution of a Web-friendly marketing plan.

Skyline Develops Partnerships with Advertising Agencies

Early in our company's development we saw the opportunity to help the advertising community reach into the World Wide Web. We worked to develop partnerships with advertising agencies and firms so that we could assist them developing effective marketing plans for the Web. By doing this, we enabled the advertising agencies to continue doing what they do best—and it allowed us to do what we are most suited to doing. At Skyline, we continue to develop partnerships with outside advertising firms.

All of these solutions will enable your marketing department to concentrate on what it does best—developing creative and inventive ideas to help your company sell more products or services.

Say you use an outside firm to do all of your current marketing work. Here again, there is no guarantee that they are up to speed on the Web, either. Many advertising firms have just begun to recognize the power of the Web and are only now establishing multimedia departments. You should ask your advertising firm what Web experience they have; have them spell out their plans for taking your company into this new arena. If their answers do not jive with what you've learned in this book, consider yourself warned.

Many advertising agencies are developing partnerships with Web providers to gain the instant expertise this field requires. A 1995 survey conducted by Forrester Research revealed that full-service advertising agencies built only 26 percent of the sites on the Web. Another 23 percent partially developed Web sites. In fact, more than half (51 percent) of all sites were built without any assistance from full-service ad-agencies.

Will inside advertising and marketing departments as well as outside agencies go the way of the dinosaurs on the Web? The answer is probably, "It depends." The Web demands expertise often lacking among current marketing circles. Those marketing people who can adapt will more than likely find a home on the Web. Those that do not prepare themselves for this transition will find no place for themselves or their customers on the Web.

WHO HAS MADE THE TRANSITION?

They say history is the best teacher. You can analyze the successes and failures of those who have gone before you, learn from their mistakes, and save yourself the time and trouble it took them to figure out the right way to do it. Let's examine a few of these pioneering companies and what they did to make it all work.

MAGAZINES AND OTHER PUBLICATIONS COME TO THE WEB

With their slick graphic appeal, tight demographics-based targeting, and reader-friendly presentation of information, magazines are a natural for the Web. Not surprisingly, many periodicals have made the transition the Web successfully. In this section, we will examine two of the larger magazines, *Time* and *U.S. News and World Report*, that have done just that.

Time magazine is a periodical with world-wide exposure and coverage. Because of this, its advertisers are willing to spend large sums of money to buy its advertising pages. Hoping to capitalize on its print success, *Time* operates a Web site (http://www.timeinc.com/time/magazine/magazine.html). *Time* offers its advertisers another option of where they can spend their advertising dollars. Useful and well planned, the site offers the articles and pictures from both the U.S. and International versions of its current issue. A unique feature allows surfers to search by key word through past issues of the magazine. This feature alone makes the *Time* site a true Web resource.

A smart move on *Time*'s part: surfers can view the site in a text-only format. This opens the *Time* site up to the entire Internet community—including all those with slightly slower connections or incompatible browsers.

The only true interaction the site offers is the ability to write a letter to the editor online. This enables surfers to voice their concerns and opinions quickly and easily while viewing the site.

Another news magazine that's made the plunge to the Web is *U.S. News and World Report* (http://www.USNews.com/). This well-conceived Web site offers the same type of information *Time* does, but the *U.S. News and World Report* site is much more clearly organized. Its homepage is visually more stimulating and interesting; the *Time* homepage is little more than a picture of the cover of the latest magazine, while *U.S. News and World Report* offers a periodical-style layout with columns and accompanying visuals. (As we have said before, the homepage is the most important part of a site; as the first thing surfers see on your site, the homepage often determines whether they stay or surf on.)

Apart from this homepage difference, these sites are quite similar in content and approach. They both offer their advertisers a venue to reach a different audience—a way for the two magazines to increase their advertising revenue and their marketability.

Both the *Time* and *U.S. News & World Report* sites could offer some greater forms of interaction, such as chat rooms on current events or message boards on domestic political affairs. This way they might be viewed as something more than an information resource by the Web community.

THE WEB IS A NEW BATTLEFIELD FOR SOFT DRINK WARS

For the last twenty years, television, radio, and print media have served as a battleground for one of the fiercest battles ever fought on this planet—the control of the world's soft drink market. There have been many combatants in this arena, but the main two have been Coca Cola and Pepsi. These two giants have spent billions of dollars to convince the world they offer the most satisfying beverages on the planet, developing memorable slogans and tactics that have become a part of the pop culture. These two colossal companies are now taking their marketing battle into cyberspace—and specifically the Web.

Both soft drink giants have transformed their marketing juggernauts into working Web battle plans. Coca Cola has pulled out all the stops for its online presence, making its transition to the Web an effective one. The Coca Cola Web site (http://www.cocacola.com) offers every key feature you need to succeed on the Web. Coca Cola has designed a site with memorable images which do not burden the slower surfers. The site provides unique, fun information about Coca Cola, its history, its current status, and its future plans. For the shareholder, the site offers financial information as well as projections. One unique aspect of the Coca Cola site: a mystery section where a surfer, say, clicks on an icon to find out about an interesting feature or image, such as a trip to the Grand Canyon. Besides offering this type of free information, Coke also offers downloadable images for surfers to download for their own use (see Figure 8-1). Representations of past Coca Cola advertising, these downloadable images are electronic postcards that you can send as attachments to your e-mail.

In addition to providing these great attractions, Coca Cola provides tie-ins to many of its conventional ad campaigns on its Web site. For example, the site serves up discussions about the Olympic Games, of which Coca Cola is a major sponsor. As this book goes to print, Coca Cola plans to offer some type of tie-in advertising between its Web site and the hit television show "Friends." The details of this collaboration are unknown, but nonetheless it illustrates how effectively Coca Cola ties in its conventional advertising with its market strategies for the Web.

Coca Cola also uses its Web site as a place for commerce. Although selling six packs of Diet Coke is not the company's primary objective, the Web site does have an online catalog of Coca Cola related merchandise. This is an effective way for Coca Cola to market itself and its main product, the soft drinks, while also utilizing its Web site as a sales mechanism.

One unique aspect of Coke's site: a message board called the Soda Fountain, where designated questions—such as "What would you do if you were the President of the United States?"—prompts surfers to post an insightful or entertaining answer.

FIGURE 8-1

These are some of the images
Coca Cola offers as downloadable
graphics.

Pepsi, Coca Cola's chief competitor, has not done as nice a job making the move to multimedia. The company offers what amounts to two separate sites, The Fridge (http://www.pepsi.com.uk) and Club Pepsi-Max (http://www.club-pepsimax.com). Both of these sites are difficult, if not impossible, to access. From what we can gather, The Fridge is intended to be an informational site providing details about Pepsi's products. On the other hand, Club Pepsi-Max is an online nightclub where Pepsi's spokespeople—like Cindy Crawford—"spend time." As we stated earlier, obtaining information about these two sites was extremely difficult, so the information we pass on to you is sketchy as well.

In short, the battle for the best soft-drink Web site is presently no contest. Coca Cola has created a tremendous site, creating an extension of its current marketing plan—in effect a seamless transition to the World Wide Web.

GRAB A BREW OFF THE WEB

Some of the funniest and most memorable commercials on television are those associated with beer. These commercials are also found on the radio and in print media. The intent is to make customers believe that a certain beer is more tasty than another and that they'll have a better time when they drink it. Animals, animated characters, famous personalities—all try to convince us that the beer that they drink, or at least the one they are getting paid to drink, is the one that they love. This marketing scheme combines humor and product knowledge in the attempt to sell a specific brand. Beer companies are now taking such schemes onto the Web.

The Canadian conglomerate Molson Brewing Company, the largest brewer in the country of Canada, is one such beer company. The brewery markets its product heavily in the conventional forms of media, and has made a similar effort on the Web (http://www.molson.com). This outstanding Web site both incorporates and enhances the company's current conventional marketing plan. The site's members-only section, "I am online," boasts chatrooms, games, and even a section called Webmail, where all of their registered users can communicate with each other via a type of e-mail. (You can also enter this section as a guest.) Members can develop personal profiles; these profiles allow members to learn more about the people with whom they interact on the site (see Figure 8-2). Membership is free, in exchange for some valuable demographic information, including the member's actual e-mail address and verification of legal drinking age. Molson also offers a section on responsible drinking and provides a corporate overview so that surfers can learn about the company as a whole.

Molson's superb site provides most of the features necessary for effective Web marketing. Their Web is an enhancement of their conventional advertising. They use sharp, eye-catching and memorable graphics that do not slow down transmission speeds. In short, Molson is an excellent example of a large, established company that has embraced the new medium of the Web and incorporated it perfectly into their overall marketing scheme.

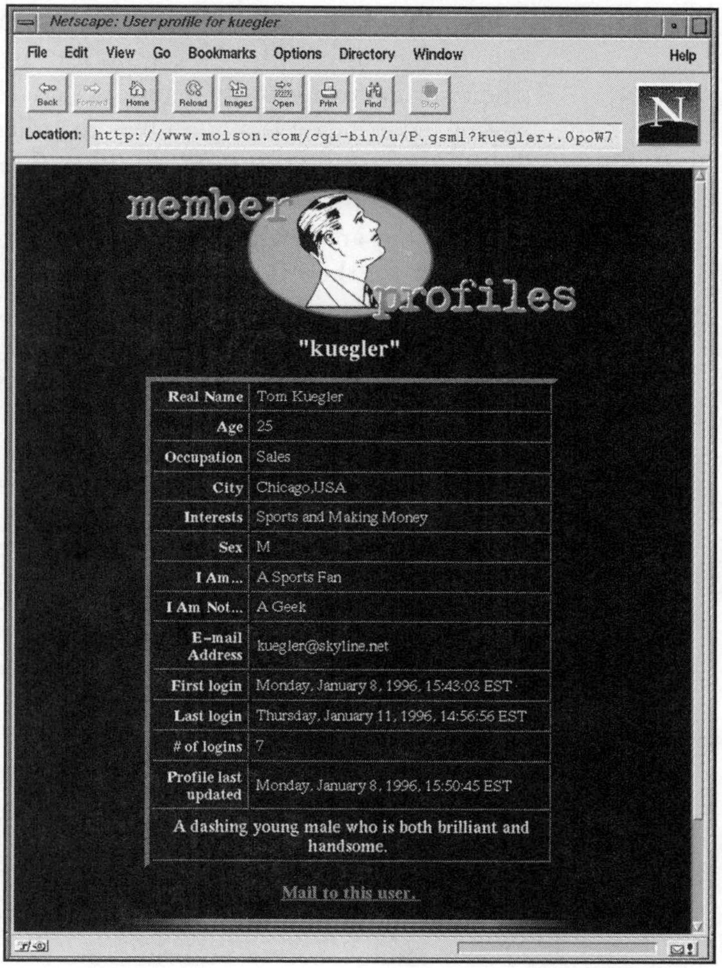

FIGURE 8-2

A personal profile from Molson's Web site.

Another beer company that has also made the transition from conventional advertising to Web marketing is the Guinness Brewing Company. Guinness is the largest brewing company in Ireland, holding a huge share of market there as well as a substantial share of America's dark beer segment. Their conventional marketing and advertising runs the gamut of media, including the sponsorship of athletic events world wide. Guinness's Web site (http://www.itl.net/guinness), called "The Local," is designed with the look and feel of the local pub. One popular enticement: an online sweepstakes competition, in which the first prize is a trip to Ireland for St. Patrick's Day. (They also give away 100 Guinness T-shirts.) This competition allows Guinness to survey the surfers who hit on the site; as a result they learn how much their surfers drink of their product and how often they drink it. The sweepstakes tactic is a good way to collect demographic information, without putting off surfers. Another fine feature of the Guinness site: surfers can download screensavers and wallpapers for their PCs. Surfers feel they are getting something for free and Guinness obtains more exposure for their product. This site also offers links to other interesting sites—always a good draw for surfers, who typically enjoy jumping from place to place on the Web.

Overall, Guinness has developed an excellent Web site for the promotion of their product. It ties in well with the company's overall marketing plan and is a nice addition to the Web. One recommendation: to incorporate more stimulating graphics. This would make the site even more memorable and entertaining.

Both the Molson and Guinness sites provide excellent examples of how to migrate to the Web; they're worth checking out since they incorporate most of the essential features you should consider to ensure the success of your ventures into this medium.

SNEAKERS SNEAK ONTO THE WEB

The world of athletics has been transformed by the marketing efforts of shoe companies. These companies have invested big advertising dollars in fast-paced ads that spur people to buy their shoes in the hope of improving their athletic performance. These companies typically hire professional athletes to act as both spokespeople and walking billboards. The stadiums, courts, and rinks are flooded with advertisements and cost these shoe companies millions of dollars. The flashy, aggressive nature of their TV and radio spots as well as their print ads translates well to the Web.

The world of athletic shoe apparel is a very competitive one—and no company competes harder than Reebok. It is surprising, then, that their Web site (http://www.planetreebok.com) is so lackluster. Known as Planet Reebok, the site includes a few of the aspects required for success, including a sweepstakes contest intended to attract surfers and obtain demographic information. You'll also find articles about current products, provided free of charge so every surfer may access.

Reebok does attempt to use both message boards and chat rooms. Unfortunately, the chat rooms are not true chat rooms at all. They are canned discussions, offered in a text format. For example, say the site offers a chat room with the New York Yankees. What you'll find there is a transcript of a few Yankee players interacting with a few other people. There is no ongoing interaction with surfers.

Reebok's site would benefit by the addition of impressive presentations and full interactivity. This said, Reebok has still done a far better job than most of their competitors, most of whom still have their sites in development.

PIZZA MAKES THE MOVE TO THE WEB

Memorable jingles, slogans, and images all characterize the marketing and advertising efforts of national pizza chains. They use these techniques to gain brand loyalty and make their food seem more enticing. They also contract famous people to push their food in their ads. Geared to make their restaurants seem like the perfect place to stop and catch a quick meal, these pizza parlors use every conventional avenue to bring their message home to the buying audience. Television and radio spots abound on all channels in every time slot, covering every possible demographic.

Indeed, the world of pizza leaves no marketing rock unturned. Given this kind of scope and depth, it should come as no surprise that two of the largest pizza makers, Pizza Hut and Little Caesar's, have both transformed their tremendous conventional marketing plans into successful multimedia blitzes.

Pizza Hut is one of the largest pizza restaurant chains in the entire world. Long known as a sit-down restaurant, the company is now attempting to compete in the world of pizza delivery as well. Pizza Hut now offers delivery at many of its restaurants; the company goal is to be as successful a pizza delivery business as it is a sit-down restaurant business. To facilitate this company transition, Pizza Hut decided to take its marketing to the Web.

In August of 1995, Pizza Hut announced a pilot program in the Santa Cruz area of California, designed to determine if surfers would order pizzas on the Web to be delivered to their homes. Although this site (http://www.pizzahut.com) is not yet fully developed as a marketing tool, it does make it easy to order pizzas. The official results of the Web pilot program are due later this year. If Pizza Hut does decide to develop this site fully, it has its work cut out for it. At this point its site is extremely plain, doing little to enhance the image of the company.

The sight of a little Greek animated character repeating the same word or phrase over and over has come to symbolize one pizza company perfectly: Little Caesar's. This pizza chain now has brought its catchy marketing and economy-priced pizza to the Web (http:// www.onthego.com/little_caesars). The approach is similar to that of Pizza Hut, only on a larger scale. Little Caesar's offers its delivery or pick-up service; you can order pizzas online, with any combination of toppings. The one thing that Little Caesar's offers, which Pizza Hut does not, is online coupons—which work well for them in their

FIGURE 8-3

The online coupons offered by Little
Caesar's Pizza.

conventional marketing efforts as well. Online specials for both pick-up and delivery are constantly updated and revised (see Figure 8-3). Another feature unique to Little Caesar's: if you enter a ZIP code not currently covered by the Web program, you are asked to complete an online form which allows the company to track the origin of all unfulfilled orders. This will help Little Caesar's determine where they need to expand their coverage.

Both of these sites view the Web as a sales tool. To exploit the full potential of the Web, they must envision it as an extension of all types of their marketing. The Web is just as useful as a publicity and name recognition tool as it is for direct sales.

THE WEB DEPARTMENT STORE

Department stores spend a lot of money putting out catalogs, publishing printed ads, and running TV and radio spots. Typically they develop all-encompassing plans designed to convince customers that 1) they offer the finest products at the lowest prices, and 2) customers should feel warm and fuzzy about their stores. A few of the large department stores have attempted to recreate this marketing magic on the Web.

Wal-Mart's excellent site (http://www.wal-mart.com) is a superb example of how an established company can incorporate the technology of the Web into its complete marketing plan. At this Web site, surfers have access to corporate information, stockholder information, and the necessary contacts for employee and personnel relations. Wal-Mart also dedicates space to its community work and minority and women-owned program—demonstrating the scope and depth of its community relations. Another added feature of the Wal-Mart site is the ability to search for the store located closest to you. Moreover, all of this information is free and simple to retrieve.

Two interesting and excellent Wal-mart practices are online circulars and online catalogs. The online circular lists all of the specials running at your local Wal-Mart. Surfers can view this circular free of charge—and it saves Wal-Mart money in printing and mailing costs.

Wal-Mart's online catalog, the "Sam's Club Express," is even more impressive. Here surfers may order almost any type of product and have it delivered to their residence or other location in two days. To gain access to this catalog surfers must fill out an online survey, which will give them a password to enter the catalog—and give Wal-Mart the demographic information they want.

This is a graphical catalog, which displays the products so surfers may see what it is they are buying (see Figure 8-4). Another feature of this catalog: the products offered online are not offered anywhere else by Wal-Mart; this encourages the public to use Wal-Mart's online service. If there is one shortcoming to the "Sam's Club Express," it is this: surfers must use an 800 number to call in their orders. Wal-Mart is not presently using an online ordering feature, but this possibility is under development.

Another major retailer using the Web to its best advantage is JCPenney Stores. In more than 100 years of doing business, JCPenney has tried every

FIGURE 8-4

A basket of pears that may be purchased at Sam's Club Express

form of media possible to promote and market its stores and products—and its Web site (http://www.jcpenny.com) is no exception.

However, its approach is different from its competitor Wal-Mart. Whereas Wal-Mart attempts to sell its products online, JCPenney uses the Web as an overall marketing tool. These two companies provide an excellent way for you to compare the different methods you can use on the Web and still be effective.

At the JCPenney site, there is a plethora of information about the company. As a surfer, you can enter the site and view the company's help wanted listings and other corporate hiring information, along with investor relations information and other corporate structure details. Recent JCPenney press releases are also available for review, and JCPenney also offers a store-locating mechanism, just as Wal-Mart does.

The concept of interactivity is not lost on JCPenney either. Its site also serves as a survey and customer satisfaction tool—enabling the company to gain needed demographic information and give surfers the opportunity to voice complaints and comments as well.

The greatest difference between the JCPenney and Wal-Mart sites is their approach to online sales. Rather than establishing an online catalog, JCPenney offers information about a multitude of topics, from home furnishing to sporting goods. This information, called "Doing It Right," is free to the surfer and is often extremely helpful. For example, one topic will address how you can decorate a room with a large bay window, suggesting JCPenney products as solutions. It would be great if surfers could order such products online; still, the JCPenney site is well-created and maintained.

The point is this: marketing on the Web doesn't necessarily mean online sales. When a company runs a TV spot, no one expects viewers to jump through the screen and buy the product from their home. The true goal is to gain exposure and name recognition from this type of advertising. Online sales is a great feature of the Web, but thinking of it as its only feature is shortsighted.

INTERNAL USES OF THE WEB

Marketing on the Web is both possible and profitable. Thus far this book has shown you how the Web can enhance your company image, increase sales, and explore new markets. Next, let's examine the ways in which you can use the Web to enhance other areas of your business.

USING THE WEB TO IMPROVE OTHER AREAS OF YOUR BUSINESS

There are many ways you can use the Web to enhance your communications. For instance, you can use the Web as a large bulletin board, where the exchange of company ideas and memos is accessible to everyone. With the Web, this bulletin board can incorporate the use of pictures and graphics. If your company is working on a large project, the status and goals of this project can be shown online so that the whole company can track its progress.

Another benefit is facilitating communications with employees offsite. When, say, employees must travel far from the office, they can use a Web site as a place to check on the latest developments at the company. They can receive the latest plans or design changes in a visual format or detailed notes from the project manager regarding the change. In return, these satellite employees can relay any necessary information back home to the office, again, in a visual manner.

Salespeople on the road can use the Web site as a part of their presentations, showing customers an up-to-the-minute update of their projects. The Web serves up this information in a visual format that's easy to understand and detailed.

We'll discuss, in great detail, many of the other internal communication possibilities available to you on the Web later on in this book. For now, it's safe to say that the Web is not only a marketing and advertising tool, but a communication and internal advisement tool as well.

OFFICE SPACE IS LIMITLESS AND CHEAP ON THE WEB

One of the largest expenditures for any large business is the cost of office facilities. Besides the lease costs of securing space, there is the cost of utilities, liability insurance, and even furnishings. All of these costs eat away at a company's bottom line. Worse, these costs do not increase the revenues of the company because they are not costs that help the company to make money; they are simply operating costs. The Web can help you reduce such costs.

As we discussed earlier, the Web provides many ways to enhance the communication of your company—including allowing many of your employees to work from home or other remote locations. Working from home is attractive to many employees: they don't have to fight traffic;

they can dress casually and comfortably; they may even increase their productivity. Many companies have tried such telecommuting with great success; the technique is now known as an effective way to increase company morale and hold down operating costs.

Although there is some cost associated with setting up telecommuting communication features on the Web, a cost analysis will show that it is much more efficient to enhance your communications than it is to add to your office space. In addition to this cost savings, there is unlimited space on the Web. Adding memory, software, or hardware is much simpler than it is to add to your office space. Your current location may have no vacant space or at least none that is applicable to your needs. This could mean relocating all of your operations to a new facility in order to handle this increased need for space.

The Web can become the largest office that you could ever imagine. There is no limit to the number of people that you can fit into your cyberoffice, and you will find that it is much cheaper than leasing another floor in an office complex.

CONVINCING YOUR STAFF TO MOVE TO THE WEB

So you're sold on the move. This book, along with everything else you have seen about the Web, convinces you that this is a place for you to go. The only problem is that you don't think that the rest of your company is as sold as you are on the Web. You anticipate a multitude of objections, ranging from cost to cyberphobia. Let's review all the issues you'll need to address to sell your staff and management on making the move to the Web—starting with the most crucial, the fear of change.

The Web opens up new realms for your company, but many of your employees may feel like they are foreigners in a strange new world. Some people fear all change; the unknown brings sweat to their brow and anxiety to their hearts. The Web is the great cyber unknown; many people in your company may have only heard about the Web from the slick sound bites of the mass media. The only way to ease their apprehension: well-explained, truthful reasoning coupled with the facts:

> The Web, although new and advanced, is just another form of communication—just like the TV you watch at home, the radio in your car, or the newspaper that you read every morning.

- The average surfer spends more time on the Web per week than using the VCR.

- More than one fourth of all of Fortune 500 companies have a Web presence—and another 65 percent plan to expand to the Web by the end of the year.

- Access to the Web will soon expand even more quickly than it already has, as the mainstream public gains access through home cable television companies.

- The low entry cost into the world of Web marketing makes any risk minimal.

If these few points do not quiet your staff's fears, tell them a story that brings the fear of technology home to them. Tell them to imagine the first time that they ever used a microwave oven. They probably thought that this process of cooking was unhealthy, unproductive, and at least unnatural. Such thinking prevailed only about 10 years ago, but now the entire country uses microwave technology. Almost 90 percent of households have microwaves, and most restaurants use microwaves for some part of the preparation process. The technology of the Web is similar to that of the microwave in the sense that it is new and foreign to many people. Time will heal all such fears, so ask your employees to recognize this and take the plunge with you.

MAKING THE MEDICINE TASTE A LITTLE BETTER

So you have quieted your staff's initial fear. They realize that they can take this step, but you want to make the transition as easy for them as possible. There are certain steps that you can take to make the transition less painful; the first is to minimize the contact that these employees have with the technical side of the Web. You want to enable as many employees as possible to surf the Web and spread the word about your site, but you will find that this can be accomplished with minimal training even with the most computer illiterate personnel.

Another possibility: perform some of the functions of the Web through other conventional office devices. For example, if you ask surfers to respond to your ad with online surveys or order forms, you can easily set the technology up so that the results of these surveys or copies of these orders come in via fax. Even the most fearful employees are probably familiar with the fax machine, so they could probably handle this feature of the Web.

One last-ditch approach is to hire an outside consulting firm to develop your Web pages at their establishment with limited input from your employees. Such a firm can handle every aspect of your Web site's creation and upkeep. Your employees will be required to do nothing.

While you can always go this route, we recommend that you get as many employees up to speed on the Web as possible. The Web is here to stay; it will become the dynamic media of the twenty-first century. Those companies with a Web-savvy employee base will be one step ahead of their competition in this new world of multimedia development.

Remember...

- Before you undergo an expansion of your marketing program to include the Web, you should first evaluate your current marketing plan to ensure its effectiveness.

- When you redesign your marketing plans to include the strategies of multimedia, and the Web specifically, make sure that you incorporate the necessary features you need to succeed.

- Both in-house marketing departments and advertising agencies may be ill-equipped for the migration to the World Wide Web; make sure they have the technical and specialized marketing expertise this venture requires.

- Many large companies, with established advertising history, have made the transition to the Web. Use the successful ones as guides for your own excursion and the less successful ones as painful lessons you should not repeat.

- The Web is excellent for many uses within your company. It can save money, time, and energy for you and your business.

- If your staff has resisted change in the past and the Web is just another reason for them to panic, approach them with reasoning and facts. If they still resist, minimize their contact with this part of your marketing and make it as easy to use as possible.

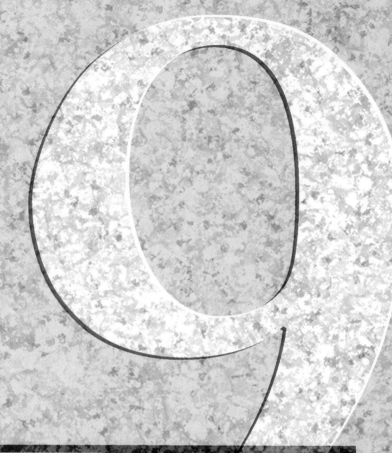

9

ATTRACTING CUSTOMERS

When we first opened our doors at Skyline.Net, we already had a basic Web site designed, up, and running. "Wow! This is great!," we all said. We plugged in our network and waited for the hits to come rolling in.

We waited, and we waited, and we waited. And we waited. But no more than a handful of drifters wandered through our little site. Eventually we realized we had to do more than just market the site to our customers. To generate the kind of interest, enthusiasm, and *traffic* that distinguishes a truly successful Web site, we had to sell our site and ourselves to the Internet community. And that, we soon learned, was as challenging as marketing any product or service in the offline world.

Attracting people to your Web site is no easy task. This fact becomes painfully evident when you do some surfing yourself. There are an awful lot of Web sites out there, thousands, in fact. Standing out in that crowd is going to require more than a little creativity, a fair measure of flexibility, and some plain old sweat. Luckily, we're here to get you started on the right foot. The following sections offer proven strategies that will have your hit counter spinning faster than the second hand on a stopwatch.

Before we begin, however, let's look at what we mean when we talk about "hits." Many sites consider a hit to be every Web-server connection where a file transfer occurs. But we agreed that that method of accounting artificially inflates a site's hit rate. After much discussion, we decided, for our purposes, to define a hit as every HTML page our server transfers and every CGI program run on the server. This was an important and difficult decision for a young company planning to sell Web space to clients who would be judging us by our "readership." This definition instantly reduced our hit rate by about five or six times. But we believed then—and do today—that it provides a much more accurate picture.

Understanding hit-rate accounting can help you determine if your Internet marketing efforts work, and whether your Web presence provider (WPP) is doing its job marketing your site.

Let's say your Web site includes 99 images, and you decide to consider the images as hits. You'd look at your hit rate and say, "Wow! We're averaging almost a hundred hits a day!" But you could be getting only *one* hit a day from users checking out all the pictures. Your results are skewed by your accounting method. Eliminating images from your hit-count criteria would give you a much more accurate picture of your

Web-site activity. You'll never develop a successful Web marketing campaign if you can't tell the difference between a hundred people visiting your site and one person visiting it a hundred times.

Why would anyone want to artificially inflate their hit rate? For many reasons: WPPs sell Web space based on the hits they attract. Marketing departments use hit-rate information to attract more customers to the site (a "bandwagon" approach). Web-page designers want to impress their bosses. Their bosses want to impress the CEO. The CEO wants to impress the stockholders. And the company wants to impress the public.

For years, when companies publicly reported the number of hits they received at a particular site, most assumed this figure reflected the actual number of people who viewed the site. It was not until 1994, when the media began informing the public about misleading hit rates, that people began calling for a consistent definition of a hit. The industry countered that technical limitations made it impossible to determine the actual number of people visiting a site, and that accurate statistics could only be generated by special machines.

All this attention to hit counts has created a more educated consumer and a more responsive Web community. Some sites now include counters that record and post each visit. Many counters also include the dates counting began. But it's still up to you to determine what your WPP's hit rate actually means, and how you want to portray your hit count to the public.

IF YOU BUILD IT, WILL THEY COME?

To develop your Web site into a viable medium for marketing your company's products, services, and image, you must first market the site itself. It's not enough to create an attractive, user-friendly site. You must also let everyone know it's out there and worth its weight in silicon.

This analogy illustrates what we're getting at: "South of the Border" is a travel plaza located in South Carolina, just off Interstate 95, a few yards south of the state line. If you've ever driven along the East Coast, you've undoubtedly seen ads for it. Billboards for "South of the Border" start cropping up more than 200 miles from the place. The closer travelers get, the more billboards they see, and each one displays the number of miles to the plaza. These are big, flashy signs, many three-dimensional, often humorous, and always informative. The billboards inform travelers that gas is five cents cheaper in South Carolina; that reduced ticket prices for many attractions in Florida and Myrtle Beach are available at the plaza; that "South of the Border" is such a great place in so many ways, stopping there simply *has* to become part of the trip. Who could resist such an enthusiastic and relentless invitation?

You can send out similarly compelling invitations by erecting your own Internet "billboards." You'll need to put up hundreds of them, all pointing the way to your site. The more you put up and the more places you put them, the greater your hit count.

So, you ask, how do I erect billboards on the Internet? Where should I put them? How can I determine who will see them?

What we're talking about here is getting your message out, and on the Internet you can do that in a number of ways. You can e-mail potential customers directly; post articles to relevant newsgroups; advise people through newsgroups or online chat forums; list your site on popular Web search sites, and ask other Web-site administrators to include links to your site on theirs.

SUBMITTING URLS TO WEB SEARCH SITES

To market Skyline's first Web site, we decided to submit our homepage URL to some popular Web search sites, such as *Yahoo*, *Lycos*, and others. There are many search sites on the Web, each with a different approach, but all with the same goal of providing a sort of yellow pages service for Internet Web browsing.

To use a site like *Yahoo*, users just enter a keyword, and the site scans its large databases of Web-site addresses. If a match is found between the user's keyword and part of a URL, part of the description of the site, or a word found within the homepage's actual HTML code, the search site displays the matching site names, descriptions, and URLs.

How do these Web search sites get their data? Sites like *Yahoo* collect electronic submissions from people who want their sites listed in the search engine's database. Other sites, such as *Webcrawler*, use an automated robot that randomly goes from site to site, following links to other sites, and recording the words it finds on each homepage.

The main problem with many Web search sites is that the shear volume of information stored in them can slow and even stall the search process. Users can find themselves buried in the hundreds of sites output during a search. It can be like looking for a "Mr. Smith" in the white pages of the Los Angeles telephone directory. Also, many sites alphabetize returned information by site name or title, not URL, keywords, or description. Imagine trying to find Mr. Smith in a directory that listed individuals by height and you'll get an idea of how frustrating this can be. Most of us would end up just throwing the directory out the window.

TIP

When submitting your URLs to search sites, you can increase your hit rate by selecting a site name or title that begins with the uppercase letter 'A.' Search sites alphabetize their outputted lists by the name/title of the site. Surfers tend to follow the links on the top of the list and ignore the remaining links.

Despite their limitations, search sites can be very useful in helping people find your Web site. Just submitting your homepage location however, is not enough. Some sites only allow a single, unique URL with a single description. This is where a more diversified Web site can allow for a greater number of hits. If you post several pages in one directory, submit each page with a different description. Table 9-1 shows an example of how you might submit multiple URLs to a Web search site, with descriptions and keywords.

TABLE 9-1   SEARCH SITE SUBMISSION EXAMPLE

Submitted URL	Description	Keyword
http://www.yoursite.com/homepage.html	The YourSite homepage offers comprehensive,up-to-date movie, music, and book reviews online.	YourSite, movie, music, book, review, entertainment, culture
http://www.yoursite.com/movie_reviews.html	Movie reviews for all movies currently playing at the box office.	YourSite, movie, review, entertainment, culture, screen, blockbuster
http://www.yoursite.com/music_review.html	Music reviews for every album on the Top Ten Music Charts.	Yoursite, music, review, entertainment, culture, cassette, CD, album
http://www.yoursite.com/book_review.html	Reviews for every book on the *New York Times* bestseller list.	Yoursite, book, print, review, entertainment, culture, library, *New York Times*, bestseller

Some sites make it possible for you to submit your Web address to several search sites at the same time. *Submit-It* (http://www.submit-it.com/), developed by Scott Banister (http://www.cen.uiuc.edu/~banister), allows you to submit your Web address to 15 different sites at once (see Figure 9-1).

FIGURE 9-1

Submit-It's homepage is an excellent place to start when beginning to advertise your Web site.

While it may be easier and take less time, descriptions and keywords submitted this way may end up briefer than many search sites actually allow. For instance, if a search site permits 100 characters of keywords and *Submit-It* only allows 50, you lose half your potential message. However, these sites give you a good idea of the number and location of sites to which you can submit.

BEG AND BARTER

Wouldn't it be great if you could swap links with other Web sites that might be of interest to your customers? Well, you can! Other sites want the same thing you do—*traffic*. People seek out Web sites with lots of useful and informative links. Many Web-site managers will be glad to set up a link to your site if you do the same for them. It's in your best interest to set up plenty of your own hot links. Every link you establish is another billboard for your Web site.

The first person you should talk to about setting up a link to your site is your Internet or Web presence provider. Your provider may have a page of links to other customers' homepages, with a small description of each site, as well as company logos or other informative images. These links may already be included in the price you're paying for your Internet service or Web page.

Next, you'll want to contact your company's own suppliers. Chances are, many businesses from which you buy products or services already have homepages with detailed information about their products and services. If these companies don't sell directly to the public or only sell at wholesale prices, they may have an online list of resellers' Web addresses and their geographical locations. Ask them to include your homepage on this list.

As you search for useful links, don't overlook your own customers. Many of them probably have Web pages with plenty of room for a link to your site.

This last link completes a kind of triad of critical connections among customers, distributors, and manufactures. These connections may be the most important links you establish on the Net. Here's how this triad might work for a company we'll call Acme Widgets.

First, a netsurfer checks out the homepage of a small mom-and-pop store. The surfer notices that the store uses Acme Widgets exclusively, and the compamy provides a link to the distributor. The surfer then checks out the distributor's homepage and learns that the Acme Widget is the best-selling widget in the country. Following another link to the Acme Widget Company itself, the surfer finds highly detailed information about the widget—what it looks like, how much it weighs, its dimensions, uses, specifications, and retail price. The surfer then views the company's list of distributor Web page, and clicks on the closest one—the mom-and-pop shop. Back at mom and pop's homepage, the surfer notes that the widget is in stock, and places an online order for two dozen.

The netsurfer doesn't have to know that the pages don't actually reside on your homepage. Say our mom-and-pop store has an online widget catalogue. Next to each widget are three links—Buy This Widget, Check Out National Widget Sales, and Widget Specifications. The first link takes the surfer to a form residing on mom and pop's Web server that allows him to place an order. The next link connects to the widget distributor, who maintains a database of national widget sales figures. The Widget Specifications link resides on the manufacture's Web site, and includes all the more technical and detailed widget info so they can focus on selling widgets.

The mom-and-pop store only has to maintain two pages in this scenario, the catalogue page and the order page. The distributor and manufacturer update and maintain their own two pages. This reduces the amount of everyone's workload. The distributor in this example could update national widget sales figures weekly, relieving the small store of the task.

Everyone benefited in this transaction by having links to and from customers, distributors, and manufactures. These kinds of connections are what netsurfers look for. They allow people to get a drill down of information without having to deal with every page in the chain.

Because you don't know where a potential client will start his or her search, put links everywhere you can. Do some surfing yourself and look for sites with links geared to your intended customer or that focus on your market niche. Look for pages that include site descriptions as well as links. As you surf, you'll find a number of sites with links but no site descriptions, typically under headings like "Some Cool Sites I Found!" Why would anyone click on "www.abcde.com" without knowing what they do or why they're "cool"?

As you find sites in which you would like your link to appear, jot them down or add them as a bookmark in your browser. Not everyone will jump at the opportunity to include a link to your site, and neither should you. All sites are not created equal, and there's a lot of competition on the Net, so choose your sites carefully.

Now, go back to the Web sites you jotted down, and look for e-mail addresses. They should be listed somewhere on the Web site. If you're unable to find an address, try sending e-mail to:

`<webmaster@theirdomain.com>`

`<www@theirdomain.com>`

`<root@theirdomain.com>`

`≤postmaster@theirdomain.com≥`.

Only use these addresses if you can't find an address online. You don't want to annoy people who are about to do you a favor.

Next, draft an e-mail message you can send to each site. Ask if they would be kind enough to include a link to your site on their list-of-links page. Specify in return that you are willing to add their site to your list of links, along with a name and description of their choice.

Better still, before you contact a site, go ahead and create a link to its homepage. This adds to your credibility when you send the e-mail. Be sure to let them know you've already added them to your site, and include the URL of the page where their site appears. You want them to feel that you found their site useful. This actually increases the probability they will include your site on their links page.

You may get e-mail from other sites proposing the same thing. While this may sound great at first—and there's no real way of stopping someone from putting up a link to your site—you may feel that being advertised on their site is inappropriate. Qualify the site before you agree. For instance, Oklahoma City may not appreciate a link from the Unabomber homepage, where it's listed as the Unabomber's favorite city. You also may feel uncomfortable adding a link to your competition.

Adding links to your Web page is a great way to create site value, get your name out to a wider range of netsurfers, make friends, and build partnerships on the Web. However, take care with your list-of-links Web page, when people visit your site you want them to take off their jackets and stay awhile. If you provide too many opportunities to go to other sites, it's like chasing them out the door as soon as they arrive. Place your list-of-links Web page slightly out of the way so browsing surfers will hang around your site awhile.

This was something we learned at Skyline with our first Web-site design. A few pages after our homepage, we included a page titled, "Best of the Net—Our Picks for the Best Internet Sites." Surfers went right to this page, skipping over a dozen other choices. No sooner had we drawn them to our site, we quickly sent them away.

When you negotiate with other sites to trade links, make sure your company assigns this job to only one person. Think of the other sites as prospects. You wouldn't allow gangs of salespeople to hound prospects in other aspect of your business. Don't do it on the Net, either.

Contacting other Web sites to swap links should be an ongoing process. It's like putting a small classified ad in every newspaper you find. Responses will vary. Many will be favorable starts leading to long and mutually satisfying relationships. Some sites won't respond to your mail and won't include the link. Others won't respond, but will include the link. Some sites may send you well-crafted hate mail for even asking.

NEWSGROUPS

Welcome to the Internet marketer's dream! Newsgroups offer a wealth of knowledge, free exchange of ideas, and help on thousands of different topics. The best thing about newsgroups is that they're specific enough for you to effectively target your market. This is where your advertising can get really creative.

Suppose an insurance company wants to post to some newsgroups. Where should it begin? It could start with some obvious business or high-risk activity groups, but that's not very imaginative. How about posting to rec.humor? But wait, rec.humor has nothing to do with insurance—or does it? Your company could post a humorous "Top 10 List" like, "The Top 10 Funniest Insurance Claims," or "The Top 10 Reasons Insurance Agents Make Better Lovers." Your number-one reason on the list could relate in some way to your company and include the URL address to your site.

TIP

Always put your signature file at the bottom of your newsgroup posting. This is a sort of digital signature that makes you unique and recognizable in public forum areas, such as newsgroups, as well as in e-mail transactions. Include this in all your newsgroup postings. Your signature file should incorporate the name of your company, your e-mail address, and the URL address of your Web site. You might also include your company address, phone number, and slogan. These should typically be four lines or fewer and no more than 80 characters across. Example:

```
| Wild Western Widget Company       <URL:http://www.yoursite.com/> |
| WebMaster@YourSite.Com    "A Widget For Every Cowpoke's Needs!" |
```

Because it is a popular source of Web-site information, one of the first newsgroups you should post to is alt.infosystems.www.announce. This is a moderated newsgroup; that is, someone actually reviews what people submit before posting the information. The moderator ensures that people don't abuse the newsgroup by posting 800 messages that scream, "***VISIT MY SITE!!! GREATEST SITE IN THE WORLD!!!"

Because alt.infosystems.www.announce is a moderated site, you must follow certain rules when you post to it. The moderator posts these rules to the newsgroup every couple of weeks; be sure to read them before you submit your posting. Failure to follow the rules ensures the moderator never posts your message. Even after it's been accepted, someone has to actually check every post, so it may take some time before your message appears in the newsgroup. Harassing the moderator won't get you posted any sooner.

Besides posting commercial messages about your site, product, or service, you can post personal replies to people asking for help. For example, let's say you work for a law firm specializing in business incorporation. You could monitor the alt.entrepreneurs newsgroup for questions about incorporating a business. Once spotting a question calling for your expertise, you could post an answer. Toward the end of your message, you would identify yourself as a lawyer specializing in this field, and you mention that you'd be willing to help on a more professional level, if the questioner so desired. You might even list the reasons hiring a lawyer to do the actual incorporation can possibly prevent future lawsuits.

Once you establish your reputation as a knowledgeable resource on particular topics, other posters will refer questions directly to you and your company. This holds true for mailing lists, as well. However, don't

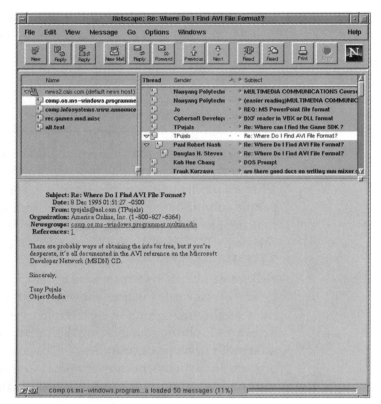

FIGURE 9-2

Netscape's news interface allows you to read and post articles to newsgroups. If an article includes an image, the Netscape news interface displays the picture on the screen.

make the mistake of trying to respond to every post or in areas where you have little or no experience. In other words, do nothing that might jeopardize your credibility as a reliable source of information.

Do whatever it takes to establish and maintain a reputation for honesty in all your online business dealings. Cyberspace scams are more common than most of us would like to admit. They irritate users and erode confidence in anyone doing business on the Web.

These concerns about online larceny are well-founded. For example, quite of bit of online business is conducted COD, giving rise to at least a couple of scams we've heard about. The first involves shippers collecting cash for bogus deliveries. After the receiver pays for the package, he or she opens the box to find broken parts, the wrong parts, or sometimes only newspapers. The other isn't a true scam, but it can create tremendous ill will. In this situation, the package arrives as promised, but the receiver refuses to pay for it. The shipper is now out the cost of shipping and COD fees.

Many Internet users post regular announcements to newsgroups, alerting the public to Net scam artists. There's even an Internet "black list." How does someone get black-listed? All it takes is an accusing e-mail message. An irate user writes to the list owner, declaring that "YourCompany.Com" scammed them, and you're on the list. However, getting black-listed isn't the end of the world, it's an online version of the Better Business Bureau. If your name or company name ever appears on the list, contact the list owner and let him or her know the circumstances of the transaction. They may not remove your name from the list, but they may add your side of the story below the complaint.

The Better Business Bureau actually has an online complaint form logging complaints about a customer or other company. It's located at http://www.bbb.org/bbb/. You can also use their site to research customers and vendors on the World Wide Web.

Newsgroup posting affects traffic to your site in a sporadic and largely unmeasurable way. If you post only one message to alt.infosystems.www.announce, you might see your hits rise quickly as soon as the message reaches the Internet community. You'll ride high for about a week, but then the traffic will quickly subside. Why this remarkable rise and fall? Most news postings remain on the system for only a few days or weeks. It's the Internet service provider on the receiver's end who determines the amount of time news remains on the system. The posting also may take longer to reach some sites than others.

The alt.infosystems.www.announce newsgroup charter states that postings to the group are for new and revised Web-site addresses. Only post to this group once for each unique URL. Using the YourSite.Com example from Table 9-1, you could post to the newsgroup over a four-week period, posting a different URL each week. The first week you could post homepage.html; the second week, movie_reviews.html; and so on. This gives you a month of increased traffic and reaches people who don't check the newsgroup every week.

When posting a message to a general newsgroup, both the title and the message play an important role. Because the *tone* of an online message is difficult to convey, Internet users developed typographical conventions to make their vocal inflections known. When someone uses capital letters, for example, it signifies that they are shouting. Leaving your CAPS LOCK key on for an entire message would make it seem as though you were SHOUTING AT THEM. Underlining a word indicates emphasis. It's impossible to actually underline the text of the basic ASCII character set, so a word beginning and ending with the shifted-dash is considered to be underlined (for example: _word_).

Want to ensure no one finishes reading your posting all the way though? Just post your press release as you would send it to a newspaper. This says you haven't done your homework and makes you look like a "newbie." You may have paid thousands of dollars to an advertising agency to write your press release, but that doesn't mean the Internet will find it even remotely interesting.

A "newbie" is a person who is new to the Web or Internet and is uneducated in "netiquette"—Internet etiquette.

An effective online press release is far more vibrant than its hard copy counterpart. We're talking glitz and glamour here. You need contests, giveaways, sound, graphics, animation, or something equally cool.

A good online release includes your Web-site address, company name, and a short description of your site. Try to include an image or video clip to pique viewers' interest and lure them to your site. This is a good way to showcase your product to relevant newsgroups. Mistral Windsurfing (http://www.sccsi.com/Mistral/mistral_welcome.html) provides video clips for surfers (both Web and wind!) to download and view. The clips and images feature famous windsurfers, like Robby Naish, using Mistral windsurfing equipment (captions disclose which products the windsurfers are using). While the video is certainly entertaining, it also works as a tool to boost Mistral's windsurfing equipment sales. The titles of the still photos and movies reflect the products the windsurfers are using in the pictures.

Mistral doesn't include its logo on the pictures themselves; nothing is stopping you from incorporating such company-specific information into your images. Just be sure the stills or video clips are original, to avoid copyright infringements.

Many Web browsers now include a newsgroup interface. These interfaces allow readers to view an image embedded in a news posting as they read the article. This feature greatly enhances your ability to develop rich, compelling postings, using both text *and* pictures.

Be sure, however, to post such documents to the appropriate newsgroups. Most groups accept text-only postings. The alt.binaries.* newsgroups are for posting binary files—text messages that incorporate pictures, sounds, multimedia, and so on.

HOW OFTEN TO ADVERTISE YOUR WEB SITE

Another delicate issue facing Internet marketers concerns the frequency with which you advertise your Web site. You may ask, "If I can advertise in newsgroups for free, why not do it every minute of the day?" The answer isn't simple. A fairly substantial Web Browser population believes commercial advertising is an inappropriate and even dangerous use of the Net. Some users still pay for each news article they receive, and would probably resent receiving your advertising. The rule of thumb here is to *post in moderation*.

The weapon of choice for frequent news readers to combat excessive postings is the so-called "kill" file. This file contains selected words, phrases, and news titles that should be ignored and not displayed to the viewer. If you post, "**BEST WWW SITE IN THE WORLD!!!! CHECK OUT NOW!!!**" to 700 newsgroups, 10 times a day, many people will just add that headline to their kill files and never see it again. And they'll probably send several nasty e-mail messages to your company, and irate replies to the newsgroup. Change the subject of your post often and keep the content fresh to ensure your readership remains high.

Remember, your goal is to cast your company in a positive light to the Internet community. Anything you say on the Internet is out there for everyone to see. If you wouldn't say it on the 6 o'clock news, don't say it on the Internet. Even a private e-mail session can become a public announcement, so be just as careful about what you say to individuals as you are about what you say in newsgroups. If people are displeased with your reply or find it offensive, they may post it to several newsgroups for all to see. This is not a good way to win support for your product or service.

The 24-by-7 Nature of the Internet

While working with a company that had already set up a Web site, Skyline was asked to include a link to their site from ours. So we set up a phone conference to work out a few details. While on the phone, we asked for their URL so we could take a look at their site. When we typed the URL into our browser, the browser responded, "Unable to contact host." The company verified that it was the correct URL. When we mentioned the connection problem, the representative said, "Oh, it's probably turned off. We turn it off at night when we go home." They didn't understand the 24-by-7 nature of the Web.

Keep your Web site up and available around the clock whenever possible. If you can't, specify its hours in your postings.

You can limit the hours of operation for certain Web-site areas. For example, if you have a customer support staff that takes care of inquiries during specific hours, make sure you give these hours in your newsgroup postings.

TAPPING INTO TRADITIONAL CHANNELS

Promoting your Web site shouldn't stop with the Internet. Other media provide important opportunities to increase traffic at your site, and you shouldn't ignore them. You've probably noticed that almost every TV commercial now displays a company Web-site address at the end. The Sci-Fi Channel regularly airs a commercial solely dedicated to information about their Web site. The Sports Channel and ESPN continually promote their Web site on television, and flash their URL at the bottom of the TV screen allowing surfers to browse for sports scores at their leisure.

FIGURE 9-3

The Wings America homepage is an online catalogue incorporating pictures and detailed descriptions of aviation merchandise.

Anyone driving along California's Highway 101 near San Francisco sees plenty of billboards advertising Web sites. C|Net (http://www.cnet.com), a cable television show about Internet advances, has its own Web site. Every week they advertise their site on the show, and they've also taken out ads on *Yahoo*'s search site. C|Net promotes its site on all major fronts, relying on no single medium to get the word out.

Wings America (http://www.carmelnet.com/Wings/), a small store in Carmel, California, sells wooden plane replicas and other aviation goodies (see Figure 9-3). If you walk into their store and ask for a catalogue, they'll probably say something like, "It's on the Web," and hand you a business card with their Web-site address. Most patrons take the card and walk out without asking what "the Web" is, or insisting on a printed catalogue. Imagine the savings! No more printed catalogues. No more expensive mailing costs. No more "Wrong Address" stamped on returned mail.

Which brings us to the business card and the letterhead, two simple, inexpensive, and surprisingly effective ways to promote your Web site. Businesspersons are used to keeping stacks of business cards around their desks. Including your Web-site address on your card makes it easy for people to find you online. Consider adding your e-mail address to your card, as well (see Figure 9-4).

Your letterhead is just as important and convenient a Web-site marketing tool as your business cards. Your letterhead may find its way into the hands of people you'd never expect to check out your Web site. For example, you may include a note to a creditor about a payment or

FIGURE 9-4

Including your e-mail and Web site addresses on your company's business cards and letterhead is a great way to advertise in traditional channels.

Skyline
Network Technologies, Inc.

Thomas J. Kuegler Jr.

Internet Publishing, Consulting, and Marketing

P.O. Box 43162
Baltimore, MD 21236
http://www.skyline.net

Phone: 410-882-3781
Fax: 410-882-3782
kuegler@skyline.net

to an IRS agent, explaining why the cost of this book need not be depreciated over five years. One glance at your letterhead, and they'll know your Web-site address.

Including your Web-site and e-mail addresses in a direct mail piece give prospects who've never heard of your company a chance to go online and learn more about you. While they may have no interest in the product you initially contacted them about, they may find something else of interest on your site.

The purpose of your Web site often determines how you market it in other media. Are you looking for direct online sales, or just broader name recognition?

A prominent soft drink company won't look to sell 16-ounce cans of pop over the Internet. It may, however, want to provide information about its current promotional offers and giveaways. The soda company could even print its Web-site and e-mail addresses right on the can! Why not include a "comment and complaint" e-mail address along with the traditional 800 number?

Anytime you advertise in the "mainstream" media, include your Web-site address. Soon your company's URL will be as important as its phone number.

Precisely how you advertise your site in traditional media is up to you. It can be as simple as adding your URL to a business card or the bottom of a newspaper ad; it can be as complex as producing your own Web-savvy cable TV show. Your traditional media marketing plan should, however, focus on bringing more surfers to your Web site.

VALUE-ADDED MARKETING

The whole purpose of advertising and marketing your Web site on the Net is to increase traffic at your site. But Net users need a reason to click on your link. You can give them that reason by adding value to your site. Value can mean something as simple as free investment tips, or as complex as a Web-search engine. But the operative word is "free." Remember, people surf the Net every day, looking for as much free stuff as they can download in a sitting. When you give something away on your Web site, you enhance its value and greatly increase the chances of someone stopping by. You don't have to give away the farm, but you must give netsurfers something. At the very least, give them all the information they need to make an informed decision about your company.

Getting the most from your Web page should be an ongoing, company-wide project. Involve everybody, from the CEO and stockholders to your clerical and maintenance staff. And don't forget your customers! They know your company, and they can help you find the best way to add value to your Web site. Take care, though, when asking stockholders what they'd like to see online. Your annual report may be a real page-turner in the boardroom, but it won't attract many netsurfers on your site but it might attract investors looking to buy stock in your company.

Don't gear your added value to one small group of people. It should be more general. For example, many employment agencies offer free online access to job listings in particular areas of the country, or in a particular field. Your site might list job openings in your company. This also gives your company the opportunity to post information about your Web site on several additional newsgroups (see Table 9-2).

Just as some companies diversify their assets, your company should diversify its Web offerings. Providing "multiple draws" gives your site a broader demographic appeal.

When Skyline began advertising and marketing our site, we found we could reach a broader group of people this way. We came up with online magazines, Web indexes, games, MUDs, business programs—the works! Middle-aged users found our business programs interesting, and young surfers found the games and MUDs more exciting. Our Web indexes created a wider, more general draw.

Of course you could use the ideas presented in this section as your own. However, many of these examples are already in use on a lot of Web sites. They'll still create a draw, but they won't help you stand out from the crowd. No one wants to re-invent the wheel, but something

TABLE 9-2 EMPLOYMENT NEWSGROUPS

Newsgroup	Description
biz.jobs.offered	Jobs offered in business fields
comp.jobs.offered	Companies looking for computer professionals
bionet.jobs.offered	Jobs available in the bio-technical fields
misc.jobs.offered	Jobs that don't fit in other categories
misc.jobs.offered.entry	Miscellaneous entry-level positions
dc.jobs	Jobs available in the Washington, DC area

new and exciting always attracts a larger audience, especially on the Internet. Look for an original idea, something no other Web-site offers. That's what the Internet is all about, and if you have the pioneer spirit to venture onto this new medium, prepare to cut your own path.

FINDING YOUR COMPANY'S ADDED VALUE

Many online companies have found their added value on the Net. UPS, for example, allows customers to track packages, view shipping rates, and check estimated delivery times on its Web site. While UPS has no direct online sales component, the company has realized the value of allowing customers to track their packages via the Web.

Was UPS's decision to put a Web interface on their internal database designed purely to increase customer satisfaction? Maybe not. Cost savings may have been a factor as well. The more people who track packages online, the fewer will call their 800 number. The fewer people calling their 800 number, the fewer employees needed to answer the phones. So UPS's decision to add value to their Web site saves them money in the long run.

Look at the information your company typically offers for free: Do you have an internal price quote system allowing callers to use your 800 number to get immediate price quotes? If your telephone sales staff spends more time giving out price quotes than taking orders, why not put a Web front-end on your price-quote system and allow surfers immediate access over the Net?

The Web is an easy and painless way for people to download software. If your company currently offers a free software product by mail or on its company bulletin board system, why not try putting it out on the Web? Part of your Web site could contain software documentation, license restrictions, troubleshooting—and, of course, a copy of the program.

One Company's Venture into Internet Software Distribution

A few years ago a mortgage company approached us about Web advertising. When we arrived at their offices and gave them our pitch, everyone became very excited. They said they had a shareware program they wanted to mail to people who responded to an online form. When we told them how they could use the Web to distribute software, and that the software would be a draw in itself, the company president nearly kissed us! (And we're not the prettiest people!)

Putting software you already give away for free on the Web can add significantly to your site's value. Software demos, insurance-rate quote programs, sample source code from a book you're selling—all add value to your Web site.

If you have an in-house programming staff, have them create new games, business programs, or other useful programs for the Web. Take the example of the mortgage company trying to attract more traffic to its Web site. The company created a program that calculates loan amortization tables from user input. It then put together a Web page with a form with three input variables—loan amount, interest rate, and term of loan. Once users completed the form, the mortgage company's Web server would calculate a loan amortization table with monthly payment amounts, total interest paid on the loan, and total amount paid over the full term of the loan.

After outputting the loan amortization table, they gave the user a choice between trying new input variables and displaying a new table, or filling out a loan application to one of the company's mortgage brokers. The broker would then respond to the inquiry via e-mail or by phone.

In this scenario, the mortgage company's loan amortization program attracted users who may have had no intention of going through this particular mortgage company for a loan. With a little thought, and very little effort, the company added tremendous value to its Web site.

TAPPING INTO THE ADDED VALUE OF OTHER COMPANIES

Perhaps your company has neither the ability nor the finances to modify its in-house database systems to make them accessible from the Web. Computers may even be new to your company, part of your CEO's commitment to catching up with technology. That doesn't mean your business can't establish a valuable online presence. You can take advantage of the groundwork laid by other companies. You can beg, barter, or buy technologies from other firms that have developed Web pages or programs that can greatly enhance your site.

You can also "steal" others' technology. No, we're not talking about corporate espionage or software piracy. Here's what we mean: Suppose you're a small, local shipping company that does business with UPS. You want to make it possible for your customers to track UPS packages instantly from your Web site. One way to

Ask and You Shall Receive

Skyline has received many requests for some of our CGI programs. If we believe the company asking is not a competitor, we may give the technology away for free, or offer to host their information on our system. It never hurts to ask. The worst a company can say is no.

accomplish this is to link your site to UPS's package tracking page. The method is simple; unfortunately it means people will enter their information on a UPS Web page, and spend less time looking at your logo, slogan, and other company hallmarks.

Another way to approach this project is with a little investigative work. Check out the code for the UPS tracking submission page, or have a Web consultant do it for you. They list the variable names, types, and methods for submitting the page to their CGI program. Using this information, you can create a form on *your* Web site, with *your* logo, through which users can access the UPS system.

Forrest Stroud (http://uts.cc.utexas.edu/~neuroses), a student at the University of Texas at Austin, set up a Web page to help Windows users find the best and latest Internet software using the program *WinSock* (http://cwsapps.texas.net). Figure 9-5 is an example of Stroud's "Consummate WinSock Applications List." He searched for links to other sites, wrote reviews on the various software available on the Net, and put it all together in an easy-to-read format. What happened? Thousands of Web surfers hungry for the *WinSock* information and programs he showcased quickly overwhelmed his school's Internet connection. Now Forrest "mirrors" his site on many other sites around the globe. (When two sites offer identical Web pages, they're considered "mirrored.") To do this, he regularly posts his HTML code so sponsoring providers can download it and offer the page on their own sites.

You can mirror your Web-site code from many different places. Mirroring attracts many users who'd otherwise go to another site for the information. Why would surfers choose your site? In many cases, the original site is mirrored because heavy traffic has created a logjam. Plus, mirroring a site closer to the surfer's actual locale often provides faster response times.

Whether you beg, buy, borrow, barter, or steal your added site value, make sure what you do supports your Web site's purpose. There's no sense in adding value to your site if it keeps surfers from viewing your stuff, and little value is added if your project takes up so much bandwidth that serious inquiries can't get though.

Examine your options carefully. If you find you've committed too many resources to add value to your site, pull the plug. Web code is easy to change. If the site isn't used to your advantage, you can always try something else.

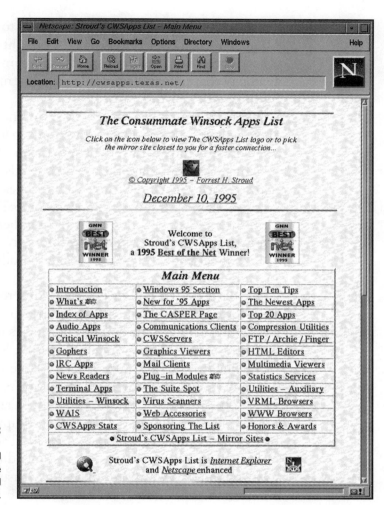

FIGURE 9-5

Stroud's CWSApps List is mirrored
around the world because the
original site was overwhelmed
with hits.

WILL THEY SHOP?

Nothing in life is guaranteed, and this is especially true when it comes
to Internet shopping. If you follow the advice we offer in this chapter,
yes, they will shop. The real question is, will they buy? In most retail
sales environments, the most commonly heard phrase is, "No, thank
you. I'm just looking." Advertising and marketing your site effectively
will attract customers who stop in and take a look around. The site's
actual content determines how many shoppers will part with their hard-
earned cash.

Let's say you've put some of our ideas to work, and generate about 100,000 hits an hour, but no one has bought a single item from the site. As with traditional advertising, the medium may not be at fault. It may be the product, price, acceptable payment methods, lackluster site—or a thousand other things.

Because consumers connect to the Internet from a single access point, they can check out several online stores in a matter of minutes. This is an incredible advantage for comparison shoppers, and a great disadvantage for you. If another company sells the same product online at a lower price with similar service, the user can learn about it in minutes, or even seconds, and buy from your competitor without wasting a micron of shoe leather. The growing number of Web sites and search engines gives the consumer even more freedom to roam the Web in search of bargains. A few mouse clicks produce price lists from dozens of online stores.

In this environment it's critical to differentiate your company from your competitors. Offer a 30-day money-back guarantee, free shipping in the continental U.S.—whatever it takes to stand out.

Because the Web is a medium with a low cost of entry, everyone from small mom-and-pop shops to large corporations competes for consumer dollars on the Internet. If you're a small company with no storefront and low overhead, you may be able to compete with larger operations strictly on price. A larger company with branch offices in every major city may be able to offer local service nationwide.

If your goal is to sell products online, directly from your Web site, gear your marketing toward that end. Measure the effectiveness of your Internet advertising and marketing efforts by calculating the actual sales the site has generated. If your online sales don't improve over time, don't be afraid to go back to the drawing board and rethink your site design and marketing strategy.

Rather than become a "Web-order" company, perhaps your goal is to increase sales at your storefront locations. Your Web site should complement your products and services, providing information that may not be available in stores. Your Web catalogue could include warranty information, more information on extended service plans, detailed manufacturer specifications, and other information store personnel may have difficulty finding. Include directions to store locations, business hours, telephone numbers, and names of store managers. Let surfers know they can visit your store to experience your products' exceptional quality for themselves.

Mail-order sales are similar to storefront sales, but the customer must take an extra step to purchase the product or service. Using your Web site as an online catalogue can save on printing and postage costs. Include your telephone number on every page, as well as accepted modes of payment. Include as much information as possible so the customer can make an informed decision.

In all cases, tell your customers *why* they should shop with your company. The rules and practices that dictate how you advertise in other media hold true for the Internet: If you have the lowest prices or best customer service on the Net, let people know.

Customer relations are just as important on the Web as they are in the non-electronic world. As Harvey Mackey points out in his book, *Swim With the Sharks*, getting a customer is easy; *maintaining* one is where real salesmanship and customer relations count. Did you ever buy a car from a dealership that followed up with postcard oil-change reminders—and included their current oil-change specials? When taking an order from the Web, ask your customers to include their e-mail addresses so you can let them know about special deals or new products, for repeat customers only. Send them an e-mail thank-you letter, telling them you appreciate their business and hope they'll shop on your Web site again in the future. Include an e-mail address where people can send comments or complaints.

Keeping customers happy makes for repeat business. Satisfied customers may even tell the rest of the Internet about the great experience they had with you.

Remember...

- When trying to attract customers to your Web site be sure to:

    Trade links with other Web sites

    Submit your company's URL to Web search sites

    Include your Web and e-mail addresses in other traditional forms of advertising

    For a short-term increase in hit numbers, post creative messages to newsgroups

- To find your company's added value, solicit ideas from everyone in the company. Make your draw general, or focus on having many specific draws. Multiple draws provide a more demographically mixed group of surfers.

- If your company is short on Web designing ability or finances, tap other companies' established added value.

- To attract surfers to buy, find your company's online niche. Then determine the type of sale that works best for you: online, in-store, or mail order. Tell customers why they should shop at your site—lowest online prices, best customer service, and so on.

- Maintaining good customer relations ensures repeat customers.

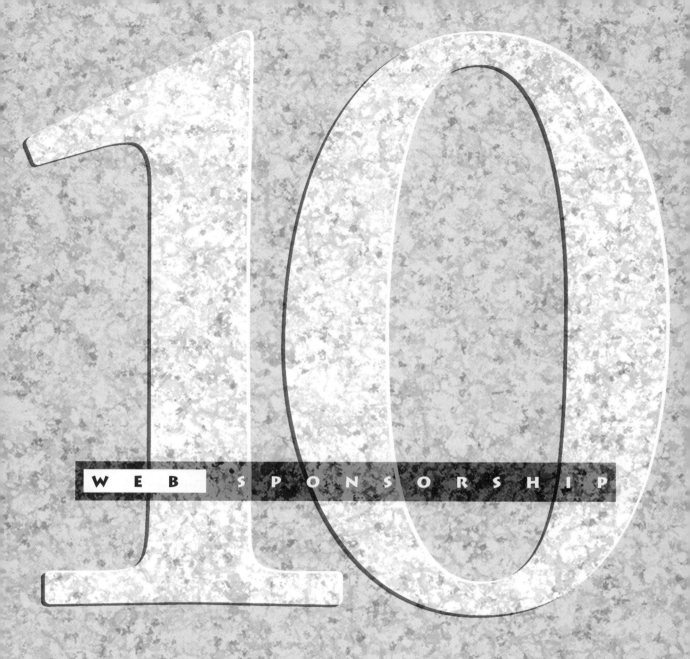

10 **WEB** SPONSORSHIP

Of the many strategies put forward in this book to increase traffic to your Web site, sponsoring someone else's site is one of the easiest and most effective. In this chapter, we look at several aspects of Web-site sponsorship, including hit rates, targeting strategies, the importance of strategic links, and cost. We also discuss the advantages and disadvantages of sponsoring various types of sites, and explore some of the ways Web-site sponsorship can help you in your never-ending quest for accurate online demographics.

ALL THE HITS, ALL THE TIME

Sponsoring a Web site is a lot like sponsoring a program on Public Television or a race car in the Daytona 500. Basically, your company pays a fee to an established Web site to post your company's logo on its pages, along with a link back to your site. (Race car sponsors would kill to connect with potential customers this directly and easily!) Web-page sponsorship quickly increases traffic at your site by giving you almost instant access to the established viewer bases of other sites.

Magazines and newspapers sell advertising space based on circulation rates. That's how it's done on the Internet, too, except that a Web site's "circulation" is defined by its "hit rate." Sites with high hit rates (lots of surfer traffic) can demand more for sponsorship dollars. However, paying $20,000 a quarter to sponsor a site that gets a million hits a week could end up being more expensive than sponsoring several smaller sites. Hosting 10 sites that typically draw only 100,000 hits a week can give your company the same overall exposure, but often at a lower total cost.

Paid advertising on a Web site often takes the form of a *banner* or other small graphic. A banner is, as the name implies, a wide, short graphic advertisement displayed somewhere on the Web page. On high-traffic sites, banners can be expensive. Currently, sites that sell advertising space just break even, because they must spend large amounts of money to attract Web surfers, which generates the big hit rates, which attracts online advertisers. It's a catch-22. Of course, everybody's betting that, as the Internet grows, the scales will shift.

The most popular companies for sponsoring Web pages are Internet providers. Always looking for ways to increase their own hit counts, they typically add the hits of sponsored sites to their own hit count figure in their own Web advertising.

Your company can—and should—sponsor as many Web sites as it can afford, but you should be somewhat selective about the sites you sponsor. Be sure the sites you choose are of a general nature or are in some way related to your field of business. And make absolutely certain they don't *conflict* with the goals and/or themes of your site. The National Organization for Women (NOW) (http://now.org/now/home.html), for example, would be ill advised to sponsor a page on the Playboy site (http://www.playboy.com).

Most of the larger magazines and newspapers are beginning to venture onto the Web in hopes of generating additional advertising dollars. Because these types of publications already have an advertiser base, they can simply call up their clients and ask if they want to join them online. Initially, advertising fees may be kept low to entice advertisers to take the Internet plunge.

WEB SITES AT THE HEAD OF THE CLASS

Hooking up with a Web page with lots of traffic is one of the fastest ways to increase hits to your site, but paying for the connection isn't the only way to do it. Some Web-page authors, hoping to showcase their ideas without going to the expense of setting up sites of their own, need space on a Web server, for which they are often willing to exchange links. You could provide that space and automatically add the new site's audience to your own.

You can find plenty of examples of these young designers on college campuses around the country. Many students are creative and have plenty of time on their hands to design interesting pages utilizing the latest, greatest features of the hottest Web browsers. In-house designers may be a little slower to adopt newer technology and are probably 9-to-5ers anyway. Students have time to surf the Web to find and emulate sites they think are popular or interesting.

A student at a local university could, for example, create some Web pages that become extremely popular. Hundreds of thousands of Web surfers could find out about the student's pages and begin overloading the university's Internet connection. The university could then decide to remove the pages from the school's Web server. The student would, of course, want to continue offering such a popular site, but, being a starving college student, wouldn't have the resources to pay a Web-presence provider to maintain the pages. The student would be highly motivated to solicit help from organizations already on the Web. Some company could then agree to put the student's pages on the company Web server for free, as long as a banner or logo was included, stating that the company, out of the kindness of its heart, had graciously provided the Web space.

Sound farfetched? Well, that's more or less the story behind "Yahoo!," one of the most successful Web sites in the history of the Net. "Yahoo!" debuted in April 1994, the inspiration of two Stanford University graduate students. David Filo and Jerry Yang assembled a wide array of links that personally interested them, and broke them down by topic. They customized the site so it could efficiently locate, identify, and edit material stored throughout the Web. Before long, their online Web site directory became so popular that they just had to start their own company. (They were only three months away from obtaining their graduate degrees, which they put on hold to pursue their business.) With $1 million in venture capital from Sequoia Capital, the two launched the Yahoo! Corporation of Mountain View, California.

The venture capitalists who invested in "Yahoo!" initially thought the site should charge users, but Filo and Yang disagreed. The two former grad students, who knew well the giveaway culture of the Net, thought the advertisers should support the site, so it could remain free to Web surfers. They recognized the importance of sponsorship early in the game, and today their site is an advertising leader.

The only real drawback to this kind of sponsorship is that you never know which sites will become the next "Yahoo!" and which will flop. On the other hand, the only thing your company has to lose is a little time and a few bytes of disk space. If the pages become very successful, you may even want to hire the students to design your company's Web pages!

You can find advertisements by students or others hoping to find sponsors for their Web pages in newsgroups and on the Web pages themselves. If the pages are successful, you'll have a lot of competition for bringing the pages to your site. It's not unheard of to offer students money to include your link on their pages.

ON TARGET WITH THE RIGHT SITE

Sponsoring someone else's Web pages is an excellent way to get instant exposure to a quantifiable surfer population. In other words, with this type of sponsorship, your company can automatically target specific demographic groups. In the case of "Yahoo!," the demographics are rather general. A better example of a targeted site is "PoliticsUSA" (http//www.politicsusa.com).

The creators of "PoliticsUSA" are taking their Web site in a different direction from sites like "Yahoo!" They plan to charge a modest monthly fee for the use of certain areas of the site. But probably the biggest difference between the two sites is market. "Yahoo!" reaches a large number of mainstream surfers, while "PoliticsUSA" connects with a specific group of Web surfers with an interest in U.S. political events. Steve Hull, president and CEO of "PoliticsUSA," believes that "the Internet is the most important development in politics since the coming of television, and that ultimately it could be even more important." His publication is a sort of daily newspaper focusing on political events and information. While the online publication doesn't currently charge users a monthly fee, the company sells ad space, Web space, and products within the site.

Hull feels the Internet can provide a way for politicians to speak directly to the public, and more importantly, a way for the public to respond. Certain areas of the site require registration, but Hull's group asks for no personal demographic information other than your name and address. "PoliticsUSA" is a new Web site offering its services free while the company makes the site more stable and robust. The efficacy of charging Web surfers for site access has yet to be demonstrated.

Sponsoring other Web sites is an excellent way to target previously established audiences, and it will help generate qualified leads. If you stick to sites that target your specific audience, you'll not only increase your chances for success, you'll also avoid offending netizens who feel blatant advertising on the Internet is wrong.

BEING "COOL" ON A BROWSER SITE

Among the companies getting the greatest number of hits from new users are Web-browser developers. One of the reasons their sites are so popular is that they often include their site addresses on the software, so the company's site is the first one a newcomer sees. This gives browser developers a huge advantage; if a company sells or gives away 100,000 browsers, that company's Web site is all but guaranteed 100,000 hits.

Most Web-browser applications allow users to change that initial site listing, but many users may be too lazy or technically unsophisticated to make this change on their own. Consequently, every time the user pulls the browser up on the screen, the developer's Web site displays. It's no wonder Netscape and NCSA have such vast hit numbers. Netscape even keeps a large portion of browser documentation on its Web site, which encourages people to return. While browser developers have yet to charge surfers to view their sites, they have begun to sell advertising space.

Private online networks such as *CompuServe* (http://www.compuserve.com) and *America Online (AOL)* (http://www.aol.com) have taken a similar approach by including their online software in modem packaging. These companies learned early on that when customers buy a modem, they don't always understand just how to use it. With the CompuServe disk right there in the box, it's easy for new users to begin exploring the private network's online offerings. The hope is that once users try an online service, they'll be hooked and want to sign up.

There are two ways to get exposure on a browser developer's Web site. The obvious way is by buying advertising space on the Web server. But you could also try to get your company mentioned on the site's "What's Cool" or "What's New" pages. These lists are usually the first Internet directory listings a new user sees, and they can be very effective. If your site is included on one of these lists, prepare to be bombarded with hits. The lists typically maintain links to "new" or "cool" sites for about a week before updating or replacing them. If your Web traffic skyrockets for no apparent reason, check some of the browser developers sites to see if you've been noticed.

E-ZINES FOR EVERYBODY

"E-zines" are electronic magazines that distribute over the Internet. Just like their hard-copy counterparts, e-zines are numerous and cover a wide variety of topics. Many traditional magazines now supplement their publications with Web sites. These make up the majority of professionally created and maintained e-zines. Because e-zines are inexpensive to create and distribute, many amateurs are also getting into online publishing. Advertising in e-zines, both professional and amateur, can be a great way to target your audience.

Many e-zines, such as *HotWired* (http://www.hotwired.com), require users to register before they can view the site. Registration can be free, as in the case of *HotWired*, or there can be a fee involved, as in the case of *Hustler Magazine* (http://hustler.onprod.com/ns/home.html).

Registration typically is used to collect demographic information about subscribers. Publishers use this data to focus the e-zine's stories and articles, as well as to provide sponsors and advertisers with the information they need to determine whether the 'zine targets their markets. We'll say more about e-zine demographics later in this chapter.

If your company is unable to find an e-zine that targets your market niche, consider creating your own e-zine in-house. This is an excellent way to add value to your Web site and offer free information to other netizens. In addition, an in-house 'zine enables your company to continually promote itself. Take care not to put too much company propaganda into the publication; endless boasting turns people off or scares them away. Save the bombast for your company's main Web site. The e-zine should be informative, educational, entertaining, or a combination of the three. All the pages can provide links to your company's homepage, with a little tag next to the link stating something like, "This page sponsored by the Wild Western Widget Company of Provo, Utah!"

Setting up a new Web site on the Internet is adventure enough without adding the complexities of e-zine publishing. In many ways, publishing an e-zine is just as involved as offline publishing; you'll need a constant influx of new articles, stories, pictures, and possibly other advertisers. Any company can create a bad e-zine; it takes talent, time, and commitment to maintain a quality publication other Web surfers will want to spend time with. This may be something your company will want to try later.

On the other hand, your company's e-zine doesn't have to offer anything it isn't already publishing. For example, if you already publish a monthly customer newsletter, putting that publication on the Web won't require any additional employees to write articles, the documents can be saved in a format used for Web pages, and with a relatively small amount of creative HTML magic, your company has an e-zine. Compared to writing the articles that appear in your e-zine, the actual design work involved in creating the HTML format is easy. (A word of advice: Don't involve your computer department in the content of your e-zine. Let the writers, editors, and others who do such a good job of publishing your newsletter crank out the articles, and send the technical people home.)

Currently, online publishing looks a lot like broadcast television. Viewers don't expect to pay to see locally broadcast shows. The programming is paid for by commercial sponsors. We can watch Monday Night Football or the Sunday Evening Movie at no additional cost because Purina Dog Chow, Quaker Oats, and Summer's Eve foot the bill. It wasn't until the proliferation of cable television that producers began finding ways to charge viewers for programming. In the case of ShowTime and HBO, advertising-free viewing is a selling point.

Almost every offline magazine with an online publication accepts sponsorships, or is seriously considering offering them, soon. Some offer free subscriptions and depend exclusively on sponsorships to generate revenues. Web sponsorship is becoming popular, cropping up on many sites. If a site doesn't offer outside sponsorship, chances are it showcases its own pages using banners. As Web sponsorships become more common, more and more netizens will come to accept the Internet as a commercial medium.

Buying advertising space on an e-zine is much the same as buying print advertising. In some cases, the 'zine will want all the images, art, and text ready to go when you place the ad, while others will help your company develop an effective banner advertisement to place on the site. However, if the advertisement is going to link to your company's homepage, many advertisers will assume you have your own staff or contractors to handle ad development.

TABLE 10-1 LIST OF SITES THAT ACCEPT SPONSORSHIPS

Site Name	Site Address	Number of Visitors Per Week	Description	Monthly Cost
ESPNet	http://espnet.sportszone.com	400,000	Sports news and information	$33,000
Yahoo!	http://www.yahoo.com	250,000	The most popular Internet search site	$20,000
Pathfinder	http://www.pathfinder.com	187,000	Contains the Time-Warner magazines *Fortune*, *People*, and *Time*	$10,000
The Spot	http://www.mtv.com	30,000	The online version of MTV's "Real World"	$16,500
HotWired	http://www.hotwired.com	25,000	News and features for the hip online community	$15,000

Before you place your advertising in an e-zine, consider three things—the 'zine's "circulation," its audience, and the cost. While advertising on *HotWired* may seem cheaper than advertising on ESPNet, the cost per visitor is higher. Their respective audiences are also very different. The demographics of offline magazines that publish on the Web should carry over into the online world, but don't be afraid to call and ask hard questions.

Sponsoring Web sites is a great way to increase your hit rate and target your market. Knowing the e-zine's demographics will help you target your marketing efforts to a particular audience. Unless your company has found a way to grow money on trees, make sure your advertisements reach the right people and that you get the most bang for your buck.

SPONSORING COOL PAGES

Sponsoring "cool" pages is another way to attract a very specific crowd with specific tastes and interests. What makes a page cool is up to the surfer. A computer programmer may find the site cool because of the extensive programming design that went into it; a fashion designer may like the excellent use and integration of color; a child may find the site interesting because it offers entertaining games.

Cool Pages, Hot Pages, Hip Pages, and Pages of the Week are all popular Web site raters that attract a lot of traffic.

An example of a site many men will undoubtedly find "cool," is "Toupsie's Babes of the Web" (http://www.tyrell.net/~robtoups/BABE.html) (see Figure 10-1.). Toupsie has scoured the Net for women with homepages and set up a list of links to them. His site also includes a rating of the women's attractiveness. Women who find their pages listed on Toupsie's site see their hit count shoot up almost immediately. Toupsie doesn't currently accept any outside sponsorship of his pages.

Sites offering lists of links often put out lists of the most popular surfer-selected sites, along with some kind of site rating. Because a surfer has no idea where a link will lead, sites that rate other sites offer a way to determine site quality.

TAKING A RIDE ON THE ROULETTE WHEEL

One of the greatest challenges of the Web is *finding* anything. With so many sites going online every day, no listing service can really keep up.

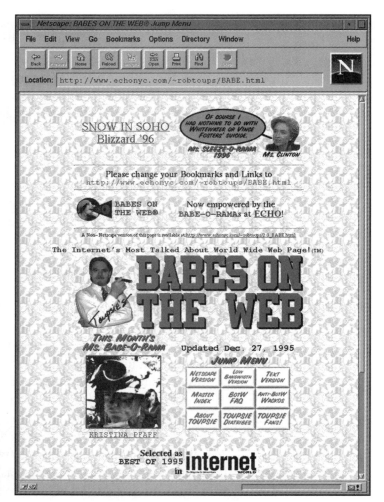

FIGURE 10-1

The "Babes of the Web" site is very difficult to get to at times, because thousands of people are trying to access it.

And to get to a site, you must know the exact "address"; key words won't work.

Some sites have managed to capitalize on the Net's irregular nature with random Web search engines called "roulette wheels." To use a roulette wheel, users simply click on the icon and the program sends them to a randomly generated URL. Roulette wheels give users a chance to view Web sites they may never have thought to visit. They can also take surfers to lesser-known areas of your Web site. Your site may offer pages your company feels are informative and interesting, yet people

Skyline's Rating System

After setting up our Web site, we noticed that our most popular item was our list of links to other Web sites. The list was compiled by us and our employees, and simply included sites we liked. Our first thought was that the list was popular because it was such a prominent item on the menu. So we changed our menu layout, and even tried hiding the list to see how users would react. To our surprise, they continued to find and use our list of links more than any other item on the site.

We then decided to make our list of links are entirely separate section of our site, and to organize the links into more specific categories. We decided to use the name Resource Exchanger, or REX. Because REX also sounded like the name of a dog, we used a canine motif. We came up with a cute picture of a scruffy old mutt to serve as the page's logo. We also made it possible for users to add sites *they* thought were cool to the list. They could even add their own Web sites. REX quickly became one of our most popular attractions.

We liked the concept of rating sites and came up with a rating system of our own. We used a scale of 1 to 5, and because our motif was already rather doggy, we used tiny fire hydrants instead of, say, stars, to bullet each rating. Skyline plans to offer hydrant awards to sites we deem excellent and worthy of note.

---

just won't visit them. Sponsoring an online URL roulette wheel, or creating one in-house, will allow your company to point surfers to those lesser-known regions of your site (see Figure 10-2).

This type of "game" is an effective way of getting surfers to at least glance at the more obscure pages on your Web site. When you sponsor sites offering roulette-type programs, you can even negotiate a higher percentage of appearances for your site. You don't want to skew the program too much, but you do want to increase the odds that surfers will reach your site.

TARGETING YOUR MARKET WITH SEARCH ENGINES

Focusing your company's marketing efforts on the people most likely to become customers is as important on the Internet as it is in the offline world. Yet targeting your market on the Internet is slightly more difficult than finding your audience in other media, because your customers must find *you*. That's why they created search engines.

Search-engine advertising is gaining popularity on the Net as a very effective target-marketing tool. In March 1995, InfoSeek Corporation

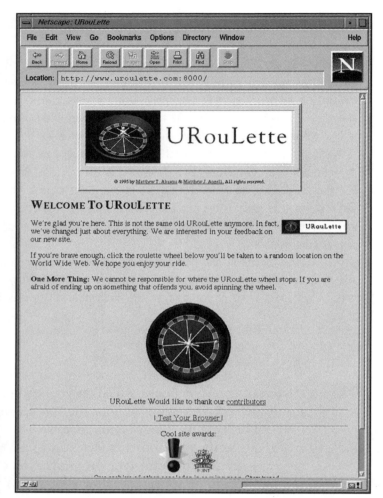

FIGURE 10-2

Web roulette wheel programs allow surfers to visit randomly selected sites or pages. This adds value to your Web site and takes surfers to lesser-known pages.

(http://www.infoseek.com) of Santa Clara, California, introduced the first search-engine ads to the Web; many others soon followed. Bill Peck, director of interactive advertising at InfoSeek, feels that search-engine advertising "is the ultimate qualification tool for the Internet." Many search sites match only a relatively small number of sites to a particular key word, returning just 10 to 25 sites at a time. This allows a search site to display several ads at the same time relating to a single key word.

One type of search engine, called a "spider" or "Web crawler," goes out unattended and gathers information found on Web pages. These programs gather the links in their search-engine databases and use the words found in the pages' text of key words. Using search engines based on this technology is a great way to locate obscure information on the Web, because the authors of the page may not have used the same key words to describe their site or page that you use in looking for the information.

Web crawlers have their downside, however. The chief disadvantage to these types of search engines is that they are key word–dependent; that is, a student doing a research project about penguins may end up at a site featuring Batman's archenemy.

The beauty of search-engine advertising is that your site gets qualified leads in addition to advertising space. The information currently returned by search sites is limited to text-only descriptions, displaying no graphical images. Yet some advertisers include images at the top of the display that relate in some way to the entered key word. A slight drawback to this approach is that some surfers browsing the Net over slow connections may not wait for the graphical elements to download.

Industry experts believe search-engine advertising is poised for exponential growth. The emergence of the technology marks one of the first uses of the Web to generate qualified leads. According to Robert Davis, CEO of Lycos Inc. (http://www.lycos.com), a company that maintains a Web-search site offering search-engine advertising, "The search-engine marketplace is explosive."

But James Kennedy, managing editor of WebTrack's *InterAd Monthly*, feels that search-engine advertising isn't suited to everyone. "When you go out to buy links, you should look at two sources—those that give you mass reach, and those that give you targeted advertising," Kennedy says. He believes that advertising in high-traffic areas should be used mostly to promote well-known brands or for name recognition.

Search-engine ad rates vary from a couple of thousand dollars to $20,000-plus. This form of advertising benefits companies looking for niche products and services and may not be particularly suited to companies looking to reach the masses. However, you can use the key words targeting your advertising to supplement your banner advertising program, rather than replace it.

HOW CAN I GET NET USAGE DEMOGRAPHICS?

Gathering reliable demographic data on Web surfers is no easy task. You've heard the joke about the Internet survey that tried to determine how many people on the Net could use e-mail. It utilized a simple form that read something like, "Those that know how to use e-mail, send an e-mail message to yes_survey@yoursite.com; those who don't, send an e-mail message to no_survey@yoursite.com."

The frustrating fact is, the only way to learn anything about these netizens of cyberspace is by asking them what you want to know. Many sites request visitor registration in an effort to collect demographic data.

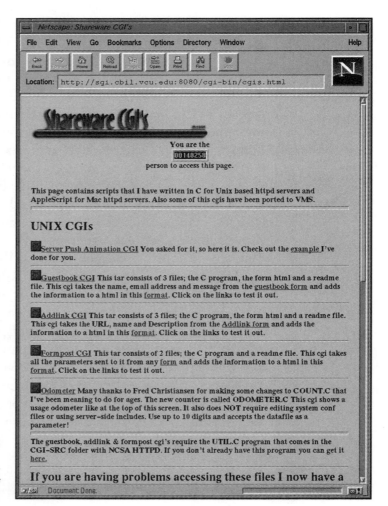

FIGURE 10-3

A mileage counter is a simple and easy way to approximate the number of people who have visited your site.

But even if users do fill out your forms, you have no way of knowing whether anything they enter is true.

One of the most obvious things you'll want to know about the people who visit your site is their number. You must be able to count your hits. Any good Web-presence provider will furnish your company with some means of gathering hit information. (They may also give you some ideas about gathering user data.) A simple "mileage counter" is an easy solution (see Figure 10-3). This program counts the number of times a Web page is viewed. But a hit rate of 100 can mean 100 people have seen a page, or that one person saw it 100 times.

"Guestbooks" offer another way to learn about visitors to your site. A guestbook program can ask users for particular demographic information without requiring it. They're a lot like real-world guest books used at museums or weddings. Users enter personal information and comments in a sort of log that your company can review. Many users with personal homepages have guest books where visitors can comments on the Web page, or through which they contact the person whose site they're visiting. (Surfers may feel uncomfortable contacting your company this way.)

The problem with guestbooks is that they provide no incentive to enter the personal information you want. Why would anybody spend their Web time filling out your guestbook if they don't have to? Many people like the anonymity the Internet provides, and prefer to remain nameless. Optional guestbooks also skew your demographics. The only thing you can know for certain is that you have a population of users who actually fill out guestbooks!

A good place to look for simple shareware mileage-counter and guestbook programs is:

http://sgi.cbil.vcu.edu:8080/cgi-bin/cgis.html.

REGISTRATION? WE DON'T NEED NO STINKING REGISTRATION!

The best way to get demographic information about visitors to your Web site is with some type of registration form. Registration forms require users to give minimal information to gain access to the site. This could include names, user names, and e-mail addresses. They also ask users to select passwords, which they must use for future access to the site. In addition to this minimal required information, you can include space for optional information that allows your company to massage your output to better fit your audience.

When sponsoring other Web sites or paying for banner advertising, you'll want to determine whether the sites require registration. If they do, ask if you can access registration information on the surfers that click on your ads. This information will help determine whether your banner advertisements target the right people. Your Web site may generate thousands of hits, but if your potential customers don't see it, you're wasting your marketing money. An ad stating "Click here for the greatest product ever invented for the mouth!" may attract lots of hits, but if the product is denture creme and your company is advertising on a Generation X Web site, you won't reach the appropriate demographic.

As more and more sites try registration forms to gather demographic information, more and more users will get sick of the process. No one wants to keep track of hundreds of user names and passwords for different Web sites. This may also inspire users to enter bogus or otherwise misleading information on your registration forms—when they don't just avoid your site altogether. The last thing you want to do is alienate users.

One way to mellow the process is to provide the forms, but make registration completely optional. Surfers won't be burdened by red tape, and, because you're asking, not telling, you'll be surprised how many will fill out your forms honestly.

DEMANDING MORE

As commercial advertising on the Internet becomes more commonplace and more companies find themselves marketing products and services on the Web, advertisers will begin demanding more sophisticated demographic information, and ads targeting specific audiences. Advertisers are becoming Web savvy. They know the difference between a "hit" and a *person*, and they consider hit counts nothing more than Internet traffic reports. A figure like 200,000 hits a day is almost meaningless. It's like a television station saying that the station's ads and programming were viewed 200,000 times a day; the station could be running 100 commercials and 100 programs a day with a viewing audience of only 1,000.

When you're ready to advertise online, you'll want to determine the number of people that see your ad—not the number of hits the site receives. You may even want to ask for the average number of hits per person; this will give you some idea as to the number of pages a person actually views. Make sure the site places your ad prominently.

You should know the specific traffic count or hit rate for the page displaying your ad, and where your ad is placed on the page. Most users surfing the Internet won't have the largest monitors or the best graphics cards, so the resolution at which the people you want to reach view the Web pages often is limited. They won't have the fastest Internet connections, either. Make sure your ad is placed close to the top of the page, or between two of the most traveled links. This ensures that every surfer who downloads the Web page sees your ad.

Amid this discussion of target marketing and demographics, it's important to remember that the Internet has its own peculiar demographic makeup. The Net boasts about 30 million users worldwide as of this writing. That's about 10 percent of the U.S. population (although netizens are found in every corner of the planet). It's a diverse group, and making generalizations about the online community—as many Web-presence providers and online service reps do—is a difficult and distorting exercise. And yet, it's also a group with many things in common. After all, they're all online.

THE COST OF WEB ADVERTISING

Advertising a Web site can be far more expensive than designing one. A banner ad on a high-traffic Web site can cost more than $20,000 a month! That's more than the start-up cost of a simple Web site and Internet connection. However, if you're going to spend a lot of money on advertising, make sure you spend it well.

If your company plans to spend a lot on advertising, make sure the investment is proportionate to your investment in the Web site itself. Site content must be dynamic and informative to keep surfers coming back. Spending lots of money on advertising does no good if people leave your homepage as soon as they see it!

Consider advertising after you develop the site and test it for a certain period of time. For example, you wouldn't want to put an 800 number in a newspaper or television ad if you were unsure your telephone lines were working properly. Similarly, make sure your Web site is well-designed and fully functional before telling the world it exists.

To test your site and determine whether it's ready for prime time, use the free methods of advertising we discussed Chapter 9. When posting to newsgroups, include in your message that your company is testing a new Web site and you'd appreciate comments or complaints about it. This encourages users to test your site and gives your company a feel for the pulse of the Web.

Asking Netizens for Comments

Whenever Skyline develops a new Web-based program or interactive page, we post to newsgroups and search sites hoping to attract a small but steady stream of surfers. We include a note in the newsgroup posting stating that this program or page is new, and that we would appreciate comments or suggestions. Users have been more than forthcoming. We've had a wide range of responses, from complaints about lack of functionality to competitors offering ideas about potential clients to whom we should market our program.

These responses have helped us better determine user demographics. Users also like to know if we implement their ideas or suggestions. If we make a change based on a user's suggestion, we e-mail that user, thank him or her for the suggestion, and attach the URL where the change can be found. This provides customer service before the sale, and keeps surfers coming back.

When Yahoo! opened its doors as a commercial venture, the founders charged advertisers $60,000 for a three-month run. "We were unusual in that we already had a product that people liked," says company co-founder Jerry Yang. "Yahoo!" attracts more than 750,000 people daily, and provides links to more than 100,000 Web sites. "Yahoo!" also lists products sold on the Internet, and even has links to contests and surveys.

"Commercialism has made it a more complex medium," says Yang.

Yahoo! already sports a "Who's Who" of Internet advertisers, including MCI, Netscape, MasterCard, and NECX.

You say you don't have $60,000 sitting around to spend for online advertising? Well, "Yahoo!" can still help you out. For only $1000 a week, you can get a screen shot, logo, or thumbnail sketch; a two-line description of your Web site, and a link to your site from one of Yahoo!'s heavily traveled pages. They call the program "Web Launch" and expect the price to rise as traffic increases to the pages.

Netscape, on the other hand, charges advertisers by the number of times a surfer sees an advertiser's banner. (Netscape calls these "exposures.") Different pages and sections of Netscape's site receive varying levels of hits, and advertising is sold based on the average number of hits in prior months. They charge $25 to $30 per thousand exposures. Table 10-2 provides a breakdown of levels and costs.

Another Web site that sells Web-based advertising based on monthly rates is that of Ziff-Davis Interactive (http://www.zdnet.com). Packages range in cost from $2,000 a month for advertising on a single, lightly

TABLE 10-2 NETSCAPE'S ADVERTISING PROGRAMS

Advertising Package	Estimated Number of Exposures	Approximate Price
Platinum	1,000,000	$25,000–$30,000
Gold	750,000	$18,750–$22,500
Silver	500,000	$12,500–15,000
Static Page	100,000	$2,500–$3,000
Global Edition Sponsorship Programs		
Global Edition (except US)	250,000	$6,250–$7,500
Japanese Edition	200,000	$5,000–$6,000
German Edition	150,000	$3,750–$4,500
French Edition	150,000	$3,750–$4,500

traveled page, or up to $40,000 for a three-month package. Package deals include an additional "middle" page on the Ziff-Davis Web server, the page where links from banner ads go. The middle page can then link the surfer to your own Web server, or to other links of your choice.

ESPN (http://espnet.sportszone.com), a leader in sports news and information on the Web, charges $100,000 a quarter for an ad on their e-zine, but e-zine content is free. ESPN's Web site receives almost 400,000 visits weekly.

So, you ask, do any of these companies actually generate revenue? Yes, they do, and in many cases they do very well (see Table 10-3).

The advertising revenue of these companies is sure to increase over time. Alex Brown and Sons estimates that Web-generated ad revenue will jump from $20 million a year in 1995 to $1.4 billion in 1998. Forrester Research of Cambridge, Massachusetts, makes a slightly more conservative estimate, putting 1998 ad revenue at $727 million, up from $37 million in 1995. WebTrack Information Services (http://www.webtrack.com), of New York City, surveyed 270 U.S. companies. Those companies spent $12.4 million to advertise on 175 different Web sites.

TABLE 10-3 4TH QUARTER 1995 ADVERTISING REVENUE FIGURES

Company	Web Site Address	Revenue
Netscape	http://www.netscape.com	$1,766,000
Lycos	http://www.lycos.com	$1,300,000
Infoseek	http://www.infoseek.com	$1,200,000
Yahoo	http://www.yahoo.com	$1,086,000
Pathfinder	http://www.pathfinder.com	$810,000
Hot Wired	http://www.hotwired.com	$720,000
WebCrawler	http://www.webcrawler.com	$660,000
ESPNet SportZone	http://espnet.sportszone.com	$600,000
cnn	http://www.cnn.com	$594,000
c|net	http://www.cnet.com	$540,000

As the foregoing figures illustrate, companies that charge for ad space on their Web sites advertise on other Web sites, as well. Table 10-3 also reveals that half of the top 10 revenue-generating companies are Web-search sites. It's also interesting to note that Web-search sites don't even show up in the top 10 biggest advertisers shown on Table 10-4. Web-search sites seem to attract surfers without much paid advertising. Most individuals include links to search sites from their own homepages, because they find the search engines of such value, and because the search sites include their links at no charge.

Currently, the cost of advertising on the Internet varies widely from site to site, and there seems to be no shortage of places to advertise. Shop around for high-traffic sites that appeal to your particular audience. If your product or service appeals to a broader audience, try advertising on Web-search sites, or the opening sites of Web browsers.

MULTIPLE PRESENCES

When you invest your company's advertising dollars in online marketing, spread the money around, just as you would in other media. Advertising on a single site severely limits your ad's reach. You can't advertise on the Web too much or too widely. The more people who

TABLE 10-4 TOP 10 LARGEST INTERNET ADVERTISERS
ACCORDING TO WEBTRACK

Company	Web Site Address	Amount Spent on Advertising
AT&T	http://www.att.com	$567,000
Netscape	http://www.netscape.com	$556,000
Internet Shopping Network	http://www.internet.net	$329,000
NECX	http://www.necx.com	$322,000
MasterCard	http://www.mastercard.com	$278,000
American Airlines	http://www.amrcorp.com/aa_home/aa_home.htm	$254,000
C|Net	http://www.cnet.com	$237,000
MCI	http://www.mci.com	$231,000
SportsLine	http://www.sportsline.com	$218,000

view your site, the farther your marketing message will go. You may have built a better mousetrap…er…Web site, but the world won't beat a path to your door—*unless* they know how to get there. The more routes you create to your Web site, the greater your exposure. Establishing multiple presences can help ensure the greatest number of people learn where and how to find you.

By "multiple presences" we don't necessarily mean additional Web sites. In the offline world, you may have to franchise in a dozen towns to make your products or services available to a large population of potential customers. On the Net, your Web site is only a mouse-click away from surfers all over the world. In many cases, surfers have no idea of the physical locations of the sites they love.

The key to establishing multiple presences in cyberspace is posting a lot of road signs. You can post your road signs in a variety of ways and media. Almost every television commercial and magazine advertisement you see displays a Web site address. Most of these addresses are easy to remember —they start with "http://www.," end with ".com," and usually contain some form of the company's name in between. Seeing these ads, you'd almost think advertisers expect you to keep an Internet-connected computer on your lap at all times (and in some cases you may wish you could!).

When you ask other sites to include your Web site address in their list of links or on a search site, you have no idea who you're inviting to your door. It's a little like throwing a party and posting invitations all over town; the different kinds of people who show up will amaze you.

In some cases, your company may not be responsible for posting your site to other sites. Web-surfers are encouraged to share the things they discover in their online travels. They love to share locations of great sites. Unfortunately, they also like to pass along their opinions. The word could be out on your site, good or bad, without your having done a thing.

People who add your site to their list of links or to other sites are marketing your site for you, whether they know it or not. They're like professional athletes who wear a given brand of athletic shoes. It's tantamount to a personal endorsement.

After you read this book, we're confident yours will become one of the Web's most popular sites. As your site attracts attention, some very popular sites may add your site to their "What's New!" or "What's Cool" page—with spectacular results

Cathie Walker's (http://www2.islandnet.com/~cwalker/homepage.html) Internet provider had a problem with her Web page (see Figure 10-4.)—it became too popular. The site's popularity created such a burden on the system the provider was forced to reduce access to her homepage, "Centre for the Easily Amused." Like anyone promoting a Web site, Walker had submitted her site to the normal Web search engines. Then, on August 1, 1995, her homepage was featured on Netscape's "What's New?" list, generating even more traffic. Her pages alone generated 25,000–50,000 hits a day, and brought the Internet provider's Web server to its knees.

What initially drew so many people to Walker's homepage? Were they looking for ways to amuse themselves? Hoping to find out what Walker looked like? Or maybe someone clicked on the link by accident. It's difficult to determine the exact reason people come to your Web site. If your company hopes to sell products or services online, you hope people come to your site to learn more about your products and order them. But the real reason they show up may have nothing to do with your product or service. (You can even generate an incredible hit if someone includes you on their list of the 10 *worst* Web sites.)

It's rarely worthwhile to maintain more than one company Web site, but it's important to maintain several links to your site. Web advertising

FIGURE 10-4

Cathie Walker's "Centre for the Easily Amused" became so popular it nearly shut down her Internet provider.

will help funnel users from other popular sites into yours. Don't be afraid to advertise in more than one place.

AD SPACE VS. SHELF SPACE

When you advertise your products or services online, you're not just buying ad space, you're buying "shelf space." As with supermarkets and retail establishments, banner placement on a site is crucial. So are the headings your site is listed under. It's also important to know where surfers are coming *from* when they visit your site. Manufacturers and retailers spend big bucks studying their customers' in-store traffic patterns to determine the best product placement. This is done using complex scientific methods or by placing a product in random locations and varying display sizes.

Note where visitors to your site come from. Your Web-presence provider can provide this information (perhaps at additional cost), or your in-house computer people can set this up. If you pay $20,000 a month for a banner advertisement and you find that more people come to your site because of in-house newsgroup postings, you may want to reconsider how your online advertising dollars should be spent.

When you list your company with search sites, you might want to do so under several headings. This makes it easier for surfers to find you. On some search sites, listing your company more than once means it will come up several times in displays of search results. This is similar to advertising your company in different places in the telephone book. (For example, an Internet advertising agency might list itself under "Advertising" and "Computers.")

Maintaining multiple Web presences helps surfers find your Web site and avoid getting lost in the maze of links crisscrossing cyberspace. The greater the number of links and routes to your Web site, the more shelf space it takes up—and the more traffic you'll generate.

Remember...

- Sponsoring Web pages is currently the most popular form of Internet advertising.

- When you begin sponsoring Web pages, keep three things in mind—the number of people who will see your ad, the target audience of the publication, and the cost.

- Sponsoring currently unsponsored, high-traffic Web sites is one way for your company to get good exposure at a low cost.

- Targeting your online marketing helps attract surfers to your Web site and increase product sales. Look for sites that know their user demographics. Talk with your provider or computer consultant to determine how to get better demographics on the surfers visiting your Web site.

- Including links on a variety of other sites will help surfers find your site. Links are like road signs: The more you have, the easier it will be for surfers to find your company online.

11

OTHER USES OF THE NET

When business first put computers on desktops, it did so in hopes of decreasing numbers of employees, increasing productivity, and reducing the overall cost of operations. The business community saw the new computer technology as the wave of the future, and embraced it enthusiastically. The result? Companies ended up hiring more employees to support the new technology, productivity remained virtually the same, and no measurable cost benefit could be found.

Similarly, the Internet can't work instant miracles for your company. You won't be able to reduce entire departments to a Web site, and, at least for the present time, money is not going pour in without additional work.

Putting your products or services on the Web is a great way to begin your online advertising or marketing, but if you use the Internet exclusively for sales, you're missing a bigger picture. The Net is an extremely flexible environment, with a lot to offer your organization as a whole (not just your bottom line).

So, although your company can certainly make money on the Internet, it's also worthwhile to consider other online benefits. The Internet is much more than just the Web. It's a dynamic and expanding medium teeming with potential uses. If your company decides to invest in an online venture, consider *everything* the Internet has to offer.

Combining different Internet technologies gives your company the ability to reach a wider audience. Not every person using the Internet has a graphical browser, and some still use text-based displays. Text-based solutions, while not as visually stimulating, do allow Internet users to read and send e-mail, transfer files, and dig up a few gopher sites. In contrast, some users access the Net from high-powered graphics workstations with plenty of graphics and sound capabilities. You'll want to offer these browsers something flashy to make the most of their powerful systems. Just as your radio advertising differs significantly from your television advertising, your approach to Web marketing should acknowledge differences in browser technologies. Put simply, you want to appeal to as many people as possible.

OTHER WAYS THE WEB CAN HELP YOUR BUSINESS

The end of the Cold War, and ensuing cuts in U.S. government defense spending, forced many defense contractors with cutting edge technology to change their target markets. Many turned their attention to the entertainment industry. Military simulations technology, for example, has made video games faster and more lifelike. And with such technological improvements, computer gaming is drawing the attention of a growing number of adult enthusiasts, further expanding the market. What might have seemed an unlikely market shift has proved to be highly profitable, indeed, for the defense industry.

The defense industry learned a valuable lesson that will serve you as you go online: People love to be entertained. The more you entertain people, the longer they'll remain at your Web site viewing your advertisements. Just as people will watch an entertaining commercial and then tell their friends about it, surfers will stay at a Web site if they find it interesting or of value, and pass the URL on to others. Remember the Wendy's "Where's the beef?" commercials? Thousands of TV viewers do. Like other forms of advertising, you have to have a "hook." If you put as much entertainment value into your Web site, people will remember your Internet marketing offerings, too.

Providing software utilities to your users also keeps them coming back. A program that calculates loan amortization tables is probably not all that entertaining, but it offers value and utility. Online catalogues, free software, new recipes—all provide something besides entertainment that adds value to your Web page.

Internet advertising should incorporate entertainment *and* utility. When people first start net-surfing, they usually stay online because they find it entertaining. Eventually, though, they want something more.

INTERNAL WEB USE

We've devoted much of this book to helping you develop a Web presence outside your company. Up to now, we've focused on creating a dynamic and effective Web page for clients and customers, primarily for marketing purposes. But the Web is also flexible enough to allow for a variety of internal uses. Using the Web inside your company is a great way to get information quickly to and from different departments and people.

An internal Web offers a number of distinct advantages over other internal networks. Web browsers are excellent database front-ends. Web programs can be written to use the browser interface. Making changes to Web programs takes a few days, as opposed to months for traditional operating-system-specific programs. Many database vendors are releasing graphical development environments so nonprogrammers can build Web-site programs. Some software companies, such as Microsoft, take an approach similar to the Visual Basic programming environment. As these programs proliferate, Web site design will become more interactive and less static.

Fears that developing complicated database programs for internal Web sites will require too many programmers have no foundation. The new product offerings lessen the resources required for building Web sites.

Suppose, for example, that your company wants to add a program to view employee purchase requests and compare them to that year's budget. If your operation utilizes a mix of Macs, PCs, and UNIX workstations, creating a user interface on these disparate platforms would take a full team of programmers months. By using the Web browser as your user interface, the project now requires only a single database programmer and a few weeks. Need to display images with your data? No problem. How about adding sound? Piece of cake. Visual programming environments for Web development are just beginning to hit the market and will encourage the advancement of Web-site technology.

If your company traditionally issues hard-copy fliers to communicate general information to your employees, consider putting them online. A weekly or monthly online newsletter will significantly reduce printing costs. And the newsletter you create will be a dynamic, full-color, interactive communiqué, complete with sound and video.

Other possible internal Web applications include tutorials and tours for new or promoted employees. Web browsers handle multimedia with ease, making for truly dynamic programs. Find an employee who knows a given job well, and record his or her explanation of how he or she performs the task. You can even include videotape of the work being performed. The added sights and sounds will enhance the employee's learning experience. Given today's "MTV generation," multimedia educational training is an excellent way to keep an employee's attention focused on the tutorial.

When we suggest giving employees Web access, companies commonly object that the enterprise will become a time-waster. "It'll be just like the screen-savers," the critics say. "The employees waste so much time configuring the darned things that we'd save more money just replacing monitors! "

While this is a valid concern—there will always be those who abuse their privileges-we strongly believe most employees will use your internal Web as an opportunity to advance and grow. A few may consider a Web browser a toy, but to those who count, it is very much a business tool.

Besides, the fact that net-surfing can be "addictive" only improves your chances of triggering an employee's interest in doing a better job. Many employees already use the Web to find answers to work-related problems—to find cheaper equipment vendors and product information for future purchases, to keep abreast of industry news, and to educate themselves about their specific job.

If you're concerned about security, remember: Most Web servers allow for some sort of password authorization procedure. While this may not be the most secure method of data transfer on all servers, it's effective enough for some kinds of sensitive information. In addition to providing a measure of security, this procedure will also track viewers of certain documents or directories.

This authorization procedure also allows you to limit access to data on your internal Web site. For example, you can restrict the ability of an employee to view anyone else's budget or purchase requests. You can also configure the program to generate a report whenever a user enters his or her name and password. It's easy. Traditionally, writing useful programs follows the 80/20 rule—writing the user interface takes 80 percent of the time, while writing the code that actually performs the work takes 20 percent. Using the Web as a user interface for an internal programming project cuts time normally spent on the interface.

4 out of 5 Systems Managers Agree

A recent Dataquest study of medium and large U.S. corporate information systems usage strategies found that 70 percent of information systems (IS) managers consider the Internet a useful tool. Of the IS managers surveyed, 80 percent felt the Internet was a reliable source for researching information.

CUSTOMER SUPPORT

In a recent Gallop poll, top American company executives ranked service improvement the number one challenge facing business today. Customer service is becoming a major factor in consumer purchasing decisions. Providing online product support is a great way to alleviate those "on hold" customer headaches.

A dedicated e-mail account is the easiest way for a company to set up online customer support. Customers with complaints or comments can contact a specific e-mail address like <support@yourcompany.com>. If you set up a specific account for customer support, be sure someone checks for mail throughout the day. Assign more than one person to handle the support account to prevent response delays due to sickness, vacation, or travel. (The customer doesn't care about your scheduling problems.) And be especially sure to respond to all customer e-mail messages within 24 hours.

You can create mail aliases so you don't have to create a specific account for support. This setup automatically forwards customer mail to the appropriate person. This technique works well for multiple mail addresses, where different people handle different problems. Create mail aliases for different problem areas, like <hardware_support@ yourcompany.com> for hardware questions; <software_support@your company.com> for software questions, and <installation_support@ yourcompany.com> for installation questions. All hardware support questions could go to Jane, all software support questions to John, and installation questions to both Jane and John.

A similar Web-based approach includes a Web-site customer support form, making it simple for customers to communicate their problems and comments. You can provide a place for them to include their product serial numbers. If your product is software, you can even make it possible for them to enter problematic keystrokes. Telling customers what kind of information to include in a message can reduce confusion and the number of e-mail transactions.

Creating an online "help desk" can also reduce customer frustration, though at a slightly higher cost in personnel and resources. Your online help desk could include common problems customers encounter, a searchable database of online help, and the e-mail addresses of personnel with answers not available on your Web site.

The site could incorporate much more in-depth explanations or detailed list of problem solutions. And if you discover a flaw in your product, you can update your customers at the help desk without clogging your phone lines or incurring a huge postage expense.

When determining which questions and answers to include on your online help desk, survey your own employees for suggestions. They probably know the product better than anyone, and can anticipate many problems your customers will report. And don't leave out the secretaries! Secretaries hear an abbreviated version of nearly every complaint before passing it along.

Include survey results in the most accessible form possible. "Question-and-answer" may work well for shorter lists, but you'll probably need a topic or key word search for larger ones.

Your help desk could also provide forms for questions the site doesn't address. Later you can post the answers to these new questions to your site, and add them to your help desk. This is a great way for start-up companies to build up a support database. The new information may help the next customer with the same question, reducing the number of problems requiring staff intervention.

Another form of online support is the Frequently Asked Questions list (FAQ). This is a mailing list or list maintained on an FTP site that provides answers to questions people ask most frequently. Many companies on the Net provide this type of support. And when they don't, interested users often start and maintain their own lists. It's very easy to turn an FAQ list into an HTML document. In most cases, it's only about a page long.

You'll find an excellent example of online customer service in action at the Hewlett-Packard Web site (http://www.hp.com). Hewlett-Packard's customer support Web site incorporates many of the foregoing ideas (http://support.mayfield.hp.com). HP began providing Internet support before the advent of the Web in 1991, offering its customers downloadable software patches from an FTP site. The company eventually set up eight mailing lists (HP calls them "electronic digests") so customers could learn which software patches were available and request them by e-mail. The mailing lists include a variety of information on new products, security, technical tips, and general news (see Figure 11-1).

Investing some of your resources in online customer support means big dividends for your company in the long run—if you take the time to set it up right, and maintain it conscientiously. Take online customer satisfaction surveys. Send e-mail to users who submit questions to ask

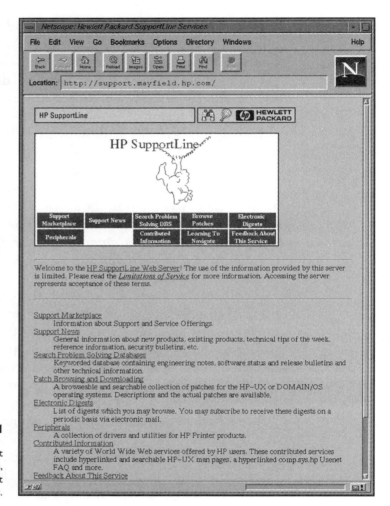

FIGURE 11-1

Hewlett-Packard's customer support homepage offers users a variety of files, help, and information about its products.

about the treatment they received from online service personnel. Survey your site's content often. Ask yourself what types of information your customers want. Solicit customer and employee input for improving the site. Keep your customers happy and they'll keep coming back. Your marketing efforts are wasted if you don't support them after the sale.

NAME RECOGNITION

Generating online sales isn't the only reason to put up a billboard on the Information Superhighway. Increasing consumer awareness of your company's name or brand is another valid reason for going online.

The next time you drive through town, notice the signs for some of the smaller pizza parlors and submarine sandwich shops. There's the shop's name in big letters, often a logo, and occasionally the logo of a large soft drink company. Do you suppose the shop owner thinks promoting that particular brand of soda improves business? Our guess is, probably not. Chances are, the soda company paid for all or part of the sign in exchange for the public exposure. Your ads on the Web can work in much the same way.

Netscape Communications follows this advertising model on the Internet (though it's doesn't currently pay anyone to add the Netscape logo to a Web site). The company created a small logo design incorporating the company name and the version of its software compatible with a particular Web site (see Figure 11-2). Surfers are encouraged to click on the icon and download the latest version of Netscape software to view the Web site in its greatest glory. This is an excellent move on Netscape's part, since industry experts predict that computer industry juggernaut Microsoft will eventually enter the Web browser and Web server markets.

It has become kind of a status symbol to place the logo of the software used to create your site on your Web page. It shows you have the latest and greatest HTML code available—keeping your company on the cutting edge of the newest technology. However, not every site will jump at the opportunity to include your logo on its Web page. You may have to spend some advertising dollars to secure placement on some of the more heavily visited sites.

Advertising your site on other Web pages with just your company's logo might not provide enough information to attract people, but some sites will allow you to display a "banner." This graphic banner takes up nearly the full width of your Web browser and about a tenth of its height. You can display your logo in the banner, along with helpful,

FIGURE 11-2

Netscape Communication's iconic logos foster name recognition and provide status to the Web sites that display their logo.

descriptive text and a link directly to your Web site homepage. You have to inspire surfers to peruse your site, so make your banner as informative and provocative as you can.

Establishing name recognition on the Internet is definitely a costly venture. Only companies willing to spend a lot of advertising dollars will secure space on high-traffic sites. Advertising your name on the Internet may not cost as much as a half-time ad during the Super Bowl, but it's probably not the kind of money your company can throw around without carefully considering alternatives.

SOFTWARE BETA TESTING PROGRAMS

Say your company is writing a piece of software it's planning to release in several weeks. Your internally sponsored beta testing confirms that the software is relatively bug-free, and you're readying the product for distribution. But how can your company be absolutely sure it's found all the bugs and fixed all the security vulnerabilities? You have no way to know for sure—or do you?

Why not release a beta version of your product on the Internet? Subjecting your software to the scrutiny of the online community provides you with a much broader range of beta testers. For some time now, many large software companies have expressed their frustration with current beta testing programs. These programs frequently pay testers with nothing more than a free version of the final product—hardly an incentive to test thoroughly. The latest beta testing programs are paying testers in cash for bugs found.

By far the most innovative beta testing strategy to date is Netscape's "Bugs Bounty" program, kicked off in October 1995. Bugs Bounty rewards users who find and report security vulnerabilities in the beta versions of Netscape's Navigator 2.0 software. Users that find serious problems can receive cash rewards or free Netscape products for locating minor bugs. Netscape offers free beta versions of the software on its FTP servers, so users can download the program and begin the bug search. This beta testing approach is unique because the software was released to the Internet community first in hopes of creating a truly bug-free final product.

"We are continuing to encourage users to provide feedback on new versions of our software, and the Netscape Bugs Bounty is a natural extension of that process," wrote Mike Homer, Netscape's vice president of marketing, in a company press release. "By rewarding users for quickly identifying and reporting bugs back to us, this program will encourage an extensive, open review of Netscape Navigator 2.0 and will help us to continue to create products of the highest quality."

Sun Microsystems supports the Netscape Bugs Bounty program and hopes the program will supplement Sun's own extensive beta testing program for the Java language. Both Sun and Netscape expect these broad, Internet-based testing programs to virtually eliminate security vulnerabilities in their respective products.

RECRUITING PERSONNEL AND LOCATING CONTRACTORS

No matter how good your current personnel lineup is, chances are, you're always on the lookout for top-notch people. But finding those people isn't easy, or cheap. Advertising a position nationally can be an expensive endeavor—unless you post it on the Web.

A growing number of recruiters, employment agencies, companies, and individuals are turning to the Web to find that ideal worker or dream job. Though recruiters and employment agencies are responsible for most current Web sites dealing with employment, a healthy mix of commercial and public sites offers employment advertising. Some sites allow individuals to post their resumes in ASCII or PostScript format.

TABLE 11-1   WEB EMPLOYMENT SITES

Web Site	Location
Stanford University	http://rescomp.stanford.edu
JobWeb	http://www.jobweb.com
Online Career Center	http://www.iquest.net/occ
Interactive Employment Network	http://www.espan.com
HelpWanted	http://www.helpwanted.com
The Monster Board	http://www.monster.com
CareerMosiac	http://www.careermosaic.com
ChicagoTribune Career Finder	http://www.chicago.tribune.com

The Internet offers a tremendously powerful tool to anyone conducting a job search. Traditional job listings, like want ads, can provide only limited details about the job. Discerning actual job requirements and understanding the abilities and qualifications needed for an advertised position can be difficult and frustrating. Web-based classified employment advertising overcomes this problem with database search engines. These search engines are similar to the ones found on *Yahoo* (http://www.yahoo.com) and *Lycos* (http://www.lycos.com), but they search for job information rather than Web-site information. Surfing job seekers can use this technology to narrow their online searches to include specific locations, salary ranges, job titles, and even specific company names.

For example, a computer programmer in Miami looking for a change links to his favorite classified employment Web site. On the search form he enters his preferred city as Denver, his salary range as greater than $50,000, and his job title as computer programmer. Search results include only computer programming jobs available in Denver paying over $50,000. Each listing gives the name of the company offering the position, the job title, and salary as a link. These links point to Web pages with more detailed information about the position. Our Miami-based programmer can perform all these searches in a matter of minutes. He doesn't have to track down a source for Colorado newspapers hoping to find an interesting job listed that particular week.

In addition to finding qualified employees or prospective employers, a company can locate other businesses online. Do you need an ISDN modem to connect your home to your office? Is your company looking for an inexpensive printer? Before you turn to the Yellow Pages, why not try the Web? It's fast becoming one of the largest business-to-business directories on the Internet. You can surf the Web looking for vendors offering products your company typically buys, and contact them online or through traditional channels.

Let's suppose you've found a vendor with the ability to accept orders online, either through a Web page that includes an order form or via e-mail. Your purchasing department logs on to the vendor's Web site, enters the product information on the form, includes the purchase order number, and submits the form. That's it! No more waiting on hold! No more misunderstandings, costly faxes, wrong items shipped, or difficulties in understanding the sales person's dialect.

This kind of online transaction also benefits vendors. They can set up a Web-based order-form program to send orders to their shipping and accounts receivable departments at the same time. They process customers' orders quickly and efficiently, with fewer errors. The customer gets great service and comes back. The vendor's operation becomes more efficient, he greatly decreases his paperwork load (reducing lost orders) and he needs a much smaller staff.

Want to get real tricky? With an internal Web site that monitors inventory, your company can automatically place orders with your vendor's Web site when your stock is low. The program can get the next P.O. number from the purchase-order database, check the budget to make sure money is available, and place the order. Everything takes place online, thanks to the World Wide Web.

Whether you need an experienced new employee or a new vendor with whom to do business, you'll find it all online.

PEOPLE ARE TALKING—AND YOU BETTER BE LISTENING

Want to catch bad publicity before it starts? Try reading online newsgroups related to your particular product or market. Newsgroups are great places for people to praise or condemn your product or service. And reading and posting to newsgroups on a regular basis can head off problems and answer questions before a disgruntled customer tells the world of your company's alleged incompetence. Once you establish your company's presence on a particular newsgroup, users will send questions directly to your company before posting irate messages to the Internet.

Building an online reputation takes careful work and planning. Responding to newsgroup postings with direct connection to your product or service, but for which your company has answers, can greatly enhance that reputation. Remember: We all want something for nothing. The more information you give away, the closer you come to landing a new customer. Use information as your loss-leader to attract potential customers.

Newsgroup postings and Web pages can also reveal what your competitors are saying about you. Ads and marketing hype in other media are easy to spot. If a competing company takes out a full-page ad in the *Wall Street Journal*, you'll definitely hear about any slanderous claims the ad makes against you. That's not necessarily true of the Internet. Competitors may make false comments and accusations about your company on the Web; you'd never know about it if you never went online.

It's a good idea, therefore, to have some of your public relations people surf the Net, looking at your competition's Web sites, checking their online ads, and watching for their newsgroup postings. Most companies probably won't create Web sites just to spread false publicity about your company, but it doesn't hurt to keep a watchful eye on the Internet.

NON-WEB-RELATED TOOLS

To much of the business community, Web advertising represents something of a California gold rush. Many companies find the Web to be an effective communications medium and a wise investment of advertising dollars. But what about prospectors already looking for future online opportunities?

As dynamic as it is, the World Wide Web may not be the only place to advertise your product or service on the Internet. Several other new and existing Internet technologies offer excellent potential, as well. The Web is a fairly recent Internet development, but companies have successfully used e-mail, gopher, Archie, and FTP to promote their products and services for years.

E-MAIL

Remember when a fax number on your letterhead made your company look cutting-edge? Now even your mother's got one. Remember when wearing a beeper made you look important? Now junior high school kids wear them. Cellular phones are the status symbols of the moment, and now even the *type* of cellular phone can influence your image.

The first high-tech status symbol embraced by the business community was e-mail. An e-mail address made a company look technologically savvy and light-years ahead of its competition. Today, every business card in your Rolodex includes an e-mail address. Web sites appear on many business cards, as well, but it's e-mail that maintains the vital communication link on the Internet. Figure 11-3 provides an example of a graphical e-mail program.

Companies use e-mail internally to quickly disseminate information and allow for a less formal means of communication. E-mail allows employees to collaborate with people worldwide. The content of an

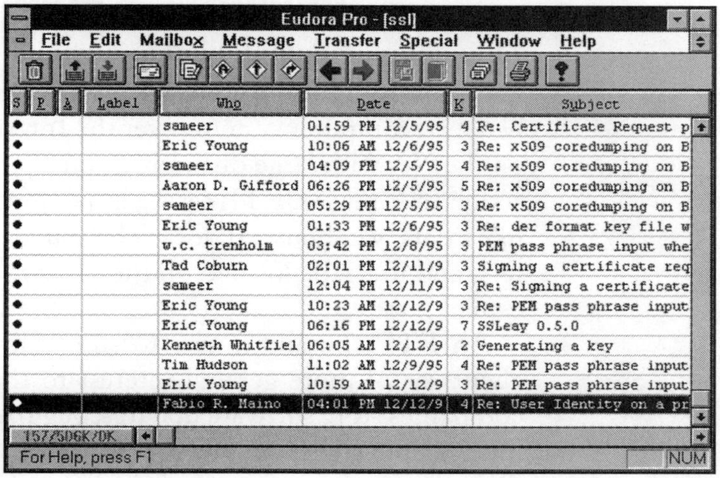

FIGURE 11-3

The Eudora e-mail package is a
graphical e-mail program for PCs.

e-mail message can be much more thorough and thoughtful than a
phone call or even a face-to-face conversation. E-mail defeats the barriers of race, age, disability, sex, religion, and even physical attractiveness.
When you receive an e-mail message from someone you've never met,
the only criteria by which you can judge that person is the content of
his or her message.

E-mail message content says a lot about a person, and employers
should take the time to establish company guidelines and show their
employees how to write these kinds of messages properly. Treat e-mail
with the same respect as a memo. The writer should reread the message to correct spelling or grammatical mistakes, and to ensure that the
content is coherent and makes sense and that no one can misinterpret
its tone.

Need to get documents to a distant corporate office inexpensively?
Attach the document to an e-mail message, or if you only have a paper
copy of the document, scan it in and attach it. We measure overnight
delivery in terms of days, faxes in terms of minutes—and e-mail in
terms of seconds.

If you set up a Web site to take orders online, ask your customers to
include their e-mail addresses. When your Web site finishes processing orders, the program can generate and send e-mail thank-yous to
each customer. And you can use your e-mail address list to notify customers of special pricing, new products, product upgrades, and bug fixes.

FILE TRANSFER PROTOCOL (FTP)

Most up-to-date Web browsers will transfer files. The File Transfer Protocol (FTP) is the underlying software method for transferring files between computer systems over the Internet. Thousands of computers on the Net with large disk drives full of software and information subscribe to FTP. An FTP server is a computer on the Internet that acts like a data warehouse. It doesn't have to be solely dedicated to file transfers, and it can be located on the same machine as your Web server or e-mail hub.

An FTP site allows you to store files of specific interest to your clients or of more general interest to the Internet community. Data companies store software updates, bug fixes, updated hardware drivers, images, sound files, and technical papers and much more on FTP sites. A recent Dataquest survey found that 60 percent of the information systems (IS) professionals polled bought software over the Internet, and 70 percent downloaded bug fixes and patches. The survey further showed that IS managers are rethinking their strategies as software distribution and sales move to the Internet.

Utilizing FTP sites can help your organization, but devise a plan before putting information and programs on an FTP site.

FTP site access can be private or anonymous. With private FTP, a user must enter a valid user name and password before the system admits him or her. Anonymous FTP means that the user may log on with a user name of "anonymous" and give the name of the computer he or she is using as a password (username@my_machine.mycompany.com). Private FTP users are authorized to access only files typically located in their home directories, while anonymous FTP puts users into a group directory where the business stores data for public consumption.

An FTP site is an inexpensive way for companies to distribute large amounts of data to people with Internet connections. For example, MicroProse Software (http://www.microprose.com) has an anonymous FTP site (ftp.microprose.com) that allows Internet users to download demos of the company's latest games or bug fixes. This method of distributing software allows anyone to download and play a demo of the latest game before buying it, saving MicroProse both the cost of floppies or CD-ROMs and the shipping and packaging expenses.

The downside of an FTP site is that it can bog down if too many people log on to it. This is especially true if you store something of great interest to the Internet community. In the rush to download your latest product offering, things can jam up. This puts a serious burden on your Internet connection and may keep other, more vital information from getting though. Avoid this problem by limiting the number of users who can simultaneously download files from your FTP site.

Netscape Communications distributes the company's Web browser software via several anonymous FTP sites. Because the demand can at times overwhelm even several sites, Netscape has partnered with other FTP sites around the world to distribute its software. If someone wants to download the latest version of Netscape's Web browser and all the FTP sites are at their user limits, the Netscape FTP server gracefully informs users that it has reached its limit and suggests other sites to try. In many cases, another FTP site may be geographically closer to the user, resulting in faster downloads.

Although FTP sites are just beginning to feature more attractive graphical interfaces, FTP began as a text-driven program. Many popular graphical FTP interfaces now exist for the Mac and PC. Most Macintosh users know of the popular Fetch (see Figure 11-4) program developed by the National Center for Supercomputing Applications (NCSA). Such graphical interfaces help simplify the file transfer process. Fetch, for example, uses a cute dog motif—the cursor turns into a running dog as the file downloads.

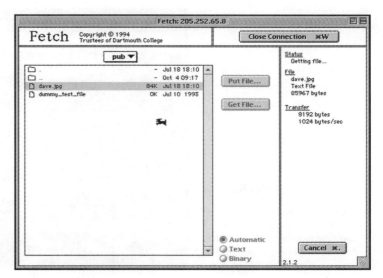

FIGURE 11-4

Fetch is a graphically oriented file transfer program for the Macintosh.

Fitting an FTP site into your company's Internet advertising plans can draw surfers to your Web site. You don't have to give away the farm to increase traffic or boost sales. Netsurfers look for free information and programs, but selling full-blown versions of the software or detailed reports of the information you offered as free samples may be a better avenue for your company. Dataquest (htttp://www. dataquest.com) includes online previews of reports and surveys, but requires a user to enter credit card information to purchase complete reports.

CU-SeeME

CU-SeeMe (pronounced See-You-See-Me) was developed at Cornell University and could become the Internet's next great advertising vehicle.

Similar to the "videophone" telephone companies invented years ago, CU-SeeMe is a type of video-conferencing software for personal computers on the Internet. A picture of the person you're communicating with appears on your screen, and if you have a video input device attached, that person can see your picture, as well (see Figure 11-5).

A "reflector" is a UNIX system that allows several people to meet and connect visually at the same time. Multiple users sign on and the system "reflects" their images and audio to other connected users.

FIGURE 11-5

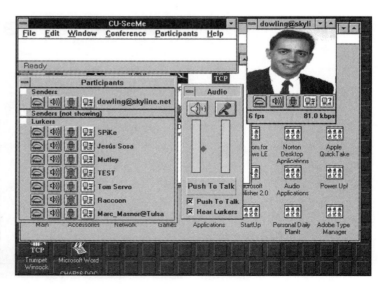

CU-SeeMe, developed at Cornell University, allows video conferencing over the Internet. You'll need a fast Internet connection to get anything close to full-motion video.

Because CU-SeeMe was originally designed for video conferencing, it's primarily used to connect distant corporate offices around the world—and it does so for the price of a local Internet connection.

While this technology isn't as fast as running a dedicated line between two offices with specialized machines, it does a good job of connecting several single users working on their own individual machines. The software also works over dial-up modem connections, but a fast Internet connection allows the software to work at its fullest potential.

As Internet bandwidth increases and the cost of Internet connections decreases, CU-SeeMe technology could lead to the development of interactive Internet TV. Talk about target marketing! How about sending ads directly to people whose exact demographics you know?

Comcast Cablevision in Baltimore, Maryland, states that it will have the ability to supply an Internet connection to every subscriber by 1997. Fiber optic cable is replacing traditional wire cable lines to increase signal quality and bandwidth. In the early days of cable television, subscribers had to rent a converter box from the cable company to decode the signal. In the future, cable subscribers will be able to rent a small keyboard with a built-in computer to use the Internet through their TV sets.

The Innovation Group, Inc. (http://innovation.com/) of Santa Rosa, California, is currently running market trials of PC-to-cable Internet connections. These cable Internet connections offer greater speed than any of today's dial-up services. The Innovation Group's product can be used on existing CATV cables with no rewiring. They also claim the Internet connection is close to ethernet speeds. Internet use over regular cable systems, using TV sets, will soon be commonplace.

Using this new and emerging technology, commercials will no longer be broadcast to an entire subscriber area, when only a small percentage of viewers constitute the target audience. Local politicians, for example, will target their particular districts by showing their commercials only to those living in specific ZIP code areas. This feature alone will save advertisers of every stripe a lot of money.

Two other companies are developing competing video standards for the Internet—Xing Technology Corp. (http://www.xingtech.com) of Arroyo Grande, California, and VDOnet Corp. (http://www.vdolive.com) of Santa Clara, California. In the past, users had to download video clips to their hard drives and run them on video players to view them. Both Xing and VDOnet have developed technologies allowing surfers to view video clips in real time straight off the Net. This allows for the delivery of video as normal Web data, rather than a special file.

In November 1995 both Xing and VDOnet showcased their products by sending live video over the Net. VDOnet broadcast the keynote address and reports from the show floor of the Internet World Trade Show. Xing broadcast live video coverage of the Comdex trade show in Las Vegas, Nevada.

Putting a video clip on your Web site may draw a few curious surfers willing to go to the trouble of downloading it to their hard drives, but the new interactive video technology will ensure that everyone visiting your site will watch.

INTERNET TELEPHONES

Several companies now offer Internet telephone connectivity. The leader, VocalTec (http://www.vocaltec.com/) of Northvale, New Jersey, offers a product called *Internet Phone* which permits real-time voice conversations over the Internet. Telephone companies surely are not welcoming this product with open arms; it allows people from all over the world to communicate for the cost of your local Internet service. No more long-distance rates. No more dialing codes. No more operators. No more calling circles. Just a simple way for people to communicate over the Internet. Now connected families can "call" each other and talk as long as they want without worrying about cost.

This technology serves a business purpose, as well. The Internet telephone can virtually eliminate expensive phone costs between distant, even international, corporate offices. While cost savings is the initial benefit for both companies and families, the possibilities are as vast as those of the telephone.

Imagine sitting at your PC one day surfing the Web. A ringing sound emanates from your stereo sound-card speakers. You switch applications to an Internet telephone program and answer the "call." On the other end a vacuum cleaner salesperson asks to set up an appointment to demonstrate one of his or her company's latest models. You thank the solicitor for calling and politely inform him or her of your lack of interest. Sound farfetched? Do you think Alexander Graham Bell thought vacuum cleaner salespeople would use his invention to harass people at dinnertime? Imagine your 14-year-old daughter begging you to get off your computer so she can "call" her friends on the Internet.

The Internet telephone will finally establish a true global village. Are your kids working on a school project about Ireland? Why not call some children in Ireland and ask them about their country? Learning French as a new language? Call someone in France to practice conjugating your verbs.

The only real barrier to creating such a global village is bandwidth. Homes will need speedier connections, Internet providers will need super—high-speed network connections, and the Internet backbone will have to become a true "superhighway." Right now it's just the yellow brick road.

INTERNET RADIO

Internet radio is much like the radio we're all familiar with, but instead of transmitting a signal over air waves, the Internet is the transport medium. Internet radio is also a one-way technology, allowing for no interactivity.

The concept of Internet talk radio first emerged in November 1992, when Carl Malamud envisioned an entirely new way of providing information to the Internet world. You may have heard of his famous Internet talk radio program, "Geek of the Week," featuring weekly interviews with famous Internet personalities. "Geek of the Week" first aired April 1, 1993. The show is sponsored by Internet Multicasting Service, O'Reilly and Associates, and Sun Microsystems.

The sponsorship arrangement of Malamud's show is reminiscent of early television, when a program might have a single sponsor. Sponsoring an Internet radio program could be an important opportunity for advertisers looking to take advantage of this technology in its infancy. In the future, advertisers will probably buy time-based ad space similar to radio and TV ad time. Radio stations will store programs online at FTP sites so listeners can "tune in" to their favorite "stations" whenever they choose. This may present a new problem for advertisers or companies selling ad space. Since the commercials will remain part of the program as long as the file stays on the system, it won't be easy to add new sponsors or advertisers to "reruns."

VocalTec's *Internet Wave* program allows Web surfers to hear audio on demand. Incorporating *Internet Wave* into your Web sites makes it possible for users to hear audio files as the transfer takes place. This technology opens up the possibility of Internet radio and broadcast radio stations simultaneously "broadcasting" over the Internet and the air. Advertising and marketing over online radio will be similar to traditional radio marketing, but with greater demographic focus.

Internet radio suggests some truly interesting applications. Years ago WordPerfect Corp. set up WordPerfect Radio, which broadcast over the telephone. When a user called WordPerfect's 800 number, entertaining music played during their hold time. The radio "station's" DJs took requests from waiting listeners, and played WordPerfect product commercials between songs. The same idea will work for users waiting for an available technician at your online help desk. The first company to implement this technology on the Web may attract people based on its novelty.

ANARCHY OR UTOPIA? THE ALL-ENCOMPASSING NET

All forms of traditional media and advertising may someday converge on the Internet. Print media is going online. National Public Radio runs syndicated programs over Internet talk radio. Television and radio stations have Web sites. And more and more people are sending mail electronically. The Internet is changing the way we do business. The question is, will this convergence of media produce Utopia, or anarchy?

One problem with the infant Internet is its lack of standards. The computer industry has struggled with it for years. Typically, the first company out of the gate or with the biggest pocketbook gets to set the standards.

In today's Internet environment, many companies that entered the arena early, such as Netscape, are going head-to-head with Internet newcomers like Microsoft. As of this writing, Netscape, Sun, and Microsoft are fighting for dominance in the Web scripting language wars. Each company wants its version of the language to become the standard. Without defined standards, people are reluctant to invest. No one wants to spend large sums of money only to have a change in standards render his or her investment obsolete.

Web scripting language is a computer programming language for Web brows-ers. The language looks similar to the C programming language and is for writing programs that run on the client side of the connection, instead of on the Web server.

A lack of standards also hurts consumers. The modem debates are a good example. A few years ago, several companies came out with modems that adhered to the V.Fast proprietary standard for 28.8 k devices. But then the CCITT (International Telegraph and Telephone Consultative Committee) specifications committee announced it would consider V.34 the industry standard. People who bought V.Fast or V.FC modems were now unable to communicate with owners of the new V.34 standard modems at 28.8 k bps. To combat this problem, modem manufacturers developed modems that adhered to all available standards.

The Internet has revolutionized the way we communicate. It has changed virtually every traditional communications delivery medium, from private letters to broadcast television, and its influence on our daily lives continues to grow. Its long-term effect on American business has yet to be measured, but the possibilities appear endless.

Remember...

- The Internet offers many advertising opportunities besides the Web. Traditional methods such as e-mail, FTP, and gopher still have marketing potential.

- An internal Web can expedite information transfer between departments and help create job-training tutorials.

- Web-based customer service allows customers to get the information they need when they need it. Post answers to frequently asked questions to reduce the workload on customer support personnel and your phone lines.

- Putting up "billboards" on the Information Superhighway is a great way to increase name recognition. It's an expensive venture, so put your money to good use on high-traffic sites.

- Advertising jobs online can be a draw in itself. Whether searching the Web for qualified candidates, or posting available positions on your Web site, the Internet is a great place for recruiters and job seekers to meet.

- Other Internet technologies offer excellent advertising potential. While your company may have had a late start in the Web advertising game, it can still be a visionary in non—Web-related advertising markets.

12

WHAT WILL THIS COST?

In previous chapters, we touched here and there on the subject of the cost of marketing your products and/or services on the World Wide Web. But in order to present you with the biggest picture possible, we generally omitted monetary considerations from our discussions. It's time now to take a hard look at the numbers.

In this chapter, we delve into the specific costs of advertising and marketing your company online. We examine in detail the expenses associated with each of the eight steps you'll take to develop a Web presence. We offer real-world cost estimates of doing the project on your own, as well as the typical price of the hands-free approach. Throughout the discussion, we consider the costs and advantages of hiring a consultant at each step. In the last section, we attach some numbers to the seemingly intangible, but very real losses resulting from *not* being on the Web.

THE COSTS OF MAKING YOUR SITE RUN

Earlier in this book, we defined most of the technical and administrative tasks associated with taking your company and your marketing plan onto the Web, breaking them down into eight steps. Within each step, we highlighted a number of options. The following section defines the costs of every option for every step.

ACQUIRING AN INTERNET CONNECTION AND DOMAIN NAME

Your first expense is your Internet connection. You establish this connection by purchasing services from an Internet access provider or Internet service provider (ISP) These service providers offer a variety of connections, each of which transmits data at a different speed, or bandwidth. Think of bandwidth as a water supply pipe; the larger the pipe, the more water gets through during a given time period. Bigger pipes cost more to use, and so do fast Internet connections.

You'll choose from two basic types of Internet connections—a SLIP or PPP account, or a dedicated line. A SLIP or PPP account is by far the least desirable. The fact that it operates over a modem renders it quite susceptible to signal interruption. The Web runs 24 hours a day, seven days a week; your site must, too, or it's worthless. The cost of establishing this type of connection is usually between $50 and $150 per month, with a one-time setup fee of $50 to $100. This option isn't particularly viable for anyone who hopes to run a reputable Web site.

The second type of connection, a dedicated line, is a continuous and largely dependable link to the Net. You can establish this connection at a number of bandwidths. A 56-Kbps line transmits data at 56 kilobytes per second; this is the minimum speed at which your company should connect to the Net. The price for this type of connection ranges from $300 to $450 per month, with a one-time setup charge of between $450 and $700. A T-1 line is a faster connection, providing a data transfer rate of 1.54 Mbs (megabits) per second. The charge for this type of line ranges from $2,500 to $5,000 per month, with a one-time setup charge of between $2,500 and $8,500. By far the fastest and most expensive connection is the T-3 line, which transfers data at 45 Mbs per second. This is an extremely pricey option and only a large corporation seeking a deep and broad Web presence should consider it. The charge for this type of connection is between $12,000 and $20,000 per month, with a setup fee of between $25,000 and $35,000.

We recommend a dedicated line with a bandwidth of either 56 Kbps, a T-1 running at 1.54 Mbs, or a fractional T-1 somewhere between these two rates. However, we understand that the type of connection you choose depends to a large extent on your budget, the amount of Web traffic you expect, and the content you want to include on your site. But don't forget to consider the costs of future connection upgrades. If you start with a 56 Kbps connection, for example, and decide after six months that you really need a T-1 line, you may have to shell out another setup fee. Just be sure to get the fastest and most dependable connection you can afford.

The next phase of establishing your Internet connection is dealing with your local telephone company. If you plan to utilize a dial-up line—and we don't recommend this—then the only phone connection you'll need is a normal telephone line. For all other types of connections, you'll need a specialized hookup that your telephone company must provide. This connection is slightly more expensive than a normal phone line. A number of factors will determine the exact cost, including the distance between your business and your Internet provider, the type of connection you have, and your location. Fees range from $75 to $200 per month, with a one-time setup charge between

$100 and $300 per line. These fees only bring the line to your building; they don't include establishing the connection inside. In other words, the telephone company will provide a data connection to your office building, but if your office is located on the 14th floor, you'll have to pay extra hourly fees to bring the data connection all the way to your office.

Your service provider may deal with the telephone company for you, and establish all the lines you need for your connection. But it will almost certainly pass all the costs on to you. Ask about this as you compare prices.

After looking at some of these numbers, you might wonder how on earth we could say, as we have again and again, that advertising and marketing on the Web is an inexpensive way to gain worldwide exposure. The truth is, establishing a Web presence doesn't have to involve paying any of the fees we've described in this section. You can always hire a Web-presence provider to do it all for you. Web presence providers already have high-speed Net connections, and they run their clients' Web pages on their own servers. By going this route, you not only avoid all the charges this section details, but the charges covered in the next two sections, "Purchasing and Installing Server Hardware" and "Purchasing, Installing, and Configuring Server Software," as well.

Web-presence providers do charge a fee for their services. These range from $150 to $400 per month, but can go up significantly depending on the number of pages you publish, the amount of interactivity you need, and the amount of disk space your site requires. Later in this chapter, we examine the long-term costs and effects of working with a Web-presence provider. If you plan to use this kind of service, you may want to skip ahead to "Developing Basic Web Strategy and Structure."

Once you establish your Internet connection, you'll need a domain name. As we explained earlier, a domain name is the identifier surfers will use to locate your company online. To secure a domain name, you must deal with Internic, the authority that assigns Internet domain names. This process isn't all that costly. Internic charges $50 per year for the use of the domain name, and you must pay for two years in advance.

If you hire a Web-presence provider, the consultant either will get the domain name for you, or simply post your pages as part of its own site without a domain name. For example, the homepage address of

Stryker Industries, Inc., one of Skyline's clients, is (http://www. skyline.net/home/stryker/). The company doesn't need a domain name because its homepage is part of our site. If you want a domain name, your presence provider can secure one for you, including the Internic fees and related consulting fees in its charges to you (typically $150–$200).

PURCHASING AND INSTALLING SERVER HARDWARE

As we've explained, a Web server is a constantly running computer that handles surfers' requests for information from your site. This server can be almost any machine, from a high-powered workstation to a PC. In most cases, we recommend using a Pentium or Pentium Pro PC with at least a 133 MHz CPU and running on a UNIX operating system. Your server should also have at least 40 MB of RAM. A machine with these qualifications will cost $6,000–$7,500. If you need a more powerful server, you may want to move up to a Sparc20 or DEC alpha, but the cost for these workstations ranges from $20,000 to $25,000.

The purchase price of the server doesn't include hardware setup, installation, and maintenance costs. If your company has the expertise to handle this technical work, your costs will be much lower. But if you lack the on-site skills to crank up your Web server, you'll have to hire someone at a cost of between $1,000 and $4,000. Any troubleshooting down the road will cost you about $100 per hour.

PURCHASING, INSTALLING, AND CONFIGURING SERVER SOFTWARE

Believe it or not, the software you'll need to run your site is one of your least expenses. In fact, it may even be available cost-free. Many Internet sources offer popular server software packages as freeware. However, you must choose from dozens of applications. If your company has the expertise to install your hardware, odds are you've also got the knowledge to install and configure the server software. You may want to hire an outside consultant to help choose the software, however. The cost for this service should be minimal

It's possible the available freeware won't meet your site's needs. In this case, you'll have to buy something else. One of the most popular Web server software packages is Netscape's *Secure Server*, which costs around $3,000. For a little less, you could pick up *Open Market's Secure WebServer*, a server software package comparable to the Netscape software.

DEVELOPING BASIC WEB STRATEGY AND STRUCTURE

Our overall purpose in writing this book is to help you develop a Web strategy and structure. Not to blow our own horn too loudly, but between these pages, you'll find everything you need to know to successfully market and advertise your products and services on the World Wide Web. So the cost of developing a basic Web strategy and structure is…well, just look on the cover.

DESIGNING WEB PAGES

The three distinct but connected phases in the process of designing successful Web pages include artistic design, marketing design, and technical design. The costs of the artistic design phase depend largely on whether your company has an art department. If it does, the people who design your company's graphics can probably handle the graphical aspects—the *look*—of your Web pages. Your in-house artists must understand how online graphics work, as well as a few aspects unique to successful Web site design, but we provide everything they'll need to know about those subjects in this book. (Get a copy for the art department.)

If you use an outside graphic design firm, you'll still need to make sure the people who design your Web site understand thoroughly how their designs will be applied online on your site. The total cost of using an independent graphic designer depends on how much time the artists spend on your design. The standard rates for art development range from $100 to $200 per page, but this figure can vary drastically, depending on the firm and what you want them to do.

The next phase of Web page development is marketing design. We don't want to sound like a broken record, but this book should give you everything you need to develop perfectly marketed Web pages.

The last phase of designing a Web page is technical design. This phase probably will prove the most costly. Companies with the in-house expertise to turn hard-copy art into online pages are rare, so you'll either have to hire new personnel or contract with a consulting firm.

In a perfect world, every company would have an in-house staff to manage and maintain its Web site. However, the cost of hiring a full-time Web team makes it a luxury in most situations. But don't dismiss the idea out of hand. You may be able to hire an individual with enough talent and experience to handle multiple phases of your entire Web project. Keeping the right person on staff could reduce your outsourcing expenses considerably. The cost for hiring an individual like this ranges from $65,000 to $90,000 per year. (These figures include all costs related to the hire.)

Your other option is to outsource this part of the project. In most cases, this is far more feasible economically. The fee for transforming your hard-copy art into effective Web pages ranges from $80 to $140 per page, depending on the consultant and the amount of work involved.

Another option is to hire an outside firm to develop all aspects of your Web pages. Unfortunately, there are a couple of drawbacks to this strategy. First, only a handful of consulting firms can do the whole thing. Most consulting firms understand only parts of the process. Question thoroughly any consultants you consider. Make sure they truly understand every aspect of Web-page design.

Second, utilizing one firm to handle every step of this process can be costly. A firm that can really do it all will charge $250–$500 dollars per page. The truth is, after reading this book, you shouldn't *need* to hire a company with all these capabilities.

DESIGNING INTERACTIVE WEB APPLICATIONS

As we discussed the marketing advantages of the Web, we stressed that one of its most important features is interactivity. It allows you to build rapport with your visitors, and separates you from everyone else marketing themselves on the Web. Unfortunately, the cost of creating interactivity on your site can be quite high, because it's unlikely your company will have the in-house expertise to develop it. But if you decide to hire someone to handle other parts of your Web-site development, you might as well try to find someone with the skills needed to make the site interactive.

When it comes to Web-site interactivity, most companies should seek the help of an outside consultant. Only an experienced programmer should tackle complex projects such as surfer registration techniques, message boards, chat areas, and MUSEs. Make sure the consultants you contract with have experience developing interactive sites, and don't be afraid to ask to see some of their work.

The cost of hiring a firm to create interactive areas on your site will be quite high. Total cost will vary, depending on what type of interactivity you want, but it can range anywhere from $1,500 for a simple message board to $30,000 for a fully developed MUSE including graphics and real-time communication.

MARKETING YOUR SITE

Making sure you let the Web community know your site is an important phase in the development of your overall marketing plan. In this book we cover many techniques for marketing your site, both online and off. Most of these strategies we put forward are simple; any company of any size can accomplish them. Because your company is almost certainly already engaged in an ongoing advertising and marketing effort, the additional costs of announcing your Web site through traditional media should be minimal.

Announcing and promoting your site via the Internet is a little more involved, but it's still fairly simple to do. If you follow our guidelines, it shouldn't cost much, if anything. Marketing your site by purchasing ad space on other site locations, however, requires some serious cash. This type of online advertising can cost from $100 to $20,000 per month.

You might also consider hiring a consulting firm to promote your site on the Internet. Many Web-presence providers will do this for an additional fee of $150–$1,000 per month.

MONITORING, MAINTAINING, AND IMPROVING YOUR SITE

Now that we've covered the initial costs of creating your Web site, let's look at the ongoing costs of maintaining and, we hope, improving your site over time.

If you've handled everything in-house, you're in a great position to improve your site on an ongoing basis. In fact, this is the most desirable and flexible situation. You have the Web people on staff to respond to changes in the company, late-breaking product announcements, or moves made by your competition. You can upgrade and add pages at will. Your greatest ongoing cost will be your Web team's salaries.

If, on the other hand, you've contracted with a Web-presence provider and consultants, you'll incur some new costs when you want to change or upgrade your site.

The first of these new costs stem from monitoring the number of visitors to your site. You'll want to determine who visits your site, where they come from, and what part of your site they visit the most. Most Web-presence providers furnish this information monthly for $200–$350 per quarter.

Beyond simply monitoring your site's progress, there's the ongoing imperative to improve and build onto your site. It's essential to offer new and different pages at least once a month. You should change your homepage that often, as well. The fees for these changes and upgrades are the same as for Web-page development.

Don't forget the cost of periodic interaction with visitors to your site who register and provide their e-mail addresses. You'll use this information periodically to inform them of changes to or new features on your site. Your Web-presence provider may conduct this type of follow-up work, typically for $50–$80 an hour.

A SUMMARY WITH REAL-WORLD SCENARIOS

We've given you the numbers, now let's explain what they mean. The five scenarios in the following section illustrate everything we've said so far about online marketing costs. These companies are fictitious, but we base the scenarios on real-world situations. We follow each scenario with a table of specific recommendations for each company. These tables include low-, medium-, and high-cost figures for each step of the process. Use this section as a ballpark guide to what you can expect to pay to establish your Web site.

SCENARIO 1: SMALL COMPANY, SMALL PLANS

Our first scenario involves a small to mid-size company with a limited budget. They can't afford all the bells and whistles, so they plan to put up a simple, five-page site. They don't have the necessary in-house expertise to handle the technical phases of Web-site development, but they have read this book and have an excellent grasp of what it takes to create an effective marketing plan. They're a creative bunch, so they plan to create their own graphics.

TABLE 12-1 FIRST YEAR ESTIMATE FOR A SMALL COMPANY WITH SMALL PLANS

Phase	Low Cost	Medium Cost	High Cost
Acquiring an Internet connection and domain name	$1,800	$3,000	$4,800
Purchasing and installing server hardware	0	0	0
Purchasing, installing, and configuring server software	0	0	0
Developing basic Web strategy	0	0	0
Designing Web pages	$400	$500	$700
Designing interactive Web applications	0	0	0
Marketing the site	0	0	0
Monitoring, maintaining, and improving the site	$600	$1,100	$1,600
Total for first year	$2,800	$4,600	$7,100

We recommend this company utilize a Web-presence provider to develop its Web site. This is the most cost-effective way to establish the online presence the company's managers want. The Web presence provider can handle the technical aspects of Web-page design, working from the company's own creative marketing plan. The company will change and amend two of its five pages at least once a quarter, and the homepage once a month. Because their Web-presence provider's machine will run their site, they don't have to worry about Internet connection or server setup costs. The company's limited budget won't allow them to utilize interactive marketing techniques, but they can

TABLE 12-2 LONG-TERM COSTS OF A SMALL COMPANY WITH SMALL PLANS

Time Duration	Low	Medium	High
3 years	$7,600	$12,800	$19,900
5 years	$12,400	$22,500	$32,700

market their site throughout the Web using the no- and low-cost strategies we describe in earlier chapters.

The long-term cost projection shown in Table 12-2 assumes that little will have changed at the end of three to five years on the small company's Web site, that the managers continue to implement their original marketing plan, and that they change and amend their five pages on schedule.

SCENARIO 2: SMALL COMPANY, BIGGER PLANS

Our next fictitious company is another small to mid-size operation, but these managers have allotted a large budget for their excursion into Web marketing, and hope to make a splash. They want Web marketing to become an integral part of their overall marketing plan by the year 2000. They also want to utilize a wide range of tactics to help them reach their long-term marketing goals. At this point, the company lacks the technical expertise to run a site on its own.

We recommend this company utilize a Web-presence provider to establish and maintain its site. The staff possesses limited technical knowledge, so the cost of hiring personnel or outsourcing continuous maintenance on an in-house site would be far too high. The company will have to pay the Web presence provider monthly fees for using its server to host the site, but this is still far cheaper than establishing an

TABLE 12-3 FIRST YEAR COST ESTIMATE FOR A SMALL COMPANY WITH BIG PLANS

Phase	Low Cost	Medium Cost	High Cost
Acquiring an Internet connection and domain name	$2,500	$3,500	$5,000
Purchasing and installing server hardware	0	0	0
Purchasing, installing, and configuring server software	0	0	0
Developing basic Web strategy	0	0	0
Designing Web pages	$800	$1,000	$1,400
Designing interactive Web applications	$2,500	$3,500	$5,000
Marketing the site	0	0	0
Monitoring, maintaining, and improving the site	$3,400	$5,600	$7,000
Total for first year	$9,200	$13,600	$18,400

TABLE 12-4 LONG-TERM COSTS OF A SMALL COMPANY WITH BIGGER PLANS			
Time Duration	**Low**	**Medium**	**High**
3 years	$21,000	$31,800	$42,400
5 years	$32,800	$50,000	$66,400

in-house Web server. The company will probably need about 10 Web pages, including a message board and registration form for interactive marketing. The Web-presence provider can design these features. Interactivity will increase monthly fees, as well as start-up costs. With this kind of expenditure on Web marketing, company managers will have to keep close tabs on the results, so a detailed hit report—provided by the presence provider—is essential to this plan. Because they have set lofty goals for their marketing, they must constantly improve and upgrade the site, altering and amending its pages on a monthly basis.

In our analysis of the long-term costs in Scenario 2, we looked at the total project costs at the end of three years and five years. We assumed the company still markets the site aggressively, and that the managers' goal is still to increase the company's Web presence on the Web with creativity, not by increasing the number of pages. This creativity will call for them to continue spending at the same rate to produce inventive ways to interact with their surfers.

SCENARIO 3: BIG COMPANY, SMALL BUT GROWING PLANS

Our third scenario involves a large company. The firm's managers aren't yet convinced the Internet should become a big part of their marketing scheme, but they want to experiment with the medium. They won't allocate a large budget for the first year, but they know they must spend some money to give it a chance to work. In fact, if the company's first year on the Web shows any promise, they've committed to going online in a bigger way. Also, the company has a large technical department with an aptitude for learning and adapting to new technology. At this time, however, the department has no experience with Internet-related technology.

Our recommendation for this company is somewhat complicated. Because the firm is testing the Web for its compatibility with their business, we recommend the company use a Web-presence provider for the first year. This will save on the non-essential costs of establishing an Internet connection and Web-server setup. To ensure the first year shows promise, however, they should establish a fundamentally sound Web site. This means 20 pages, with snappy graphics and engaging features. They should also make the most of Web interactivity with message-board and surfer-registration systems. They should assume from the start that their Web experiment will be successful.

Because this is a large company, they should capitalize on their size by using the first year to train their in-house technical staff to establish and run a Web site. This knowledge will save money during years two through five. Because they lack the Internet connection, we also advise them to pay the Web-presence provider a quarterly fee to market their site on the Internet. As always, the company should change its pages frequently to keep the site looking new and fresh.

Now let's examine year two of Scenario 3. We assume the first year showed great promise and the company managers are now convinced the Web is a viable marketing option. They're ready to make a long-term commitment to the Internet. We also assume their in-house

TABLE 12-5 FIRST YEAR COST ESTIMATE FOR A BIG COMPANY WITH SMALL GROWTH PLANS

Phase	Low Cost	Medium Cost	High Cost
Acquiring an Internet connection and domain name	$2,500	$3,500	$5,000
Purchasing and installing server hardware	0	0	0
Purchasing, installing, and configuring server software	0	0	0
Developing basic Web strategy	0	0	0
Designing Web pages	$2,000	$2,700	$3,500
Designing interactive Web applications	$2,500	$3,500	$5,000
Marketing the site	$1,000	$1,500	$2,000
Monitoring, maintaining, and improving the site	$3,500	$4,200	$5,000
Total for first year	$11,500	$14,400	$20,500

technical department has gained the expertise needed to purchase, install, and maintain a Web site, and they've added no new technical staff.

One thing we don't assume, but suggest, is that they purchase Web pages and interactive programs designed and utilized by the Web-presence provider for use in the initial setup of the in-house Web site. Many Web-presence providers state in their contracts that Web pages created by them remain their property. Other Web-presence providers state the opposite. For our purposes, we assume the company must pay a small fee for the rights to these pages initially.

The company now brings most of the site's operating and maintenance functions in-house. The Internet connection is a T-1, enabling the company to handle the large amounts of traffic to its site. We assume that even though they used a Web-presence provider the first year, they now have paid a fee to establish their own domain name. Their hardware is a Pentium Pro PC with 64 MB of RAM. They purchased a server software package, because it best suits their long-term plans.

For an analysis of long-term costs in Scenario 3, we look at overall costs at the end of three years and five years. We assume this company continues to run its site in-house, with no additional personnel or hardware. We also assume the company hasn't contracted with any

TABLE 12-6   SECOND YEAR COST ESTIMATE FOR A BIG COMPANY
WITH SMALL GROWTH PLANS

Phase	Low Cost	Medium Cost	High Cost
Acquiring an Internet connection and domain name	$32,500	$52,000	$68,500
Purchasing and installing server hardware	$8,000	$8,500	$9,000
Purchasing, installing, and configuring server software	$1,500	$2,000	$3,000
Developing basic Web strategy	0	0	0
Designing Web pages	$1,000	$1,500	$2,000
Designing interactive Web applications	0	0	0
Marketing the site	0	0	0
Monitoring, maintaining, and improving the Site	0	0	0
Total for first year	$43,000	$64,000	$73,500

TABLE 12-7 LONG-TERM COSTS OF A BIG COMPANY WITH SMALL BUT GROWING PLANS

Time Duration	Low	Medium	High
3 years	$87,000	$130,400	$162,500
5 years	$152,000	$234,400	$299,500

consultants during this time. Their current staff handled any technical developments through education and training. They still have to pay an Internet service provider for the Internet connection. These long-term figures also reflect first-year expenses, when the company outsourced Web production and maintenance.

SCENARIO 4: BIG COMPANY, BIG PLANS

Scenario 4 involves a large, well-financed company, whose managers want to create a large project on the Web. They have allocated a huge budget to create the best site money can buy. They plan to add personnel to handle the project. They've made a long-term commitment to maintaining a dynamic online presence. They want to become known as one of the best sites on the Web, a place every surfer will want to visit repeatedly.

We recommend this company bring the Web site in-house. They will have to hire three full-time employees to handle every aspect of the creation and maintenance of the Web site. This expertise will be expensive but it's the only way to effectively manage a site of the magnitude this company wants. The upside is, they won't have to rely on, or pay for, outside consultants to develop their Web pages.

The company will have to establish a T-1 connection to the Internet. We also recommend using a UNIX-based workstation as the Web server. This machine will be able to handle the traffic and future expansion this site will experience. The company should purchase the software to run the site; this software will offer features to better meet the company's goals.

The company should buy three months' advertising on an already popular Web site, such as "Yahoo!" or "Lycos," to help establish it as one of the best places to visit.

TABLE 12-8   FIRST YEAR COST ESTIMATE FOR A BIG COMPANY WITH BIG PLANS

Phase	Low Cost	Medium Cost	High Cost
Acquiring an Internet connection and domain name	$32,500	$52,000	$68,500
Purchasing and installing server hardware	$20,000	$22,000	$25,000
Purchasing, installing, and configuring server software	$1,500	$2,000	$3,000
Developing basic Web strategy	0	0	0
Designing Web pages	0	0	0
Designing interactive Web applications	0	0	0
Marketing the site	$50,000	$60,000	$70,000
Monitoring, maintaining, and improving the site	0	0	0
New personnel	$195,000	$225,000	$270,000
Total for first year	$299,000	$361,000	$436,500

For our analysis of the long-term costs in Scenario 4, we looked at the project at three years and five years. We assume the long-term plans stay on track, that the company won't need to hire additional personnel to handle the expansion of the site, and that the company continues to purchase three months' advertising every year to help keep its site in the limelight.

To keep the site state-of-the-art, the company will have to add new hardware and software technology over the course of the next four years. These additions include real-audio and full-motion video capabilities. The long-term figures reflect these additions.

TABLE 12-9   LONG TERM COSTS OF A BIG COMPANY WITH BIG PLANS

Time Duration	Low	Medium	High
3 years	$867,000	$1,053,000	$1,279,500
5 years	$1,445,000	$1,755,000	$2,132,500

SCENARIO 5: ANY SIZE COMPANY, MEDIUM PLANS, BUT COMPLETELY HANDS-FREE

We've examined large and small businesses with a variety of Web-site budgets and goals, but in Scenario 5 we look at a company that plans to use consultants and Web-presence providers to handle every aspect of the site. All the company managers want to see are the benefits and rewards of making this decision. They'll require the consulting firm to stay within a budget of $15,000 for the first year and $40,000 for three years. They believe the Web is an avenue of great promise and opportunity, so they want their site to be thoughtfully designed and marketed.

We recommend the company hire a Web-presence provider. In this case, however, not just any provider will to do. This company needs a full-service Web-presence provider that understands every aspect of Web-site production and maintenance. This kind of expertise is rather expensive, but it allows for the establishment of a well-planned site. We recommend a site of 10 pages with some interactivity, including an area for a message board with a topic related to the company's line of business. The Web-presence provider should adjust and maintain the site throughout the year, altering half the pages at least once per quarter. The provider also should post press releases to newsgroups at least once a month. Once every quarter, the Web-presence provider should

TABLE 12-10 FIRST YEAR COST ESTIMATE FOR ANY SIZE COMPANY WITH MEDIUM PLANS, BUT COMPLETELY HANDS-FREE

Phase	Low Cost	Medium Cost	High Cost
Acquiring an Internet connection and domain name	$2,000	$3,000	$4,000
Purchasing and installing server hardware	0	0	0
Purchasing, installing, and configuring server software	0	0	0
Developing basic Web strategy	$800	$1,000	$1,200
Designing Web pages	$1,200	$1,500	$2,000
Designing interactive Web applications	$2,000	$2,500	$3,000
Marketing the site	$1,000	$1,500	$2,000
Monitoring, maintaining, and improving the site	$4,000	$5,000	$6,000
Total for first year	$11,000	$14,500	$16,200

TABLE 12-11 LONG-TERM COSTS FOR ANY SIZE COMPANY WITH MEDIUM PLANS, BUT COMPLETELY HANDS-FREE

Time Duration	Low	Medium	High
3 years	$25,000	$33,500	$42,200
5 years	$39,000	$52,500	$56,700

supply a hit-rate report, including where the surfers come from, so company managers can see the results of their investment.

In analyzing the long-term costs of the company in Scenario 5, we examine the project after the site has been running for three and five years. We assume the costs of doing business haven't changed and the overall strategy of the site remains constant. We also assume the company's approach remains completely hands off.

THE COSTS OF NOT MAKING A MOVE

We discussed in some detail all of the costs of marketing your company on the Web. We analyzed every aspect of the business decisions involved in allowing your company to move into cyberspace. Now we explore the costs of *not* being on the Web.

UNSEEN REWARDS

The first loss you may see is simply an unrealized gain. Advertising and marketing on the Web presents opportunities. If you elect not to go online, you'll miss them. The Web's potential for generating direct sales is both feasible and practical. We're not talking about instant profits, but opportunities to grow your revenue base. We advise companies working with direct sales features on the Web to aim to break even the first year. Sales will increase in years to come, once your site becomes established. Breaking even the first year may not sound exciting, but the Web's growth will lead to astronomical direct-sales numbers before the decade is over. A study conducted by the Cross-Industry Working Team predicts that businesses will transact 17 *billion* Web transactions per year by the year 2005. That's a lot of money changing hands, and we're sure your company wants to be a part of it.

The Web is also a great place to get exposure. Putting a dollar figure on the benefits of this exposure is nearly impossible. We can only re-state the obvious: No other advertising or marketing medium can put your company before more people.

Remember...

- The cost of marketing on the Web includes many factors. Compare the costs of each factor and decide which best suits your needs and your budget.

- Base your decision to keep your Web site in-house or to outsource the work on your long-term goals for your site. If you plan to continually expand and build your site for years to come, your best choice may be to run your site in-house. Otherwise, outsourcing is probably the wisest choice.

- Choosing not to invest on a Web presence may cost your company both future sales and future exposure.

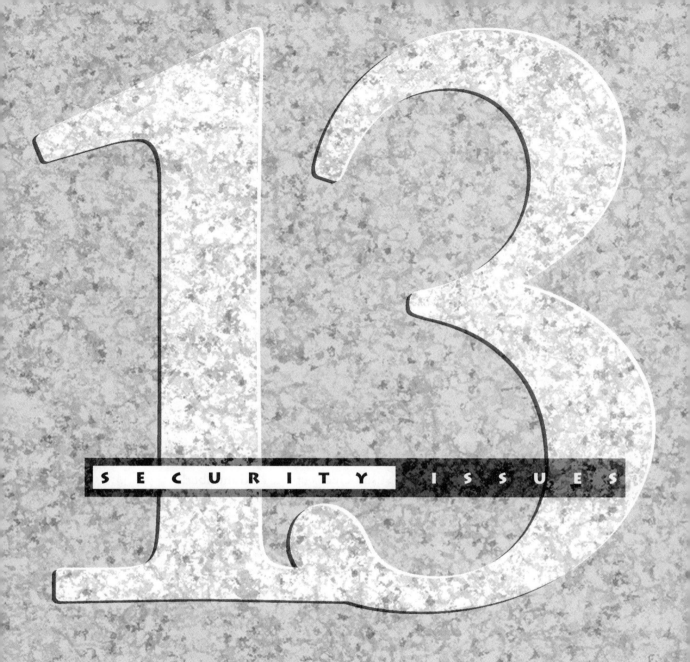

13

SECURITY ISSUES

One of our goals when we set out to write this book was to give readers a warts-and-all portrait of the Internet, and we believe we've done a good job of exploring the pros and cons of taking your company online. In this chapter we take a hard look at what may be the biggest wart in cyberspace—*security*.

The Internet is an unsecure environment. It's an open, largely unpoliced region with tremendous potential for lawlessness. In most cases, your data is no safer on the Net than your wallet would be on the dashboard of an unlocked car. In other words, your company may be locked up tight as a bank vault, but once you go online, everyone can get the combination.

When Dan Geer of OpenVision Technologies, Inc. (http://www.ov.com) spoke at the 1995 Lisa Systems Administration Conference on Electronic Commerce, he related a true story about a talk show he had appeared on with two other Internet security experts. The host asked the experts if they'd ever used their credit cards to make unsecure purchases over the Internet. The first expert said, yes, he had used his credit card to purchase flowers for his mother over the Internet. Geer responded that he, too, had purchased flowers for his mother over the Internet. The third expert admitted that he had done the same thing. The difference was he used Geer's credit card number!

Securing the Internet would require securing every individual computer connected to the Net—a virtually impossible task. One weak link would compromise the entire chain.

You can take certain steps to protect your Web site from hackers, flamers, and other intruders, however. A new generation of encryption software and hardware even makes it possible to conduct reasonably secure financial transactions online.

Before we explore some possible solutions, though, let's look at the obstacles to a secure Internet.

HACK THE PLANET

As we explained in Chapter 1, educational and scientific communities established the Internet to facilitate the free exchange of ideas and information. The idea that this valuable new resource would ever be misused was the last thing on anyone's mind. In the early days of the computer revolution, scientists frequently would share computer system passwords, if they used passwords at all. Even government and military facilities often paid little attention to protecting their systems.

They actually had little reason to worry. Thirty years ago, relatively few computers existed. No hackers with mainframes in their basements stayed up all night trying to break into the computer systems of large government and educational institutions. Encrypting the data sent over phone lines seemed to be enough. That attitude, however, has changed with the times.

Today, an average desktop PC has as much power as a roomful of computers had only 10 years ago. Data encryption schemes once thought to be unbreakable can now be cracked in a few months using supercomputer technology. Scores of highly skilled hackers live to pit their abilities against sophisticated computer security systems.

The government's first response to the hacker phenomenon was to close up shop, ignore them, and hope they'd go away. Whenever a military base suffered a computer break-in, the security breach was merely closed and the hacker ignored.

But the hackers didn't go away. The military failed to understand that what motivated these computer cowboys wasn't the data, but the hack itself. Every new security system became a new challenge. Break-ins were often no more than joyrides; the data were trophies and proofs of success to the hacker community.

Hacking was—and is—a game; the object is to break in, look around, and leave without being detected. A case in point is Kevin Mitnick, an elite hacker long sought for his illegal activities. In February 1995, authorities arrested Mitnick and charged him with computer fraud and access-device fraud. During his "reign," Mitnick stole an estimated 20,000 credit card numbers, gathered over a million dollars worth of computer data, and racked up millions of dollars in fraudulent cellular phone bills. Mitnick never used the credit card numbers, but kept them as proof of his deeds.

In 1994, the Secret Service reported 2,600 attempted break-ins to Internet-connected computers.

DON'T PASS THE PASSWORD

Widespread computer use makes computer security, on and off the Internet, a subject of ongoing concern. Do the secretaries in your company use computers? If personnel or salary information is maintained on those computers with no passwords or forms of encryption, anyone with even the most basic computer knowledge can gain access to confidential data.

Venturing onto the Internet, from a security standpoint, isn't much different than securing access to your secretary's computer. Just as much care and forethought is needed to securely conduct business on the Internet. While many people feel leaving their computers unprotected is an acceptable risk, others will want to isolate the room from any outside source, encrypt the data, remove the disk drive, and lock them in a fire- and waterproof vault.

GIVE ME THE BAD NEWS FIRST

As we said, the Internet was not conceived with security in mind. It was *supposed* to be wide open. In a way, "Internet security" is an oxymoron. The Net wasn't designed to be secure. In fact, many experts believe the only way to ensure total security is to rebuild the Internet from the ground up.

The problem stems from the way computers transmit and receive data over the Internet. After it leaves your computer, data must travel through several other computers before reaching its destination. Once the data leaves your site, you have no control over its route, and that route may not be the same every time. This process is somewhat similar to the U.S. postal service. You have no control over the path a letter travels to reach its destination. You can watch the carrier take the letter from your mailbox, but after that, it's literally out of your hands. You have no idea what treatment the letter will receive as it passes from carrier to carrier and post office to post office. How do you know your mail wasn't opened? How do you know your mail wasn't altered? How do you know who actually wrote and sent the mail?

Internet security raises the same questions. Once an e-mail message leaves your site, anyone with access to any computer it travels through along the way could open it, read it, and possibly change it. While this isn't quite as easy as it sounds, almost any competent computer user can download the necessary files from the Internet to acquire this capability. Hackers often write their own intercept programs, which look for the first four common digits of credit card numbers and only open the "letters" that contain these numbers.

It can also be difficult to determine with any certainty the actual identity of the person sending a document over the Internet. Forging e-mail is extremely easy. E-mail documents can't be signed in the conventional way. And the "From:" tag in an e-mail message isn't enough to verify a sender's identity.

To combat this problem, digital signatures were developed. A digital signature is a file containing unique information directly linked to a company or an individual. This information is as distinctive as a person's signature. Digital signatures verify that the sender and receiver are the correct people, and that the information has not been modified during transmission. The information transmitted need not be encrypted to use a digital signature; a digital signature simply verifies sender, receiver, and information integrity.

In the future, digital signatures may play a key role in protecting Internet users from online credit card theft. Just as credit card transactions at retail establishments aren't valid without signatures, future credit card orders may require digital signatures. Digital signatures will be identifiable and traceable to the card holder, making online credit card theft much more difficult.

MY KEY IS SOLID! IT HAS TO BE SECURE!

The *Netscape Navigator* software includes a feature that allows users to determine whether they're viewing a site over a secure connection. A small, graphic door key symbol displays in the bottom left corner of the browser. The key symbol can take two forms: A broken key on a gray background indicates an unsecure connection. A solid yellow key on a blue background represents a secure connection (see Figure 13-1). Also, URLs beginning with https:// instead of http://, indicate that the document comes from a secure server.

For a secure transaction to take place, a Web client must request a specific page from a Web server. The server must send the client a document that includes a list of supported encryption methods. The client must then return a message to the Web server, stating the strongest supported method of encryption. The Web server may then send documents encrypted with the agreed-upon method. Once the computers agree upon an encryption standard, *Netscape* displays the solid key signifying a secure connection.

Cryptography is the process of turning understandable and readable information into what appears to be gibberish. Encryption is the act of coding data in this way.

Unfortunately, a solid key doesn't ensure a secure transaction. Even *Netscape's* elegant security solution isn't unbreachable. On August 15, 1995, two individuals working separately shook up the world of

FIGURE 13-1

Solid and Broken Netscape Keys

electronic commerce by breaking the 40-bit encryption used in the international version of *Netscape Navigator*. It took only eight days after release of the software for a French researcher, Damien Doligez (http://pauillac.inria..fr/~doligez/sll), and Swedish cryptography enthusiast David Byers (http://dcs.ex.ac.uk/~aba/ssl) to break the code. Doligez, working at the *Institut National de Recherche en Informatique et en Automatique* (INRIA), Paris, a French research institute, used 120 networked computers to break the 40-bit key. Netscape claimed the value of the CPU time was worth approximately $10,000. Doligez disagrees with Netscape's CPU time assessment, but agrees the data returned is not worth the time and effort required to break the 40-bit key.

CPU stands for central processing unit, the microprocessor or "brains" of your computer. You may be familiar with CPU product names such as 386, 486, Intel Pentium, Intel Pentium Pro, Motorola 68040, PowerPC, or DEC Alpha.

"CPU time" refers to how much time a CPU spends on a particular program. Many companies assign this time a dollar value, and some organizations even sell their CPU time. For example, say your company buys a PC for $3000 and plans to use it over the next three years. CPU time value per day would be $2.74. ($3000 divided by three years divided by 365 days a year.)

Netscape estimates that a 40-bit, RC4 encrypted message would take, on average, 64 MIPS-years (million instructions per second—a way to rate CPU speed) to break. That would be a a full year of processing time for a 64-MIPS computer. By this estimate, Doligez's 120 computers are equivalent to 2,920 MIPS, more than 45 times faster than a 64 MIPS computer.

Then, on September 17, 1995, two graduate students at the University of California at Berkeley found a security hole in Netscape's secure server product. Ian Goldberg and David Wagner discovered that Netscape had based the random-number generator of its encryption system on the computer's internal timekeeper, the system clock.

The process of encryption relies largely on random numbers. The greater the ability of a computer or program to generate random numbers, the better the encryption. If a hacker can discover how those random numbers are generated, he or she can easily determine the "key" and decrypt all the information sent between the two computers. Nescape's use of the system clock as the basis for its encryption system is a definite no-no in cryptography circles, and proved to be a bad move.

In October 1995, the same Berkeley students and faculty reported security flaws in the basic Internet structure itself—the TCP/IP protocol (Transmission Control Protocol/Internet Protocol). A hacker, located on a segment of computer cable between the Web client and Web server, can view data transactions between the two computers. After intercepting and viewing the data, the hacker can forge a reply to the client. If the impostor message reaches the client before the actual reply from the Web server, the impostor's reply is accepted and the actual reply from the Web server is rejected, allowing the impostor to alter data without a trace.

As these examples show, even *Netscape*'s security system offers no real protection against a determined hacker. Don't be lulled into a false sense of security by the image of a solid key.

WHAT'S AN ACCEPTABLE RISK WHEN IT'S NOT MY MONEY?

In the previous section, we described several ways hackers use the Internet to intercept passwords, credit card numbers, bank statements, and other personal financial information. Some companies will say, "Hey, it's not my money they're stealing, and besides, credit card companies take the loss."

But in a roundabout way, it *is* your money. If customers dealing with your firm don't get a warm, fuzzy feeling, they won't feel safe doing business online. Given the option of purchasing a product from a secure vendor or an unsecure vendor, consumers are far more likely to spend their money where they know it's safe. You wouldn't unlimber your wallet and flash your wad on a street corner in the bad part of town, even if you really wanted that hot dog. Similarly, Internet users won't want to send unsecure credit card information out onto the Net, at least not for long.

Although many people currently do business this way on the Internet, you can bet that's going to change. The media are already exposing the Internet's most insignificant security flaws, scaring off would-be online shoppers. And your competitors won't hesitate to highlight the fact that they use a secure server to protect their customers' financial information, and you don't. This can make your company look careless in handling online financial transactions.

You probably won't see your customers switch from your unsecure Web site to a secure site. The Net isn't like a real-world shopping mall, where customers can walk up to a counter and complain. Your online customers could send you e-mail, but they probably won't. Sales will simply drop, and you won't know why.

The cost of getting a secure server up and running is relatively high for most companies and providers, but, as is true of almost all computer technology, the price is dropping. Because of the added expense, you may be willing to take risk using a non-secure Web server. But your company won't appreciate the public complaints of customers whose credit card information was stolen while purchasing products from your Web site. How much will that cost you?

When your program saves credit card information to the Web server, be sure it places the information outside the reach of the Web server software. Storing credit card information in the same directory as the form or CGI program that collects customer information is a dangerous practice. Have your CGI program write the data to a secure directory and remove it

Being Unsecure Can Lose a Sale

In the process of selling Web advertising to several companies, we came across a federal credit union interested in going online. We entered the bidding process with a competitive proposal, and it looked like we had the deal tied up.

But two days before the credit union was to award the contract, an outside consultant asked union officials if they had any plans to put account information online. The officials replied that they didn't plan to do so immediately, but might consider it in the future. The consultant remarked that they might want to consider going with a provider offering a secure server. The credit union called all the Web-presence providers involved in the bidding process to determine those with secure servers. Only the provider with the highest bid had a secure server in operation.

Can you guess who won the contract? The highest bidder nailed the contract because it had a secure server. The credit union only had immediate plans to put advertising on the Web and was at least a year and a half away from putting account information online. Nonetheless, Skyline lost the sale because we didn't have a secure server in operation. At this point we made plans to develop or purchase a secure Web server.

from the Web server as soon as possible. Keep credit card information offline as much as possible. Kevin Mitnick clearly demonstrated the dangers of failing to do so.

Some experts say using your credit card online in an unsecure manner is an acceptable risk. The chances of someone actually getting your credit card numbers off the Net and using them, they say, are very low. However, the media constantly spotlights Internet security vulnerabilities, raising public anxiety about doing business online.

It's up to you to make your online customers feel safe and secure in their dealings with your company. And it's your responsibility to reduce their actual risk. Your customers have entrusted their money to your company; the least your company can do is safeguard it. Many of your online customers know nothing about the potential dangers of online commerce. Don't teach them the hard way.

SMELL SOMETHING FUNNY?

One of the biggest dangers and main causes of today's mass Internet break-ins is the availability of so called "sniffer programs." These programs "sniff" out and intercept predetermined data moving across the Internet. A sniffer program easily can find super user passwords to computer systems, credit card numbers that begin with well-known number sequences—any data a hacker may find of interest.

A computer system's "super user" or "root user" has God-like powers in administering the computer. ("Root" and "super" are interchangeable in this context.) It can modify, delete, update, or add new information anywhere in a system. About the only thing a super user can't do is read information encrypted by other users.

There is nothing special or secretive about sniffer programs. Company network professionals use them to analyze and repair network connections. A sniffer can be as simple and inexpensive as a software program downloaded from the Internet and used in conjunction with a network card, or as expensive as dedicated hardware that attaches to the cable supplying Internet service.

A bug in some Sun Corp. computers allowed users to read a device that showed the first pieces of each packet of information going across the local connection. This small security hole allowed hackers to see user names and passwords as valid users logged into systems connected to Sun computers.

In December 1994, Scotland Yard arrested a British teenager for allegedly using a sniffer program to hack into some of the U.S. government's most sensitive computers. He had been monitoring secret communications between U.S. agents in North Korea. What made the crime particularly upsetting to authorities was that after the youth finished reading the documents, he put them on computer bulletin boards set up for hackers. The systems he obtained access to included those for ballistic weapons research, aircraft design, payroll, procurement, personnel records, and electronic mail. This teenager (and the hackers who subsequently found the information on the bulletin boards) compromised more than a million passwords.

The Air Force Office of Special Investigations reported that such a break-in required more than just remedial computer knowledge. The teenager used a special sniffer program to find user names and passwords for various computers located on the Internet. He was caught only after he left his computer online overnight connected to a U.S. Department of Defense computer. The U.S. Defense Information Systems Agency reported that the hackers had adversely affected military readiness.

Although sniffers are extremely effective hacker weaponry, they're limited in scope. A sniffer can only detect information that travels across a single local area network (LAN). In other words, sniffers can't view all Internet traffic, just a small subset. However, once hackers learn other systems' passwords, they can set up sniffers on those systems as well, extending their reach.

Sniffers also work in reverse, and can assist computer administrators in catching hackers. Even if a hacker erases all traces of evidence on the machine he broke into, a sniffer still knows the machine from which the hacker returned.

A sort of caller ID system was built into the Internet's TCP/IP protocol. It contains the addresses of source and destination machines for data traveling across the Net. When data reaches its destination, the address of the source machine can be recorded. Hackers typically circumnavigate this identifier by going through several machines to hide their original location, like movie spies routing telephone calls through several cities and countries to throw off a trace. Sniffer programs can view every piece of data flowing across the local network connection to log incoming and outgoing addresses.

To locate data of interest, hackers set up sniffers to find predetermined number and letter sequences. Finding credit card numbers is relatively easy; the hacker just sets up the sniffer to search for the first four common numbers. Every time a packet goes across the local network, the sniffer looks inside until it finds a match. It outputs the packet data to the hacker, or stores it in a file. Sniffers can also search packets for other common information. The words "login," "password," and "root" are commonly used to gain access to a wide variety of systems. "Root" is the most dangerous of these, because it's typically used for a system's super user account. With super user privileges, a hacker has total control of the computer system.

Tracing a sniffer is difficult and should be left to a network administrator or outside consultant. On a large network, sniffers can place a heavy demand on the machine sniffing the network, making it easier to identify. Sniffers also create large information logs; if disk space is shrinking rapidly for no apparent reason, a sniffer may be the cause.

The difficult task of hiding information from a sniffer requires extensive computer knowledge. Some solutions are hardware-based. For example, "active hubs" allow the hacker to gain information from only a single computer system. (A hub is a piece of equipment that splits a network connection to connect individual computers to the network.) Software solutions can be more difficult because a hacker can replace the commands used to look for sniffers.

Kerberos is one program used to beat the sniffers. The program encrypts data entered after login. Unfortunately, using *Kerberos* still leaves the login name and password vulnerable. *Kerberos* reportedly is also difficult to install, and the program requires that all password information be maintained on a single system. If that system were broken into, the entire network would be compromised. But *Kerberos* does a good job of encrypting information after login, and is considered a secure means of communication.

UNIX systems are the primary host machines for sniffer software programs. Windows-based PCs can also run sniffers but require someone on the inside, since PCs lack the ability to execute commands remotely from the network.

Sniffers continue to be one of the hacker's favorite and most effective tools. But encrypting important data transmitted across the Internet significantly reduces a sniffer's effectiveness. Because of the volume of data that typically travels over network connections, hackers usually go after only the most easily decipherable information. Encryption encourages them to leave your data for more easily targeted information.

SHUTTING DOWN INSTEAD OF BREAKING IN

Besides these annoying-but-innocuous joyriding hackers, there is a poisonous breed of hacker who breaks into computers for profit. These hired industrial spies are determined, not just to break into your system, but to shut down your system.

Shutting down your system is actually easier than breaking into it, as a Cornell University graduate student proved. In November 1988, Robert Tappan Morris Jr. wrote a program that came to be known as an "Internet worm." Morris took advantage of lax password policies and a program used to send and receive e-mail to enter UNIX systems. His worm program spread as an e-mail message that replicated itself on host systems, and then sent the same message to other computers. Using a simple e-mail account, Morris shut down thousands of computers.

Hackers can send thousands of messages to your e-mail account, inundating available disk space and making it difficult for your company to find actual sales and information inquiries.

Occasionally a company may bring this kind of electronic "mail-bombing" on itself. The case of the spam-happy law firm cited in Chapter 6 provides a good example. The volume of hate mail sent to Canter & Siegel cost the firm its Internet accounts. Using this book as a guide, your company is bound to fare better online.

Hackers and non-hackers alike also play "jokes" on the Internet. Posting fake messages to newsgroups, for example, is simple, and programs like *Netscape Navigator*, with its "Netscape News" interface, simplify it further. A third party posting a message like "40-year-old male looking for 12-year-old boys" to the newsgroup alt.religion.christian with your company as the ostensible source almost certainly will generate a paralyzing avalanche of hate mail; posting "All pedophiles will burn in hell!" to the alt.sex.pedophilia newsgroup will result in a similar response. Hackers sometimes get creative and post to newsgroups using the name of your company's CEO, including the appropriate return e-mail address. While everyone in your office may get a kick out of the e-mail response to your "pedophile" CEO, the boss won't be laughing.

Another way to virtually shut down Internet traffic to your site is to "ping" or "spray" it. A ping is similar to the procedure of the same name used on submarines to verify target distance. The ping command sends a small packet of information to a site, which then returns the packet to the sender. It's a way to determine whether a site is up and operating. A ping also reveals the relative distance from site to site based on the time it takes for the packet to travel both ways.

When the hacker sends a series of pings with no time between each ping, the command is called a spray (see Figure 13-2). Pings operate on a very low level, getting through when other connections won't. A hacker can spray your site to the point where no higher-level connections can get through, effectively shutting down your site.

A slight variation on the spray strategy involves sending thousands of requests for large graphic images to your Web server; your server spends all its time trying to send these large files back to the host, flooding your Internet connection.

Sometimes shutting down your system has more impact than breaking into it. Once an intruder breaks into a system and the systems administrator finds the method of access, the open door to the intruder can be closed. But it's difficult to protect your system from hackers posting slanderous information to the Internet in hopes that netizens who fall for the bait will flame your company.

FIGURE 13-2

Hackers can use ping and spray strategies to bring activity on your Web site to a grinding halt.

```
horizon 13% ping www.skyline.netPING
horizon.SKYLINE.NET (205.252.65.8): 56 data
bytes64 bytes from 205.252.65.8: icmp_seq=0
ttl=255 time=0.7 ms64 bytes from 205.252.65.8:
icmp_seq=1 ttl=255 time=0.5 ms64 bytes from
205.252.65.8: icmp_seq=2 ttl=255 time=0.5 ms64
bytes from 205.252.65.8: icmp_seq=3 ttl=255
time=0.6 ms64 bytes from 205.252.65.8: icmp_seq=4
ttl=255 time=0.6 ms64 bytes from 205.252.65.8:
icmp_seq=5 ttl=255 time=0.5 ms64 bytes from
205.252.65.8: icmp_seq=6 ttl=255 time=0.7 ms—
horizon.SKYLINE.NET ping statistics —7 packets
transmitted, 7 packets received, 0% packet
lossround-trip min/avg/max = 0.5/0.5/0.7 mshorizon
14% spray www.skyline.netsending 1162 packets of
lnth 86 to www.skyline.net ...          in 10.3
seconds elapsed time,          332 packets (28.57%)
droppedSent:   112 packets/sec, 9.4K bytes/
secRcvd:   80 packets/sec, 6.7K bytes/sec
```

OKAY, LET'S HEAR THE GOOD NEWS

The good news is that there are good guys in white hats trying to protect the Internet from hackers. (Okay, they probably don't wear hats.) No Internet police force goes out looking for computer hackers. However, groups of netizens have banded together to combat computer-related crime. Companies sell computer security hardware and software; colleges and universities help look for security vulnerabilities in the Internet, and concerned individuals write programs for better data encryption and to check a computer's vulnerabilities.

So far in this chapter, we've focused mainly on hacker horror stories. Although the following section deals with what we consider the good news about Internet security, you'll find no "success" stories here. A hacker who failed to breach a system's security won't make the evening news. For every system a hacker breaks into, many others stand their ground and hold up against a hacker's attacks. Unfortunately, claiming that your computer site is impregnable is enough to attract hackers who'll work day and night to break into your system. The only time a success story gets publicity is when a hacker is captured—usually after the hacker has done some damage.

CERT DOES MORE THAN FRESHEN YOUR BREATH

The Computer Emergency Response Team (CERT) is a government-sponsored organization formed in November 1988 after the Internet worm attack brought several thousand computers to their knees. Headquartered at Carnegie Mellon University's Software Engineering Institute (SEI), CERT develops strategies for responding to Internet security events.

The people at CERT and other security consultants are definitely the good guys. CERT helps ferret out hackers before they can do any damage. The organization works hand-in-glove with many systems administrators to help fight computer-related crime. Once a system is broken into, CERT tracks down the hacker using logs showing where the hacker came from and where he or she went. CERT then notifies other sites the hacker may have tried to infiltrate of the attempted attack. This kind of cooperation helps the Internet community fight and find hackers, and in some cases, secure their prosecution.

Since the Internet never sleeps, CERT is available around the clock. It maintains a 24-hour hotline at (412) 268-7090; an FTP site (ftp://info.cert.org) containing information on Internet security topics, and an electronic mailbox (cert@cert.sei.cmu.edu) that is continually checked during business hours. The FTP site (see Figure 13-3) includes security-related documents, past CERT advisories, and security tools for testing your system's vulnerabilities. CERT also maintains a

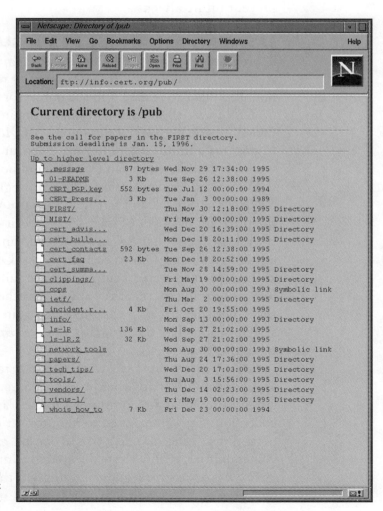

FIGURE 13-3

CERT's FTP site contains information and programs related to Internet security topics.

mailing list to inform subscribers of possible security vulnerabilities and bug fixes. To join the list, send an e-mail message to cert-advisory-request@cert.org. You'll also find these advisories on the Usenet newsgroup comp.security.announce.

If your company is concerned about Internet security, join CERT's mailing list to keep abreast of possible vulnerabilities in your system. Whether you join the list or not, CERT will inform your system administrator, via e-mail, of any possible attacks or break-ins they discover at your site. Working with CERT will help your site remain secure and prevent future attacks.

IS SATAN AN ANGEL IN DISGUISE?

A program known as *SATAN* (*Security Administrator Tool for Analyzing Networks*) shook up the Internet security world when its authors announced plans to release it to the public for free. The authors designed *SATAN* to assist systems administrators in determining security vulnerabilities on networked computers. *SATAN* may sound like a godsend to systems administrators hoping to ensure the security of their networks, but hackers too can use it to find holes in a system's defenses.

Why would anyone release such a program to the general public? *SATAN*'s authors, Dan Farmer and Wietse Venena, claim they released the program in hopes of increasing security awareness. Proponents of the release argue that *SATAN* doesn't do anything new, it simply takes advantage of well-known security holes. Opponents counter that not all Internet-connected computers have full-time systems administrators monitoring for security gaps, and furthermore, that *SATAN* allows those with no hacking experience to gain relatively easy access to a system scanned by the program, thus *increasing* the overall vulnerability of the Net.

SATAN isn't the first security program to raise hackles on the Internet. *Crack* and *COPS*, two other popular programs, have come under similar scrutiny. *COPS* (Computer Oracle Password and Security) is a collection of programs used to monitor various computer security vulnerabilities. Like *SATAN*, *COPS* doesn't *correct* the system's security vulnerabilities; it only alerts the system administrator to the problems.

Crack is a password-guessing program that tries to "crack" a system by trying easy passwords or words found in dictionaries. In Skyline's experience, *Crack* is an effective tool for finding users who've made the mistake of using easily guessed passwords. Programs like *npasswd* ensure a user enters a password the systems administrator feels is secure. The program is used in place of the password programs, *passwd* or *yppasswd*. On UNIX systems, *npasswd* forces users to enter a secure password the first time. These programs provide the same type of password-guessing techniques programs like *Crack* use, but guess in real time as the user enters his or her password, not after it's been updated on the system.

When setting up a Web server on a network, using programs like *SATAN*, *COPS*, and *Crack* lessens the chances of a hacker break-in. These programs expose well-known security vulnerabilities to systems administrators. However, since the source code for many operating systems and programs is widely available on the Internet, hackers can always sift through the code to find new, undiscovered security holes.

Eric Allman, the author of the *sendmail* program, stated at the 1995 Lisa Systems Administration Conference that he has turned his paranoia level to the maximum setting. *Sendmail* is the program responsible for sending and receiving mail on UNIX-based systems; hackers have used it many times to gain access to systems. In several cases, the hacker simply sent an e-mail message to the mail server to crash the machine or to gain access.

Some experts recommend that companies continually upgrade their *sendmail* software as a way of thwarting potential break-ins. Tom Coppeto of the Massachusetts Institute of Technology takes an entirely different approach. Every year he challenges his students to break into his *sendmail* system, with the condition that if they break in, they let him know how they did it so he can fix the hole. A student has yet to succeed. His secret? He uses an outdated version of *sendmail* that most people have forgotten how to break into.

ADVANCES IN INTERNET SECURITY PRODUCTS

New security systems, devices, and gimmicks seem to appear on the market every day. Short of locking your computer in a room with no outside connections and a guard on the door, nothing can make your system absolutely secure. However, the products discussed in this section can help reduce your risk.

Security products can take the form of software or hardware. Software is the least effective of the two. Hackers can get the source code for software security products and find ways to beat it, or they can "reverse engineer" (or "decompile") the software to see how it was written. While a similar process can be done to hardware products, it's typically extremely difficult and costly.

Security means different things to different people. The online security needs of the National Security Agency (NSA) will differ from the security needs of a local supermarket. However, both will probably want some kind of protection (see the NSA Web site, Figure 13-4). The NSA probably needs a product that strictly limits access to

FIGURE 13-4

The National Security Agency maintains this Web site to provide general information to the public. Notice the broken key in the bottom left-hand corner, signifying the document is not secure.

particular data to one or two people. But that might not work for the supermarket. When the main office tries to get payroll out every week, strict security standards can get in the way. A security system requiring passwords for each computer and every employee on every file, encrypting every file, and storing all data on removable disks is bound to delay the payroll. Your organization should take care to choose a security product that fits your needs, not one that stands in the way of your business.

SIMPLE SECURITY

Let's not overlook the first and most simple security product ever invented—the password. Passwords are your first line of defense in the fight to keep your data secure. Not establishing passwords on your computer system is the same as leaving the locks off your doors. The more passwords, the more difficult it is to get into your system. Passwords may not only be used for gaining entry to a system, but for gaining access to files and directories, as well.

The second level of computer system security is the encryption program. Most UNIX systems feature pre-installed encryption software. Two widely used UNIX commands are *des* and *crypt*. *Crypt* implements an encryption technique based on the German "Enigma" machine used during World War II, while *des* implements the government's Digital Encryption Standard (DES) form of encryption. *Crypt* encrypts passwords on UNIX systems. It can be used to encrypt other files, as well.

Both *des* and *crypt* should be used for low-level security files. For anything of importance, use stronger security, and truly sensitive data should not be stored on networked computers. Techniques for breaking *crypt*'s coding scheme are well-known among hackers. (Figure 13-5 shows an example of the *crypt* command encrypting a clear-text message using the password, "my_password.")

FIGURE 13-5

The crypt program turns ordinary text into gibberish.

```
horizon 1% cat unsecure.txtThis file contains text
that is not encrypted. Look, mom! Anyone canread
this file!horizon 2% crypt my_password <
unsecure.txt > secure.txthorizon 3% cat
secure.txt;™O» ™-Xo@†:at≥µÎd˘¢˜<-
:‰´™¸∞Û´7∆¤tO™3BAÓÛÕïDC†Oû`¥¿|Ëâ9Z>≤Yâ<V=ÏofiR
```

Another important step is to keep log files of all security-related information. Keeping logs of failed logins, attempted unauthorized access, new accounts, logins outside of normal business hours, and mystery files will alert you to potential attacks and help identify anyone trying to gain access to your system. A trail of failed logins may indicate that a hacker is trying to break a password, or an employee is trying to gain unauthorized access to information. New account creation is just as dangerous. This could mean a hacker already has entered your system and installed a backdoor. A "backdoor" is a way for the hacker to continue to enter your system even after the initial security hole has been closed. The hacker may have created a valid account for himself to gain "legitimate" access at will. Logins outside normal business hours may indicate that hackers have access to your system. Most hackers work between 9 P.M. and 6 A.M. HST (Hacker's Standard Time). It's the best time to access a system, since no one is sitting around the office wondering why the hard disk was just accessed for no apparent reason. On the other hand, an off-hours login could simply be an employee with insomnia.

Tracking down mystery files is another important security precaution. If you notice that the login program has a more recent date than the date it was installed, it could mean that someone has replaced it with a "Trojan Horse" program. A Trojan Horse, as its name implies, looks like an innocent program, but it's used to infiltrate your system and surreptitiously record passwords and other information.

WRAP THAT RASCAL!

A "wrapper" is a type of software package that logs requests for Internet services and provides a form of password control. Install a wrapper to limit access to certain programs and to log every request made to run those programs. For example, the program *finger* reports users located on a particular system, or to get more information on a particular user (see Figure 13-6). A wrapper can be placed on the *finger* program so that every time a request is made to get more information on a user, the Internet address of the requesting machine is logged to a file and the request is accepted or denied based on the information found in a type of password file.

Two types of password files exist for wrapper programs—"Allow" and "Deny." The Allow file includes the addresses of machines that

FIGURE 13-6

The finger program finds additional information about a user on a system.

```
horizon 14% finger dowlingLogin: dowling
Name: Paul J. DowlingDirectory: /home/dowling
Shell: /bin/tcshOffice:  Jr.On since Wed Dec 27
09:26 (EST) on ttyp0 from horizon.SKYLINE .Mail
last read Wed Dec 27 13:45 1995 (EST)No Plan.
```

may request the service, and the Deny file denies access to the included machines. Each file can incorporate a list of services the requesting machines can or can't access. For example, a machine may not have the ability to use FTP to transfer files, but may use *finger* to see other logged-in users.

The log files the wrapper program creates are helpful for determining whether a hacker has tried to attack your machine. For example, an unknown machine may make many attempts to obtain information from your system. Without the log facility of the wrapper program, these "inquiries" would go unnoticed. But because of the wrapper's log files, you can add the unknown machine to your systems Deny file and deny access.

SECURE WEB PRODUCTS

As we said at the beginning of the chapter, transactions between a Web client and server are inherently unsecure. To increase the level of security on the Web, companies have created secure Web-server and Web-client products. Secure Web servers and browsers are probably the most mainstream Web security products. As online financial transactions increase, so do the numbers of companies utilizing secure Web servers. Consumer demand will no doubt continue to influence more companies to supply secure Web browsers.

Netscape Communications (http://www.netscape.com) is probably the largest and most visible secure Web server and client software developer. The *Netscape Navigator* is the most secure browser available, and it works hand-in-glove with the *Netscape Commerce Server*. The *Navigator*, available free from Netscape's FTP site (ftp:// ftp1.netscape.com), includes 40-bit encryption to protect online transactions. The U.S. domestic version includes 128-bit encryption, exponentially better. According to independent Web-search sites such as *Yahoo*, over 75 percent of people using Web browsers use *Netscape Navigator*. This means that at least 75 percent of your online customers will have a secure Web browser. Netscape includes SSL (Secure Socket Layer) support in its *Navigator* product, allowing users to connect to any SSL-enabled Web server. The *Navigator* incorporates support for the Secure Courier Payment Protocol, providing payment support from the desktop to the financial institution.

The *Netscape Commerce Server* ensures data security with features such as server authentication, data encryption, data integrity, and user authorization. The *Commerce Server* incorporates Netscape's SSL protocol for secure transactions. Netscape has patched the security vulnerability mentioned earlier in the chapter, and no longer bases its encryption algorithms for the *Commerce Server* on the time stored in the computer system clock.

Open Market, Inc. (http://www.openmarket.com) (Cambridge, Massachusetts) sells the Open Market *Secure Web Server* to provide secure Web transactions. The Open Market *Secure Web Server* offers both S-HTTP (Secure HyperText Transport Protocol) and SSL security protocols, so that applications can be written to support any secure Web browser.

Spry, Inc. (http://www.spry.com) sells the Spry *SafetyWEB Server* to protect communication and commerce (see Figure 13-7). The Spry Web servers provide built-in database support, allowing companies to update their Web pages from company-created databases. The Spry server package includes additional software applications to help companies create and generate HTML pages without traditional programming knowledge or coding. They include a text indexing and search engine to help companies create Web search engines like *Yahoo* (http://www.yahoo.com). *SafetyWEB* also offers S-HTTP and SSL to protect online transactions.

HARDWARE-BASED SECURITY

While the algorithms may be similar to those of software encryption programs, hardware-based encryption is much more difficult to override. Hardware encryption can be placed at almost any point along a network—on the computer itself, to encrypt all data stored to the hard disk drive; between modems, to encrypt all data as it's transmitted; from computers to routers, and from routers to routers.

FIGURE 13-7

Spry offers Web clients and servers a free trial version of its Web server.

While this sounds easy and practical in theory, it's very expensive and difficult to install hardware-based encryption equipment. Securing the channel between you and your Internet provider requires that both parties have the same encryption hardware. As soon as the data is sent from your Internet provider to the Internet, the data is unsecure again.

The U.S. government is currently seeking to standardize the type of hardware encryption your company may use through mandated application of the Clipper Chip, a small, tamper-proof computer chip that's compatible with all communications standards. Its encryption capability is stronger than DES encryption and uses an 80-bit key. Almost any communications or computer device may incorporate it.

One of the problems blocking widespread implementation of the Clipper Chip standard is the rumor that the NSA, which developed the algorithm used for the encryption process, built a secret backdoor into the algorithm, giving them immediate decrypting capability.

SecurID is a hardware-based product that keeps users from forgetting or revealing passwords. SecurID was designed for companies with users who login from remote sites. The SecurID is a credit-card-sized device with a small screen that displays a random six-digit number once every minute. To log into a system using SecurID, the user must have a user name and password, just like other systems, and the six-digit SecurID number. The software on the host side of the network is in sync with the SecurID card to accept the randomly generated numbers. The user name and password prevent unauthorized use if the device is stolen; without the device, even knowing the user name and password is useless.

SecurID does have limitations. The system is only designed to prevent unauthorized access from conventional means, such as password guessing or password theft. Also, if a user loses the card, that user won't be able to access the system until he or she receives a new one. SecurID doesn't protect against hackers that break into systems through less conventional means.

A secure router can provide respectable levels of security without infringing too much on your local system. A router is a specific piece of hardware that allows your local network to talk to the Internet. A secure router allows only certain specific information you authorize it to accept to pass through the router. For instance, let's say you want only Web traffic to come through the secure router. You would then set up the secure router to block every request to the system except requests for Web data transfers. Secure routers pass packets of data from the Internet to the computer located on your local network, and vice versa.

FIREWALLS

Looking for one of the best hardware security solutions on the market? Firewalls take you as close to absolute security as is currently possible on the Internet. A firewall is a piece of equipment installed between

your network and the Internet that blocks data being transferred between the two. Just as the firewall in a car protects the passenger
compartment from the engine, a firewall computer system protects your
computer network from the Internet. Firewalls are similar to secure
routers; the difference is that firewalls don't pass packets between networks or computers (see Figure 13-8).

Firewalls isolate computers or networks that contain secure information. They're not needed for all Internet communications and should
be used only to block systems containing credit card numbers or other
sensitive data. The company puts all the information it wants the outside world to see on the firewall, and all other information on the
network inside the firewall.

The main advantage of a firewall is also its main disadvantage. While
a firewall can keep hackers from reaching internal systems, it also keeps
internal users from reaching the outside world. For instance, a Web
surfer can view files stored on the Web server located on the firewall,
but users on the internal network can't browse outside Internet
Web sites.

A firewall doesn't prevent all access to the outside world. But with a
firewall in place, access is only possible from the firewall. If an internal
user wants to log on to a remote machine, he or she must first log on to

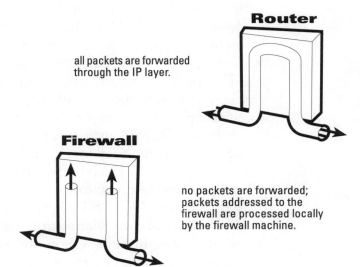

all packets are forwarded
through the IP layer.

Router

Firewall

no packets are forwarded;
packets addressed to the
firewall are processed locally
by the firewall machine.

FIGURE 13-8

A firewall blocks all network traffic
from reaching internal computers or
networks, while a secure router blocks
only certain traffic.

the firewall. E-mail from the outside world comes first to the firewall, which forwards the mail to the internal network. Mail aliases conceal the real user names of the people on the internal network. The real user name on inside network mail destined for the outside world is replaced with an alias and shows the firewall as the e-mail return address.

The firewall provides only four services: domain name service for the outside world; e-mail forwarding; FTP service, and Telnet service. Firewalls are set up and maintained for security, not service. If service is an important issue for your company, consider placing a non-secure machine on the outside of the firewall for general access.

Because firewalls are meant for security, systems administrators shouldn't administer them. A security administrator should take on that responsibility. Systems administrators typically have broad, general knowledge, and are concerned with getting systems to work together seamlessly. But a firewall is a specific piece of equipment with a specific duty, not a general host or server machine. The security administrator should have more training in firewall management, and a greater respect for security.

NON-STANDARD STANDARDS

Standards allow everyone's product to work with everyone else's, which in turn provides the consumer a wider range of choices. But who should establish the accepted standard of encryption and authenticity to the network world? The NSA? Or the National Institute of Standards and Technology (NIST)? How about RSA Data Security, Inc.? All three offer competing forms of encryption and authenticity verification, but who will win the battle over the standard?

NIST (http://www.nist.gov) holds a congressional mandate to develop digital signature standards for government; RSA, however, holds significant patents on digital signature algorithms and wants to be paid for their use. The RSA algorithm allows companies and individuals to create secure communications channels, which scares the NSA (http://www.nsa.gov:8080). The NSA would like everyone to use the Clipper Chip for secure communication, and entirely different methods of authentication. The RSA algorithm, however, provides both authentication and encryption security. Current government regulations allow companies to freely export software based on simple digital signature algorithms incorporating encryption of 40 bits or less.

However, companies incorporating the RSA algorithm may not export their software outside the United States and Canada.

In the spring of 1994, NIST announced a final Digital Signature Standard (DSS). The NIST announcement directly affects only U.S. civilian government agencies; however, its choices often become the de facto standards due to the government's large impact on the marketplace. After establishing the DSS standard, NIST announced that the standard could be used without royalties. RSA isn't at all happy about NIST's decision, since RSA holds patents on the technology used in the DSS standard. According to RSA, anyone using DSS should be required to pay RSA royalties and obtain a license. However, the government is sticking to its guns and has offered to pay the litigation fees of any government contractor sued by RSA (see Figure 13-9).

Will any of these technologies emerge as a standard? Or will they become standards only through government mandates? The battle is raging, and the outcome remains uncertain. While these entities slug it out, the ultimate casualties are business and the consumer.

The good news is that digital signature programs currently exist to protect Internet communications. The closer the government comes to a dispute-free standard, the faster the general public will accept the digital signature programs. Computer users in other countries already have access to this technology, and are free to use it at will, because U.S. patents aren't valid worldwide.

As the mainstream population goes online, standards will emerge, and utilizing digital signatures will become as simple as signing your name.

WHEN THE GOOD NEWS ISN'T GOOD

Philip Zimmerman, a Boulder, Colorado–based computer programmer, is currently under criminal investigation for exporting munitions. No, he isn't selling arms to the Contras or supplying explosives to the Iranians. He just put his encryption software on an FTP site. Since the Internet is global, some overseas users downloaded his software. The U.S. State Department places export restrictions on powerful encryption software, labeling them "munitions" under the International Traffic in Arms Regulation Act.

What exactly did Zimmerman write that landed him in such hot water? The program he wrote is called *PGP: Pretty Good Privacy*. The

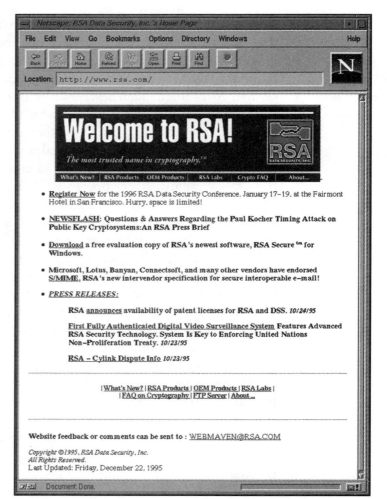

FIGURE 13-9

Users can download free evaluation copies of RSA Data Security software at its Web site.

PGP software uses the RSA algorithm to encrypt e-mail, which provides all the benefits of RSA encryption, including authentication and message integrity.

The government's investigation may have slowed Zimmerman, but he isn't stopping. He released additional software based on the *PGP* algorithm called *PGPfone*, which uses speech compression and cryptography to turn a notebook PC into a secure telephone. All of the software Zimmerman has written and distributed using the *PGP* algorithm is available free on FTP sites. Zimmerman hopes millions of people embrace his software. If the government outlaws it, millions of people will be criminals.

The export restrictions on this kind of software were imposed supposedly in the interest of national security. When foreign governments, pedophiles, terrorists, and drug dealers can encrypt data transmissions, the U.S. government has difficulty finding these criminals. If two suspected drug felons communicate with unencrypted e-mail messages, the government has a much easier time figuring out their content.

This may be true, but these software restrictions may, in the long run, pose a greater hardship on American companies. Currently, the U.S. government's export restrictions prevent encryption vendors from exporting security products based on greater than 40-bit encryption algorithms. The thinking behind the government policy is that strong encryption could become a shield for criminal activity. The problem is that 40-bit algorithms expose U.S.–based merchants and companies in the international cyberspace arena. Companies located outside U.S. borders are free to use the strongest encryption technology available. Projects are already under way in Australia and other countries to create a commercial 80-bit encryption code. The irony is that most of the algorithms are based on U.S. research.

Although Zimmerman's intent was good, the government considers his software a threat to national security. Zimmerman, however, fears the government will abuse its "point-and-click" wiretap ability. He also fears the government is creating a "society optimized for surveillance." He wants cryptography to give privacy back to the individuals who lost it during the information age.

Stewart A. Baker, formal NSA general counsel, says that since he's been on the "inside," he has "been struck by the extent to which the rules are observed, not to the extent to which they have been violated."

Most companies doing business on the Internet aren't up to anything illegal, but they still want to keep their company secrets. And most want the government to keep its nose out of their business.

So what are Zimmerman's future plans? "I intend to work full-time on making more encryption tools available to the general public for free," he says.

In August 1995, the White House announced it would permit the export of stronger encryption products. The draft policy would allow the export of 64-bit encryption keys, allowing encryption 16 million times harder to break than 40-bit encryption. But there's a hitch: Users would have to "escrow" their encryption keys with a government-certified third party. This third party would act as a kind of encryption key bank, holding the name of the company or individual registered to the key and the key itself. (A "key" is a password used to encrypt or decrypt a message.)

Putting these passwords in escrow would enable the government to decrypt messages in court-approved wiretaps.

Software vendors who want the ability to create a single version of their products for sale domestically, as well as abroad, accuse the government of forcing them to use key-escrow encryption in all their encryption products. The Business Software Alliance stated in a sternly worded letter to Vice President Al Gore, "In the name of 'national security,' it appears that the administration really is attempting to satisfy domestic law-enforcement concerns—without industry input, public debate, or congressional involvement." The government responded that the policy was based on public concerns raised in two public meetings.

TYPES OF SECURITY

Like online commerce, online security is on the Internet. New online security companies are emerging much the same way personal computer companies appeared during the 1980s. These new companies want to establish their technologies as the de facto standards of Internet security. In addition to the new companies, many larger companies are using their reputations and marketing muscle to offer security standards to the online community. In the end, the winners of this contest will be those whose technology is embraced by the most consumers and merchants.

ON A PACKET AND A PRAYER

Encrypting data at the packet level is becoming an attractive alternative to simply securing links between a client and a host. Craig Hunt, in *TCP/IP Network Administration*, defines "packet" as "a block of data that carries with it the information necessary to deliver it—in a manner similar to a postal letter, which has an address written on its envelope."

Since TCP/IP is the protocol of choice for use on the Internet, packet encryption technologies are gaining ground in the Internet security wars. Packet encryption uses a kind of secure router to encrypt the entire packet of information, including the header, and replace it with a new header and the encrypted old packet as data. The new header contains the address of the secure router on the other end, which receives the packet, removes the header, decrypts the old packet, and sends it to the proper receiver. This method of encryption is much better than encrypting a link because a new key can be used for each encrypted packet, rather than just for each connection.

Packet encryption technology is the best defense against hackers using sniffers. The unencrypted header on the secure packet allows the router to act as a firewall; only specific encrypted packets may pass through the router. Public key encryption not only secures the data, but authenticates the sender, as well. Packets can also be time-stamped with this technology. Hackers could capture encrypted packets and send them back at a high rate, much like pinging or spraying, to shut down a system. Time-stamping allows the system to ignore replayed packets so legitimate packets can get through.

Because the TCP/IP headers remain in place, the protocol of the Internet can stay in place and continue to send clear-text packets. This offers the flexibility of sending and receiving secure as well as unsecure packets, for business as usual without a major overhaul of the entire Internet. The ability to continue to send clear-text packets allows other security schemes to work on top or in place of packet encryption. Imagine encrypting packets of encrypted data—now *that's* secure! Since the algorithms will be pressed in silicon, the level of security is that much greater.

Packet encryption isn't Web-specific, so it works with every application that uses TCP/IP. Where other encryption schemes fail, packet encryption comes to the rescue. For example, when using the software encryption scheme *Kerberos*, you must send the clear-text user name and password ahead of the encrypted transmission. When using packet encryption, the user name and password also are encrypted. Because special hardware handles encryption and decryption, computers and operating systems run at their full speeds.

Packet-encrypting routers eliminate the need to dedicate links between routers. This allows you to set up a backup router as a standby in case the main router goes down. When the main packet encryption router goes down, the backup takes over, so no communications are lost. Because the technology doesn't use dedicated links, packet encryption routers can send data to any source, not just systems connected at the same speed with the same technology.

At the present time, packet encryption isn't ready for prime time. Standards must be developed, the industry must embrace the technology, and low-cost packet encryption must become available for home and small-business use. However, packet encryption will probably become the secure connection of the future, enabling companies and Internet users to adopt packet-level encryption without having to rely on their Internet service providers.

In October 1995, Atalla (http://www.tandem.com/prod/atalla.html), a San Jose, California–based subsidiary of Tandem Computers, Inc. (http://www.tandem.com), unveiled a product designed to provide secure Internet commerce. The company claims its WebSafe Internet Security Processor hardware device helps make Internet transactions more secure than existing security methods, such as Netscape's Secure Socket Layer or EIT's Secure HyperText Transport Protocol. Atalla provides companies with back-end hardware for transaction processing and front-end hardware for automated teller machines.

MasterCard is examining the WebSafe product for potential use in its current Secure Electronic Payment Protocol (SEPP). Jeff Stapleton, project manager for electronic commerce at MasterCard International (http://www.mastercard.com), says that the current version of MasterCard's SEPP proposal is software-only security, but the company expects to incorporate hardware-based encryption in the future.

Atalla plans to target companies and financial institutions planning to do business online who need greater security for Internet commerce. Hardware-based security such as WebSafe is considered better for Internet security because of its greater tamper resistance. WebSafe clams up when hackers try to pirate data by zeroing out its stored encryption information and denying the transaction. WebSafe implements both RSA (public key) and DES (private key) encryption technologies, making the product more useful.

Atalla directly competes with VeriFone, Inc. (http://www.verifone.com), a Redwood City, California–based company also in the Internet payment business. VeriFone provides front-end verification terminals that allow merchants to accept and verify credit cards electronically. VeriFone is primarily a dial-up business; merchants swipe credit cards at verification terminals that call to verify funds availability.

Atalla maintains that WebSafe encrypts the PIN number as well as the credit card number, making it applicable to bank and ATM cards.

Currently, hardware security solutions are more expensive than software security applications. But Atalla believes that, in the long run, companies will spend as much on security software as hardware, because software solutions require more powerful Web servers. The hardware may be a better spend, since it's a lot harder for hackers to get through tamper-resistant hardware than it is for them to crack even the most sophisticated software.

THE CLIENT/SERVER MODEL

Unlike packet encryption, the client/server model only encrypts data between the client and the server. Both hardware and software client/server encryption methods exist, but in this section we'll focus on the two main software standards.

The Secure Socket Layer protocol (SSL) is Netscape's protocol for secure transmission of data over the Internet. Released in December 1994, SSL works on a low level, just above the TCP/IP protocol (again, the dominant transmission protocol used on the Internet). This allows SSL to work with more applications than just Web-based programs. Just about any program using high-level TCP/IP program calls can work with SSL. SSL-compatible protocols include HTTP (Hyper Text Transport Protocol); Telnet; FTP; gopher, and NNTP (Network News Transport Protocol). *Netscape Navigator* (http://www.netscape.com/comprod/products/navigator/version_2.0/index.html) currently employs the SSL protocol for secure Web transactions.

The SSL protocol ensures three types of security— authentication, encryption, and data integrity. These three types of security also happen to be the major elements required for Internet commerce.

To provide this level of security, Netscape licenses public-key encryption technology from RSA Data Security, Inc. (http://www.rsa.com). Public-key cryptography is considered one of the strongest encryption technologies available. MIT developers Rivest, Shamir, and Adelman created RSA. Everyone using RSA has a public and a private key. To send and encrypt a message, the sender uses the private key and the receiver's public key. Once encrypted, only the receiver's private key can decode the message. Even the sender can't decrypt it.

The RSA algorithm is far more secure than the DES algorithm, which uses the same key for encrypting and decrypting messages. The sender must transmit the DES key to the receiver for the message to be read.

Also, because the sender's and receiver's private keys are never divulged, RSA authenticates the sender and receiver. With the DES standard, anyone with the key can encode or decode a message.

Netscape created SSL as an open standard. The company offers it free of charge for non-commercial use, or for licensed commercial application. SSL provides more than just secure Web transactions. It also works with a variety of other modified Internet programs to secure Telnet sessions and FTP file transfers.

Netscape hopes SSL will become a standard on the World Wide Web and has presented it to the W3 Consortium (W3C) and the Internet Engineering Task Force (IETF). According to the company, more than 3 million people currently use SSL in SSL-enabled products.

The second client/server model encryption software standard is an open protocol also based on the RSA algorithm. S-HTTP, from Enterprise Integration Technologies (EIT) (http://www.eit.com), is a secure version of the HyperText Transport Protocol (HTTP). Whereas SSL is application-independent, S-HTTP is used only for secure Web transfers.

Many key industry players originally backed S-HTTP, because Netscape's SSL is a proprietary protocol. In April 1995, Terisa Systems (http://www.terisa.com) of Menlo Park, California, was launched as a joint venture between EIT and RSA Data Security, Inc. Terisa now develops, markets, licenses, and supports technologies that make secure Internet transactions possible. SSL and S-HTTP had emerged as competing standards and a bloody standards battle was about to ensue. Then, in September 1995, Terisa announced it had received investments and technology from Netscape Corp., effectively calling a truce between the feuding technologies.

Terisa now markets and licenses both technologies and continues to develop software to help companies conduct secure electronic commerce. Some Terisa customers that use S-HTTP and SSL include Bank of America, CyberCash, First Data Corporation, MasterCard, Open Market, Spyglass, Spry, and Sybase.

To use S-HTTP a surfer accesses a merchant's Web site with an S-HTTP-capable browser, selects the items he or she wants to order, and enters credit card information into the browser. The Web browser uses S-HTTP to encrypt the card number, and then transmits the encrypted file to the merchant. The merchant's Web server then uses S-HTTP to decrypt the file and sends the digital signature included in the file back to the surfer's browser for authentication. Once the Web server receives confirmation of the verified signature, all transactions between the Web server and client are secure.

S-HTTP is extremely flexible, allowing each application to configure the amount of security required. Transmissions from client to server and vice versa can be signed, encrypted, both, or neither. Two browsers supporting the S-HTTP protocol are *Secure NCSA Mosaic* (http://www.commerce.net/software/SMosaic) and Spry's *Internet In A Box* (http://www.spry.com/products/internet.html). With SSL, the degree of authentication is optional; however, encryption and data verification always remain in effect for this lower-level protocol. It takes a lot of time for computers to compute encryption and data verification algorithms, and the ability to change or remove them will increase the speed and number of transactions a Web server can perform.

Because it's an application-level protocol, S-HTTP works much better with secure routers. The data is encrypted with SSL, so a secure router has no idea what type of data is passing through the router. With S-HTTP, the router knows the type of connection being established.

Unlike SSL, S-HTTP also provides for the non-repudiation of individual requests or responses through digital signatures. This allows the data receiver to verify to a third party that the sender actually sent the data. This is a lot like sending a registered letter, except S-HTTP verifies the sender instead of the receiver.

Client/server technology is currently the basis of most secure information transfers on the Internet. Most secure Web-presence providers currently use client/server–based security. This technology will continue to grow and meet the needs of most companies and consumers doing business online.

THIRD-PARTY AUTHENTICATION

Third-party authentication involves using an impartial third party to verify client and server identity. This type of authentication is being developed and used mostly for financial transactions on the Internet. For example, let's say you're sending credit card information over the

Internet to make a purchase. The form for credit card information passes from the Web server to the client, who sends the credit card information to a bank—the third party. The bank then sends a message to the Web server confirming that it accepts the credit card number and amount and has authenticated the client. The Web server receives a confirmation number from the bank and returns a successful reply to the client. (Figure 13-10 illustrates an example of this transaction.)

This model has reduced fraud substantially because the merchant never receives the actual credit card information; the credit card number and amount are verified; the credit card holder is verified to the merchant, and the merchant is verified to the customer. Everyone is happy. Will SSL eliminate online credit card fraud? Of course not. Nothing is absolutely secure on the Internet (or anywhere else in the world, for that matter). However, SSL will substantially reduce the likelihood of fraud.

The problem with third-party authentication is that a third Web site now enters the picture. Remember waiting at a retail checkout counter during the Christmas season for what seemed like hours for

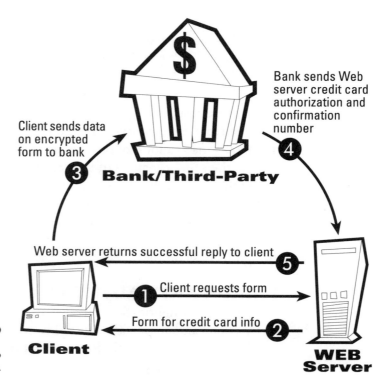

FIGURE 13-10

Client and server use a third party to handle the transfer of funds.

confirmation of your credit card number? The system slows when credit card verification volume is high. Imagine what would happen if a customer placing an order on your Web site had the same difficulty obtaining a connection to the third party. If the customer tires of waiting and closes the connection, you lose a sale.

The third party can also store secure information, even though your company has an unsecure Web site. Having another company handle your online financial transactions frees you from having to deal continually with security problems and maintain security hardware and software. Find a provider you trust to handle your online collections. (We'll discuss this further in the last section of the chapter.)

A Redwood City, California–based company, VeriSign, Inc. (http://www.verisign.com), has positioned itself to step in as a neutral third party who can verify buyer and seller identity and vouch for Internet data integrity. A spin-off of RSA Data Security, Inc., VeriSign uses the RSA encryption algorithm to perform authentication, encryption, and message integrity verifications. When using the Netscape or Open Market secure servers, your company must obtain a digital certificate from VeriSign before the secure servers can become operational.

Beginning in early 1996, VeriSign will offer digital signature certificates to individual users to enable the company to verify both buyers and sellers. Offering users digital signature certificates will reduce fraud, since VeriSign will then be able to verify buyers before purchases are made. VeriSign won't accept any form of payment, nor will it offer secure Web space. The company will remain an impartial third party, vouching for the identities of buyers and sellers.

Using third parties can help your company remain outside the payment loop and even save time in authorizing and sending credit card information to the bank. Having a third party authenticate the buyer and seller can make everyone feel warm and cozy about the transaction. However, utilizing a third party adds another potential failure point to your system. If the third party's computers are down, or the network connection between the buyer or seller is down, the transaction won't go through.

WHICH SECURITY METHOD IS RIGHT FOR YOU?

Unless your company has plenty of in-house computer experts, it's best to leave security to your Internet provider. When selecting your provider, choose one that implements security appropriate for your needs, and takes into consideration future growth. While your company may not be considering more stringent forms of security now, as your information needs grow with the Internet, your need for tighter security will grow as well.

The more valuable the data on your the computer system or network, the more money you must spend to make the system safe. For example, a large bank probably will spend hundreds of thousands of dollars making sure data is secure on the Net, while a small, online business accepting credit card orders may need only a secure server.

RSA President Jim Bidzos believes that "You need to use a level of protection that is consistent with what you're using it for. . . . For example, if you're protecting e-mail, why bother with hardware? But I think for financial transactions, hardware is the sensible way to go. It raises the fence significantly for those who want to attack a system."

Your company must weigh the cost of implementing a secure Web server against anticipated profits. If your company expects to make only $10,000 its first year online, why spend $100,000 protecting the investment? Software is easily upgradable. If a security vulnerability is found in a program, the user need only download the patch from the Internet. Fixing hardware holes requires down time while you return the hardware to the manufacture or upgrade components in-house.

How you plan to handle online sales is yet another factor. The methods of payment your site accepts will determine the necessary security level. (We cover this in more detail in the next chapter.) We strongly encourage businesses considering accepting online payments to make the transactions as secure as financially feasible.

A bank setting up shop on the Internet may consider using a combination of hardware and software to handle financial transactions on the Web. Because of the risk involved, security should be the number-one concern. The bank should incorporate nearly all of the security products mentioned in this chapter, including a Web server running secure server software; a firewall to protect information located at the bank; WebSafe to offer and perform additional hardware-based encryption, and, once it becomes available, packet encryption. Doing the work in-house assures the bank and its customers of the highest level of security.

Because a mom-and-pop store probably doesn't have the financial resources of a bank, purchasing Web space from a Web presence provider that runs a secure Web server is probably the most feasible option, and a good start when cautiously venturing online. This will enable the small store to accept payment on the Web and determine the store's online marketing efforts before it establishes a larger presence on the Web.

Even if your company has no plans to conduct online financial transactions, security is still an issue. Just because there's nothing of much value in your office doesn't mean you leave the office doors unlocked at night. You'll want to lock your Internet-connected computers up tight to keep hackers out.

YOUR WEB PROVIDER'S SECURITY

Many people taking their companies online for the first time will opt to leave Internet security worries to their Web-presence provider (WPP). Unfortunately, not all WPPs provide the same level or efficacy of online security. Investigate the security provisions of any WPP you consider before you trust it to look after your site. Among other things, make sure it has firewalls, secure servers, and no outside login access to the Web server. Make sure hardware and equipment are as secure as they can be.

Is Your Internet Service Provider Safe?

In March of 1994, some of the current employees of Skyline Network Technologies were involved in catching a hacker who broke into a government facility. One Skyline employee just missed catching the hacker by 30 minutes. Over 25 GB of data were destroyed in a little over an hour. Luckily, good backup procedures and other recovery technology ensured the recovery of almost all of the data. The hacker continued to taunt the government installation, sending e-mail messages with copies of current password files attached, and sending faxes with the same content.

The hacker in this case was easy to identify. He was a disgruntled former employee, fired earlier that day, who turned around and maliciously attacked government computers that night. Shortly after his termination and the initial attack on the computer systems, he decided to start a small Internet provider company in the community surrounding the government installation. As the taunting of the government facility continued, he began to connect to the computers from the root account of the main computer of his new company, which was housed in his home. By tracing Internet connections and phone records, it was easy to determine who was committing this crime.

Slightly over one year later, he pleaded guilty and was convicted. The judge's sentence wasn't much more than a slap on the wrist.

So, what happened to his Internet provider company? He's still in business and doing quite well. Would you trust your company's and clients' sensitive data to this Internet provider? We wouldn't.

Now can you sleep at night? Not quite yet. How do you know the WPP and employees are on the up-and-up? That's a far more difficult question to answer.

We're not suggesting that you conduct an extensive FBI-style background check of the WPP and its employees. But before you trust an Internet provider with your business, take some time to check out the company. Ask for some references. Talk to others using their service. Call the Better Business Bureau and see if anyone has registered a complaint. A little legwork now can save a lot of heartache later on.

Remember...

- The Internet, like the real world, is not a secure place to conduct business. Many products and services have been created to make the Web a more secure environment for consumers and merchants.

- All software contains bugs, even though many companies like to label them as features, and the Internet is no exception. Hackers use the bugs in software providing security for Internet-connected computers to gain access to the system or to shut the system down.

- Not providing security for your customers' financial data can result in sales losses. As consumers become more educated about the Internet, they're less likely to enter financial data into unsecure Web documents.

- While there is no Internet police force, there are good guys looking out for everyone's best interests. The Computer Emergency Response Team (CERT) helps look for hackers before damage is done and works to fight computer-related crime.

- Advances in Internet security products help make the Net a more secure place to conduct business. Companies have developed hardware and software products to help protect consumer financial information.

- Netscape's Secure Socket Layer (SSL) and EIT's Secure HyperText Transport Protocol (S-HTTP) are the current software standards for providing secure Web document exchange on the Internet.

- Firewalls are the best security your company can invest in. However, just as they limit a hacker's ability to enter your system, they limit a valid user's ability to reach the outside world.

- You can use a third party to verify both merchant and customer in an online transaction, and even provide a secure Web server for your financial transactions.

- Choose a reputable Internet provider that makes it a policy not to hire computer hackers as employees.

14

PASSING THE BUCK: GETTING PAID ON THE WEB

As more and more companies find their way to the World Wide Web, and as the stigma of online "commercialism" fades, business transactions conducted over the Internet become increasingly common. Unfortunately, sending personal financial information into cyberspace is still a risky business, and the current media fascination with those risks can scare away potential online customers.

Getting paid on the Web ultimately testifies to your marketing plan's effectiveness. And when everything goes as it should, customers *will* place the order. In this chapter we examine some ways companies are making it possible—and safe—for their customers to buy online. We also look at present efforts and future strategies to make the Net truly secure for online financial transactions, from secure third parties to cybercash.

THE ONLINE BUSINESS BOOM

Commerce on today's Internet involves much more than just sending credit card information through e-mail. Many other forms of payment exist, and more crop up every day. Banks have been slow to venture online, mostly because of security issues, but MasterCard and Visa are working on strategies to aid in making electronic commerce safe and secure for consumers and merchants alike. Sophisticated new hardware and software solutions are being developed to support current technology and to ensure that online transactions remain secure.

In a study of online spending patterns, BIS Strategic Decisions estimated that $4.8 billion was spent online for products and services in 1994. The total value of the market for electronic commerce products and services is expected to grow to almost $14 billion by 1998. With that much money flowing through the Net, consumers will demand new ways to pay for online products and services. In retail establishments, consumers can use just about any form of payment: cash, check, credit card, or debit card. Consumers will want the same options online, and they'll want the method of payment to be secure.

A variety of companies and organizations are moving to the Web as a way to improve customer service and increase sales. In December 1995, Alaska Airlines (http://www.alaska-air.com) became the first U.S. national carrier to offer customers the option of using the Internet to book travel and purchase tickets. Bill Ayer, Alaska's vice president of marketing and planning, said, "We surveyed our frequent fliers and nearly half said they wanted the convenience of making travel plans on their home or office computer." Airlines have been looking for a way to offer home computer-based reservations for years, but have been unable to find a workable solution. The Web provides carriers with the means to help travelers find complete travel information, book travel arrangements, and pay, all at the same time.

Alaska Airlines' Web site (see Figure 14-1) enables consumers to pay online, using virtually every form of credit card or a pre-established

FIGURE 14-1

Alaska Airlines offers an attractive site that allows travelers to pay for tickets online.

commercial account. The site's only drawback is that the transmission of credit card data is unsecure. Many of the larger air carriers may be waiting for more secure payment methods before venturing onto the Web. However, Alaska Airlines does offer a well-laid-out, attractive, and easy-to-use-Web site for checking prices and ordering online.

The Web is also used as a means of accepting political campaign contributions. Lamar Alexander, 1996 presidential candidate from Tennessee, has a homepage on the Web. Jim Brandell, the Alexander campaign's 26-year-old director of Internet Services, says the site has attracted more than 160 volunteers and a number of campaign contributions. While the campaign still relies on Web surfers to mail in their contributions, candidates like Alexander may be accepting contributions over the Web before the next election.

Many campaigns will be able to use the Web to solicit funds from sources outside a local candidate's home state or district. A person not residing in a candidate's home state who wanted to support his or her position on, say, protecting firearm rights, would normally have to do a lot of leg work to find out the candidate's position and where to send a check. As mainstream politics finds a home on the Internet, more voters are able to connect online with candidates from across the country.

The low cost of entry has attracted hundreds of companies, large and small, to the level playing field of cyberspace. An entrepreneur can get Internet access and set up a homepage for under $30 a month. On the Internet, a small, one-man operation can look as good or better than a large, multi-national corporation. But whether it's an individual working out of a virtual office, or a CEO sitting in an expensive downtown office building, they're going online for one purpose—to *sell*. And they're leaving no stone unturned in their efforts to make it safe and easy for their customers to *buy*.

TAKING THE ORDER—"WILL THAT BE PAPER OR PLASTIC?"

Payment options abound on the Web, from offline COD to online banks, and just about everything in between. To stay competitive and make the sale, your company will want to offer customers a wide range of payment options. Safeguarding their security and privacy should be the highest priority of any online vendor.

Arranging to receive payment on the Internet can be a tricky task. Many believe that sending credit card information through unsecure e-mail or Web-based forms is an acceptable risk; many others do not. Often, it's not the mode of transportation but *how* the data is transported that's at fault. Banks and high-volume stores don't send out the day's receipts in brightly painted Yugos with "MONEY" written in bold letters on the side. They use reputable armored truck companies with armed guards. When transmitting financial and personal information over the Internet, you should take similar precautions. Several recent technical advances have made online commerce easy and much more secure, but these options aren't free. Your company will have to balance its desire for online commerce with the cost of securing those transactions.

PAYMENT OPTIONS

Before you even set foot in a retail establishment, you'll notice most have a list of payment options stickered to the door. This list not only informs customers of the payment methods the store accepts, but it may actually draw someone in to take a look around. Customers may like to use the Discover Card because of its 1 percent cash-back offer, or American Express because it extends most manufacturers' warranties. Some sponsored cards offer customers product or service discounts and premiums. Your company should make just as many payment methods available to your online customers, and post "stickers" of accepted methods of payment on your Web site. These notices can take the form of color graphics of credit cards, bank cards, and the like, or simple text announcements.

The payment methods you accept on your site are very important. They can add value to your product or service because of the ease or security they afford your customers. Accepting several payment options will make your Web site more customer-friendly and allow customers to use the method of payment most comfortable and familiar to them. We highlight several online payment methods in this section. Each has specific applications, risks, and conveniences.

CREDIT CARDS—DON'T LEAVE CYBERSPACE WITHOUT THEM

Credit cards are by far the simplest and easiest way to order online. Completing the transaction requires no elaborate steps. Your company can determine whether money is available before shipping the requested item, and the customer need not belong to a special service, or set up any special bank accounts. Ordering online with a credit card is simply an electronic mail-order transaction.

Unfortunately, if your company doesn't currently accept credit cards, setting up a merchant account with a bank can be a hassle—especially if your company sells computers. Banks have been burned by mail-order computer resellers so many times they're extremely reluctant to offer such companies merchant accounts.

Accepting credit cards is relatively easy for you, as well. All your company really needs is some Web space. If you sell widgets, for example, you need only set up two Web pages—one to promote the widget and your company, and another to accept product orders. On the order-taking page, you include a form with a list of widgets and a place to enter a credit card number and shipping address. Done! Now your company is ready to receive online orders. People feel more comfortable paying by credit card; they know there's a third party involved who can intervene should the merchant fail to honor its promises. It's much simpler to call a credit card company and tell them to cancel a payment than it is to get your cash back.

You may decide to take steps to secure your online transactions using one or more of the foregoing technological solutions, but keep in mind that Internet credit card transactions are no riskier online than they are in the real world. Years ago, it was discovered that some dishonest store clerks kept the carbons from credit card receipts and used them to rack up thousands of dollars in unauthorized charges. It was a huge scandal. Neither the consumers nor the merchants were really at fault. It was *the mode of transmission*—the store clerk. Just because the store clerk's security check turns up nothing negative, that doesn't mean they're honest. It could just mean they've never been caught! Credit card companies eventually developed carbonless credit slips and even magnetic card readers that automatically entered the information with minimal sales clerk intervention. Credit card companies developed a technological means of securing that particular mode of transmission.

As we noted in Chapter 13, several technologies are available to ensure that the mode of transmission for Web shoppers—the Internet—is secure. In the United States, consumers and merchants have access to some of the most effective encryption applications available. However, current laws have weakened encryption standards for Internet activity outside the U.S. The reason for these different standards, of course, is national security. But the laws make it very difficult to secure international commercial traffic on the Net. While many groups inside and outside the U.S. are lobbying the government to change the laws, it doesn't look as though any changes are forthcoming.

Credit card companies make their money by charging you, the merchant, a fee based on a percentage of the sale. The percentage varies from 1 to 5 percent, depending on dollar amount and type of items your company usually sells. Shop around for the lowest bank rate you can find. A good place to begin your search is on the Web! Several credit card companies have Web sites that include rate information and online forms you can use to apply for an account.

As commerce on the Web becomes more commonplace, banks will step in to ensure greater financial security when handling online credit card orders. This third-party involvement will simplify credit card transactions on the Net, and require fewer resources for processing orders. Ultimately this could remove any need for a secure Web server, since the bank will actually handle the financial transactions.

In the third-party scenario, everyone is happy. The customers are happy knowing their credit card numbers go directly to the bank via a secure channel, and not to the merchant. The merchant is happy because the bank authenticates the charge, resulting in fewer charge backs and reduced processing costs. The bank benefits from the overall control; should the customer be unhappy with the product or service for any reason, the credit card company can act as a mediator between the customer and the merchant.

Credit cards will continue to be the method of choice for online transactions for the near future. It's the way most people like to pay, and it's the easiest and most secure method for everyone involved. However, one of the problems with credit card business is that it's not very well suited to small-ticket items. Much of your lower-priced inventory has a price floor where the transaction's cost begins to exceed its profit. Your company probably pays around 15 cents per transaction in processing fees to enable your customers to pay with credit cards. So it doesn't make sense to sell, say, a 10-cent comic strip to a credit card customer. For this reason, online merchants and consumers alike will seek alternatives to credit cards.

DIGITAL CASH

An increasing number of companies conduct online commercial transactions using "digital cash," a kind of electronic currency. Internet users transfer money from their checking accounts to their online digital cash accounts, converting real-world dollars into digital coins stored on their computers' hard drives.

Digital cash allows Internet users to buy at their own convenience, 24 hours a day, seven days a week. From a consumer standpoint, the chief benefit of this form of online payment is obvious: The interest clock doesn't start ticking when a purchase is made with digital cash the way it does with credit cards.

Digital cash is especially well-suited for "micropayments"—small, inexpensive items a person might normally purchase with change. Brochures, pamphlets, booklets, short stories, and other very low-cost items can now be marketed and sold worldwide with the help of digital cash. This is a great way for individual vendors to sell their wares on the Internet. Have a short story you want to publish? Sell it online for a couple of dimes. A micropayment could be used to pay the postage on an informative pamphlet you want to order. Budding cartoonists can offer their comic strips online for a couple of cents. And computer programmers who write shareware programs can accept digital cash as a method of payment.

True digital cash also will provide much the same kind of anonymity paper currency does. Because some fear that computers and connectivity are bringing us all closer to George Orwell's *1984*, many will be relieved to learn that digital cash will keep Big Brother from knowing our every financial move. This also will scare a lot of law enforcement officials, because illegal activities normally rely on cash. Imagine drug dealers setting up Web sites and accepting digital cash for dope. The worst part is that the Web sites could be set up in another country, such as Colombia, allowing drug dealers to operate completely outside U.S. borders.

Digital cash also allows people to pay anonymously for items they'd be embarrassed to shop for in public, or which they don't want showing up on their credit card statements. Weight-loss products, acne products, condoms, hair-loss products, presents for a special someone—all may be bought anonymously over the Internet using digital cash. As long as no one keeps records of the transaction, the transaction remains anonymous. It's the same principle as paper money; no one keeps track of the serial numbers on their fives, tens, and twenties.

The technology behind digital cash is public-key encryption systems. A file is created containing the face value of the "bill," a serial number, and other information authenticating the note. The file also contains the digital signature of the issuing bank, as well as the digital signature of each person who received the money.

Digital signatures are an important part of the digital cash system because they prevent forgery. Decoding digital signatures contained in the digital cash is only possible if the cash has been spent more than once. Once the issuing bank receives two copies of the same "bill," the bills can be used against each other to break the encoded digital signatures, immediately revealing the forger. The purchaser's PC generates the bills' individual serial numbers. The thief's PC also generates a digital signature, so identification is relatively simple.

Because it's tied to the money that eventually will be transferred from the issuing bank, you can't spend digital cash twice, just as you can't write checks on money not in your account. (Well, you can, but when the checks start bouncing, you go to jail.)

The biggest problem with digital cash is that no standards have been established. This is very inconvenient for consumers, who must install several payment software programs on their Internet-connected PCs. In many cases, they must register with the company providing the software, and then download it before each purchase.

Digital cash is very much in its infancy right now, but someday it probably will become as prevalent as the ATM card. For now, you can expect people to embrace it in much the same way they embraced paper money—that is, *slowly*—though while it's still new, a number of people use it just for the gee-whiz effect.

A leader in the digital cash movement is DigiCash™ (http://www.digicash.com). Founded in 1990 by Dr. David Chaum, the mission of this Netherlands-based company is "to develop and license payment technology products." DigiCash developed a virtual currency it calls "ecash." Initially, ecash has taken the form of a kind of play money called CyberBucks™. According to Dr. Chaum, "It will catalyze enormous growth in electronic commerce on the Internet, and prove of enduring value through its improved protection of consumers and society at large."

Mark Twain Bank (http://www.marktwain.com), located in St. Louis, Missouri, has begun accepting applications for accounts that can be used to deposit and withdraw ecash over the Internet. Mark Twain Bank customers must fill out online forms and mail or fax them to the bank. The bank then issues a password by return mail. Setting up a merchant account is just as easy. Mark Twain Bank can move the ecash into a regular bank account on any business or scheduled day, or the money can be sent by check or wire.

CyberCash, Inc. (http://www.cybercash.com) was formed by Dan Lynch and William Melton who are experts in their respective fields. (Melton is the founder of Verifone (http://www.verifone.com), a company that brought real-time credit card authorization to consumers and merchants. Lynch has long been tied to the Internet; he converted ARPAnet to TCP/IP back in 1983.) CyberCash is more like an electronic money order than digital cash. CyberCash provides a way for consumers to use a method of payment already seen as money, like credit cards, debit cards, and checks. It guarantees payment to the merchant before the product is shipped. More a *method* than a *form* of payment, CyberCash provides a relatively secure way to use credit cards on the Internet.

Handling a CyberCash transaction requires a separate program, available free online. Once the consumer installs the CyberCash software, he or she is ready to make online purchases. The merchant displays CyberCash's onscreen graphical button on the Web site to notify potential customers that CyberCash is an acceptable form of payment. When the customer clicks on the button, the program informs the Web server to send an electronic invoice to the customer, who then enters his or her name and credit card information on the order blank. The program encrypts the data and returns it to the merchant. The merchant then sends the invoice and customer identification information to the CyberCash server.

Once the CyberCash computer receives the information, it sends the credit card information to the merchant's bank for authorization. The merchant's bank sends a response to the merchant, letting the merchant know that the purchase has been authorized. The customer is charged for each transaction, which amounts to less than the cost of a postage stamp.

In July 1995, CheckFree Corp. (http://www.checkfree.com) joined forces with CyberCash to help consumers safely conduct payment transactions in real time over the Internet using credit cards, debit cards, checks, or cash (see Figure 14-2). To buy goods and services using CheckFree and

FIGURE 14-2

CheckFree offers a secure way for consumers to pay for products using cash, check, credit cards, or debit cards.

CyberCash, the user must first download the *CheckFree Wallet* software, a stand-alone program that works in conjunction with all major Web browsers. CheckFree charges the consumer no transaction fees or service charges. A 768 dual-key encryption system legal for export outside the U.S. protects credit card information. RSA Data Security licenses the technology to ensure safety and security on purchases made with the *CheckFree Wallet*. Since the software is legal for export outside of the U.S., companies also can tap into foreign markets securely.

CyberCash differs from DigiCash in that CyberCash accepts most current forms of payment, in addition to some digital alternatives. While only Mark Twain Bank currently accepts DigiCash, over 80 percent of U.S. banks accept CyberCash. CyberCash is the only company with worldwide license to export a 768-bit RSA encryption algorithm, making international CyberCash transactions extremely secure.

The oldest form of digital cash is a product called NetCash, developed by Software Agents, Inc. (http://www.netbank.com/~netcash/). This system requires users to send check or credit card information to the NetBank (not a real bank, but a part of the NetCash system) to purchase NetCash. Within minutes, the NetBank returns an e-mail message including a NetCash "coupon" that looks like this:

```
NetCash US$ 25.00 A123456B789012C
```

The coupon consists of three parts—"NetCash US$" (signifying the currency), the dollar amount, and the serial number, located at the end of the coupon. It's like an online travelers check.

NetCash is issued as soon as the NetBank receives the request. But, just as with a check, unless the merchant calls the issuing bank to verify funds availability, there's no way of knowing whether the NetCash is actually valid. The merchant who receives the NetCash can send the merchandise immediately on good faith, or wait for the NetCash to become valid. Waiting for the NetCash to become valid is like waiting for a check to clear.

NetCash is entirely e-mail- or Web-based. Every time customers want to get "change" for their NetCash coupon, they must e-mail or fill out a Web form at the NetBank. This adds a lot of additional steps to the online buying process.

NetBank takes a 2 percent cut of the NetCash redeemed. There's no minimum transaction fee, making the NetCash system ideal for small purchases. In fact, NetCash places a $100 ceiling on what merchants can sell. NetCash isn't totally secure because the length of the verification key is so short, and thus shouldn't be used for large-ticket items. In the security chapter, we noted that Netscape placed a value of $10,000 on the cost of breaking a 40-bit key; few hackers are going to go after the small NetCash transactions.

Eventually, people using the Net probably will have digital cash on their computer much the same as they have bills and coins in their wallet or purse. Digital cash could make it easy for companies to charge surfers for browsing their sites. People might be likely to pay a couple of cents to view a site they find interesting. For the site, those few cents can add up quickly. Digital cash is best suited for online newspapers and magazines. Many magazines currently require users to pay a yearly subscription fee with digital cash. They might also charge users for only the particular day or for the individual columns they read.

A recent trend in many newsgroups is to sell graphic images for a penny per image. In this way, photographers or models can charge interested viewers for their work and still offer it inexpensively. A reduced-size version of the image can be posted to a newsgroup or placed on a Web site. If surfers find the image interesting enough to add to their collection, they can cough up 1 cent worth of digital cash. Those interested can thus purchase hundreds of images for only a few dollars, and pay artists and photographers for their work.

Digital cash offers a unique way to pay for goods and services online, but it's not quite ready for prime time. To gain widespread acceptance, the technology must be simplified into a true plug-and-play solution. It must be integrated into Web browsers so that using it becomes as easy as opening a wallet or a pocket book.

THE OLD-FASHIONED WAY

For the present, the most secure way to handle online commerce is do it offline, the old-fashioned way. You can include an address and phone number on your site (an 800 number is best, of course) and forget about cybercurrency altogether. It's really the safest and most secure way to conduct commercial transactions through the Internet.

However, playing it safe on the Web won't generate a lot of sales. A1 Internet Services (http://www.a1co.com), of Hudson, Canada, found that less than five percent of its clients receive Internet orders by check or money order. Studies show that 30–80 percent of businesses can increase their profits by accepting credit cards for online purchases. People surfing the Net move in and out of sites so quickly many of them simply won't bother to take the time to write down your payment address or call your 800 number.

Cash-On-Delivery (COD) is another old fashioned way to bill for sales. COD has the same drawbacks in electronic commerce as it has in the mail-order industry. There's no way to ensure that the customer will pay for the package when it arrives, that the package isn't simply a prank, or even that it's not a form of industrial espionage. With COD, you ship the product, pay for the shipping and the additional cost for COD, all with the expectation that the customer who ordered it will accept and pay for the package. If for some reason the customer doesn't accept delivery, your company is out the cost of shipping and COD extras, which typically run more than $10. It could also take your company several additional days to get the merchandise back. UPS, for example, will hold on to a delivery for a minimum of eight days—three days for the first three attempts to deliver; five days on will-call; two days for the weekend. The longer your company goes without payment or product, the longer your company's money is tied up. In addition, losing $10 for every package returned isn't the greatest way to make money with your online venture.

But your biggest problem with traditional billing and collection methods won't be undeliverable orders. It's getting any orders at all. As soon as you add that extra step—writing down your address or phone number, sending out a check or dialing the phone—you give them another chance to reevaluate their decision to buy. When prospective clients click on your "Order Now!" button, they'd better be able to do just that. If they find an address for sending a check or money order, or a phone number, chances are, they'll just move on. (Many customers don't have two telephone lines, so they'd have to sign off to free the line for the call.)

Fortunately, there is a way to allow customers to use checks without requiring them to physically write out and mail a hard-copy document. Checks are really just bank numbers on a piece of paper. The numbers don't necessarily have to be on that piece of paper to work. It's possible to set up an online form on a Web site that allows users to enter check information, and which the merchant can then submit to a bank. This digital check has many of the same characteristics as the paper version: It takes the same amount of time to clear and process, and doesn't guarantee that funds are available. The main difference is that the customer doesn't have to put it in the mail. The check can be deposited immediately instead of the merchant waiting for the check to arrive. The merchant still has the option to wait for the check to clear before sending merchandise, and the customer must make sure money is available in the account to avoid a bounced check fee.

This method of payment may sound new, but it's been around as long as the check itself. The biggest problem with digital checks is the same as with credit cards—no signature. How can a bank determine whether someone actually authorized the transfer of funds without a signature? This is another area where digital signature technology comes into play. Banks will be able to register a customer's digital signature to verify the customer's identity and authenticate the request for funds transfer.

The risks of fraud with digital checks is about the same as the risk associated with credit cards. Merchants should take steps to ensure that the financial data on the check is kept from prying eyes on the Internet. A secure method of transfer, such as Netscape's Secure Socket Layer (SSL) or EIT's Secure-HyperText Transport Protocol (S-HTTP), should be used when transmitting the numbers on the check to the merchant or bank.

Redi-Check (http://www.redi-check.com), of Salt Lake City, Utah, offers a secure way for customers to order online using their checking accounts. The program, called Secure Pay, requires customers to enter their account only once at Redi-Check's secure Web site. Once account information has been stored at Redi-Check's site, it need never be entered on a merchant's site, reducing the risk of fraud. When Redi-Check receives the information, they issue the user a unique user name and password to enter at any Web site that accepts Secure Pay.

The program benefits merchants because they don't need an expensive secure Web site in order to take online transactions. The consumer needs no additional hardware or software. The cost to the merchant is an initial $250 setup charge and 2 percent of the total of each check submitted. The service is free to consumers. Secure Pay is currently in use by many companies, a partial list of which can be found on Redi-Check's Web site.

While surfing Redi-Check's Web site to obtain the information for this section, we went through the process of setting up a Secure Pay account. After the user enters all of the information into the form, a button appears at the bottom of the form that reads, "Submit my information securely and verify my account information."

The only problem with this transaction is that neither the site nor the form are secure. Most people don't realize it, but the entire process of submitting your account information to the Redi-Check site is unsecure and potentially dangerous. To verify our conclusions, we used the Netscape Navigator Version 2.0 Beta 3; none of the methods used to indicate a secure link were visible.

We feel that once the account is set up, future transactions are secure, but entering your initial bank account information insecurely over the Internet is a risk. Redi-Check provides an 800 number for customers who would rather not submit their bank account information over the Internet.

Digital checks offer consumers and merchants the advantages of ordering products and services online using a more traditional form of payment. Their one drawback is that most consumers are not familiar with reading or entering the information found on their checks. The less comfortable people are with a payment method, the less likely they'll be to use it. Redi-Check has made the process of entering your checking account information easy, and uses images to help consumers locate the proper numbers on their checks.

Remember, the easier you make it for customers to order online, the more orders you'll receive. Traditional forms of payment, although secure, require an additional step in the purchasing process. This extra step may mean the difference between making a sale and losing it.

ESTABLISHING PAYMENT STANDARDS

MasterCard International, Inc. (http://www.mastercard.com) and Visa International (http://www.visa.com) are currently battling to determine which bank's standard will become the de facto standard for secure transactions on the Internet. Initially, MasterCard and Visa worked jointly on a standard, but MasterCard terminated the joint effort and teamed up with Netscape Communications Corp. and IBM Corp. Reportedly, MasterCard severed relations with Visa because Visa brought Microsoft into the picture. MasterCard feared that Microsoft would try to dominate the market.

MasterCard has sent its standard, called "secure electronic payment protocol" (SEPP), to the ANSI standards body, hoping to win industry approval. Visa took a different route with its "secure transaction technology" (STT). Visa prefers to release the technology into the marketplace in hopes that industry will embrace it and public demand will make it a standard. Visa has not yet submitted STT to the ANSI body for approval. Visa believes ANSI will take as long as two years to make a decision. Two years on the Web at this stage of the game is an eternity.

Visa has already signed a deal with Sony Corporation of America (http://www.sony.com) in an effort to expose the industry to the Visa/Microsoft technology. In April 1996, it's expected that Sony will launch an online entertainment theme park, offering entertainment, information, and consumer transactions on the Web. Visa will provide the secure electronic payment capabilities.

MasterCard has said they will charge no additional fee to online merchants over their offline counterparts while using SEPP. Visa claims it's too early to determine whether they will charge any merchant fees. Additional fees typically arise when extra risk is involved for the financial community. MasterCard feels that its SEPP technology ensures the same, if not better, security than traditional offline transactions.

CyberCash states that its method of electronic payment will be compatible with either Visa or MasterCard standards. Both MasterCard and Visa are competing with the CyberCash method, so once a standard is accepted, CyberCash will have to rely on its partner, CheckFree, to remain a viable payment method. Once the credit card giants agree on a secure protocol, CyberCash would become redundant, adding another point of potential failure in the transaction.

The problem with choosing an online standard too soon is that it can backfire and end up costing more money in the long run. Some of the foregoing online payment groups will require your company to pay a setup fee. For example, Visa's STT product may sound like the way to go with industry giant Microsoft's backing. However, if ANSI accepts MasterCard's standard, and consumers begin using the MasterCard technology, switching may be rather expensive. If Visa gains industry-wide approval, your company will sit in the catbird seat.

The outcome of the standards war remains uncertain as of this writing.

ONLINE BANKS

Online banks are a more recent development in Web history. Banks are venturing online more hesitantly than other organizations because of the Internet's security limitations, but they're getting there. Most online banks provide general information about the banks themselves, and allow surfers to enter credit card applications over the Internet. Several banks now make it possible to view your account information using a Web browser. At least one bank we know of allows you to open an account online.

BankNet is a joint venture between MarketNet (http://www.marketnet.com) and Secure Trust Bank of Bradford, United Kingdom. BankNet allows Web surfers to open accounts online. The procedure is this: The surfer enters the information into a Web form, prints it out, signs the hard-copy document, and sends it to the bank along with a photocopy of his or her driver's license or passport. Once an account is established, BankNet allows account holders to look at their account information using a Web browser, and to write electronic checks. (To write electronic checks on a BankNet account, the user must download Netscape's *WorkHorse* program.) Public- and private-key encryption tools ensure secure delivery for the electronic checks. In the future, BankNet hopes to offer electronic check deposits from other online banks, as well. Use of electronic checks—BankNet calls them EChecks— currently is limited to other companies or individuals within the BankNet network.

This method isn't yet practical for Web-wide use. Users must follow several steps to establish an account online, sending information via snail-mail, downloading and installing software, and then viewing participating merchants' homepages. Entering the initial information securely requires a secure browser. A customer can just as easily provide the merchant his or her credit card information safely using secure Web technology available now.

Wells Fargo Bank (http://www.wellsfargo.com) also offers online banking services. (See Figure 14-3.) Wells Fargo's first online payment venture began in April 1995, when merchants began accepting online payments for products and services sold on the Internet with the help of the bank. Then, in May, Wells Fargo set up a secure Web server to offer customers secure Internet access to the current balances in their checking, savings, line of credit, and credit card accounts, as well as transaction histories for checking, savings and credit card accounts. Wells Fargo offers an easy-to-use, attractive site that includes information aimed at providing the information customers need, online. For example, they offer an ATM locator to help customers find ATMs in their area.

In September 1995, Wells Fargo Bank introduced a software application—the Wells Fargo MasterCard Purchasing Card—allowing merchants to give their business customers electronic cash-register receipts when a transaction is made online. Cardholders benefit from

FIGURE 14-3

Wells Fargo Bank is definitely on the leading edge of Internet banking, offering account holders many online services.

reduced costs, orders are placed quickly, and the process is secure. Merchants typically receive their money in one to three business days, instead of the usual 30–60 days. Merchants are required to send additional data to Wells Fargo, along with the usual authorization information, for the receipts to be generated.

Online banks add significantly to the emerging online commercial environment. They fit right in, and might be the force that finally stabilizes things. Take, for example, the process of buying a car. Say a user wants to buy a car online. He or she searches several online databases and finds a list of cool cars. The user then goes to several automobile and consumer e-zines to find reviews of the vehicles, and narrows the list. To get a broader and more unbiased view, the consumer may post messages to several automobile newsgroups, asking others what they think about the cars on the narrowed-down list. Finally, the user selects a car. Now, he or she wants the lowest financing available for the vehicle. An online automobile buying service could offer links to various financial institutions that take credit applications over the Web. The user submits credit information on a form located on the bank's Web server, and the bank returns the results of its credit check via e-mail. Once the amount of the loan has been established, the user contacts the buying service. The buying service orders the car from a local dealership, which in turn contacts the bank. The loan is issued and the car is delivered directly to the user's house, where he or she completes the transaction by signing the loan and ownership papers.

In this example, the entire process is handled online, without the pressure of visiting car dealership after car dealership, looking for the right car at the right price. No more pushy salespeople. No more waiting for hours in the dealership for loans to be approved. Finding the relevant loan rates and automobile prices was quick, easy, and inexpensive because the customer used the Web.

One bank that takes loan applications online is First Union Bank (http://www.firstunion.com), headquartered in Charlotte, North Carolina. First Union accepts MasterCard, consumer loan, and home equity loan applications online. Their retirement services also allow customers to check the status of existing IRA accounts and open new ones. The products currently offered set the stage for the company's move into full-service banking through the Internet. First Union's Community Commerce program, aimed at helping merchants offer their wares to online consumers, uses a variety of payment systems and interfaces to help encourage commerce on the Web and test available technologies. Many features offered at First Union's Web site require additional snail-mail or phone interaction with the bank.

Barnett Bank (http://www.barnett.com) takes a different approach to providing customers with online banking services. Together with Time-Warner's Full Service Network (FSN), the bank offers customers home-banking services through their TV sets. Barnett Bank customers can access their accounts by entering the Services venue on the FSN Carousel™ navigation system.

Barnett Bank launched the program in December 1994, in Orlando, Florida. "We believe that our customers will find the Barnett Bank service to be easier to use than other interactive banking services they might have seen on the Internet," said Jon Palmer, chief retail banking and technology executive. "Interactive television is a very powerful new medium for presenting our products and services to customers and prospects alike."

The new network, while not relying on the Internet, still takes security concerns very seriously. All financial information resides on computers located at Barnett Bank, and not on any outside computers. All data is encrypted via special hardware embedded in the interactive cable-TV controller. The network uses a special, proprietary operating system. Barnett also offers desktop banking through the Prodigy network to customers located outside the Orlando area. Security for these transactions can be maintained through Prodigy, since the financial data never travels over the Internet.

Barnett Bank uses a variety of techniques to attract surfers to its Web site. One such technique is the site's "Free Lunch" section, offering online games, screen-saver programs and images, and banking tools. All games and programs are cost-free, one of the best ways to attract crowds of Web surfers. The bank definitely shows a commitment to establishing an electronic presence, and we predict it will continue to grow online as more consumers look for banking alternatives.

Banks use digital signature technology to verify users and safely conduct more banking business online. Soon banks will extend their reach to a greater number of customers by offering services online. A bank with a limited number of branches in outlying areas can maintain contact with and offer services to customers located a great distance from a branch office. Online banks currently offer different programs and levels of online banking, but soon will standardize their online features. The banking industry has the most to lose in electronic commerce, and understandably will remain apprehensive until better methods of security are developed, or until customers demand more online banking services.

SECURE THIRD PARTIES

You say your company doesn't want to spend the money to create a secure Web site? Luckily for you, other options are available. Secure third parties, for example, are institutions set up between customers and merchants to handle the financial transactions between the two. Renting secure Web space from a third party may be the best way to achieve security while keeping costs down. As commerce continues to spread across the Web, many more secure-third-party companies will appear.

One such company is VersaNet International, Inc. (http://www.versanet.com), of Staunton, Virginia. Here's how that company's service works: When surfers click on the "Enter Payment" button on the sites of VersaNet clients, they are transferred to a secure Web site. There they find forms and programs tailored to the specific payment and ordering needs of the site of origin. The customer enters the payment information on the secure server, and VersaNet returns an e-mail message to both the purchaser and the merchant, verifying that funds were accepted and transferred. This method allows merchants to ship products more quickly, since the funds transfer is verified.

VersaNet uses Netscape's Netsite Commerce Server and charges a single $295 one-time setup charge. To use VersaNet's SecureOrder™ payment system, your company must set up a merchant account with Automated Transaction Services, Inc. (ATS) (http://www.calypso.com/ats). ATS provides the software to perform authorization services needed to allow instant, online credit card authorizations. Once an account is established with ATS your company can accept both checks and credit cards on the Web.

Secure third parties will become more popular as smaller merchants with fewer resources continue migrating online. While a small company may want to keep Web operations in-house, it may not want to purchase or maintain a secure Web server. Third-party solutions offer an affordable alternative to expensive, secure servers and local Internet providers that don't offer secure transaction capability.

A1 Internet Services offers inexpensive secure Web space for only $29.95 a month and a one-time $29.95 setup charge. To use A1's service you must have an established merchant account. A1 merely provides the secure Web space. The company's Web page (see Figure 14-4) uses Netscape's SSL to provide online transaction security. The A1 secure Web service setup is similar to VersaNet's secure online offering, but doesn't provide the ability to authorize payments online.

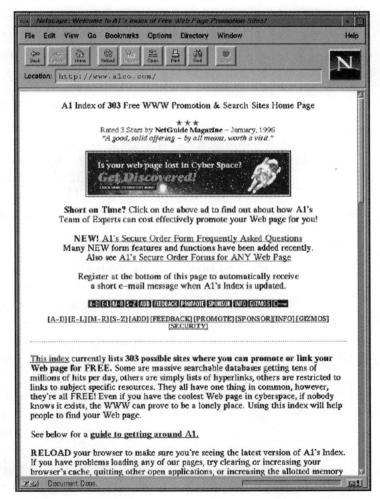

FIGURE 14-4

A1 Internet Services makes it possible for companies to lease space on a secure server.

Almost 80 percent of credit card fraud flows from the merchant. Once credit card information is placed on a Web server, almost any employee with access to the server can find it. Using a third party to handle your site's financial transactions permanently removes your company from suspicion; you never see the credit card information. Third parties provide peace of mind for both you and your customers.

As standards emerge for credit card processing and the software to perform secure transactions comes down in price, the need for third parties may diminish, but for now they comprise a viable solution to security and economic concerns.

HANDLING FOREIGN ORDERS

Once you establish a Web presence you may be surprised by the number of foreign customers you generate. Your marketing message travels literally worldwide. That global reach may even be one of the reasons you went online in the first place. (Or maybe not.) But handling foreign orders can be daunting in more ways than one.

It's almost impossible to block foreign surfers from your Web site. If you're doing business on your site, you can bet some of them will want to become customers. This is good, of course, if you want to break into foreign markets. In fact, you already may be used to filling foreign orders. If you are, this section will hold no surprises for you. If, however, you are new to the export business, or you never meant to get into it in the first place, read on.

Currency exchange is a problem every international merchant must face, and now that the Web offers low-cost international advertising, international orders are more likely for the ordinary merchant. Like interest rates, banks offer different rates for different currency. Shopping around for the best deal can save you or your customers some cash. Credit card companies offer currency exchange services for a fee, but you can bet the rates won't be the best available. Like the rates themselves, fees vary widely.

Although credit cards seem to offer the easiest way to handle foreign orders, this isn't necessarily so. Unless the credit card was issued from a U.S. bank working with U.S. currency, you will run into the currency exchange problem. Your customers will be required to pay the currency exchange rate offered by that bank on that particular day. This may surprise the foreign customer when he or she receives the bill.

OK, let's say you have the currency problem under control and everything is going smoothly. You still have many opportunities to get into trouble with customs and unforeseen export restrictions. Export of the product your company sells may not be allowed, or its importation may not be allowed by the country where your customer resides.

You need look no further than Chapter 13 for an example of this kind of problem. Remember Philip Zimmerman, the guy who made his encryption software available on an FTP site? Someone outside the U.S. downloaded his software, and he's now under investigation for selling munitions. Something as simple as offering a program for free on the Internet can get you or your company in trouble when it starts crossing borders.

Package delivery is another headache international merchants endure. Outside the U.S., such delivery involves greater delays, since the package changes hands so often and is out of your control for so long. Customs agents can slow package delivery. So can military conflicts and bad weather. The ship may not reach port at the specified time, or the plane may not land at the initially specified airport. Trade embargoes may be established after the package leaves your facility, resulting in delays or losses in some *Twilight Zone* holding pattern.

Many companies conduct foreign sales over the Internet successfully, and have for quite some time. As your company increases sales to foreign lands, the process of handling orders outside the U.S. will become more routine. If your company needs help with import and export commerce, check some of the Web search sites for import/export companies that already have a Web presence.

ACCOUNT HOLDER NOT PRESENT—FRAUD AND CHARGE BACK ISSUES

Using credit cards and other forms of payment has the same drawbacks in cyberspace as it does in the real world. It's just as difficult to determine whether the person staring at you across the counter is really authorized to use the card he's handing you as it is to verify identities on the Internet. Even though credit cards are signed on the back, the space provided for the signature is so narrow it's usually distorted. Not that anyone ever really looks at signatures, anyway. And when a customer believes someone has used his or her card without authorization, the merchant ends up getting the shaft.

Taking credit orders online involves the same risks. Even having a cardholder's PC verify the purchase will not completely prevent fraud. Separated spouses, children, baby-sitters, guests, friends, and others may have access to the computer and could make unauthorized online purchases. The purchase may not hurt the consumer directly, but someone pays in the end. Credit card companies pass along the costs in higher interest rates; merchants divert the costs with higher prices.

Secure connections don't prevent fraudulent purchases, they only protect the information as it's transmitted. A secure connection merely ensures that the thief who has stolen the credit card number won't compete with other thieves trying to steal credit card numbers from unsecure connections. The card number may even have been stolen from a source outside the Internet, providing the thief with near total anonymity. Until banks can find a way to identify credit card holders with a greater degree of certainty, online merchants will have to pay higher processing fees to accept online orders.

Because ordering on the Internet is so much like buying from a mail-order company, you should follow the same procedures and precautions. The main difference is that credit card companies are working on ways to make online commerce safe for merchants and consumers.

Remember...

- Getting paid on the Web is the ultimate testament that your online marketing plan is working.

- Sending personal financial information over the Internet is an acceptable risk—but a risk, nonetheless.

- You should include a list of accepted methods of payment on your homepage. If a customer's method of payment isn't listed on your site, he or she may not place an order.

- Credit cards are the simplest and easiest forms of online payment. People are used to sending credit card information over the phone to order products. Studies show that businesses can increase profits 30–80 percent by accepting credit cards.

- Digital cash is a form of electronic currency used to transfer money over the Internet. Although many online merchants don't currently accept digital cash, it may become a popular payment method in the future.

- Relying on customers to mail checks or call toll-free numbers is the safest way to conduct commerce on the Internet. However, the principle of "nothing ventured, nothing gained" holds true for traditional payment methods online.

- Banks are moving to the Internet and are beginning to offer virtual offices in cyberspace. Soon, many banking matters normally requiring a customer to appear in person may be handled online.

- Renting secure Web space from a third party may be the best way to achieve security and keep costs down. A few companies offering secure Web space also have the ability to authorize transactions in real-time over the Internet.

- Accepting orders online involves risks similar to the risks of mail order. Fraud is a potential problem, and you should take the same precautions mail-order companies do.

15

THE INTERNET AND THE LAW

You have a working knowledge of the Web. You've taken the time to develop your marketing plan, figured out how much it's going to cost you, convinced your staff that it's the right thing to do, and even protected yourself against hacker trespass. You're ready to take the online plunge, right?

Well, there's one more thing you ought to prepare yourself for—the legal ramifications of giving your company a Web presence.

In this chapter we discuss some of the emerging issues of law confronting the adolescent Internet. As you take your company online, you'll want to have at least a passing familiarity with copyright law, the concept of obscenity, your tax liabilities, international commerce proscriptions, U.S. government regulations, and legal actions you can take against hackers.

Although we will cover these topics in some detail, this chapter is not meant as a substitute for professional legal advice. Use it as a checklist of legal issues you should know about and understand before going online. When you have serious questions about the law or your rights on the Internet, it's always best to seek the advice of an attorney who specializes in media and computer-related law.

THE CENTRAL LEGAL ISSUE ON THE NET: COPYRIGHT

The Net was designed to facilitate the free and open exchange of information. Who in a free society would criticize such a noble goal? (Not us.) But what happens when that free and open exchange involves intellectual property? When is a piece of writing, a graphic, a photograph, a song, or a concept merely information, and when is it the protected property of its creator?

Activities on the Internet have sparked a legal debate over issues of copyright infringement and intellectual property that promises to heat up as the online population grows. Aside from the technical challenges of protecting the rights of authors, artists, programmers, and others in cyberspace, how does current copyright law impact your Web presence?

WHAT THE COURT HAS SAID

The codes and regulations that make up U.S. copyright law are quite specific about the rights of ownership of intellectual property. The owner of a copyright has exclusive and total rights to the distribution of the work. These rights cover everything from books to music, from paintings to sculptures. To allow for museum exhibits and live performances, the law includes a special clause stating that these rights extend only to the works when a material object physically changes hands. This is where the Internet and the Web tend to run into a legal gray area because it's difficult to ascertain what changes hands over the Internet.

Those who would like to spend some additional time researching U.S. copyright laws can start their research on the Web. The Cornell University Law School site includes the complete United States Copyright Act (http://www.law.cornell.edu//usc/17/overview.html).

Traditionally, information, files, data, articles, and essays published online have been free for the taking. Most of the time, you didn't even have to ask for things; you could just log on, pick up what you needed, and take it with you. But as cases involving copyright disputes on the Internet make their way to the courts, this tradition not only is being challenged, it will most certainly change forever.

A recent court case underscoring the problem of online copyright protection involved a Massachusetts Institute of Technology student named David LaMacchia. In brief, LaMacchia set up an Internet directory where he stored copyrighted software programs. Because he was online, other users could easily access his directory and copy these programs for themselves. LaMacchia claimed he had no idea anyone was making illegal copies of these programs, but federal prosecutors charged him with wire fraud. A federal judge later dismissed the case, ruling that existing wire fraud laws did not cover the crime. Prosecutors had hoped to charge LaMacchia with copyright infringement, but at that time, those laws didn't cover online services.

One of the most prominent cases to deal with online copyright infringement involved a lawsuit filed by The Church of Scientology against Netcom Online Communication Services, Inc., a San Francisco Bay Area–based Internet access provider. In this case, Netcom was accused of allowing one of its users to post copyrighted articles that were the property of The Church of Scientology. After the church complained, Netcom took no steps to remove the copyrighted material from its system, claiming they did not have responsibility to shut off bulletin boards or monitor for infringments. So the church sued. In

November 1995, a federal court in California ruled that Netcom could, in fact, be held liable for "contributory" copyright infringements, but could not be held responsible for direct copyright infringement if they had knowledge of the crime and failed to act. This ruling allows the church to proceed with its lawsuit, which probably will come to trial sometime in 1996.

HOW THIS IS DIFFERENT, BUT THE SAME

To understand U.S. copyright law, you must first consider two established legal doctrines. The first of these is the fair-use doctrine, which states that someone may use portions of someone else's work without infringing on the copyright. The doctrine doesn't attempt to define the exact limits of use, but states the factors to be considered in a particular case. The factors include the purpose, nature, amount, and effect of the use of a copyrighted work. Many people in the publishing community wish that this doctrine didn't apply to the Internet, since the ease with which data may be copied online makes it very difficult to police fair uses of copyrighted material.

The so-called "first sale" doctrine forms a cornerstone of U.S. copyright law. This is the tenet that enables libraries and video stores to exist. The first sale doctrine holds that, once a tangible copy of a copyrighted piece is sold, the particular copy may be leased, lent, resold, or rented in any way the purchasing party wishes. In other words, since a library has purchased the books in its collection, it may lend them out at any time or in any way without securing the permission from the copyright owner.

Audio recordings and computer programs are exempt from this doctrine, because these works are so easy to copy. Some publishers want this exemption to apply to works posted on the Internet, as well. Since the Internet allows for the easy duplication of copyrighted work, they argue, it should be illegal for anyone to distribute copyrighted materials online, even if the materials were purchased legally.

These two cases underscore the ambiguity that seems to prevail in the legal system when it comes to dealing with copyright law and the Information Superhighway. Some people view this as a brand-new medium that should be regulated with brand-new rules and regulations. Others view the Internet as an extension of all other types of communication, and believe, therefore, that it ought not receive any special treatment.

Those who see the Web as a bastion of free information, where ideas are shared and communicated without ownership concerns, want to protect the status quo. They feel any outside interference impedes the flow of information and violates the purpose of the Net. They see the imposition of strict copyright laws on the Net as akin to charging people to borrow books from the library.

Those who believe the Web is just another form of communication worry that authors, artists, designers, and programmers seem to be losing the right to control the fates of their works. They fear that if the Net is allowed to run free and unregulated, no intellectual property will be safe. Once something is posted online, it can be copied and downloaded by users all over the world in a matter of minutes, sometimes even seconds. With no regulations in cyberspace, they argue, creators will lose, not only control of their works, but also the profits they rightfully deserve.

Software companies are currently developing packages that eventually will make is possible to charge people each time they view a document online. Many people favor this "per-hit" method of compensating a copyright holder. Another strategy involves the use of encryption software that would scramble documents or files to make them unreadable by Web surfers. To view the documents, users would have to buy the code that unscrambles them.

Another option already being utilized on some Web sites is called a *members-only section*. Sites employing this feature set up pages that are free for the browsing, but charge a fee for access to other parts of the site. Again, users pay a fee to get a password that opens the restricted area (see figure 15-1).

We believe the answer to the copyright quandary lies with some version of the members-only approach. Completely restricting access to information on the Web will quickly diminish its popularity and its usefulness as a marketing medium. But there's room for a compromise that protects the rights of creators, while maintaining the freedom that makes the Net what it is.

As far as making marketing and advertising decisions about the Web, we advise putting out only information you are sure you have the rights to. The copyright debate will almost certainly heat up in the next few years and it's better to comply now than to rush to make changes.

FIGURE 15-1

ESPNET marks its homepage "members-only" areas with little ticket icons.

AM I ALLOWED TO SAY OR DO THIS?

What if your advertising plan calls for something that pushes the envelope? How do you decide whether an ad is risqué or obscene? How can you tell whether something you post will be considered satire or slander? What you can and can't say on the Internet has been the subject of much recent discussion, and it should be a major concern of any company planning to establish a Web presence. In this section we'll look at how decisions in recent court cases may affect the way you market your products or services online.

PROTECTION OF FIRST AMENDMENT RIGHTS: HOW FAR DOES IT EXTEND?

When the Web first caught the attention of the general public a couple of years ago, it boasted what we can only describe as an anything-goes environment. You could find vulgarity, nudity, and violence without even searching for it. The Web, and the Internet in general, was considered a haven of First Amendment rights. There seemed to be no line you couldn't cross, no barriers to any kind of expression.

As the Web grew in popularity, and more and more John and Jane Q. Publics joined the environment, the chances that someone would see something online that they found offensive dramatically increased. And, in the truest tradition of modern America, so did the lawsuits.

In a recent case, a University of Michigan student named Jake Baker posted messages to an online newsgroup that described his fantasy rape and torture of one of his female classmates. To make matters worse, Baker used the actual name of his classmate in his postings. That incident drew the attention of FBI officials, who arrested Baker and charged him with transporting threatening materials across state lines. He was held without bond by a federal judge, but his case eventually was thrown out by a judge who ruled that the Constitution guarantees the right to broadcast any message, no matter how disgusting it may be.

A recent case that has captured the attention of the national media involves a group of America Online subscribers who used the service to post lewd pictures of children. FBI agents rounded up some of the organizers of these postings, and prosecuted them under federal laws forbidding the distribution of child pornography. At the time of this writing, the outcome of these cases is undecided.

A case involving another online service drew quite a bit of attention from the business community. In this case a New York–based securities firm Stratton Oakmont filed suit against Prodigy for $200 million over several libelous statements posted to one of Prodigy's money-related bulletin board systems. The statements falsely suggested that Stratton Oakmont was unethical and guilty of committing Securities and Exchange Commission (SEC) violations. Stratton Oakmont argued that Prodigy was responsible for the content of messages posted on its service. Prodigy argued that it was no more liable than a telephone company when someone makes a libelous statement over the phone. A New York court decided that Prodigy was a publisher and could be held liable. After this ruling, Stratton Oakmont agreed to drop the suit if Prodigy would offer an apology.

WHOSE LAWS MUST I OBEY?

One knotty question emerging from all this is, whose legal jurisdiction covers whom? If a man sitting at home in Baton Rouge, Louisiana, happens to download pictures of a naked child that originated from a Web server located in Thailand, does the state of Louisiana have the right to prosecute the man under local laws that prohibit the transmission of child pornography? This question lies at the true heart of legal issues on the Web, and so far, no branch of the government has been able to provide any definitive answers.

Among the most publicized Internet criminal cases confronting this issue are those involving gambling. A few ambitious entrepreneurs have established "virtual gambling" establishments on the Web. A server located on an island or foreign country where gambling is legal provides these online "casinos." Users send their money to a bank account located outside U.S. borders, then fund their gambling endeavors out of this account. They can play almost any casino game, from craps to blackjack, and all of it happens right on the Web. To further protect themselves, these casino operators allow nonmembers to browse their site, and even allow them to gamble with fake money. This keeps the sites very busy, and with all the activity, U.S. officials are unable to track who's gambling for real and who's playing with funny money.

THE TRUTH, THE WHOLE TRUTH, AND NOTHING BUT THE TRUTH

When you testify in court or before Congress, you are required to swear that the testimony you give is the complete truth as you know it, and that you are not attempting to deceive anyone. U.S. advertisers operate under basically the same standards. It's illegal to publish ads that are substantially untrue, made to deceive, or unfair. This standard was established to protect consumers. A variety of government agencies are charged with enforcing the regulatory guidelines to which advertisers must adhere. Until recently, little has been done to apply these guidelines to the Web.

In this section, we examine the general guidelines advertising must adhere to, and how this translates to the Web. We also examine how federal regulatory agencies have recently enforced these codes on the Web.

ADVERTISING GUIDELINES

The Federal Trade Commission (FTC) is the agency charged with establishing advertising guidelines. The FTC also is in charge of prosecuting violators of the guidelines it establishes. The FTC concentrates its efforts on three main areas—unfairness, deception, and advertising substantiation.

In the area of unfairness, the FTC relies on three criteria. First, an ad may not be "immoral, unethical, oppressive, or unscrupulous." Second, an advertisement may not cause "unjustified consumer injury." Third, an ad is never allowed to "violate any law as it has been established by statute, common law, industry practice, or otherwise." In other words, advertisers in this country must be conscientious and ensure their messages violate no laws of the land.

In the area of deception, the FTC states, "The Commission will find an act or practice deceptive if there is a misrepresentation, omission, or other practice, that misleads the consumer acting reasonably in the circumstances, to the consumer's detriment. The commission will not generally require extrinsic evidence concerning the representations understood by reasonable consumers or the materiality of a challenged claim, but in some instances extrinsic evidence will be necessary." In other words, the FTC will deem deceptive and subject to FTC prosecution any advertising that would deceive the ordinary, logically thinking person.

The criteria the FTC applies to advertising substantiation is similar to the rules the commission uses to define deception. If an advertisement's claims can't be validated, then it is considered in violation of the FTC rules. The FTC utilizes independent research groups as well as in-house study groups to determine whether ads act in violation of their substantiation guidelines.

WHAT HAVE REGULATORS BEEN DOING?

Up to now, the federal government has not regulated advertising posted on the Web. Many of the federal agencies charged with advertising regulation are still becoming familiar with Web technology. However, there have been a few cases dealing with the regulation of advertising online.

A case in point involved the U.S. Department of Transportation, which regulates the advertising of all transportation firms, and Virgin Atlantic Airlines. In November 1995, the airline posted an advertisement on the Web that displayed the fare between Newark, New Jersey, and London, England. But the posted fare failed to include taxes, and wasn't even available most of the time. The Department of Transportation fined Virgin for the misleading advertisement, and made the airline remove the ad from the Web.

This was one of the first cases brought by a federal agency against an online advertiser, but the number is sure to rise as federal agencies get up to speed with Web technology.

UNCLE SAM'S SHARE

As a businessperson, there's probably nothing in the world that gets your knickers in a twist like the thought of paying more taxes. As you prepare to put your Web marketing plan into action, you might wonder, Are there any tax surprises waiting for me online? Do I have any special tax obligations from online revenues? What about new IRS Internet regulations I haven't heard about? What about local regulations? This section will try to answer these questions so that you might avoid the wrath of a short-changed Uncle Sam.

IF I SHIP IT, WHO DO I PAY ?

Your online marketing efforts really seem to be working. You put your site up only last week and already you've got 100 orders for widgets. Now you're getting ready to ship the orders from your factory in Osh Kosh, Wisconsin, to locations all around the U.S. Now you wonder, To which customers do I charge sales tax?

Luckily, state and local governments treat Web sales much the same as mail-order catalog sales. Presently, you have to charge sales tax only on items you ship within the state where you're located. In other words, if your factory is located in Osh Kosh, you only have to charge sales tax on the widgets that you ship to customers living in Wisconsin. All your other widget customers get a break and pay no sales tax.

This is true for sales within the United States. We'll cover orders traveling outside the country later on in this chapter in the section about import/export laws.

NO NEW RED TAPE

Wouldn't it be wonderful if you weren't required to fill out a slew of new paperwork enabling the IRS to track your Web transactions? Well, believe it or not, the IRS has issued no additional forms for your online activities. At this time, the IRS and the great majority of state and local governments allow you to lump Web revenues in with all other forms of revenue your company generates. In the future, there may be so-called "new media" forms to fill out, but for now nothing extra is required. Enjoy it while you can.

HACKERS

Costly security breaches seem to be on the rise in the Internet's expanding universe. A 1994 study conducted by the accounting firm Ernst & Young revealed that of 1,271 North American companies surveyed, over 50 percent reported financial losses in 1992 or 1993 due to information security breaches. In 1993, the Computer Emergency Response Team (CERT), a federally funded organization that monitors and investigates computer security issues, reported a total of 132 computer security breaches in North America. By 1994, this number had grown to 2,341.

In an earlier chapter, we discussed technological strategies for protecting yourself from unwanted hacker intrusions. In this section, we look at legal solutions to this problem.

WHAT TO DO IF THEY GET IN

In spite of all your efforts, a hacker may still manage to break into your system. When this happens, you must first assess the damage. Hackers often break into a system just to prove they can do it, and they may not have caused any trouble or stolen any files.

Despite widespread concern about online security, few hacker intrusion cases make it to the papers. Most corporations don't release the news that their systems have been violated, fearing the publicity will undermine their business. Because many hacker intrusions don't involve the malicious destruction of files or the theft of corporate secrets, many corporations deal with them internally, or quietly hire outside experts.

If a hacker breaches your system's security, you'll have to examine this issue carefully and determine what course of action you want to take. If your property is stolen, or if a hacker causes any damage, we recommend that you report the incident to the proper authorities.

WHAT THE LONG ARM OF THE LAW CAN DO TO THE BAD GUYS

If the security lapse is one of great magnitude, incurring serious damage to your system, or the hacker has escaped with valuable data, then you may want to bring in the authorities. Unfortunately, hackers tend to be hard to catch. (It's not like you can pick one out of a mug book.) Still, even the best of the bunch slips up once in a while.

A case in point is Kevin D. Mitnick. Mitnick is one of the world's most famous and most elite hackers. He's been accused of stealing thousands of data files and at least 20,000 credit card numbers. He accomplished this by breaking into the systems of large companies such as Apple Computer and Motorola and taking information files. He also preyed on commercial network services, like CompuServe and America Online, where he was able to capture users' identification numbers and necessary passwords. A true hacker, Mitnick seems never to have used the credit card numbers he captured, keeping them only as "trophies" to show off his hacking proficiency.

Authorities knew about his activities, yet Mitnick eluded capture for almost three years. (He gained access to a phone company switching station where he could disguise the point of origin of his initial connection.) Finally, in February 1995, Mitnick was captured in Duraleigh Hills, North Carolina, with the help of computer security expert, Tsutomu Shimomura. In December 1994, Mitnick had broken into Shimomura's home computer system and stole hundreds of data files. He then harassed Shimomura with taunting voicemail messages about how easy it was for him to break into his system. Mitnick didn't realize that this harassment would only infuriate Shimomura and drive him to capture the hacker.

Two books about this case—one written by Shimomura, the other written by Mitnick, and both co-authored by journalists—recently hit the book stores. A third book probably will be on the shelves by the time you read this. We recommend them all. They make fascinating reading and it's always a good idea to know your enemy.

It often takes an extremely coordinated effort to catch a skilled hacker. If this kind of security failure occurs at your site, you should contact CERT and the FBI to determine your best course of action.

You can reach CERT online at <ftp://cert.org>. This FTP site is filled with information about online security. It offers software that tests your system's security, as well as information about the general state of online security. It also provides contact numbers for reporting security break-ins.

CAN WE GET THIS IN OR OUT OF THE COUNTRY?

As you use your Web site to reach out to customers beyond U.S. borders, eventually you'll have to deal with unfamiliar issues like local product restrictions, tariffs, and export duties. And these are only a few of the hurdles you might have to clear. In this section, we examine some ramifications of using the Web to break into foreign markets.

THE WHOLE WORLD IS NOW YOUR MARKET

Whatever doubts we may have about the future of the World Wide Web, of one thing we are certain: It will continue to expand into a global marketplace. As the Web expands, so will your opportunities— and your headaches. Making your way safely through the labyrinth of import/export laws to reach your new international customers may give you a real migraine.

First, you must decide whether you really want to move into international trade. Nobody says your company *has* to sell to overseas customers. Maybe you don't feel like jumping through those hoops right now. Maybe yours is a product or service that doesn't lend itself to foreign trade. Dealing with foreign customs is a time-consuming and expensive venture that many people simply decide to forgo.

It can be time-consuming, confusing, frustrating, and an all-around pain in the back forty. Before you dismiss altogether the idea of selling to customers outside the U.S., however, take a moment to weigh the hassles against the potential to expand your markets and increase your profits. A lot of people have struck gold in foreign markets. And after all, making money is what Web marketing is all about.

The first rule to remember about international trade is that customs laws differ from country to country. You won't be able to establish a single international shipping procedure that works everywhere. When you sell to foreign markets, you must customize your shipping procedure by product, region, and country.

Maybe You Won't Be Able to Ship It Everywhere

A Skyline client had a product that was manufactured from shredded U.S. currency. He had an arrangement with the U.S. government that allowed him to use the shredded currency, but in return they set many restrictions on what he could do with his product. One of these stipulations was that he could not sell his product outside the U.S. When we created Web ads for this company, we always had to include a line that limited the offer to shipping addresses within the U.S.

To assist you in the processing, shipping, and delivery of your products overseas, you may want to hire a customs clearing agent in the country where you'll be doing business. Clearing agents help companies outside the country get their products smoothly through customs (or as smoothly as possible). In most cases, they also compute tariffs for you, and some will invoice you separately for tariffs, so you can pay them after your product goes through customs.

The paying of tariffs and other taxes is another expense you must take into account when deciding whether to sell to international customers. One tax you can almost count on paying every time is the so-called value-added tax (VAT). This tax is computed as a flat percentage and tacked onto the price of the goods. Although not used in the U.S., this tax is very prevalent in Europe and South America. These taxes are designed to increase the prices of your products and make them less attractive to foreign buyers. Make sure you calculate these increases, and inform your potential customers through your Web site that prices they pay will be higher.

The one possible escape clause here the "minimum price threshold." If your product is priced below a certain minimum, most countries won't charge a VAT. By pricing your products carefully, you can avoid many of the foregoing shipping problems. Once again, each country's laws are different, so check each threshold price.

GOVERNMENT VIEWS AND PRECEDENCE

In 1992, Vice President Al Gore made a speech about his vision of the future. It was in that speech that he first used the phrase "Information

Superhighway." This was a signal that the government was beginning to recognize the influence of the Internet. It wasn't long before the feds decided the Information Superhighway could use a few rules and regulations—a few speed limits and stop signs.

In this section we discuss actions the U.S. government has begun to take to bring "order" to the Internet. We look at some of the activities of each branch of government vis-à-vis the Net, and the progress they've made in their efforts to tame cyberspace.

CONGRESS SPEAKS OUT

Recently, the legislative branch of the federal government has been contemplating legislation that would affect the Internet community dramatically. Most of this legislation deals with controlling the "smut" that may be found on some computer networks. In late 1995, Congress became aggressive in attempting to pass legislation to control the transmission of sexually explicit information to minors on the Internet. As of this writing, no "anti-smut" legislation has passed both houses of Congress, but two bills had entered the final stages of enactment.

Presently two sets of legislators are attempting to get their bills through Congress. One group of lawmakers wants to make it illegal for users of the Internet, or any networking service, such as Prodigy or America Online, to "knowingly send or directly send" sexually explicit material to minors. Representative Henry Hyde of Illinois is spearheading this plan, which would call for fines of $100,000 and up to two years in jail. One provision of Representative Hyde's plan would exempt companies providing access to networks such as America Online, CompuServe, and Prodigyfrom liability if one of their users violates the law.

The other group of legislators, led by Representative Rick White also wishes to regulate the exchange of information on the Internet. However, Representative White's proposed law makes illegal the transmission of information deemed "harmful to minors." This description is more ambiguous, but also allows for more latitude in the publishing of sexually explicit material. The penalties are similar to those in Representative Hyde's legislation, and the proposed law also calls for immunity for network providers.

No matter which piece of legislation finally passes into law, one thing is certain: Censorship is coming to the Net. These laws almost certainly will force judges to lay down guidelines, as groups challenge the censorship of cyberspace in the courts.

THE PRESIDENT'S TURN AT THE PLATE: INFORMATION INFRASTRUCTURE TASK FORCE

In February 1993, the White House established a standing committee to examine the world of "The Information Superhighway," and to make specific recommendations regarding the development and growth of cyberspace. This committee was named the Information Infrastructure Task Force (IITF).

The presidential task force was developed to investigate a broad spectrum of telecommunications systems. Our primary concern is with the IITF's Information Policy Committee (IPC). This committee's purpose, in its own words, is to "identify and suggest critical information policy that must be addressed if the National Information Infrastructure is to be fully deployed and utilized, particularly those issues which may serve as barriers to the utilization of the infrastructure as the Nation's primary communications channel."

Out of this large committee, several subcommittees were formed. The actions of one of those subcommittees, the Intellectual Property Working Group, is of particular interest. This subcommittee, once again in its own words, "is seeking to develop an appropriate balance among the rights of copyright owners and users in the development of the information infrastructure."

On September 5, 1995, the Intellectual Property Working Group released a report on its findings. The product of months of hearings and testimony from many people in the publishing and Internet industry, the report summarized in detail every aspect of the copyright question plaguing the Web. The report is huge, so we won't reprint it here verbatim, but we should look at some of the subcommittee's recommendations.

You can view the entire report presented by The Intellectual Property Working Group (if that's how you want to spend a week or so) by going to <gopher:/ /ntiantl.ntia.doc.gov>. The document is a big one (560k), so it may take a while to download. We recommend checking it out. It's a good example of the way the government spends your tax money.

The subcommittee first recommended that the privileges of the fair-use doctrine of copyright law should not extend to the Internet. Their reasoning was simple: Monitoring fair use of copyrighted material in cyberspace is impossible, and the only way to stop abuses is to make an exception to the doctrine.

The subcommittee also recommended that the first-sale doctrine not extend to activities on the Internet, for similar reasons.

The task force also discussed the issue of encryption. They recommended making it illegal for anyone to circumvent encryption methods that copyright holders used to secure electronic copies of their documents. It also recommended making it illegal for anyone to pass on the knowledge or technology that would enable others to go around any coding or encryption an online publisher may utilize.

Although none of these recommendations has yet to take effect as law, it should only be a matter of time before these or similar restrictions are enforced in cyberspace.

HERE COMES THE JUDGE—RECENT COURT RULINGS

Earlier in this chapter, we discussed recent court rulings dealing with Web activities. None of these cases, however, answered any of the basic questions about the Internet.

Where exactly does the freedom to exchange information online infringe on the rights of creators of original works? What kinds of online speech does the First Amendment protect, and what constitutes slander, libel, and pornography? What legal jurisdiction applies in cyberspace?

One of the biggest problems the judges faced in these cases was an utter lack of legal precedents. Up to now, the U.S. Supreme Court has made no ruling on any of the basic questions affecting the Internet. The High Court is unlikely to act before the other two branches of government have taken a shot at establishing a few Internet laws.

Remember...

- The Internet was designed as a free forum for the exchange of information; users could grab and take any information they could find. As user numbers increase, however, this policy of grab and take became more ambiguous. Take care how you utilize other people's information, and make sure that you have the rights to publish it.

- Publishing sexually explicit material and other work that may be considered offensive on the Internet has become a recent target of prosecutors. Although laws are not yet developed to effectively prosecute users who deal in this type of material online, it's probably better to steer clear of it for now.

- Paying taxes from business on the Web is not a complicated procedure at this point. It's similar to tracking the tax liability from a mail-order catalog business.

- When someone hacks into your system and enters areas they're unauthorized to enter, your best bet for legal action is to contact CERT and the FBI.

- The Web makes the world your oyster, but that doesn't make international commerce any easier. You must examine the cost benefits of doing business overseas and determine whether it's in your best interest to conduct foreign trade.

- The U.S. government recently started taking action to regulate the Internet. Although no clear-cut laws and regulations have been established yet, some regulation is inevitable.

- The most important message we want this chapter to communicate is, if you have any questions about the legal implications of doing business on the Web, get the expert advice of an attorney who specializes in media and computer-related law.

16

THE CARE AND FEEDING OF YOUR WEB SITE

In this chapter, we'll be looking at a number of issues you'll be confronted with once your site is up and running. Most of these issues will have more meaning for you once you've established your site, and we recommend waiting until you have a Web site before addressing many of them. Of course, we definitely recommend that you read this chapter *before* you launch your site. You'll still need to consider most of these issues from the very beginning of the development of your company's online presence.

In this chapter, we'll be looking at the Web as an excellent resource for fast, inexpensive market research. We'll be discussing various ways to keep track of how often surfers visit your site, and the different tools that can help you analyze that data and apply the results your Web development. We'll also be explaining how to use registration to gather valuable information about your customers *without* offending them. And finally, we'll be showing you how to use your site to expand into new and distant markets.

TRACKING WEB TRAFFIC

The first thing you'll want to do after your Web site is set up and your company has gone online is begin counting the number of visits to your site. This number is a very important, and can be a good indicator of the popularity of various aspects of your site. Not only should you keep track of the number of visits to your entire Web site over time, you should also pay attention to which sections are receiving the most attention.

WHEN A HIT ISN'T A HIT

Earlier in these pages, we discussed some of the different ways people keep track of the number of times surfers "hit" their sites. There are literally dozens of different methods of counting hits. This can be very confusing, both to clients and others in the Web advertising industry. To help clarify things, we've defined a few of the most useful types of hit counts in the next section. (Table 16-1 at the end of the section provides a summary.)

RAW HIT COUNT

The *raw hit count* includes every file sent from the server to a Web browser. This means that every Web page, every image (large or small), every sound file, and every CGI program accessed is counted as a hit.

(You'll remember from Chapter 3 that CGI stands for Common Gateway Interface.) Web-presence providers and webmasters often use raw hit counts to measure the traffic at a Web site. If the raw hit count is very high, it may be time to upgrade the Web server or Internet connection.

This type of hit count produces the highest numbers, but not necessarily the most accurate account of the traffic at your site, since a single Web surfer could rack up a dozen hits or more. It's not a very accurate measure of the number of *people* who visit your site.

Raw hit counts are often used by Web-presence providers and Web sites that offer sponsorships to boost the confidence of their advertisers. These companies want potential Web advertisers to see how much exposure the Internet can provide, so naturally they quote the highest numbers they can. Some Web presence providers bill their advertisers based on the number of hits each advertiser receives. In that case, "hits" usually refers to the raw hit count because it's the larger number.

CLICK COUNT

The *click count* includes only those files specifically requested by the user. The count is increased exactly once every time a user clicks on a link. The count may go up every time a CGI is executed, but only if the user clicked on the link. If the user clicked on a standard Web page that happened to execute the CGI on its own, it wouldn't count. If the user clicks on a link to a page that contains five images, only the original click is counted. In contrast, the raw hit count would have included the original page and each image for a total of six hits. If, however, the user clicks on an image and views it separately (sometimes sites allow you to click on an image and receive a larger, higher resolution image), that specifically requested image is included in the count.

The click count is very useful to the Web advertiser because it gives a better indication of how many people visited the site and how popular are specific features. The click count can be significantly lower than the raw hit count; it's a much more accurate reflection of activity on your site. However, counting the number of specifically requested images can be difficult, so advertisers often rely instead on the page count.

PAGE COUNT

Next to raw hit counts, the *page count* is the most popular way to measure site traffic. It's really a simplified way of estimating the click count.

It includes every Web document sent to the users, including those pages that were generated by a CGI program. It never includes images, even if a user specifically requests them since it's rare for a user to specifically request an image without it's accompanying Web page, and it can be difficult to discern when this happens.

Always be careful when people (especially Web-presence providers) simply quote some number and call it a hit count. Unless they tell you which type of hit count they're referring to, the number is useless.

IMAGE COUNT

The *image count* is the number of times an image (and graphic file) has been sent from your server to a user on the Web. This count is a subset of the raw hit count, and it's usually the largest contributor to its total. It is useful to know this number because image requests typically account for about 80 to 95 percent of Web site traffic. When a site is running on a slow server or with a slow Internet connection, it may be necessary to take steps to reduce the image count somewhat. This can be accomplished simply by including fewer images in your HTML pages, or by making more efficient use of the disk caching performed by many popular Web browsers.

VISITOR COUNT

The *visitor count* is a measure of the number of individuals who have visited a Web site. This is by far the most difficult Web site activity to measure. In fact, current Web technology makes it impossible to provide an accurate number without requiring user registration (covered later in this chapter). Most advertisers use the browser count (described in this section) as the best substitute for the visitor count.

The usefulness of the visitor count is obvious. The number of times a particular Web document has been viewed isn't nearly as important to advertisers as the number of people who actually saw that document. Because this number is so important, you can expect some changes in Web technology to allow a more accurate visitor count.

REPEAT VISITOR COUNT

Like the name implies, the *repeat visitor* count is a measure of the number of individuals who return to a Web site a second (or third) time. This count tells the advertiser how many people were interested enough in the Web site to come back. It's a subset of the visitor count and is generally a significantly lower number. Like the visitor count, the repeat visitor count is difficult to obtain with current technology. Most advertisers use the repeat browser count as an approximation of the repeat visitor count.

BROWSER COUNT

The *browser count* is a measure of the number of computers that have connected to a Web site. While this approach is often used as a substitute for the visitor count, it's not as accurate a measure of individual activities at a site. You don't know, for example, that every computer has only one user. Several people may have accessed your site from the same machine. Or a single person may have visited your site from both the office PC and the computer at home.

The biggest problem with the browser count is caused by *dynamic dialup accounts* (see Tech Note). Users of these accounts may have different Internet addresses each time they connect to the Internet. This makes a single user's computer look like a different machine every time, which skews the browser count. This problem is balanced somewhat by the fact that several users may connect through the same address.

Most home users of the Internet connect to their Internet service provider (ISP) with a modem. They dial the phone number given to them by their ISP, and they're instantly on the Net. Most of these companies provide service to so many customers that they cannot give an individual Internet address to each user. Instead, users are assigned different addresses each time they connect. These are called dynamic dialup accounts.

For Web sites, this means the same user may connect to their sites from several different addresses, which makes it look like the connections are from several different computers or users.

At Skyline, we find that we receive a lot of hits from Baltimore area ISP customers. Since their Internet addresses are assigned dynamically, we have no way of knowing if many of those connections are from just a handful of users or from hundreds.

REPEAT BROWSER COUNT

The *repeat browser count* is an approximation of the repeat visitor count. Instead of counting the number of users that return to the site, the repeat browser count measures the number of computers that return to the site. This approach has the same accuracy problems as the browser count.

INTERESTED HIT COUNT

The *interested hit* count is a measure of the number of pages that were seen by visitors who were actually interested in them. In truth, there isn't a way to count such a thing, but there are techniques that can help approximate it (see Tech Note). Be warned: estimating the interested hit count isn't for the squeamish. And frankly, the calculations are much too tedious and subjective to be worth the inaccurate results.

Estimating the Interested Hit Count

Before we discuss one of the techniques for estimating the interested hit count, we should define one more term: second click. The second click is the link users select from the first page they view on a Web site. The first click is the one that brought them to your site (usually to your homepage). They may have been sent there from another site and have no idea what to expect. Only when they're interested in what they've seen on the homepage will they make a second click.

There are several ways to calculate the interested hit count; unfortunately, all of them are inaccurate. You start by subtracting from the page count all the first clicks that didn't result in a second click. You're not interested those users who saw your homepage and didn't find it interesting enough to continue browsing your site. This step will cut your numbers (and perhaps your ego) down significantly. Next, subtract 50 percent of all last clicks—the last page viewed by each visitor. You can assume that the visitor was loosing interest at this point or he or she would have kept clicking. Last, subtract all page visits where the user didn't stay long enough to read a significant portion of it. The only way to approximate the amount of time a user viewed a particular page is to look at how much time elapsed before he or she chose another page. Obviously, the approximation will not work for the visitor's last click: there is no next click to measure against. The cutoff time you choose will depend on the length of the page and the estimated time required for the user to receive and display it.

Another, simpler method of estimating interested hits is to search through your access logs (the record the server keeps of every file it has ever sent) and find users that viewed three or more of your Web pages in one visit. Three clicks is a fairly accurate sign that that visitor was interested in your site.

IMPRESSION COUNT

The *impression count* is a measure of the number of times visitors have viewed your company hallmark or Web sponsorship. It's used most often by those companies that offer Web sponsorships. It's becoming common for the sponsor to be billed based on the number of impressions it generates rather than the amount of time a sponsorship is available on the site.

A company with its own Web site can use this number to measure the site's ability to increase company name recognition. The impression count is an easy hit count to generate and should be provided by most Web presence providers.

CGI COUNT

The *CGI count* is simply a measure of how many times a given CGI program has been executed. It's used primarily for billing purposes. A Web-presence provider may charge the Web advertiser a higher rate for CGI programs than for regular Web documents. The CGI count is also useful for determining if a CGI is being utilized enough to be worth keeping on the Web site.

TRANSACTION COUNT

The *transaction count* does exactly what you would expect—it counts the number of transactions completed online. Like the CGI count, Web presence providers may keep track of this count so they can collect a "per transaction" fee from their advertisers. The advertisers can use this count to measure the success of their online sales endeavors.

INDIVIDUAL HIT COUNTS AND CUSTOMIZED REPORTS

Most Web-presence providers can furnish you with a list of every file you have on the Web, along with the number of times each of those files has been accessed. This list is called an *individual hit count list* and it shows you exactly which files are most and least popular. You can use it to generate the statistics that are most useful to your company. Unfortunately, this list can be very long and tedious to break down into useful data, so you may prefer to have your Web-presence provider generate a customized report. Tell them what data you need and see what they can do for you. If they can't give you what you want, read on and learn how to generate your own statistics.

The most common types of hit counts are summarized in Table 16-1. (*Billable hit counts* are those counts that are sometimes used by Web-presence providers to determine the monthly charges to their advertisers.) The hit count types are arranged in the approximate order from most inclusive (highest count) to least inclusive (lowest count).

THE RIGHT TOOL FOR THE JOB

If you maintain your own Web site, you'll want to learn to calculate hit counts on your own. To do this, you'll need the access logs from your Webmaster and at least one of the tools we will discuss. Even if you don't maintain your own Web site, you may want to generate your own statistics anyway—especially if you can't get useful, customized data from your provider. If this is your situation, simply ask your provider for the access logs that pertain to your Web site, and use some of the tools we are about to discuss to analyze those logs. These tools are just a sampling of the many programs designed to help you analyze the usage statistics for your Web site.

TABLE 16-1   MANAGING AND TRACKING HIT COUNTS

Type	Counts	Billable
Raw Hit Count	Every document, image, sound, and CGI	Yes
Image Count	All image files sent from the server	Yes
Click Count	Specifically requested documents, images, etc.	No
Impression Count	Company hallmarks and sponsorships	Yes
Page Count	Entire documents and CGIs; estimates click count	No
Interested Hit Count	Documents that were found interesting by the user	No
Browser Count	Number of computers that visited the site (or page)	No
Visitor Count	Number of people that visited the site (or page)	No
Repeat Browser Count	Number of computers that returned to the site at a later time	No
Repeat Visitor Count	Number of people that returned to the site at a later time	No
CGI Count	Number of times a CGI program was executed	Yes
Transaction Count	Number of online transactions (sales)	Yes

WUSAGE

According to its own documentation:

Wusage maintains usage statistics for a WWW server. Specifically, it updates the following information, week by week:

- *Total server usage, each week*

- *Index usage, each week (responses to ISINDEX pages)*

- *The top ten sites by frequency of access, each week*

- *The top ten documents accessed, each week*

- *A graph of server usage over many weeks*

- *An icon version of the graph for your homepage*

Wusage is an extremely popular tool for conducting basic analysis of a Web site. It's available free of charge on the Web. It was written by Thomas Boutell. You can find more information on Wusage at:

```
http.//siva.cshl.org/wusage.html
```

REFSTATS

RefStats is a small program that works with NCSA and Apache Web server software (both are free servers). It scans the logs produced by these servers, and produces a list summarizing the URLs that referred the user to your site. In other words, this program tells you how people are finding your site. For instance, the analysis of Skyline's logs shows that a large number of people are finding us by using *Yahoo!* (a Web index site) and searching for "Maryland" or "Baltimore." This tells us that people are actively seeking information about Maryland and Baltimore on our site, so we should continue to expand such information. You can use RefStats to see how effective your Web sponsorships have been. It can tell you if somebody found your site by clicking on an advertisement you sponsored on somebody else's page. This is an invaluable tool.

RefStats is available free on the Internet at:

```
http://www.netimages.com/~snowhare/utilities/
refstats.html
```

Just access the Web site and follow the instructions.

ACCESSWATCH

AccessWatch is a program designed for UNIX-style Web servers. It analyzes the log files from NCSA and CERN Web servers, along with the countless other servers that use the same style of log file. Written by Dave Maher, a student at Bucknell University, this program produces very attractive and useful output that can be viewed with a Web browser. It generates statistics for hourly server load, page demand, accesses by domain, and accesses by host. It performs a browser count and calculates the average number of pages viewed by each visitor. The product is free for government, academic, and non-commercial use. All of you Web advertisers will have to pay $40 per year to use the product—and believe us, that's a bargain. (Figure 16-1 shows a sample of the output from AccessWatch.)

WEBREPORTER

Open Market has designed a "sophisticated tool for analyzing Web server access activity and generating customized reports." The product appears to be fairly comprehensive, and it does offer some nice customization features. The drawback to this product is its price: $495. (Hey, who said all Web statistics tools were free?) It might be worth it, if there were not so many similar tools available for free. For the $495 price tag, you get the chance to create a few new reports, and an easy-to-use interface.

Cache Confusion

Hit counts are clearly the most useful indicators of the amount of interest users have in a particular Web site or page. The log files generated by practically all Web servers can be analyzed quickly to produce detailed reports showing how many times each element of a Web site has been accessed. The reports can show, to some degree, how many different visitors are viewing a site, and how long they're staying. All of this information is invaluable to the Web developer—especially when deciding which areas of the site to change or remove and which to expand.

Unfortunately, hit counts have a few enemies out there, including an otherwise quite useful process called caching.

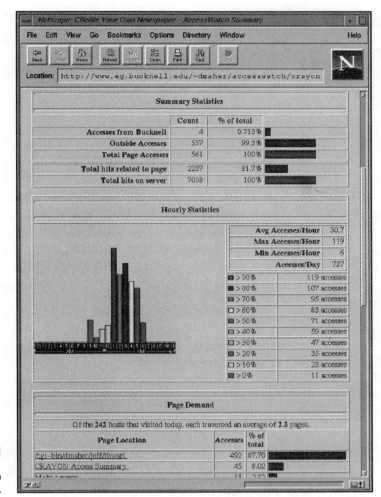

FIGURE 16-1

This is an example of the output from AccessWatch.

PERSONAL CACHE CONFUSION

When a user visits a site, many Web browsers will *cache* (store for reuse) the documents and images contained on the site. This allows the user to re-visit that document or image without re-retrieving it from the Web server. This *personal caching* helps to cut down on the amount of Web traffic in the Internet.

But the unfortunate side effect of personal caching is that it causes your hits to be undercounted. If a user re-visits your page without contacting your Web server for a new copy, your server has no way of knowing that the user returned.

INSTITUTIONAL CACHE CONFUSION

When an organization finds itself accessing the same Web sites over and over again, it may decide to cache several Web documents on a local server. This allows everybody in the organization to access those popular files without wasting the time and money involved in retrieving the files from across the Net. (We won't get into the details of how this is done.)

This kind of *institutional caching* has the same effect on hit counts as personal caching, only on a larger scale. Some organizations (including most commercial online services) have established such large caches that their users are finding that the documents they receive are no longer up-to-date. At Skyline, for example, we continue to get comments on Web pages that have been removed from our server for several months. The comments usually come from users of America Online or one of the other commercial online services. The users of these services are victims of *over-caching*; the services have established caches that don't check to see if a document has changed, even after long periods of time.

ADVANCED SITE AUDITS

When you want serious, detailed information about the usage of your Web site, there are experts out there who can help. A few highly specialized companies have made a business out of snooping through people's Web sites and generating all kinds of interesting statistics. Don't set your hopes too high; these companies can't really provide any more data than was already in your log files. But they have developed some excellent methods for turning that data into understandable and useable statistics.

WEBAUDIT

WebAudit is becoming one of the more popular services for analyzing Web statistics. (Figure 16-2 shows one of the company's sample reports.) According to the company's Web site:

> *WebAudit will sort your website statistics by page name, hits, groups, first time viewed, last time viewed, and produce 2-week, 3-month and 1-year histories in split seconds! All instantly before your eyes with up-to-the-minute Cool reports!*

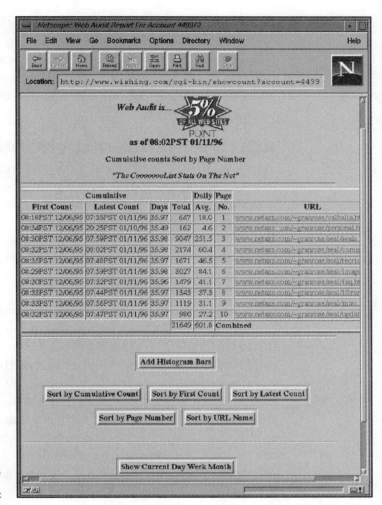

FIGURE 16-2

A sample report from WebAudit

INSTANT MARKET RESEARCH

It's not enough to simply collect hit count information. You must also use that information to conduct market research. If you come from a big company with a significant advertising budget, you probably have some experience conducting or purchasing conventional forms of market research. Market research gives you information about the needs and preferences of your consumers. This research is used as a guide when establishing new products and services and also to help direct the modification and marketing of existing services.

Market research can be an expensive part of a complete conventional marketing campaign—unless your company is on the Web. Fortunately for Web advertisers, market research is an inexpensive addition to any online marketing strategy. Businesses can use the hit counts generated by their Web sites to measure consumer demand for their products and services.

REAL VS. INCIDENTAL PRODUCTS

To understand the usefulness and limitations of using Web page traffic to measure consumer demand for your products and services, you must first understand the difference between real products and incidental products. *Real products* are those products and services that are manufactured and marketed to be sold themselves. *Incidental products* are those products and services that are by-products of real products, generally not intended to be sold.

For example, a record store's real products may consist of compact discs, cassette tapes, and vinyl albums (they still actually sell those things here and there). If the store gives away T-shirts every Saturday morning to the first 500 customers, those T-shirts are considered incidental products. The shirts are of some value to the consumer, and they help to bring business into the store (hopefully), but the retailer doesn't intend to make any money directly from the shirts; instead, he hopes they will increase the sales of his real products.

When a company goes online, the Web site itself—especially the site's added value—is usually considered an incidental product. The company is probably not in the business of providing Web sites, and doesn't intend for the site to produce income directly. Whether or not the site is used to generate sales of real products, it's usually not the product being sold and is therefore not a real product.

Remember that hit counts simultaneously measure consumer interest in both real and incidental products. It can be difficult to separate whether the visitor's interest was in your real product or the added value of your Web site. In the record store example, the retailer must realize that many of the Saturday morning shoppers were attracted by the free T-shirt and not by the selection of music at the store. And he cannot assume that just because the shirts attracted an additional 400 shoppers, the giveaway was successful. His success must be measured by the increase in sales.

In the same manner, you cannot assume that just because one section of your Web site attracted more visitors than another, that any products included in that section were more desirable to visitors. It may just be that the visitors were attracted by the incidental products in that section. Your added value will bring a lot of people to your site who have no interest in your product at the time. But if your site is properly designed, they will remember you when they do need your products or services.

It can be useful to set up your Web site so that it allows you to separate customer interest in your real products from interest in your incidental products. Figures 16-3 shows two Web pages that are identical except for the way they handle the price of the album. In the first figure the price is given automatically, while the second figure requires that the user click on the word "here" to receive the latest price. By using the second method, the retailer can receive two different hit counts: one from those users who look at the lyrics, and another from those users who go on to look at the price. The retailer can assume that a visitor who requests the price has some interest in purchasing the album. With the first method, the retailer receives only one hit count and has no way of knowing whether the visitor was interested in the lyrics or the price. Perhaps the visitor already owns the album and only wants to be able to sing along.

SOLICITED VS. UNSOLICITED MARKET RESEARCH

Hit counts are a form of unsolicited market research. When visitors browse your Web site, they may not even be aware that their visit is being counted. In fact, many Web users don't realize that any records are kept of their activities while visiting a site. (Perhaps ignorance is bliss; denizens of the Web don't usually like hearing that their actions are being recorded.) Because you aren't asking the user to furnish any information, and the user isn't taking any special action to provide information, hit counts are totally unbiased and non-intrusive.

But what happens when you want more information than a hit count can provide? After all, counting hits only tells you how many people saw a particular advertisement, viewed a specific Web page, or conducted an online order. If you have the time to analyze them, the logs generated by your Web site will also tell you, to some degree, where

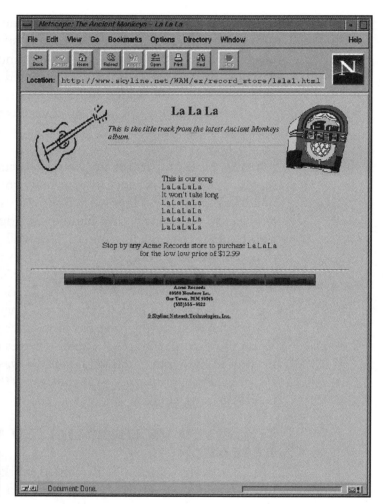

FIGURE 16-3 A

By isolating specific product data in a Web site, a company can improve its ability to turn hit counts into useful market research.

your visitors are coming from. But that isn't enough information to satisfy many marketing departments. Can't the Web be used to conduct more in-depth market research?

Indeed, it can. You can use the Web to survey consumers just like you would use telephone or direct mail surveys. Online surveys are cheaper for you and easier for participants. Online surveys can be interactive, asking additional questions based on the answers to previous questions. And when an online survey is submitted, the information can be automatically entered into a statistical database; there is no need for the surveyor to manually enter or scan the answers, as is necessary

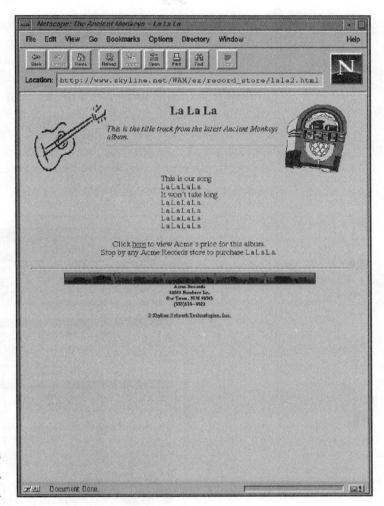

FIGURE 16-3 B

Note the isolated link, "Click here...," which qualifies hit counts.

with conventional surveys. The trouble with online surveys is that they survey only online consumers. Their results cannot be applied directly to entire consumer populations.

Online surveys can be used to gather information about consumer demographics and consumer interests. They can ask the participants what products they may own that compete with or complement the products of the surveyor. They can collect all sorts of information, as long as the surveys are conducted properly. Most of the rules that apply to user registration apply to online surveys (see "The Downside to User Registration" and "Getting The Most from User Registration" later in this chapter).

Conducting an online survey isn't the only way to gather solicited market research from your Web site. Many advertisers simply ask for general feedback from visitors. These comments may be about the advertiser's real products or the Web site itself. Such comments can be invaluable to any business, and make consumers feel like they have a voice in the marketplace. You can gather this feedback with online forms, or through e-mail. Regardless of how you obtain your information, be sure to assign somebody with the task of reading, analyzing, and perhaps responding to the market research you have gathered.

FIGURE 16-4A

The Photography & Video On Location, Inc., Web site contains an e-mail button that makes it easy to send comments and business inquiries. url=http://digiserve.com/loiodice/

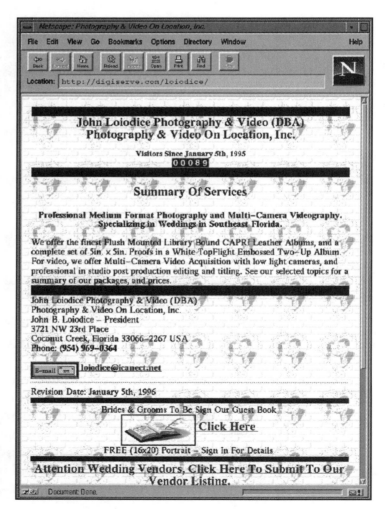

Many Web browsers now include support for e-mail. This means a Web page can provide a link that sends an e-mail message. Take a look at Figure 16-4A. About halfway down the page is a button that says "E-mail." Visitors with compatible Web browsers can click on that button to quickly send e-mail to the company. Figure 16-4B shows the automatic e-mail message as a Netscape user would see it. Notice how the "Mail To" address is already filled in. That was done by the browser. This feature makes sending feedback or business inquiries simple for the user and it reduces the risk that a user may mistype the company's e-mail address.

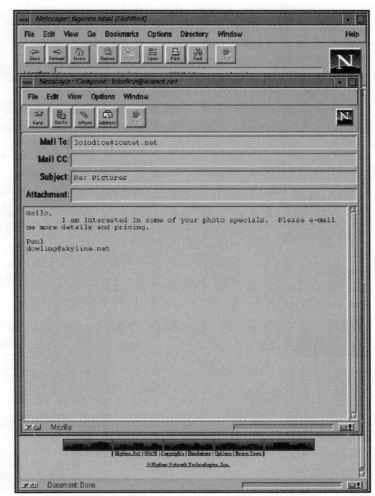

FIGURE 16-4B

When a Netscape user clicks on an e-mail link, he or she sees something like this. url=mailto:loiodice@icanet.net

HOW TO USE THE RESEARCH

As we said earlier, it's not enough just to gather information from your hit counts and user feedback. You must analyze that information and use it to guide your marketing strategies (both online and off). Use your hit counts and Web site logs (the unsolicited research) to discover:

- Which real products are most interesting to the online community

- Which Web pages are most interesting to the online community

- How users are discovering your Web site (sponsorships, searches, etc.)

- What about your site attracts users

- Whether your visitors are browsing from home or work (this is an approximation)

- Where, geographically, your visitors are coming from (requires some effort and isn't completely accurate)

Some of the information in the above list requires some effort and additional knowledge. If you plan to analyze your unsolicited research on your own, we recommend hiring a consultant first to show you how to get all you can out of the data. A skilled consultant can walk you through an analysis of your first month of logs and teach you how to do it yourself the next time. Before choosing a consultant, make sure he or she already knows how to extract all of the above information from your Web site logs. In truth, most Web consultants pay very little attention to logs and hit counts.

Information gathered from hit counts and site logs is subject to the errors and restrictions discussed above under "When a Hit Isn't a Hit."

Feedback and surveys gathered via online forms or e-mail (solicited research) can be used for a variety of purposes. Use this data to:

- Determine (more accurately) the geographic location of your visitors

- Determine the economic status of your visitors

- Discover the needs of your visitors (in terms of your products and services)

- Find out how consumers rate your products (real and incidental) compared to those of your competitors

- Learn how to improve your Web site and attract more consumers

Once you've gathered all of the information you can from your online market research (both solicited and unsolicited), send that information to the folks in your marketing department (or firm) and have them suggest ways of applying that research to future business developments and marketing strategies. For starters, you should use the information to:

- Modify the appearance of your Web site to suit the suggestions of your visitors

- Modify or expand your site's added value to reflect the interests of your visitors

- Highlight products online that seem most appealing to the online community

- Adjust your online marketing strategies to concur with any demographic statistics you have discovered

USER REGISTRATION

As we've said, registration is an excellent way to acquire additional demographic information about your users, as well as other market research. A company may either encourage or require users to register with the Web site. Web site registration forms may be simple or complex (though simple forms are more likely to be filled out).

In its simplest form, user registration involves assigning a name and password to Web site visitors. Visitors can then use that name and password to connect with the site at a later time. A company can restrict access to individual Web pages or entire Web sites based on whether a visitor has registered or not. It's also possible to limit access to specific individuals. For example, online pricing information may be made available only to a company's sales force and not the entire Web community.

Along with gathering demographic information, there are other advantages to utilizing user registration. User registration can provide the following:

- It allows you to restrict Web access to registered users only. This can be done on a page-per-page basis, or for the entire Web site.

- It allows you to limit the amount of time a user may spend on your Web site. If you have a very busy feature on your site, you may want to keep visitors from continuously hogging your resources—particularly if that feature doesn't generate sales.

- It allows you to charge fees for certain information, or for access to particular features.

- It allows you to track the usage patterns of each user. You can analyze a single visitor and learn exactly what products he or she seems most interested in.

- It opens up opportunities for *profile-driven marketing*.

Profile-driven marketing refers to the use of customer preferences and behaviors to customize future visits. A site could allow users to enter their interests into a database, and then use that data to modify the site so that each time a user connected, the site would report any new information it had gathered that was relevant to those interests.

Another site might keep track of customer purchases, and then modify the site to automatically suggest items or warranties that might complement previous purchases each time the user visits.

THE DOWNSIDE TO USER REGISTRATION

For all its uses, user registration is hardly the solution for every company. It has several drawbacks that have kept the majority of Web sites from implementing it. For starters, registration invades the privacy of the visitor. It's very unappealing among netizens to have to provide personal information to complete strangers just to gain access to their Web sites. Many people are just not comfortable giving their names, addresses (even cities and states), ages, and sex.

The other drawback to user registration is the amount of time it takes for the visitor to fill out a registration form. By forcing the visitor to pause before moving on to examine your commercial content, you risk that he or she may lose momentum or interest in browsing your site. Many visitors will simply be looking for a quick bit of information, and won't want to take the time to fill out a form, wait for a password, and then figure out how to use it (many people still have trouble logging in).

GETTING THE MOST FROM USER REGISTRATION

So what can you do to ensure you get the most from user registration? The first thing you should do is decide whether you really need to use it at all. You can get quite a bit of demographic information simply from hit counts, logs, and solicited market research. Most businesses should be more interested in attracting a large audience than in identifying individuals within that audience. Adding a registration process will scare away many users.

If you're going to request that users register with your Web site, you must give them some incentive to do so. You have to let them know what they stand to gain by registering. You may need to show them a sampling of the services your site has to offer, and tell them they may register to experience the site fully. Do *not* set things up so that they must register in order to get *anything* out of your Web site—and make sure they don't think this is the case. If the homepage of your Web site offers only two options—register or leave—you can bet most surfers will bolt. Like everything else on the Web, convincing users to register on your site requires a soft sell.

Also, it's very important to choose carefully the information you request when you seek to register users. You'll scare them away with too many questions or questions that are too personal.

Generally, you won't be out of line to ask for an e-mail address on your registration form. You'll need this to get the password back to the user. When the user registers, the form is often (but not always) processed immediately, and the password is sent directly to the e-mail address. Among other things, this ensures that the e-mail address was correct.

Requiring registered users to include an accurate e-mail address helps the Web site to identify when a single user has registered more than once; people can register under hundreds of names, but most people have only one e-mail address. The registered user's e-mail address can also be used later to contact him or her about site problems and additions, and to send relevant commercial information (discussed later).

Including the e-mail address also helps remove some of the visitor's feelings of anonymity. This is especially useful on sites that provide highly interactive features, such as chat rooms and MUSEs. By ensuring that you have at least one piece of accurate information about the user's identity, you're helping to force that user to take responsibility for his or her actions online. Even though the user is still anonymous to the rest of your users, he realizes that somebody can contact him and confront him about his actions.

Aside from the e-mail address, you're free to choose whatever information you feel you'll need from registered users. But remember, you don't want to intrude on the user's privacy, and you don't want to waste the user's time. We recommend asking for a user's ZIP code rather than city and state. It feels less obtrusive to the user, and the ZIP code can be easily converted into useful geographic information. (You'll also want to acquire a database of ZIP codes.)

And don't forget to give users the opportunity to enter a country. You're on the World Wide Web, remember, and not everybody surfing your site is from the United States.

The Skyline Registration Process

Figure 16-5 shows the Skyline Network Technologies' registration page. Some of our interactive features require registration. Otherwise the features would have no way of keeping track of a user from one visit to the next. Our registration page specifies how users will benefit by registering. It then goes on to ask for only four pieces of required information. Notice how we specifically asked for both first and last name: It's the only way to be sure you get both names and that the computer can easily decipher which is which.

Notice the separate section for optional information. We begin that section with a message that encourages users to fill in the information honestly and promises that we will respect the user's privacy. This has helped to increase the number of users who provide us with the optional information. This section asks for data we can use to enhance the demographic information we receive through unsolicited market research. All of the information is of particular interest to us. We don't waste the user's time by asking for data we don't use.

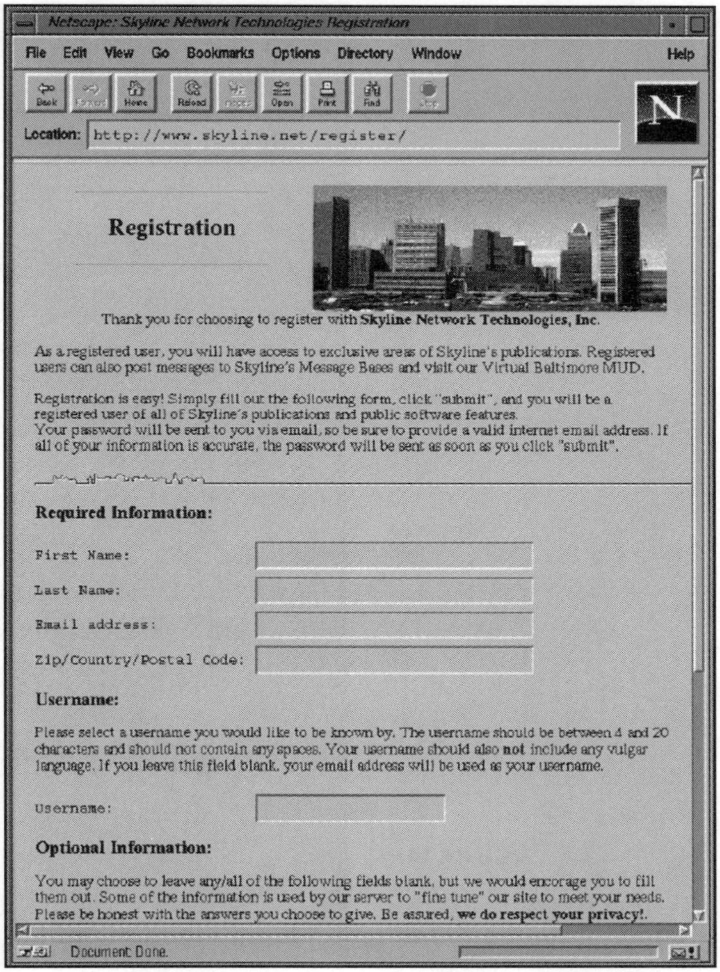

FIGURE 16-5

The Skyline registration page can be used as a model for most Web sites.

If you want your registration form to include more than five or six items, we suggest making some of the information optional. You'll be surprised how many people will answer the optional questions.

After users have registered, be sure to tell them their passwords and anything else they may need when using your site. Figure 16-6 shows the message displayed on the Web browser of a newly registered Skyline user. This message appears as soon as the users submit their registration. It tells them that the registration succeeded, how to get their passwords, and what to do if they have questions. It also asks

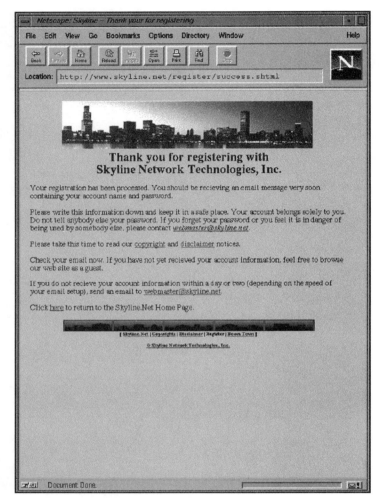

FIGURE 16-6

Skyline's "Thank you for registering"
page provides all of the information
new users will need.

them to read the disclaimer and copyright notices. Every site that implements registration should have a similar page.

CONTACTING REGISTERED USERS

If you've decided to implement user registration, odds are you'll be accumulating a lot of e-mail addresses. You'll probably want to cash in on this bounty by contacting those users and telling them about your products and services. *Don't do it!* These users have trusted you with their e-mail addresses only to obtain access to your Web site. Don't violate that trust by sending unsolicited commercial messages. Besides, your commercial information is already online, where your registered users have complete access to it 24 hours a day.

That said, there are times when it's okay to contact your registered users by e-mail. It's generally acceptable to contact a user when:

- That user seems to be having trouble online (you'll know this from your logs)

- You've had problems with your server that may have significantly affected the user

- You believe somebody else may be using the user's account

- There have been major changes to your Web site that the user may want to know about

- The user has not used the account in several months and you would like to know if you should disable it

When you do need to contact a registered user, remember that your e-mail message is probably unsolicited. You must make it clear from the start of your message that you have good, non-commercial intentions, and then state your message concisely and accurately. After you've done this, it's acceptable to provide a small piece of commercial information. For example, you may want to mention a new product and tell the user that more information is available on the Web. If you include any commercial information, it must be only one or two sentences and appear at the end of the e-mail message. Anything else is really not much different from sending unsolicited commercial messages to Usenet.

Every time you send an unsolicited message to a registered user (or any Net user), you should give that user the opportunity to request not to receive another unsolicited message from you again. This is similar to a person's right to tell telephone solicitors to remove their names from their calling lists. On the Net, if you don't honor a user's request not to send unsolicited messages, they can have you blocked from their e-mail accounts, and they can flame you to the rest of the Internet world. Take a look at the following e-mail messages; they're both samples of unsolicited communications. And both are too commercialized to be truly acceptable, but you'll see how the second one is clearly less offensive.

TO: "Jane Doe" jane.doe@your.email.account

FROM: "Widget World's Webmaster" webmaster@widget-world.com

SUBJECT: 173 Weekly Newsletter

Ms. Doe,

Hello from all of us at the Widget World Web Site. Welcome to

our 173rd weekly e-mail newsletter. This newsletter is sent to

all registered users of the Widget World Web Site.

The Widget World corporation was founded in 1823 by William H.

Klein Sr. Since then, it has grown into the world's largest

supplier of commercial and residential widgets.

This week's specials include our new family size widget and the

commemorative Elvis widget. Both are available at 20% off

through the Widget World Web Site.

As always, the Widget World Web Site will be featuring the

sights and sounds of Rome. Use your Web browser to walk the

streets of this magnificent city. Buon Divertimento!

We look forward to seeing you again on the Widget World Web

Site.

William H. Klein VIII

This first message is clearly a commercial message. Unless the recipient of this message has knowingly signed up to receive a weekly newsletter from Widget World, Widget World is guilty of abusing the recipient's e-mail account. The company doesn't even try to hide the fact that their message is strictly commercial. All of the information in the e-mail message is probably available online and most of the information isn't even timely: it's not something the recipient needed to know immediately. Now consider the second message.

TO: "Jane Doe" jane.doe@your.email.account

FROM: "Widget World's Webmaster" webmaster@widget-world.com

SUBJECT: See more of Italy

Ms. Doe,

Recently, there have been some very exciting changes at the

Widget World Web Site. We simply had to write to you and tell

you about them.

Starting this month, our "Sites and Sounds of Rome" has been

expanded to include the lovely city of Venice. You should stop

by — you'll be amazed at the realism of our guided tour.

Our site has recently won the Widget Industry Technology Award

for most creative use of technology to advance the use of

widgets world-wide. thank you to all of our visitors you helped

make this possible.

We look forward to seeing you again on the Widget World Web

```
Site. If you do not wish to receive future updates on the

Widget World Web Site, please reply to this message
and let

us know.

+ - - - - - - - - - - - - + - - - - - - - - - - - - - +
|  William H. Klein VIII  |   CIO, Widget World      |
|   klein@widget-world.com |    (212)555-5533         |
|                          |                          |
| Visit the Widget World Web Site at http://widget-world.com |
+ - - - - - - - - - - - - - - - - - - - - - - - - - - +
```

Avoiding the Mass E-mail

Skyline has been utilizing registration, on an optional basis, for quite some time. We've acquired well over 1,000 accounts, each with its own e-mail address. As of this writing, we have not sent out a single mass e-mailing to our registered users, though we've considered it on many occasions. We have, however, sent individual messages to users who seem to be having trouble with our site. We do plan to send out a mass e-mailing or two at some point, but we are patiently waiting until we have a lot of non-commercial information to share. We will probably send a message that is 75 percent about the entertainment value of our site, 20 percent about the Web as a whole, and 5 percent (one or two sentences) about new, commercialized features on our Web site.

This message was more acceptable because it focuses less on commercial information and more on information that may interest the recipient. The company sounds like it's trying to help the recipient find some online entertainment on its "Sights and Sounds of Rome" Web pages. This second e-mail also provides the means for the recipient to prevent future unsolicited contact.

KEEPING UP WITH NEW WEB TECHNOLOGIES

You've heard this several times by now, but it bears repeating: The Web, as a technology, is in its infancy. At this point in its development, the Web is still constantly growing and changing, acquiring new users, uses, and features. No business can expect a site put up today to have any value on tomorrow's Web. As the capabilities of the Web continue to grow, Web site owners must face the constant challenge of keeping up. Every day your site remains unimproved, it loses a step on the competition. Because of course you know, all of them *are* improving their sites.

When the color television was introduced, broadcasters rushed to provide color programming to their viewers. In the same manner, Web designers watch for new features of the Web and rush to provide Web sites that exploit the new technology. These designers devote several hours each week (if not each day) to reading trade publications and browsing relevant Web sites, trying to keep up with the newest Web applications. And once they learn about an innovation, they search for ways to use it in their Web site designs.

If you're designing your own Web pages and don't have the time to keep up with the new technologies, we recommend hiring a consultant review your site occasionally. The consultant has already spent countless hours reading the trade publications and browsing the Web. He or she can tell you what new features would benefit your site the most. Then you can implement those features, or pay somebody else to do it. The important thing is to make sure your site reflects, as much as possible, the state of the art of Web advertising and marketing.

Note to Small Businesses
Most small businesses use the "hands free" method of developing a small Web site. These businesses often cannot afford to have their sites redesigned every time a new Web feature arrives. Don't worry. Web users don't expect small sites to keep up in the same way the larger sites do. Just make sure that the company that hosts your Web site is providing a state-of-the-art atmosphere throughout its site. That will help to attract an audience to its Web server, and in turn, to your site.

KEEPING UP WITH NEW MARKETING IDEAS

It's not enough to keep up with the technological developments of the Internet and the World Wide Web. You must also stay on top of new marketing ideas and trends throughout the Web. As a Web advertiser, it's in your best interest to:

- Follow the trends in user demographics

- Keep up with the Internet community's views on Web commercialization

- Follow (and influence) changes in laws relating to copyright, security, privacy, import/export, and censorship (all of these are becoming major issues within the United States)

- Learn from the online successes and failures of other businesses (especially those in your field)

- Fight to ensure that the Internet remains a safe and profitable place to do business

You can accomplish most of these objectives using the Internet as your primary tool, because:

- Most Web demographic studies are published, at least in part, on the Web

- You can keep up with the current views on Web marketing simply by listening in on a few Usenet newsgroups

- Most of the laws relating to the Internet and Web marketing are discussed throughout the Net, mostly in the form of petitions and protests

- You can discover the online successes and failures of other businesses simply by browsing the Web and looking for yourself

- You can fight to ensure that the Internet remains a safe and profitable place to do business by e-mailing your government representatives

One popular source of Internet marketing information is the Internet Marketing Discussion List. You can participate in this discussion through the Web. Point your browser to:

```
http://www.popco.com/hyper/internet-marketing/
```

This Web site maintains a database of the current discussions and keeps archives of previous discussions that you can browse through. Unfortunately, it can be difficult to find specific information on the Internet Marketing Discussion List. You'll have to participate in (or at least follow) the discussions to fully benefit from the site.

Skyline's Web Advertising and Marketing Site Debuts

To help new Web marketers learn more about the Net and keep up with new marketing trends, Skyline is establishing a Web Advertising and Marketing (WAM) Web site on our corporate server. By the time this book reaches stores, we should have a significant resource online. We encourage you to check out the site. We will try to keep it updated with new information that was not provided in this book, and we will report any corrections (not that there are any mistakes) and changes to the topics we've covered in these pages. You can find the WAM site by pointing your Web browser to:

`http://www.skyline.net/WAM/`

EXPANDING YOUR MARKETS

With the use of the World Wide Web, many companies are finding they can reach a much larger market than every before. Small companies that used to serve only one town from their single shop are now taking orders from around the country and around the world. But they're quickly finding that launching a Web site isn't the only preparation to make before expanding their markets—especially when expanding into international markets.

We've saved this discussion on international markets until now because most companies should wait until they have some online experience before considering international markets.

ENTERING INTERNATIONAL MARKETS

The Internet has often been described as the "global marketplace" because it allows businesses to reach markets in all corners of the world. In truth, the only global marketplace is the globe itself. A Web site doesn't establish a company as a player in the global marketplace; it's simply one of the tools you can use to get there. The site doesn't excuse the company from import/export laws, cultural conformity, or international market research.

ARE YOU INTERESTED?

The first thing to decide about global markets is whether or not you're really interested in them. As we mentioned in the last chapter, providing your products and services to customers beyond the borders of the United States can be a migraine-producing experience. To answer this question, you should consider all of the preparations, all of the costs, all of the hassles of opening international markets, and weigh that against the benefits. In other words, ask yourself, Can I actually profit from international markets?

As you consider all this, don't assume that the rest of the world is one big market. The earth is covered by a quilt of cultures. Every country has different laws, monetary systems, and customs. You'll probably want to consider which of these widely divergent markets would be most profitable for your company. Don't forget to make sure that the people in those markets have sufficient Web access.

ARE YOU PREPARED?

If you're going to expand into international markets, you'll need to make all sorts of preparations. The issues you need to address fall into two categories: technical and cultural. The major technical issue is *speed*. We've told you before that when data travels over the Internet, it travels through several different networks. The overall speed of a connection depends on the slowest, most congested network the data travels through (the weakest link). Just think how many slow, congested networks there must be between San Francisco and Taiwan. How long do you think it would take a graphically intensive homepage to squeeze through the slowest one?

The number of transatlantic-Atlantic Internet links is on the rise, but oversees traffic still slows down while both Europe and the U.S. are awake. In some overseas countries, Internet users pay a nickel or more each minute they're online. If your homepage takes five minutes to load into their browsers, you had better make sure they're getting their money's worth. If you really plan to deal with overseas customers, you'll need to have a text-only version of your Web site that those users can select.

If you're committed to reaching diverse markets with your Web site, you should consider mirroring. When you mirror a site, you establish an identical site in a different (usually) geographical location. That way a consumer can choose the site that is closest, and most likely fastest. This technique cuts down on international traffic and makes the most of the telecommunications infrastructure.

Usually, when you connect to a site that is mirrored, the homepage will list the locations of all of its mirror sites, leaving the choice with the user. This extra step can be somewhat clunky to the user and doesn't always result in the best choice of sites.

The technique of mirroring will become much more popular as Web servers become smart enough to automatically switch visitors to the most appropriate server. The user doesn't even have to realize the switch has been made.

The other significant technical issues include your ability to ship products safely, quickly, and economically to foreign markets and your ability to provide customer support to those markets. If your company isn't prepared in these areas, then you're probably wasting your time and money pursuing international markets.

The rest of the preparations you must take before going international involve cultural issues. For starters, there is the issue of language. In many countries, like the Netherlands and the Nordic countries, the people learn English at an early age. But in other countries, like France, Spain, and Italy, it's often to your advantage to use the local language.

Along with language, there are cultural and currency issues to consider. You should always consult with citizens of the country to make sure your site doesn't offend their culture. And you must be sure to price your products in the native currency, or specify that prices are listed in U.S. currency. Realize that not all countries use credit cards as widely as we do in the United States. In several European countries, paying with credit cards via telephone is heavily restricted or banned outright. You can expect such limitations to extend to Web purchases.

When selling to most foreign countries, you should include metric equivalents for any weights and measurements you give. And remember that the symbolism and color used in your Web site may not translate properly into other cultures. For instance, not every culture assumes that red means stop and green means go. Likewise, the meanings of your icons and buttons may not be consistent across national and cultural borders.

Swedish Postal Service Profits on the Web

The Swedish postal service expects to make a lot of money thanks to that country's restrictions on credit card purchases. The service is launching a Web site for Swedish mail-order companies. Companies can order merchandise online, but instead of credit cards, they will pay C.O.D. at their local post office.

If you're trying to reach international markets, you'll want to consider sponsoring small advertisements on Web sites in your target areas. These advertisements will help to funnel consumers from that area into your site. At the very least, you'll want to list your URL in some of the online Web indexes from that area. The following sites may help you find places to advertise or list your site:

Europe

- *Datateknik*, a popular Swedish computer magazine. This site contains a list of favorite hot links. URL=http://www.et.se/datateknik/

- EUnet, an alliance of European and North African Internet access providers. The EUnet site contains links to each of its affiliates and a "Pick of Europe" list for individual countries. URL=http://www.eu.net/

- Italian National Research Council provides a list of Italian Web sites. URL= http://www.mi.cnr.it/NIR-IT/All-IT.html

- Link Everything Online includes a comprehensive list of Web servers both in Germany and elsewhere. URL=http://www.leo.org/

- Planet Internet, an online service operated by a subsidiary of the Netherlands postal/telecommunications service. Everything is in Dutch, but it does contain several links to U.S. sites. URL=http://www.pi.net/

- The Danish Research Network provides a list of Danish Web servers. URL=http://info.denet.dk/

Asia

- Institute of High Energy Physics, Beijing, maintains the China Homepage. This site is mirrored in the United States. URL=http://solar.rtd.utk.edu/china/china.html

🌐 Nippon Telegraph and Telephone includes a list of Japanese servers. The site also offers suggestions for getting your Japanese text into HTML (not an easy task). URL=http://www.ntt.jp/

For more ideas on attracting customers from foreign markets, review Chapter 9. Many of the topics discussed can be modified to target foreign markets.

ARE YOU LEGAL?

Aside from technical and cultural issues, there are those issues most people forget to consider until it's too late. We're talking about legal issues. No matter how firmly you believe you can apply the principles from this book to the global marketplace—no matter how much potential you feel is waiting for you in foreign markets—you simply cannot proceed to these markets without first consulting a lawyer. There are many legal issues involved in international trade that we have not discussed in this book. You will want to understand all of the issues thoroughly before you seek foreign markets online (see Chapter 15).

ENTERING OTHER NEW MARKETS

For most businesses, foreign markets are not the only new places to conduct business online. Most U.S. businesses can use the Web to target geographic areas that might have been previously out of reach. Small businesses that sell shipable products have the most to gain; they suddenly have exposure all across the country. Businesses that provide services and products that are difficult or expensive to ship may find it's too expensive to support markets in distant areas of the country. These businesses may, however, use the Web to measure how much interest in their products there is in different geographical areas. They can then use those measurements to determine the most suitable places to locate additional branches.

Many large U.S. companies have already established markets throughout the country. The Web does little to expand their markets, but it does make it easier (and cheaper) to reach consumers and support customers in distant markets. Customers who might have chosen a company with a storefront of branch office in their home state may settle for a company that they can contact and seek support through their home PC.

In order to target specific areas of the U.S., businesses may need to sponsor advertisements or list their URLs on several Web servers that are "local" to their target markets. Consumers tend to look to local Web servers when searching for businesses. Most people are more comfortable with a company that is located nearby, or at least has established some sort of marketing presence in their area.

THE CONSTANT BATTLE

Large companies need to realize that there is more involved to maintaining a Web presence than keeping your Web server plugged in. It's a constant process of browsing other businesses, keeping up with new technologies, designing and redesigning Web pages, and building new interactive features. Small companies with simple Web sites can get away with fairly static data. They can get by without conducting detailed statistical analyses of their Web server logs. But any company (large or small) that is going to invest a significant amount of money into establishing a quality, technologically elaborate Web site, must plan to devote continued time and money into keeping that site in top form.

Remember...

- There are many different ways to count hits on your Web site. Don't be fooled by misleading numbers.

- The Internet is full of tools to help you analyze your Web site logs. Use these tools, and take the time to understand and apply the results to your Web development.

- The Web—the entire Internet, for that matter—is an excellent resource for fast, inexpensive market research.

- Registration can be a valuable information gathering tool, but it can also alienate many visitors to your site. Use it carefully and sparingly.

- Today's innovative Web site is tomorrow's relic. If you want to stay on top, you have to keep up with new technologies and new marketing ideas. It's often cheaper to rely on consultants for the most up-to-date information and advice.

- Establishing a Web site isn't the only step to expanding to new markets, especially if you've set your sites on foreign markets.

17

WHAT THE FUTURE HOLDS

When it comes to the future of the World Wide Web, opinions are like e-mail addresses—everybody has one. So many notions, conclusions, and predictions are floating around in and out of cyberspace, that it's hard to keep track. Some see the Web, and even the Internet, as nothing more than a techno-fad that will die out in a few years. Others fervently believe the Net will change every aspect of our lives forever (for better *and* for worse). We take this opportunity to share some of our own opinions and predictions about the Web and its role in marketing and business applications.

THE FUTURE OF INTERNET TECHNOLOGY

Many people consider today's Internet a primitive precursor to tomorrow's true global communications infrastructure. Consequently, they expect all the current technology to eventually become obsolete, superseded by a new, faster, more versatile Internet. While the lightning pace of technological development—especially in communications—certainly supports such an expectation, there's really no reason to believe that businesses are wasting their time and money investing in the current technology.

The Internet always has been a creature of constant change, the restless offspring of many creative and insightful minds. In the years to come, you can expect the Net to continue its restless evolution, but especially to grow in size and speed. For now, its population seems to be growing almost faster than the Net's capacity to hold it. But as businesses and consumers rely more and more on the Internet for everyday operations, telecommunications companies (including cable television providers) will invest in more lines and faster technologies, increasing the Net's current data capacity and speed by several times.

The Internet as we know it is truly a stepping stone to tomorrow's global infrastructure. We believe that we can, in fact, expect a complete transformation of the current technologies over the next several years.

500 Channels of Interactive Television

Forget all the hype you've heard about 500-channel interactive television systems. The cost of the in-home hardware and fiber optic connections required for such systems—not to mention the costs of producing and "broadcasting" interactive programming—precludes them for the near future. Sure, the technology itself could be developed fairly quickly, but Americans don't spend enough time in front of their TVs to warrant such an expense. Simply put, the market can't support that type of technology.

But we also believe that the changes will come as a gradual evolution, and not a sudden revamping. In our business, we've witnessed the emergence of several leading-edge network technologies (after all, that's our name). But new technologies don't begin to gain popularity until they're adapted to conform to existing standards. In other words, successful new Internet technologies almost certainly will come as improvements to old ideas, and not as sudden replacements for them.

To those of you who ask, "Why waste time and money investing in a technology and a medium that's subject to constant change?" we answer this: The most exciting, most successful, and most marketable technologies and media are generally those experiencing the most change. These are the technologies that constantly fight to meet the needs of society, of consumer and business alike. And those of you who embrace the new technologies will have the most influence over its evolution. Only by participating can you mold this ever-changing medium to fit your particular needs.

THE FUTURE OF WEB TECHNOLOGY

Earlier in these pages, we talked about how some browsers are being designed with advanced features that haven't yet been established as "official" Web (HTML) standards. What we didn't mention are the dozens of new technologies being designed to compete with or supplement HTML. The Net always has seemed to beckon large companies, small companies, and even individuals to create new applications and improve on existing ones. Web applications have been no exception.

As of this writing, we've lost count of the number of new Web technologies now fighting for recognition and acceptance on the Web. These technologies range from new online transaction methods to faster, smoother full-motion video; to complete virtual reality products. Two of the most popular and promising technologies are Sun Microsystems' Java language and the Virtual Reality Markup Language.

JAVA

Java (see Figure 17-1) is a relatively new programming language for the World-Wide Web. It was introduced by Sun Microsystems as a way to make the Web more interactive. Basically, Java allows developers to write programs and store them on Web sites (in a text-based, uncompiled format). When a Java-equipped Web browser retrieves that program, it compiles, executes, and displays the results of that program within the Web browser. This allows a Web page to include sophisticated interactions and animations the same way it includes simple pictures and text.

For Web users to take advantage of Java applications, they must have Web browsers that understand the Java language, and a computer that's powerful enough to support the applications. Today, that combination is difficult to find among typical consumers, but as more of them invest in today's (and tomorrow's) high-speed home computers, Java, or

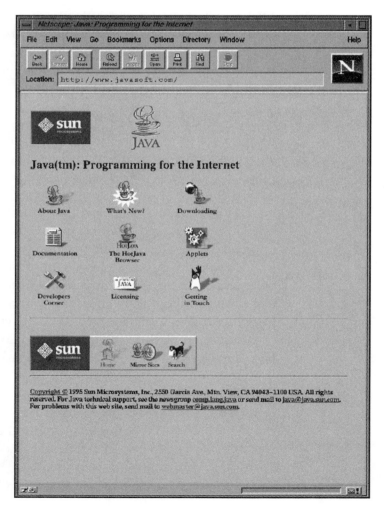

FIGURE 17-1

Sun Microsystems' Java site offers Java-equipped browsers a taste of what's to come.

a similar successor or competitor, will certainly become an integral part of tomorrow's Web. For now, Java is mainly used for testing purposes and some business-to-business applications.

Compiling is the process of turning the text-based code written by a computer programmer into the actual instructions used by a computer. When you purchase a program or retrieve it from the Net, you generally receive files already compiled for use on your type of computer (PC, Macintosh, etc.). A program compiled for a Macintosh, for example, won't work on a PC.

Java allows a single program to work on a variety of computers because it sends only the text-based code to the user's computer. That machine is free to compile the code so that it will run properly. This process can be very demanding on the user's computer; compiling can be very time and resource consuming for a computer.

VIRTUAL REALITY MARKUP LANGUAGE (VRML)

VRML was introduced by Silicon Graphics (SGI) and Template Graphics Software. It allows developers to create three-dimensional "places" to which users can travel. The WebSpace Web site (see Figure 17-2) offers more details on SGI's implementation of VRML. SGI describes the benefits of its WebSpace product as follows:

The benefits of utilizing WebSpace can be illustrated in two ways. The first is information density. Anyone who has surfed the Web for a sufficient length of time has a bookmark list that runs off the screen. Even if you subdivide it, you are going to run out of screen real estate soon enough. That is the limitation of 2D. You have limited screen space to organize your information. Utilizing a 3-dimensional interface, you have gained essentially infinite screen real estate for a finite number of pixels. Simply turn your "head" and more information pops into view. The second benefit of WebSpace is, as people, we are used to dealing with information in 3-space. Think of getting a phone call at your desk. You get a phone number from the caller, write it down on a Post-it™ and stick it on your cabinet. When you go to call that person back the next day, you recall, "I put that number here" and you turn your head to see the note. That is our spatial recall skill at work. We are hard-wired to organize information using a 3-space map in our heads.

FIGURE 17-2

Silicon Graphics, in association with Template Graphics Software, introduced WebSpace, "The first commercially available 3D viewer for the World Wide Web."

THE WEB YELLOW PAGES

An important current Web function that we expect will continue growing is its role as a kind of Yellow Pages. Every day, more and more consumers turn to the World Wide Web to find goods and services. And they do it whether or not they plan to make an online purchase. By searching the Web, consumers can find small companies and businesses too distant to appear in their phone books. The Web already gives consumers instant access to the world's largest collections of business information. AT&T maintains its entire 800 directory online—very helpful for locating companies by name or business category. Many other Web sites exist that help consumers locate companies with a Web presence (we discussed the Internet Yellow Pages earlier).

For now, consumers must roam rather wide on the Web to generate truly comprehensive lists of the information they seek. This requires a little bit of knowledge and effort. But as the Web becomes more consumer-friendly, online searches will get easier. By the end of 1996, consumers will have a few simple, comprehensive options for finding businesses with an Internet presence.

But what about those businesses that lack such a presence? How will consumers find *them* online? Remember, just because a company doesn't have a site, that doesn't mean it can't reap the benefits of Web commerce. Many of the businesses in the AT&T 800 directory don't have their own Web sites, but thanks to AT&T they do have a Web presence (albeit a small one). A company can establish a Web presence simply by placing its name, phone number, and other key information on the Web. If they place the information where some database or Web search site will index it and allow users to search for it, the company becomes instantly available to the Web community. Consequently, we can expect to see Web-presence providers offering more services to do just that. For a minimal fee, they will provide Yellow Pages-type listings on the Web. For a slightly higher fee, they'll take a few steps to help interested Web users find that listing and, consequently, the company. We expect to see an increased demand for this service as small companies who feel they can't afford a Web site realize the need to establish some sort of Web presence anyway.

THE WEB AS A SALES MEDIUM

The World Wide Web is just beginning to exploit its potential as a sales medium. As we said earlier, consumers have been a little reluctant to make final purchases on the Web. The most common reason for this reluctance is prevailing doubts about the security of Web transactions. That doubt finally is starting to dwindle.

The truth is, the Web already provides most of the tools needed for safe online transactions. All that are missing are consumer confidence in, and wide availability of, the tools. Over the next year or two, expect an increase in confidence and availability, leading to a dramatic increase in the number of online transactions. Those companies that have already established online storefronts and developed policies to handle such purchases will have a leg up.

THE FUTURE OF USER REGISTRATION

An increasingly common annoyance to Web users continues to be the number of sites requiring user registration. According to some studies, approximately 20 percent of commercial Web sites require registration. From the consumer's viewpoint, that means thousands of registration forms to complete, and hundreds of thousands of personal questions to answer. This, to many Web surfers, is a very unappealing development.

In the near future, expect an increase in the number of sites requiring registration. Companies are still desperate for demographic information, and many want to charge fees for access to specific parts of their sites. These companies are willing to alienate a few users for the sake of meeting their marketing objectives.

Another factor leading to this increase is the continuing growth of interactive Web features. As Web sites develop new ways of providing social interaction between users, they will need some way to keep track of them. The registration process allows Web sites to remember an individual user when he or she returns to the site at a later date.

Skyline's "Registration Wizard" May Change the Future of User Registration

Skyline Network Technologies is considering plans for a Web service that would make user registration easier for both consumers and online businesses. The plan involves using a centralized user database for which willing consumers could provide whatever demographic information they feel comfortable disclosing. In return, they would receive a username and password that would be valid at all participating Web sites. When the users visit a participating site, they can use that username and password to connect without going through a separate registration process.

This registration method allows users to specify exactly which information they wish to make available to any particular company. It also simplifies account management for the businesses, because they need not maintain their own copies of the database. Each business could request reports on its users directly from the main database. A lot of details must be discussed before this type of plan can work, but expect to see this, or a similar idea, reach the Web some time in 1996.

But after user registration surges and prevails for a while, its popularity will suddenly decline. Users will grow tired of filling out a registration form every time they visit a new site. They'll no longer be willing to divulge personal information to every company that asks for it. Companies will be forced to find new ways to gather demographic information and track users. Perhaps some sort of centralized database will emerge where companies will share demographic data and attempt to track usage patterns without users involvement.

THE FUTURE OF INTERNET SECURITY

The direction of Internet security is somewhat vague at this point. Security problems have existed for years and it's only now that people are devoting significant resources to solving them. The Internet originally was conceived as an open environment where people shared thoughts and ideas with few limitations. Today, those early freedoms have grown into serious security problems.

Many experts believe the Internet will need to be entirely reworked to be completely secure. Other concerns also may necessitate such a complete revision: The Internet is running out of IP numbers—the addresses given computers on the Internet—due to the explosive growth of the past few years; current hardware and software are unable to handle this problem. However, a complete overhaul of the Net is not in the immediate future at this point.

Most of the current advances in security were created to implement secured Internet commerce. As more people begin to purchase goods and services online, it becomes more important to find security for these kinds of transactions. The many companies bringing different technologies to the marketplace are fighting over which technology should be the standard. Credit card companies and banks are trying to find ways to make commerce on the Internet secure in hopes of generating more revenues. These companies are hoping that, as more people buy online, they will begin to depend less on checks and cash for purchases. The current standards proposed by MasterCard and Visa will probably be accepted rapidly by the marketplace once they're fully released. In the meantime, SSL and S-HTTP will dominate secure online commerce.

Packet encryption is an emerging technology that eventually will fill the gap between a complete reworking of the Internet and current software-based security technologies. Computers are getting faster every day, necessitating larger encryption keys. The U.S. government's current export restriction on encryption methods using keys larger than 40 bits will quickly become little more than a joke as faster computers become more affordable. Initially, hardware-based packet encryption will be an expensive investment, but as more products and companies enter the market place the price will drop. Software-based packet encryption techniques, although not as secure, will be more popular because they're more cost-effective. Packet encryption is the most promising new security technology, and will likely emerge as the security protocol of the future.

Cost is the major factor limiting the widespread use of any new Internet security product. Although many solutions currently exist, they're too expensive to implement on a broad scale. Atalla's *WebSafe* product, though an effective security application, is not priced for home computer shoppers. Any hardware-based solution on a merchant's site will require similar expensive hardware and software, on the customer's site. What good is having the best security hardware if it can't communicate with anyone? (That's as secure as you can get!) Companies will rush to fill the gaps and undersell the competition, as long as patents don't stand in the way. This is similar to the problem encountered when using public-key encryption software; if your company is U.S.-based, you must pay RSA Data Security a license fee to use it.

All Web browsers will quickly become SSL- or S-HTTP-enhanced to accommodate online commerce. Netscape's *Navigator* browser holds 75 percent of the market, and supports both SSL and S-HTTP; other browsers looking to compete in the marketplace will have to be secured as well.

Firewalls and secure routers protect in-house corporate computers from Internet trespassers. But while they provide security to the business that utilizes them, they offer no security benefits to the customer. Merchants using firewalls for Web transactions don't make the transactions secure; they only protect themselves from hackers. This may be your only concern when setting up an unsecured Web site, but eventually, most companies will want to accept payment over the Internet. When they do, they'll have to consider other forms of online security.

In the end, predicting the security protocols of tomorrow's Internet is like trying to guess the future occupation of a 5-year-old. Where does all this leave consumers and merchants today? Well, with a lot of choices. Internet sales are growing and people are feeling more comfortable ordering online. Security is rapidly becoming a major concern of both merchants and consumers. Both parties will want to eliminate the risk involved in online commerce and eventually will be able to work together to find a solution.

THE FUTURE OF WEB ADVERTISING AND MARKETING

Let's face it, the bottom line for most of us has nothing to do with the technological details of the Web. How many of you are really losing sleep over the expected number of transatlantic data lines or local Internet service providers? What most of us want to know is, what does the future hold for Web advertising and marketing? Since many experts project that the Internet population will reach 100 million by the year 2000, and the vast majority of those users will have access to the World Wide Web, there's no question that Web advertising and marketing *has* a future.

THE MEDIA

Before we reach the year 2000, you can bet some major changes will take place in the Web's media aspect. That is, the way the Web presents its information tomorrow will differ significantly from the way it works today. In a few years, the Web will be used to present more animation, more full-motion video (even in real-time), and new types of multimedia that haven't even been thought of yet.

Real-Time Multimedia

Today, much Web-site audio and full-motion video is what we call "time-delayed multimedia." This means that the audio or video is sent to the user's computer as a file. After the computer receives that file, it displays or plays it. It's called "time-delayed" because there's a delay while the file is sent to the computer. This type of multimedia is limited because it only allows the use of pre-recorded audio and video. It also requires that the user's computer have enough hard-drive space to store the multimedia file before playing it.

Web sites that want to feed live audio or video into users' computers must use what we call "real-time multimedia." Real-time multimedia allows the user to receive a continuous stream of data that converts into audio or video as it arrives, much the way a television picture displays as the signal is broadcast from the station. The only delay is the fraction of a second it takes for the television signal to reach the TV set in your living room. The television station can change what the viewer sees at any time, and it takes effect immediately. In contrast, time-delayed multimedia is like forcing viewers to record every program on the VCR before they watch it.

Time-delayed multimedia has its uses, but advertisers (and consumers) are becoming more interested in real-time multimedia. With real-time multimedia:

- *Live programs can be "broadcast" over the Web*

- *Audio and video elements can instantly be modified to reflect a user's actions*

- *Internet users can talk to each other like they would on a telephone*

- *Internet users with video cameras can conduct video conferences from their computers*

As the Web's multimedia capabilities improve, bandwidth increases, and costs decrease, the Web will undergo some drastic changes. These changes, along with improved home access to these features, will make the Web even more valuable as a medium of communication. Books, magazines, concerts, movies, and government documents published on the Web will one day outnumber those printed on paper.

Businesses will find it increasingly difficult to compete for consumer attention among the mass of available Web publications. Most businesses will find that it's cheaper to revert to the subsidized content model—now used in television—than to attempt to develop their own added value and compete with those sites devoted strictly to attracting consumers.

THE FUTURE OF INTERACTIVITY

But the aspect of the Web that will develop the most over the next few years is its interactivity. We've stressed throughout this book that Web users are becoming dissatisfied with static, stale pages. They're making it known that they expect constant change on corporate Web sites. Businesses can comply or say goodbye to their online audience.

Businesses can't treat a Web site as one big advertisement. As the Web begins to compete with television in many households, each Web site must follow the television model by providing a combination of entertainment and commercialism. The most effective way to combine the two, and do so in a way that television can't touch, is to use interactive applications. For this reason, we expect to see an increase in extremely complicated Web applications through which users can interact with other users around the world.

PROFILE-DRIVEN MARKETING

In the last chapter, we briefly discussed profile-driven marketing. What we didn't mention was that profile-driven marketing is simply another form of Web interactivity. Whenever user profiles (information gathered about a user) are utilized to tune the interactive features of a Web site in a way that encourages them to buy, that's profile-driven marketing. So naturally, future profile-driven marketing will directly result from advances in interactivity. But advances in online information-gathering techniques will have an impact, as well. As Web sites become more sophisticated, and new methods are developed for keeping track of users from one visit to the next, profile-driven marketing will enter a new era. Soon, Web sites will greet consumers by name and in their native language. The commercial site of the future will accurately suggest products and services that meet the needs and budgets of each visitor.

The next couple of years will tell exactly what new methods will develop for gathering and managing user profiles, but for the short term, the primary method will continue to be user registration and solicited user responses.

WEB DESIGN FIRMS

Today's Web boasts a lot of do-it-yourselfers—companies handling all or most of their own Web marketing process. But as the Web develops and new technical and design issues emerge, do-it-yourselfers will find it increasingly difficult to stay on top of things. Until recently, it was common for companies *not* to hire personnel specifically for Web-site development. Instead, most companies just assigned Web duties to an employee, and expected that employee to maintain the site in his or her spare time. Before long, however, most of these companies realized that managing and updating a Web site is a full-time job. We know of many companies that have teams of three to 20 people just to continue developing their corporate Web site.

The problem with expecting internal employees to manage a Web site is that they must spend half their time keeping up with and learning about all the new Web-related technologies. Many companies comparing the cost of hiring a full-time Webmaster with that of contracting with a design firm conclude that it's cheaper to hire the Webmaster. However, then they find themselves devoting a significant portion of their budgets to training the Webmaster and keeping him or her abreast of new developments. One advantage to contracting with a Web development and design firm is that you don't have to pay for hours of training and research. When you hire a design firm, you pay for fully trained Web designers (assuming you choose a quality firm).

Note to Small Businesses

Since few small businesses have the resources to design or maintain their own Web sites, Web design firms have always been a necessity. For you, Web design firms have been the cheapest and fastest way to establish an online presence. That won't change in the future. But as more large companies rely on the same Web design firms, you may find your designers becoming too expensive. You may be forced to seek new, smaller Web design firms.

Of course, if you work hard to establish a successful online presence today, you may have a larger budget by the time these changes occur.

In the future, as more companies recognize the difficulties of maintaining a state-of-the-art Web site on their own, Web design firms will find their services in greater demand. Businesses will depend on Web design firms the same way they depend on conventional graphics design firms.

TWO FOR ONE

Speaking of conventional graphics design firms, expect to see the line blur between them and Web-site design firms. As the Web becomes a major business tool, companies naturally will prefer to use a single firm for their on- and offline designs. This will be cheaper and easier for most companies. To accommodate them, expect to see:

- Web design firms buying conventional graphic design companies

- Graphic design firms buying Web design firms

- Advertising agencies merging with Web design firms

- Web design firms hiring graphic designers and restructuring to handle conventional design

- New companies forming that handle both conventional and online designs from the start

- Any other combination imaginable

THE GREAT SHAKEDOWN

As on- and offline design functions merge, the competition among Web designers will heat up. Many Web designers will find they can't compete. Web designers who don't fulfill the need for appealing, innovative designs will be the first to fail in tomorrow's market. This includes those companies lacking the resources to provide quality services. The next to go will be those who don't merge with conventional design firms or at least acquire the conventional design skills needed to compete with merged companies. Finally, those Web designers who fail to keep up with emerging trends (both technological and cultural) will lose out to those who do.

COSTS

Today, the cost of basic Web advertising and marketing is very reasonable. Considering the potential audience, it costs far less to advertise on the Web than it would to reach the same audience through any other medium. Quality Web advertising—the kind that consistently captures a large audience—could become considerably more expensive, though still more economical than any other medium. As competition increases, today's quality Web sites will become slightly cheaper in the near future, but before long, those sites will not be considered quality sites. We've said it several times: The Web is evolving. Web advertisers must be willing to develop more intense, more interactive Web sites. And you can bet they'll pay more bucks for the bang!

The future will only underscore this fact. The costs of Web marketing and advertising will someday resemble the costs of television advertising: Small companies will be able to afford lower-quality Web designs, advertised on lower-quality sites with smaller audiences; big companies will spend huge sums of money on Web development in an attempt to capture the largest audience they can. The major difference, and the advantage to small companies, is that every company will still have exactly the same available audience. When a small company with a small audience develops an innovative Web site, its popularity can soar as high as the big guys'.

Overall, the price of quality Web advertising and marketing will increase as demand increases—and demand definitely will increase if the Internet reaches its projected population of 100 million by the year 2000. But bargain-basement Web designers will always be there to help small business get started.

FIVE HURDLES

For the Web to reach its full potential in years to come, it must clear certain hurdles. Among the most obvious of these are security measures, government regulations, Web organization, cost to consumers, and the ability of the Web to compete with conventional media.

SECURITY

The Web can't mature as a marketplace until businesses and consumers learn to utilize and trust at least one of the secure methods of data transfer and online transactions.

GOVERNMENT REGULATION

Both U.S. and foreign governments must adopt clear, consistent, and unrestrictive policies and laws concerning online sales, taxation, import and export, copyrights, pornography, and cryptography.

WEB ORGANIZATION

The World Wide Web must become easier to use by establishing more versatile and comprehensive indexes to Web information. Today's indexes have made a good start, but they're woefully incomplete and congested with inaccurate and misleading information (usually because of overzealous marketers). The average consumer will find a better place to do business when it becomes easy to search for any company using a wide range of criteria.

COST TO THE CONSUMER

The Web of the future will require high-speed Internet connections and top-of-the-line home computers. If these items aren't priced within reach of most consumers, many advanced Web technologies—like Java and VRML—will die of neglect.

COMPETITION FROM CONVENTIONAL MEDIA

The final hurdle stems from the Web's ability to capture consumer attention. The Web has many competitors in this race—television, radio, motion pictures, video rentals, magazines, books, and more. It won't be easy. Fortunately, the Web already has achieved a level of interactivity and usefulness that can never be surpassed by today's conventional media. If the Web continues to grow faster than other media, it's destined to become the world's richest and most diverse marketplace.

THE NOT-SO-NEAR FUTURE

Who can say what the Internet and the Web will evolve into 10, 20, or 50 years down the road. Will the Internet eventually reach into every home? Every workplace? Every automobile? Perhaps we will all access the Internet from a wristwatch or a pocket-sized computer.

Regardless of how the Net evolves, you can bet the changes will be dramatic and geared toward the future needs of society. In the future, the Internet will continue to make it easier for us to work, play, and shop. It will bring an even more expansive and powerful collection of information into every aspect of our lives. Perhaps the Internet will completely replace many of the communications media—telephones, fax machines, televisions, even radios—that we treasure so much today.

The Internet is destined to bring nations closer, help news travel faster, and bring worldwide attention to the struggles and triumphs of everyday people, businesses, and governments. The Internet will change the lives of generations to come.

YOUR FUTURE ON THE WEB

What does the future hold for your company? That depends largely on how you respond to the issues discussed in this book. There's no question that the World Wide Web will influence and enhance business as we know it. How or when businesses begin to reap most of the benefits of the Web remains to be seen. Yet one thing remains certain about today's Web: *The stakes are low and the rewards are high.* The companies that place their bets on the most innovative, widely accepted, and expandable technologies will find a royal flush of future opportunity.

The race is on. If this book is your first introduction to the Web, you're already behind the pack. For up-to-date information and additional resources relating to Web advertising and marketing, turn to Skyline's Web Advertising and Marketing Site:

`http://www.skyline.net/WAM/`

Remember...

- The Web (and the entire Internet) is constantly evolving. Tomorrow's Web may barely resemble the Web we know today.

- In the future, it will be easier to locate both large and small companies on the Web.

- Soon, almost every business will establish some sort of presence on the Web.

- The Web will continue to expand as a sales medium.

- User registration will become such an annoyance to users that businesses will be forced to develop less intrusive methods of tracking users.

- Whatever the Internet of tomorrow becomes, advertising and marketing will have a significant impact on its development.

- Web design firms soon will provide services similar to those of conventional design firms. We can expect to see several mergers between Web design and conventional design firms.

- Your future on the Web will result directly from how you utilize Web resources throughout the next year.

MARKETING THE WIDGET ON THE WORLD WIDE WEB

The widget. It's the quintessential hypothetical product. Business literature is rife with references to it. It stands in for anything and everything that can be manufactured, manipulated, packaged, processed, sold, returned, and remanufactured. Throughout this book, we've often used the versatile widget as our imaginary commodity. In this chapter, we'll use it again as we put together a complete Web strategy for Wally's Widget Company, the manufacturer and seller of the world's finest widgets.

For the purposes of this illustration, Wally's widgets are consumable items that may be purchased and utilized by the general public. The widgets are moderately priced and easy to ship, both nationally and internationally. The company itself is rather small, with a total of only 20 employees, 17 of whom work in production. Wally Wilbert, the company's founder and namesake, is the one who'll go through the process of establishing a Web presence for his firm. No one in his company has technical experience in developing a Web site, or training in the field of computers. Wally, himself, has no special technical expertise or knowledge, but he's heard about the Web and he thinks it will help his business.

We put together this illustration to give you a complete soup-to-nuts experience of the process of developing a Web presence and marketing plan. It's a way to show you the whole process in action, from start to finish. Everything we've talked about in these pages will be demonstrated in this exercise. It's our hope that many companies will be able to use this appendix as a guide as they go online. It won't be a perfect match for every company, but it should give everyone a better idea of how it all fits together.

GETTING WALLY STARTED

Wally Wilbert has finally made his decision: He's ready to take Wally's Widget Company online. He's been listening to and reading stories about the Internet, the Information Superhighway, and something called the Web for some time now. He's heard that the Net represents the cutting-edge communications technology of the future, and that any company that doesn't market itself on the Web will be lost and hopelessly left behind. Wally, an aggressive marketer by nature, doesn't want to be left in the dust. He knows it's time to get into this game. The problem is, Wally doesn't know where to start.

Wally starts his research at the local bookstore, where he finds (believe it or not) *this* book. He wisely buys it and spends the day reading, captivated. After he finishes the book, he realizes that his next step is to see this World Wide Web for himself.

So, he turns to the Yellow Pages (the hard-copy version, because he's not online yet) and finds the phone number of a local Web access provider. He calls up the provider and establishes an online account for himself. He buys a software package at a local computer store that includes access software and a browser, and he installs it on his PC at home. At the same time, he signs up for a three-hour class at the local community college. He's got to learn the basics of accessing the Internet and navigating the Web somewhere. He completes the class and prepares to start his online research.

Wally now begins spending time on the Web, checking out various sites, and recording his observations in a journal. He accesses the successful sites he read about in this book, and quickly recognizes what works about the sites and what doesn't. He spends some time on newsgroups and chat areas to find out what other surfers like, and he begins to get a sense of what it's going to take to successfully market his widgets and at the same time create a successful Web site. After about three weeks of diligent Web surfing, Wally sits down to develop his online marketing plan.

THE WIDGET GETS A MARKETING PLAN

Wally is really starting to feel like a surfer. He spent much of the last month acquainting himself with the Web, interacting with the online natives, and taking meticulous notes about the experience. In his notes, he highlighted the sites he likes best and what it was about them that captured his attention. He's beginning to get an idea of what he wants to accomplish with his Web site. Now, before he goes any further, he must establish clear, definable goals, and use the notes he's been keeping to develop a plan that will enable him to reach those goals.

WALLY'S GOALS FOR BEING ON THE WEB

As a business owner and operator, Wally recognizes the critical need for clear goals. He would never begin any company related project without them. Goals help in the development of the plan and give purpose to the enterprise. He also knows that these goals must be both aggressive and reachable. And they must be clearly definable and understandable to everyone involved. The overall goal he establishes for his Web project is to produce the best Web site possible within his budget. This goal is important, but rather subjective, so he knows he must define some more tangible aims.

Wally's first goal is a defining one. He wants to use his Web site as a sales device. He wants to sell his widgets directly to surfers through his site. He realizes that just being on the Web is going to enhance the exposure of his company, but for Wally, that's not enough to justify the expense. To make the project work economically for the company, it must include direct sales.

The second goal Wally establishes for the Web project is the approximate date by which he wants his site to be up and running: He wants to get his project off the ground and flying within the next three months. Although he doesn't want to compromise quality to meet this deadline, he does want this project completed expeditiously. This three-month time frame is loose enough to give him the time he needs to organize his resources, but tight enough to move the project along.

The final goal Wally establishes is a financial goal. He's hoping for the best with his Web venture, but he knows he must be realistic. In the short-term, he just wants to break even. In other words, he wants the cost of his Web marketing plan covered by the additional sales it generates. Next year, however, he wants the project to turn a profit and show evidence of future steady growth.

MARKETING TECHNIQUES FOR WALLY AND HIS WIDGETS

Now that Wally has his goals established and knows where he wants to take his online venture, he begins considering the specific marketing techniques he will use. Currently, he runs a regular ad in several newspapers that invites customers to call his warehouse for a free sample widget. The ad strategy has been very successful, and he hopes to be able to continue and expand it with his Web advertising.

As a new feature specifically designed for his Web pages, Wally decides he'd like to try an online sweepstakes that requires participants to register. The prize will be a free widget, and Wally will have a drawing for a new widget each month. This feature will enable him to expand his exposure on the Web while he gathers the demographics of the surfers visiting his site. He also believes the contest will act as a draw, enticing surfers to visit his site and see his marketing information.

Wally also plans to offer a 10 percent discount on all online purchases for the first six months. This will jump-start sales from his site by encouraging customers to buy now. The discount will only be available to customers visiting his site.

To build up his online sales even more, Wally wants to harness the Web's ability to interact with its customers. To do this, he'd like to offer message boards or chat areas on his site. In particular, Wally wants to establish a discussion group in which the topic is the use of his widgets. In this interactive area, users could exchange widget tips, ideas for new widget applications, and favorite widget stories. Wally would also like to set up an interactive page dedicated to the city of Walla Walla, where Wally's Widget Company is located. The idea is to provide a place where local people and tourists can find out about what is going on in the Walla Walla area.

For now, Wally includes both interactive areas in his site plans. When he reaches the development stage, he'll reevaluate these ideas and decide which will work best in his Web scheme. The interactivity of both or one of these features will allow Wally to build the rapport he needs to take his sales to a new level.

Wally also knows, from his extensive surfing over the last few months, that the visual aspects of his site will greatly influence its success. His company's current advertising doesn't include eye-catching graphics or pictures, so he knows he'll have to do some new thinking. Using the same systematic approach that has served him so far, he sits down with a pad and paper and sketches some ideas for his Web site. Wally is quite a widget maker, but he's no artist. Yet, he doesn't worry about how well he sketches; he knows that this is only the planning stage and content is what's important right now. Wally also knows that many surfers aren't working with the latest and greatest technology, and that their connections may be poor. He would love to utilize audio and full-motion video, but decides that this is something he will hold off on. It may be worth looking into for next year, but for now he decides to use pictures and images only.

NUTS AND BOLTS OF WEB MARKETING WIDGETS

Now that Wally has established his overall and specific goals, chosen some of the online techniques he wants to use, and filled a sketch pad with layout ideas, he's ready to turn his plan into action. Being the wise person he is, Wally realizes this is an area where he may need some help. Although he believes he could eventually turn all his sketches and plans into reality, he knows he can't do it within his three-month time frame. Even if he could, it wouldn't be the truly effective Web site he wants without the help of a professional.

Since he took the time to read this book, Wally knows he will only want to work with Web-presence providers who understand all the concepts related with developing a Web site, and have the programming knowledge to utilize all the features he wants to include. After interviewing five Web presence providers and consultants, Wally chooses one with the qualifications he needs.

At their first meeting, Wally and his new Web-presence provider talk about money. To stay within his budget, Wally learns that he must streamline his project to include only the essentials. In the end, he decides to include five pages on his site.

The first will be the company's homepage. It will feature the company name and an impressive graphic, the company's slogan, "No widget in the world is made like Wally's widgets," and a picture of a widget. The homepage will also include links to all other areas of the site.

Another page will be an area for comments and registration. This will consist of an online form, which surfers will be asked to fill out. This information will be saved in a file format, which Wally will be able to use to better market his products. He will use the sweepstakes to give surfers an incentive to fill out the registration form.

Another link on the site will take surfers to a message board area. This area will consist of two pages—one for discussion of Walla Walla, and another for widgets. Wally initially had hoped to include chat rooms in his design, but the cost of including this feature was beyond his budget for the first year. One of his goals for next year is to add this feature to the site.

The last and most important page on Wally's site is the area he'll use to sell his widgets to the surfers. This area will list the various types of widgets for sale on the site. A price and feature description will accompany a picture of each widget. If a surfer has an interest in one of these widgets, he or she will be able to click on it and go to the online order form. The surfer may then fill out the order form, choose a method of payment, and complete the sale by clicking on a button at the bottom of the screen.

Links to every page on the site from every other page are key features of Wally's site plan. Navigational buttons at the bottom of each page will take surfers to any part of the site. This feature will increase traffic on all parts of Wally's site, and give it continuity.

The Web-presence provider assures Wally that he can set up this site configuration within the necessary time frame. Wally has chosen an excellent Web consultant who is able to mix all of these necessary ingredients into a workable Web marketing plan. To make Wally's site seem fresh and new all year, he can also use seasonal pictures from the Walla Walla area.

BRINGING SURFERS TO WALLY'S WEB SITE

His Web site is finally up and running and Wally is pleased with the work of his Web-presence provider. The one thing missing is *traffic*. Wally plans to rely on his own creativity to bring multitudes of surfers to see his creation. To announce his arrival in cyberspace, he'll use both on- and offline media.

A WIDGET MAKES THE ROUNDS

To begin generating traffic on his site, Wally first goes to the major search engines on the Web. The first one Wally utilizes is "Starting Point." This site is actually a program that allows you to add your site to many search engines at once. With "Starting Point," Wally adds his site to several search engines. Obviously, he uses "widgets" and his company name as key words for these search engines, but he also uses "Walla Walla" and "message boards." This broadening of his key terms will allow Wally's site to attract a more diverse audience. It probably means he'll have to go to each search engine individually to make sure they accept all the key words, but the wider audience contact is worth the extra effort.

A WIDGET MAKES THE NEWS

Another important way to get the word out about Wally's new site is by posting to newsgroups. Wally knows he can't blatantly advertise in these newsgroups, so he comes up with a little twist to draw attention to his site. He decides to offer a new widget joke every week. This joke posting can also include a line inviting people to his site if they want to learn more about widgets. For example:

```
Q: How many widgets does it take to cross the road?

A: Two, one as a left shoe and one as a right

For more interesting facts and funny stories about
widgets see:

        http://www.wallyswidgets.com
```

Wally could post the jokes to rec.humor or rec.humor.funny. He knows that this type of press release is a little less threatening to surfers, who generally don't feel like being sold.

Another idea is to publish the top five reasons you should give a widget as a present. Wally could list them in descending order (like you-know-who) and have the number one reason be:

```
        Check out < http://www.wallyswidgets.com >
```

Wally also will publicize the fact that he offers message boards on both widgets and Walla Walla by posting this information to any newsgroup he can find that's even remotely related to the subjects. Updating and posting to message boards is an ongoing chore, and Wally knows he'll have to spend a few hours every week posting messages to attract new surfers to his site and encourage past surfers to return and see what's new.

To get the ball rolling with a large group of initial visitors, Wally plans to post the following message to the moderated newsgroup, comp.infosystems.www.announce:

```
Subject: COMMERCIAL: Moderately priced Widgets shipped
Internationally!

Wally's Widget Company <URL:http://www.wallyswidgets.com>
is now offering international Widget sales over the
Internet! Wally's Widgets are factory fresh, straight
from the manufacture.
```

```
Check out our Web site: We offer free online giveaways,
message bases, and Wally's List of Wonderful Links!

So be sure and check us out at:

            URL:http://www.wallyswidgets.com

I look forward to seeing you!

Wally

+ - - - - - - - - - - - - - - - - - - - - - - - - - - - - +

| Wally Wilson              wally@wallywidgets.com |

| CEO, Wally's Widgets   <URL:http://www.wallyswidgets.com> |

+ - - - - - - - - - - - - - - - - - - - - - - - - - - - - +
```

He might also post a similar message to: misc.forsale.non-computer, dc.forsale.misc, dc.forsale, and pubnet.forsale. The dc. newsgroups are local to the Washington, D.C., area. (Check with your Internet provider to determine which newsgroups are local to your particular area.)

ELECTRONIC DIRECT MAIL FOR WIDGETS

During the production stage of Wally's project, he decided to include a registration form on his site (really a customer survey). Among the questions on Wally's survey is a request for surfers' e-mail addresses. Wally utilizes the e-mail addresses to announce new offers and items to surfers who have visited his site. He is careful to send e-mail messages only to surfers who say it's OK to keep them on the mailing list (another question on the survey). Wally knows that many netizens take offense at receiving unsolicited e-mail.

GETTING PAID

The overarching purpose of Wally's online marketing plan is to make money selling his widgets. To do that, the surfer must pay him. Wally has studied our chapter on getting paid online, and determined that he is going to accept credit cards through his Web page. He knows it's important to secure online financial transactions, so he verifies that his Web-presence provider is utilizing a secured server. For now, Wally is only going to accept credit cards because it will be the simplest way for him to track his orders and accounts receivable. He has always accepted the major credit cards from his customers, so his account is established with all of these entities.

WALLY FINDS OUT HOW HE'S DOING

Wally's site has been up and running for over three months now, but he's unsure how it's doing. He wants to know how many hits he's received and where they come from. To gather this information, he turns to his Web-presence provider. The provider tells Wally that he can give him a report of the number of hits each of his pages receives, as well as what machines they come from. This information is important because it will allow Wally to determine what parts of his marketing plan are effective, and what parts he must be rework.

WALLY'S SCORE SHEET

Wally's first year online is coming to a close. He's had some successes and some set backs, but overall, he's happy with the outcome. But was the site a success? Did it meet the goals Wally set? Did the site break

TABLE A-1 FIRST-YEAR COSTS OF PRODUCING WALLY'S ONLINE MARKETING PLAN

Item	Cost
12 months of Internet access for Wally to conduct his research and site promotion	$240.00
One copy of Web Advertising and Marketing	$34.95
12 months' fees charged by the Web presence provider to utilize their server	$3,000.00
15 pages of Web design construction	$1500.00
Production of two message boards for the site	$1200.00
CGI program for the online survey	$700.00
CGI program for online order form	$700.00
Miscellaneous changes to homepage and the rest of the site	$1,800.00
Monthly site audit reports from the Web-presence provider	$600.00
Charges from Web-presence provider to furnish information from surfers from online survey and relaying orders	$900.00
12 widgets for the sweepstakes prize (assuming a cost of production of $10 per widget)	$120.00
Total costs for the first year:	$10,794.95

even as hoped? To answer these questions, let's look at the first-year costs of producing and maintaining Wally's site.

To understand how Wally has done this first year online, you first have to know a little something about the widget business. Wally sells his widgets for $20 apiece. His costs of production and shipping and handling amount to about $10. So, his net profit is $10 per widget. During his first six months online, Wally offered a discount of 10 percent to all online shoppers. This cut his profit to $8 on each widget he sold within the first eight months. During the first six months, Wally sold 510 widgets via his Web site. During the second six months, he sold 726 widgets online.

For the first six months, Wally realized a profit of $4,080 (510 widgets @ $8). For the last half of the year, he made $7260 (726 widgets @ $10). Net revenues for his first year online came to $11,340. When you compare this to the costs of generating and operating his site for a year, you can see that Wally exceeded his goal with a net profit of $545.05.

The success of the first year convinced Wally to continue with his plans to expand and build on his site. In the next few years, he hopes to add that chat line, and to broaden the draw of his site by offering searches of widget-related information. Wally wants to accomplish all of these goals while maintaining a profitable online operation. So, as you might expect, Wally's going to go slow.

Although the revenue figures within this chapter are fictitious, they're based on the true story of a company that moved onto the Web to promote its business.

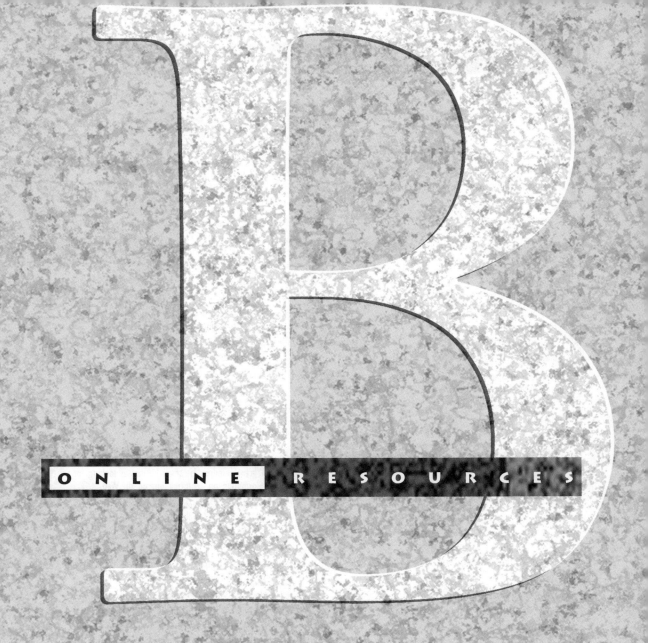
ONLINE RESOURCES

BUSINESS RESOURCES ON THE WEB

Resource	Address	Description
A1 Internet Services	`http://www.a1co.com`	A1 offers an extensive list of search sites (over 500!) in which you can include your site for free. They also offer a searchable list of e-zines.
Better Business Bureau	`http://www.bbb.org/bbb/`	Business information and links to local BBBs.
Commercial Use of the Internet	`http://www.netrex.com/ business.html`	Almost a small, online version of this book!
Dun & Bradstreet Information Services	`http://www.dbisna.com/`	This server has a wide array of articles, tutorials, and news to help your company.
Entrepreneurs on the Web	`http://www.eotw.com/`	A well-organized collection of pointers to business information resources on the Web.
Global Network Navigator's Business Pages	`http://gnn.com/gnn/bus/ index.html`	An online directory of companies offering products and services.
List of companies that lease Web space	`http://union.ncsa.uiuc. edu/HyperNews/get/www/ leasing.html`	Contains a large list of companies and rates that offer Web space as well as low-cost graphic designer services.
Mortgage Calculator	`http://www.skyline.net/ horizons/games/morcal/`	A mortgage calculator with graphs that also displays amortization tables.
RiskWeb	`http://www.riskweb.com`	A Web site about the area of risk and insurance.
Small Business and Effective Web Marketing	`http://www.wilsonweb.com/ rfwilson/webmarket/`	A great resource for small businesses looking for information on venturing out on the Web.
Standard & Poors 500 Index	`http://www.secapl.com/ secapl/quoteserver/ sp500.html`	A real-time graph of the most recent day's activity of the Standard & Poors 500 Index. Also includes data on the last 12 months, the last 5 years, and the last 10 years.
StockMaster Mutual Funds Chart	`http://www.ai.mit.edu/ stocks/mf.html`	Although not updated daily, this site has a nice selection of funds with all the historical data.
The Small Business Administration (SBA)	`http://www.sbaonline.sba. gov/`	The SBA's Web site contains information on starting, financing, and expanding your business.
Trademark Act of 1946	`http://www.law.cornell. edu/lanham/lanham. table.html`	Cornell University's law school has put the entire Trademark Act of 1946 online; you can check it out at this address.
Traffic Resource	`http://www.i-traffic.com/`	Contains a list of the top 50 sites that accept sponsorships and allows you to sort the output on many factors, such as: cost, hits, and rating.
WebTrack	`http://www.webtrack.com/`	A Web site dedicated to Web advertising and marketing. Includes their monthly newsletter, InterAd, which monitors developments in Web marketing. Also includes a list of sites that offer Web sponsorship or advertising.

BUSINESS RESOURCES ON THE WEB (CONTINUED)

Resource	Address	Description
Yahoo's Business Headlines	`http://www.yahoo.com/headlines/business/`	If you bought this book to become an Internet merchant but don't know what to sell, check out these lists of businesses.
Yahoo's Business Opportunities	`http://www.yahoo.com/Business_and_Economy/Products_and_Services/Business_Opportunity`	
Yahoo's Small Business Information	`http://www.yahoo.com/Business_and_Economy/Small_Business_Information/`	

COOL HOT SITES

Site	Address (URL)
Cool Links	`http://moose.erie.net/~rinderle/cool_links/index.html`
Dave's Web Page	`http://www.connix.com/~dberry/index.html`
Doug McGruter's Great List of Hot Sites	`http://www.digitalaire.com/DigiAire/Hot.html`
Hot Links	`http://fly.hiwaay.net/~fbeaver/`
Mike's Page of Cool Links	`http://www.twics.com/~mjm/home/html`
Netscape's What's Cool Page	`http://www.netscape.com/escapes/whats_cool.html`
Netscape's What's New Page	`http://www.netscape.com/escapes/whats_new.html`
Skyline's REX	`http://www.skyline.net/REX`
Yahoo's Cool Links	`http://www.yahoo.com/Entertainment/Cool_Links/`

WEB SEARCH SITES

Search Site	Address	Description
CUSI Services	http://pubweb.nextor.co.uk/public/cusi/doc/list.html	A single form used to search a number of different WWW search engines.
DEC's Alto Vista	http://www.altavista.digital.com/	A Web and newsgroup search engine.
DejaNews Research Service	http://dejanews.com/forms/dnquery.html	A site that searches Usenet newsgroups.
Excite	http://www.excite.com/	Allows searches of Web sites and newsgroups; reviews of over 35,000 Web sites.
Galaxy	http://galaxy.einet.net/cgi-bin/wais-text-multi?	A Web search site.
Internet Advertising Network's Internet Address Finder	http://www.iaf.net/	Helps you locate e-mail addresses based on people's names.
JumpStation	http://www.stir.ac.uk/jsbin/js	A Web search site.
Lycos	http://www.lycos.com/	A well-known search site that allows you to search for individual pages as well as entire Web sites.
The Point, Top 5% Index	http://www.pointcom.com/cgi-bin/pursuit-gif/	Allows you to search the Top 5% of the sites on their list as rated by fellow surfers.
Skyline's REX	http://www.skyline.net/REX/	Skyline's own categorized Web directory.
Starting Point	http://www.stpt.com/	A Web search site.
The All-in-One Search Page	http://www.albany.net/allinone/	All-in-One offers the ability to search just about every search site on the Internet. If they don't know about yours, feel free to add it!
WebCrawler	http://webcrawler.com/	A Web search site.
WWW Worm	http://wwwmcs.cs.colorado.edu/home/mcbryan/WWWW.html	A search site that boasts of over 3 million sites.
Yahoo	http://www.yahoo.com	A great resource for finding Web sites.

USENET NEWSGROUPS

Name	Description
alt.business.import-export	A newsgroup focusing on import and export.
alt.business.misc	A newsgroup about business and commerce of all kinds.
alt.business.multi-level	Focuses on multi-level marketing business opportunities.
comp.infosystems.www.announce	A moderated newsgroup for submitting new web sites.
dc.forsale	Items for sale in the Washington, DC area.
dc.forsale.misc	Items for sale in the Washington, DC area.
misc.entrepreneurs	Originally for entrepreneurs to share ideas and information; lately has degenerated into people selling business opportunities online.
misc.forsale.non-computer	Pretty self explainatory.
misc.invest	Investment newsgroups.
misc.invest.funds	A newsgroup on mutual funds.
misc.invest.stocks	A newsgroup on stocks.
pubnet.forsale	Another for sale group.
rec.humor	A newsgroup for humorous postings.
rec.humor.funny	A newsgroup for funny jokes and postings.

GLOSSARY

10BaseT   A protocal that allows ethernet communications over twisted copper wire that resembles a telephone cord.

24 by 7   24 hours a day, seven days a week—meaning something that is up and running constantly.

56k   A network connection that has a speed of 56-thousand bits per second.

active hub   A hub that allows communications only between the WAN and each physical LAN segment. It does not allow data to pass from one physical LAN segment to another.

authentication   A method of verifying that a person or computer is who they say they are.

back door   A way for a hacker to continue to enter a computer system even after all other security holes have been closed.

banner   A graphic advertisement that is wide and short and displayed somewhere on a Web page.

BBS   A *Bulletin Board System* is a computer system with a modem that allows people, with other computers and modems, to log in and use its services.

beta testers   People that test software to find flaws.

bookmark   Similar to a bookmark that is placed in a book, it is usually a function of a Web browser to keep track of a particular site's address and name so that users can easily return to the site.

browser   Software that allows a user to navigate the Web, retrieve documents, and follow links to other sites and documents.

cache   The process of storing data for re-use. On the Web, files that are retrieved from a Web server are often cached by the browser. That way, those files can be redisplayed without generating additional network traffic.

cache confusion   The under-counting effect that caching has on a Web server's hit counts.

CERT   The *Computer Emergency Response Team* is a government sponsored organization, formed after the Internet worm attack, whose mission is to respond to Internet security events.

CGI   *Common Gateway Interface* is used by Web server software to allow programs to interact with the Web.

CGI program   A program that uses the Common Gateway Interface to interact with the Web.

client   A computer or machine connected to the Web, used for displaying information located on a remote computer but does not host a site or distribute files to other computers.

coherence factor	The measure of a site's ability to flow smoothly from page to page, both logically and visually. The two main contributors to the coherence factor are consistency and logical arrangement.
compile	The process of turning the text-based code written by a computer programmer into the actual instructions used by a computer.
COPS	*Computer Oracle Password and Security* is a collection of programs used to monitor various computer security vulnerabilities.
CPU	The *Central Processing Unit* is the "brains" of a computer.
Crack	A password-guessing program that when fed a password file tries to "crack" the password by guessing easy passwords or words found in dictionaries.
crypt	A UNIX program that uses an encryption technique based on the German Enigma machine used during World War II.
cryptography	The process of turning usable information into what appears to be jibberish, unreadable under normal circumstances.
CU-SeeMe	A type of video-conferencing software for personal computers used to communicate over the Internet.
data integrity	The assurance that data has not been modified or deleted.
decompile	The opposite of compile, decompiling is taking the code that a computer understands and turning it into something humans can read.
decrypt	To undo the process of encryption. Turning seemingly jibberish information into readable or useable form.
des	a UNIX program that implements the government's Digital Encryption Standard (DES) form of encryption
DES	The *Digital Encryption Standard* is a private key encryption scheme that uses the same key to encrypt and decrypt data.
Digital Cash	A form of electronic currency that is used to transfer money on the Internet.
digital signature	A file containing unforgeable and unique information directly linked to a company or individual that is as unique as a person's signature.
Digital Signature Standard (DSS)	A standard for digital signatures announced by N\$\Sigma$T (National Institute of Standards) that affects U.S. civilian government agencies.
domain name service	Computers on the Internet have a unique numerical address (four numbers separated by periods) that is used to identify each computer. Names can be used instead of the numbers. The domain name service is used to convert a name into its corresponding number.
dynamic addressability	A trait applied to media formats that allow specific content to be sent to an individual based on that person's behavior.
encryption	The act of data cryptography.
finger	A program that reports the users logged into a specific computer or obtains more information on a particular user.
firewall	A piece of network security equipment that connects between your network and the Internet and blocks data being transferred between the two.
FTP	*File Transfer Protocol* is the underlying software method for transferring files between computer systems over the Internet.
GB	A *gigabyte*; equal to approximately 1000 megabytes (MB).

gopher	Gopher is a menu-driven document delivery system that organizes and helps Internet users find information. The name was chosen based on the pun, "Go For."
hacker	At one time this term was used to describe a knowledgeable and determined computer programmer. Today, however, it is used to describe a person who uses their computer abilities to commit criminal acts.
hit	The act of retrieving a file from a Web server. A file that is retrieved 5 times has recieved 5 hits.
hit count	The number of times a particular file, or set of files, is requested from a Web server.
homepage	The first page visitors are expected to see when connecting to a Web site. It is often analogous to the cover and table of contents of a book or magazine.
HTML	*HyperText Markup Language* is the principal language used to define documents on the Web. HTML allows Web designers to mark up standard text documents to include images and hypertext links to related documents or objects.
HTML page	A Web page that is composed of HTML code.
HTTP	*HyperText Transport Protocol* is the most commonly used method of transferring data on the Web.
hub	A piece of network equipment that allows several physical data networks to behave as one. Usually, each physical network consists of only one computer.
impression	The process of a consumer viewing a company hallmark, advertisement, or sponsorship.
incidental products	Those products and services that are byproducts of manufacturing or marketing real products. Incidental products generally are not intended to be sold or otherwise directly generate revenues.
interactive pricing	A form of pricing where prices rise and fall continuously in response to such issues as supply and demand.
Internet Access Provider	(or *Internet Service Provider, Internet Provider, ISP*) A company that provides individuals and businesses with Internet connections.
ISDN	*Integrated Services Digital Network.* A service that is often used to connect to the Internet because it is faster than typical telephone modems.
key	A password used to encrypt or decrypt a message
kill file	A file that contains words, phrases, and news titles that should be ignored and not displayed to the viewer.
LAN	A *Local Area Network* often refers to a single physical network or several physical networks that behave as one becuse they are connected through a hub or repeater.
link consistency	The tendency for similar links to behave in a similar manner. In other words, if two documents contain the same button, either button would be linked to the same file.
links	Connections from one hypertext documnet to another hypertext document or piece of Web data. When selecting a word or image in one document causes the retrieval of a second document, the first document is said to be linked to the second. The word or image is often called the link.
login	Utilizing a name and password to connect to a remotely located computer.
loss leader	A marketing term used to describe a product sold at a loss to attract prospective customers.
mail alias	A name, other than the username, used to send e-mail to particular person.
market research	The process of gathering and analyzing information about consumers and competitors.

MB	A *megabyte* is equal to approximately 1 million bytes.
MIPS	*Millions of Instructions Per Second* is a quantifying value for rating CPU speed.
mirror	When a duplicate of a Web site is maintained on an additional computer.
modem	A device used by computers to communicate over telephone lines.
moderated newsgroups	A Usenet newsgroup in which a person (the moderator) reviews what people submit before the information is actually posted to the newsgroup.
moderator	A person who reviews what people submit before the information is posted to a newsgroup or mailing list.
MUDS	*Multi-User Dungeon* (or occasionaly *Multi-User Domain*).
netiquette	slang for Internet Etiquette.
netizen	A citizen of the Internet.
Netscape Navigator	Netscape Corporation's Web browser.
network	A group of computers that communicate together. This term may also describe the physical medium and equipment used to facilitate that communication.
newbie	A person who is new to the Internet and is uneducated in proper Internet etiquette.
news interface	Allows users to read and post articles to newsgroups.
newsgroups	Forums where related information on a given subject is exchanged by users through the posting and reading of articles. There are over 15,000 newsgroups across the Internet, covering a broad range of subjects; many more are added daily.
NNTP	*Network News Transport Protocol* is used to transfer Internet newsgroups from the Internet to individual computers.
npasswd	A UNIX program that requires users to enter a password that the systems administrator feels is secure.
packet	A single block of data, packaged and passed over a network. It is analogous to a postal letter for computers. Small amounts of data from one computer are placed in a packet, addressed to another computer, and sent to that computer over a network.
packet encryption	The process of encrypting packets of data as they enter a network.
passwd	A program used for setting or changing passwords on a UNIX system.
ping	A command that sends out a small packet of information to networked computers. That computer quickly replies by sending another packet back to the sender. The command is used to determine if a distant computer is successfully networked, or to determine the relative distance from site to site based on the time it takes for the packet to travel round trip.
PostScript	A programming language used mostly by printers for rendering text and graphics.
price floor	The cost of a transaction exceeds the profit made on the item.
profile-driven marketing	A marketing approach where market research data is stored for each visitor. When a visitor returns, the Web site (or other sales tool) can respond in a personalized manner.
public key encryption	A public key encryption scheme uses two keys (passwords) to encrypt and decrypt data—a public and a private key. To send and encrypt a message, the sender would use her private key and the receiver's public key. Once encrypted, only the receiver's private key can decode the message. Even the sender is unable to decrypt her message. Public-key cryptography is considered some of the strongest encryption technology available and was developed by three MIT developers—Rivest, Shamir, and Adelman.

real products	Those products and services that a company offers as marketable commodities. They are intended to generate revenue directly. Compare to *incidental products*.
real-time multimedia	Audio and/or video data displayed as it arrives at a computer. All live broadcasts require the use of real-time multimedia. Compare to *time-delayed multimedia*.
registration	See *user registration*.
reverse engineer	See *decompiling*
router	A piece of network equipment that allows two or more physical networks to communicate. For example, a router will allow computers on a company LAN to communicate with the Internet. It routes packets from one network to another.
S-HTTP	*Secure HyperText Transport Protocol* is a secure version of *HTTP.*
SATAN	*Security Administrator Tool for Analyzing Networks.*
search engine	A software program that searches a database using keywords input by the user.
search site	A Web site that uses a search engine to search for information.
secure router	A router that filters out data packets that have not been authorized or may pose a security risk. Only packets that are not filtered out will be routed to their destination.
SecurID	A small, hardware-based product the size of a credit card that keeps users from forgetting or revealing passwords.
sendmail	A program responsible for sending and receiving mail on a UNIX based *system*.
server	A central computer that offers (serves) resources to other (client) computers.
site	Similar to a server.
sniffer programs	Software that allows a computer to capture and examine packets that are not addressed to it. A sniffer on the Internet can "sniff" out data that contains personal information, like credit card numbers.
spamming	The name given to the flooding of Usenet with large numbers of identical, or similar, messages.
spray	Similar to the *ping* command but sends the small packets of information as fast as possible.
SSL	*Secure Socket Layer.*
standard	A protocol or set of procedures that people all agree upon.
submission page	A page that contains a form so that Web users can send information via a Web browser to a Web server.
subsidized content	A model of commercialization where advertisers pay a media producer (such as a television station or Web site owner) for the privledge of sponsoring a program or Web page. This model provides the producer with the funds to create additional content, and the advertiser with a place to publish commercial messages.
surfer	Slang used for a person that uses the World Wide Web.
surfing	Hanging ten on the World Wide Web.
T1, T3	High speed network connections. A T1 carries 1.54 megabits of data per second and a T3 carries 45 megabits per second.
tags	The name given to any element of an HTML document that is used as instructions to format the document. Tags can be used to make certain text show up as bold or underlined. Tags are also used to create a link between two different HTML documents.

TCP/IP Protocol	*Transmission Control Protocol* and the *Internet Protocol*. This is the protocol that moves data across the Internet.
telco	Another term for telephone company.
third party authentication	An *authentication* method that requires an impartial third party to validate the identity of two computers or computer users.
time-delayed multimedia	Audio and/or video files that must be retrieved, in their entirety, from their source before they can be displayed to the user. This form of multimedia is easier than real-time multimedia, but is more restrictive and less interactive.
traffic	Network data traveling over a network connection.
trojan horse	A typically innocent looking program that is disguised as a routine command but is used to record passwords and other user information.
UNIX	A computer operating system developed at AT&T's Bell Labs and refined at Berkeley. It is used mostly by companies and is not as popular with home users. UNIX is not an acronym and does not stand for anything.
URL	A *Uniform Resource Locator* is an address used to specify the exact location of a machine, file, or piece of data on the Internet.
user registration	The process of giving a username and password to a Web user. That username and password provide access to otherwise unavailable features on a server.
variable names	Used in programming and mathematics to describe a value that changes or is unknown. Often represented by an "x" or "y."
WAN	A high-speed network that connects two or more LANs.
Web browser	See *browser*.
Web code	The text and tags that describe a Web document to a Web browser.
Web Consultant	A consultant that advises on HTML, Web server configuration, and sometimes marketing.
Web Designer	A person that turns design ideas into HTML.
Web index	A Web page or site that provides a list of other Web pages or sites. It is usually organized by topic.
Web Indices	Plural of Web index.
Web Presence Provider	A person or company that establishes Web sites for other individuals, companies, or organizations. They often host the Web site on their own server.
Web site	A grouping of Web pages that are linked together so that you may easily flow from one page to the next. It is often used to describe the information that one individual, company, or entity puts on the Web.
Webmaster	The person in charge of and responsible for a Web site.
wrapper	A program that is installed on a computer system to limit access to certain programs and to log every request that is made to run those programs.
yppasswd	A program on a UNIX machine similar to *passwd*. The difference is that by using *yppasswd* users can change their passwords on several networked computers at the same time.

INDEX

A

Abuses of Internet, 61
AccessWatch, 410, 411
Accounting services, 27
Active documents, 151
Active hubs, 325
Added-value marketing, 241-242
Addresses. *See* E-mail; Web sites
Advanced Research Projects Agency
  (ARPA), 2-3
Advanced site audits, 412-413
Advantages of Web marketing, 31-32
Advertising. *See also* Marketing
  broadcast advertising, 16-17
  copyright issues, 387
  cost of, 263-266
  in e-zines, 254-255
  FTC criteria for, 391
  FTP sites and, 288
  future of, 449-454
  by large corporations, 58
  monthly rates for, 264-265
  multiple presences, 266-269
  1995 4th quarter revenue figures, 266
  nonthreatening postings, 463-464
  print advertising, 15-16
  search-engine advertising, 259
  shelf space and, 269-270
  spamming, 125-128
  static advertising, 55-56
  techniques for, 460-461
  top 10 largest Internet
    advertisers, 267
  truth in, 390-392
  Web Advertising and Marketing
    (WAM) Web site, 433
Advertising agencies, 203-204
Aesthetics of design, 183
Age of clients, 30-31
Airlines, 26
  Alaska Airlines, 356-358
  American Airlines, 267
  United Airlines, 26

Alaska Airlines, 356-358
Alexander, Lamar, 358
Alex Brown and Sons, 265
Allman, Eric, 331
America Express, 359
American Airlines, 267
America Online, 11, 50
  Chicago Tribune and, 52-53
  hackers and, 394
  legislation involving, 397
  lesson from, 55
  liability for comments in, 143
  modem packaging, software in, 252
  over-caching, 412
Animation on Web, 102-104
Anonymous FTP sites, 6
  Netscape Communications, 287
A1 Internet Services, 367-368m
  366-378
Apache Web server software,
  RefStats, 409
Apple Computers, 394
ARPAnet, 2-3
ASCII
  art, 175
  resumes posted in, 281
Asian sites, 436-437
Atalla *WebSafe*, 346-347, 448
Athletic shoe advertising, 210-211
Atlantic Financial Consulting, 108
AT&T, 267
  800 directory online, 444-445
Audience for Web, 42
Audio features, 100-102. *See also*
  Copyrights
Automated Transaction Service,
  Inc., 376
Automobiles
  buying services, 374
  parts, 23
Ayer, Bill, 356-358

B

Back button, 166
Backdoors, 334
Baker, Jake, 389
Baker, Stewart A., 343-344
Bandwidth. *See also* Internet
    connection
  of browsers, 131-132
  CU-SeeMe technology, 289
Banister, Scott, 226
BankNet, 372
Bank of America, 348
Banks
  online banks, 371-376
  security considerations on
    Internet, 352
  services, 26-27
Banners, 248
  cost of, 263-266
  name recognition and, 279-280
Barnett Bank, 375
Barry, Dave, 87
Beer marketing on Web, 208-210
Bell, Alexander Graham, 290
Berners-Lee, Tim, 9, 133
Beta testing programs, 280-281
Better Business Bureau, 233, 354
Bidzos, Jim, 352
Billable hit counts, 408
Billing and collection methods,
    367-370
Binary files-text messages, 234
BIS Strategic Decisions, 356
Black list on Internet, 233
Blatant advertising, 61
Boldfaced text, 181
Bolt, Bernak, and Newman, 2-3
Bookmarks, 169
  links, sites for, 228-229
Boutell, Thomas, 409
Brandell, Jim, 358
Broadcast advertising, 16-17
Brochures online, 162